D0653066

SAINT JOAN OF ARC

Frontispiece
The Canonisation of St. Joan of Arc, May 16th, 1920

SAINT JOAN OF ARC

Born January 6th, 1412
Burned as a heretic, May 30th, 1431
Canonised as a saint, May 16th, 1920

V. SACKVILLE-WEST

London
COBDEN-SANDERSON
One Montague Street

First published 1936

Printed in England for
R. COBDEN-SANDERSON LTD.
by The Camelot Press Ltd.
London & Southampton
on paper supplied by
Spalding and Hodge Ltd.
and bound by the
Leighton-Straker Bookbinding Co. Ltd.

For
PHILIPPA

CONTENTS

ILLUSTRATIONS

MAPS (by J. F. Horrabin)

FOREWORD

There are many deliberate omissions in this book.

Students of the period may ask why I have not entered more closely into such things as the relations between the Dukes of Burgundy, Brittany, Bedford, and Gloucester, Cardinal Beaufort, and so on.

My answer is that I wished to concentrate on Joan of Arc herself, bringing in the minimum of outside politics.

It seemed to me that Joan of Arc was far more important and problematical than any of the figures or politics which surrounded her. It became necessary for me to refer to some of those figures and politics: but, beyond that simplified reference, I have kept her consistently in the foreground, at the expense of other interests. It seemed to me, in short, that Joan of Arc presented a fundamental problem of the deepest importance, whereas the political difficulties of her day presented only a topical and therefore secondary interest. The history of France in the fifteenth century can hold no interest to-day save for the scholar; the strange career of Joan of Arc, on the other hand, remains a story the conclusion of which is as yet unfound. I do not claim to have found it in this book. I take the view that many years, possibly hundreds of years, may elapse before it is found at all.

In the meantime, I wish to record my gratitude to several people: to my sister-in-law, Gwen St. Aubyn, who has provided and annotated many specialised books for me; to Mr. J. F. Horrabin, who has drawn the maps; to Father Herbert Thurston, S.J., who has given me his time for discussion of Saint Joan; to Dr. Baines for his views on the psychology of visionaries; to Mr. Milton Waldman, who most generously lent me his notes on the trial; to the Secretary of the Royal Observatory, Greenwich, who sent me a table of the phases of the moon during 1429 and 1430; and, finally, to the Société des Amis de la Bibliothèque Nationale (Office de Documentation), to whom I am indebted for some of the illustrations.

The question of footnotes troubled me considerably. I had at first intended to put none, but was gradually forced to the conclusion that a complete absence of reference to authorities was even more irritating to the reader than the constant check to the progress of his reading. Of two evils, I hope I have chosen the lesser.

The question of proper names troubled me also. It seemed to me that *Jeanne* was ill-translated by *Joan*, and yet I could not bring myself to write the closer rendering of *Jean*. I have therefore decided to stick to the French version of her name throughout, except in the title of the book itself.

The same problem arose over the names of French cities. It will be observed that I have elected to print Orleans without an accent on the e. This is because most English readers are accustomed to pronounce Orleans in the English way. On the other hand, I have spelt Reims in the French way. This is because the addition of an h in no way affects the pronunciation, and therefore seemed to me pointless.

I am advised on good authority that Domremy should be written without an accent on the e.

V. S.-W.

"[And it was shown to her] how serious and dangerous it is curiously to examine the things which are beyond one's understanding, and to believe in new things . . . and even to invent new and unusual things, for demons have a way of introducing themselves into such-like curiosities."

ADMONITION ADDRESSED TO JOAN OF ARC.

Procès de condamnation, Vol. I, p. 390.

"Pauvre Jeanne d'Arc! Elle a eu bien du malheur dans ce que sa mémoire a provoqué d'écrits et de compositions de diverses sortes."

SAINTE BEUVE.

Chapter I

JEANNE D'ARC

. . . Et Jehanne, la bonne Lorraine,
Qu'Englois bruslèrent à Rouan;
Où sont-elles, Vierge souveraine?
Mais où sont les neiges d'antan!

FRANÇOIS VILLON

i

No contemporary portrait of Jeanne d'Arc is known to exist. Possibly none ever existed at all. She denied having ever sat for her portrait, although she admitted having seen, at Arras, a painting of herself in full armour, kneeling on one knee, presenting a letter to the King. This painting, she affirmed, was the work of a Scotsman. Apart from that, she said she had never seen another image in her likeness, nor had she ever caused one to be made. The frescoes depicting her life, which Montaigne saw on the façade of her home at Domremy on his way to Italy a hundred and forty-nine years after her death, were already in a bad state by then and have now entirely disappeared; *l'âge*, he wrote, *en a fort corrompu la peinture.* Yet there can be no question that she was, even during her lifetime, a person whom one would expect to find portrayed in a hundred different places; a person of legend. Butterflies in clouds accompanied her standard; pigeons miraculously fluttered towards her; men fell into rivers and were drowned; dead babies yawned and came to life; flocks of little birds perched on bushes to watch her making war.[1] The magistrates of Ratisbon paid twenty-four pfennigs in 1429 for the privilege of looking at a picture showing how the Pucelle had fought in France, but the advantage as well as the expense is theirs, not ours.[2] There is nothing left to tell us what Jeanne

[1] *Procès*, Vol. V, p. 294: MS. 891 in the Queen of Sweden's collection, Vatican Library. (*N.B.* This MS. does not mention the butterflies.)

[2] *Procès*, Vol. V, p. 270: *Item, mehr haben wir gebe von dem Gamael zu schaun wie die Junkchfraw zu Frankreich gefochten hat, 24 pfennig.* Stadtrechnung, Ratisbon.

d'Arc looked like, although Eugélide, Princess of Hungary, gives us some reason to believe that she had a short neck and a little bright red mark behind her right ear.

ii

On the other hand, hundreds of fanciful posthumous representations, in stone, in bronze, in plaster, in stained glass, in fresco, on canvas, or on wood, leave us with an impression neither blurred nor doubtful but only too definite, unauthentic, and precise. Pen and ink, equally active, have lent their services to the willing imagination, so that from these various mediums of the artist and the historian a double image clearly emerges: the image of Jeanne pensive and pastoral, or the image of Jeanne embattled and heroic, the basis of truth in both interpretations heavily overlaid with all the hues of sentimentality and romance. If these interpreters are to be believed, then Jeanne the peasant sat permanently with folded hands and upturned eyes, and Jeanne the captain permanently bestrode a charger whose forelegs never touched the ground. The lover of truth sighs in vain for one plain portrait, unflattering, authentic, crude; a portrait which shall attempt no picturesque rendering of that remarkable destiny, no seizing of those dramatic moments, but a quiet statement of what Jeanne looked like, whether in daily life at her father's house, or in the few strenuous months when by popular acclaim she became known throughout France and much of Europe as a suddenly public personage; as, in short, la Pucelle, *Mulier illa quæ Puella vociferatur*.[1]

Such a statement, if ever drawn, is missing. Only by inference, only by the reasoning of probability, and with the help of certain given indications, is it possible to reconstruct to-day the physical appearance of either Jeanne the peasant or Jeanne the captain. The peasant, chronologically speaking, comes first. She breaks as an apparently ordinary little girl of twelve

1*Procès*, Vol. I, p. 409.

or thirteen into the pages of history. She comes of healthy parents, taking her share in the housework, in the work of the fields, in the care of the cattle, and in the general yearly round of a simple, practical, country family. There is every reason to presume her tough and sturdy; reasons racial, documentary, and evidential. There is every racial reason to presume her short and stocky, rather than tall and slender; every reason to suppose her muscular, with features homely (in the English, not the American, sense) rather than pretty. Many men and women who had known her in her youth came forward later to testify to her moral character, to her early avocations, to the personal impression she made on them, to the affection and respect with which they regarded her, but not a single one mentions even as a passing comment that she was pretty. Had she been pretty, her contemporary apologists would certainly have mentioned the fact, of outstanding importance, especially to Latin minds, in the case of a woman. One of them, at least, would have dragged it in, however irrelevantly, to increase the plea of her youth, her pathos, and her sex. The fact that none of them did so, not even Perceval de Boulainvilliers, whose admiration for her was great enough to allow him to remark, *Hæc Puella competentis est elegantiæ*, which one might colloquially render as "passably good-looking," may be accepted as a negative if not as a positive point in the inference that Jeanne was no prettier or more attractive than most girls of her region and class.[1]

Apart from this surely legitimate inference, other deductions may be drawn from the very nature of the life she led at home and of the hardships she proved later able to endure. The climate of Lorraine is not always soft and favoured, as those who have known it only in spring and summer might be tempted to believe, nor does the existence of the working peasant in Lorraine or elsewhere consist always of lying among the buttercups of a golden meadow while contented

[1] *Procès*, Vol. V, p. 120: Letter from Perceval de Boulainvilliers to Filippo Maria Visconti, Duke of Milan.

cattle ruminate by the waters of a sleepy stream. Jeanne had to help her mother with the housework and the spinning, and her father and brothers with the ploughing and the harvest. Roughened fingers, a skin reddened by the sun, harshened by harder weather, stolid limbs, and stout muscles, the inevitable consequences of such a life, can scarcely have added to the feminine attractions of a girl whose feminine attractions, if she ever potentially had them, are never even mentioned by those who knew and loved her first.

If common sense was one of her outstanding and most valuable characteristics, as I believe it to have been, then at least we owe it to her memory never to romanticise her unduly, as she would never have wished to be romanticised. There is enough romance, and to spare, in the facts of her life, without inventing also the legend of the china shepherdess leaning on her crook. Jeanne was not made of china, nor, except in poetic legend, was she ever much of a shepherdess. Better, and truer, to see her prosaically, sensibly, and logically, as she herself would have wished to be seen, without embellishment or false claim.

Those who describe her from either first- or second-hand knowledge give, on the whole, a consistent picture. Her hair, they say, was short and black; her complexion dark and sun-burnt, as might be expected. The author of the First Part of *King Henry VI* makes her refer to herself as *black and swart*; wildly unreliable chronicler though he was, it is still quite likely that his information on this point was derived from some handed-down tradition. The description of her hair given by witnesses who had known her received a curious little point of confirmation, when, in 1844, a letter came to light at Riom, addressed to the citizens of that town, and signed "Jehanne."[1] But more interesting even than that signature was the seal, for a single black hair had been pressed into it by a finger. It was a common custom of the time, and

---

[1] Jeanne learnt to sign her name, but never to write or read.

it is tempting to believe that both the finger-print and the hair were Jeanne's.[1]

None of these witnesses mentions her eyes, but there is on racial grounds a strong presumption in favour of their having been brown; it has been suggested also, on the analogy of other visionaries, that they were slightly prominent. They all agree that she was strong and well made: *Estoit de grande force et puissance*[2]; *Bien compassée de membres et forte*[3]; *Belle et bien formée*[4]; her breasts were well formed, said the duc d'Alençon, who had often slept beside her while on their campaigns, and, young man as he was, had watched her at her undressing; but he was careful to add that never had she aroused any carnal desire in him. So far they all seem to be in agreement. Only on the question of her height is there any apparent dissension. Was she short or tall? The *Chronique de Lorraine* describes her as *haulte et puissante*, but the *Chronique de Lorraine* is neither a reliable nor a contemporary document. On the other hand, an Italian soldier, who was present on her arrival at Chinon, told Philip of Bergamo that she was short as to her stature.[5] The truth probably is that, although sufficiently tall for a woman, she looked much shorter when dressed as a man, a contention which may be personally endorsed by anyone who has seen even a tall woman in men's clothes.

We may presume her, then, to have been a strong, healthy, plain, and sturdy girl. Strong and healthy she certainly was, for otherwise she could never have taken her ordinary part in country life as a child, nor, later, could she have endured the sudden unaccustomed weight of armour and the long rides across country—rides which, one way and another, took her over some three thousand miles of our modern computation,

[1]*Procès*, Vol. V, p. 147; and Marquis de Pimodan, *La première étape de Jeanne d'Arc*, p. 10. (Let me warn any enthusiast against making a pilgrimage to Riom in order to behold this unique relic for himself. The hair has disappeared.)

[2]*Chronique de Lorraine*.   [3]*Chronique de la Pucelle*.

[4]*Procès*, Vol. III, p. 219: Deposition of Jean d'Aulon.

[5]*Procès*, Vol. IV, p. 523.

or more than the distance from France to India.[1] No evidence exists to the effect that her mysterious inspiration upheld her in these tests in any physical sense; it seems, rather, to have worked the other way round, so that her physical fitness came usefully to hand at the service of her celestial mission. Saint Michael, Saint Catherine, and Saint Margaret had chosen their servant well. In the inexplicable way of saints, they had picked on an ignorant able-bodied girl whose early training fitted her for the exhaustive demands they proposed to make on her toughness and her endurance.

iii

All things considered, the little statue in the museum at Domremy probably comes nearest to a true presentation of Jeanne as she really was. The history of this statue is disputable and confused. Local tradition says that Louis XI, son of Charles VII, extended his royal benevolence to the preservation of the d'Arc family's humble cottage at Domremy, and that the statue now in the museum, with its replica in a niche over Jeanne's front door, represents a part of his tribute to the liberator of his father's kingdom. That is as it may be. It seems more likely that the statue in the Domremy museum is a much later reproduction, with modifications according to the ideas of the time, of a section of a sculptural group set up in 1456 by the ladies of Orleans on a bridge spanning the river in that city.[2] Certainly the statue at Domremy cannot be even an immediately posthumous portrait; it cannot be a portrait so nearly contemporary that we may suppose the sculptor to have been acquainted, if not with Jeanne in person, then at any rate with those to whom her features had been familiar, and from

[1] L. Champion, *Jeanne d'Arc écuyère*, p. 249.

[2] *Domremy-la-Pucelle*, by André Philippe (Appendix); and *Procès*, Vol. IV, pp. 448–9, description by Pontus Heuterus, a Dutchman. M. Quicherat, on the other hand, believes it to be a copy of a statue once in the Cathedral of Toul: *Procès*, Vol. V, p. 247.

THE DOMREMY STATUE

whom he could have taken advice as to her lineaments and general build. Yet there is something about this crude and clumsy little statue which carries conviction as other and more pretentious works fail to carry it. True, the portrait has been falsified in several particulars. The ruff and armour are obviously untrue to date; they are of the reign of Henri IV, or even Louis XIII, rather than of the reign of Charles VII. Then, again, Jeanne is represented with long hair: hair so long that it reaches to the buttocks in the kneeling statue; hair so ostentatiously long that she could have sat on it, were she sitting upright instead of kneeling. This is quite comprehensible when we reflect that one of the principal accusations against her was that she adopted men's clothes and fashions; naturally, her apologists and rehabilitators, awkwardly embarrassed by her masculine career, aspired to present her under as feminine an aspect as possible. They went so far as to gild her sculptured hair, and traces of this particular rehabilitation survived so late as into the nineteenth century.[1] Nevertheless, this fat untruthful little statue does contrive to suggest the common-sense, commonplace aspect of Jeanne as other more romantic portrayals fail to suggest her. There is something in those thick short thighs, those truncated arms, which evokes the unattractive peasant girl whom Saint Michael, Saint Catherine, and Saint Margaret so sagaciously selected for their purpose.

I think it is not unfair to qualify her as unattractive. Men attempted no rape, nor were women jealous. She made war, but not love. Those who choose to take the purely religious point of view may maintain that some spiritual quality in her personality exalted her above all such human failings. Possibly. But human beings are human beings, slow to recognise the exceptional spiritual qualities, and there is no reason to suppose that they were less human in the fifteenth century than they are to-day. Yet the fact remains that Jeanne travelled and slept in a comradely way with men, day after day, night after night, keeping her virginity intact to the last; and that she also came

[1] *Le Magasin pittoresque,* 1834, p. 43 *seq.*

into contact with various women who would have been among
the first to suspect her of making a, to them, dangerous
appeal. But somehow or other, for all the excitement of her
startling notoriety, she clearly aroused neither the natural
desire of men nor the competitive mistrust of women. The
men of her first escort, travelling with her in the most intimate
conditions for eleven days, sleeping beside her at night,
avowed themselves in strong and detailed terms as having been
completely free of carnal thoughts. The men-at-arms at
Vaucouleurs were even less complimentary, for when Robert
de Baudricourt, their leader, jocosely suggested turning Jeanne
over to their pleasure, there were some who would have taken
advantage of this offer; but, as soon as they saw her, desire left
them and they felt no further inclination.[1] Witness, also, the
list of women whose admiration she had gained, such as the
poet Christine de Pisan, or whom she could count among her
friends, not only the village friends of her childhood, not only
the matrons of Neufchâteau, Vaucouleurs, Chinon, Poitiers,
Bourges, Tours, and Orleans, not only the three ladies of
Luxembourg, but also princesses such as Yolande d'Aragon,
Marie d'Anjou, and the young Duchess of Alençon.

It is evident that the complications of sex presented few
difficulties to Jeanne herself or to others in regard to her.

Her views on feminism, as concerned herself, were characteristically clear-cut and bold: "It is true that at Arras and Beaurevoir I was admonished to adopt feminine clothes; I refused,
and still refuse. As for other avocations of women, there are
plenty of other women to perform them."[2]

At the same time, it is impossible to believe that her
unusual experiences had left no trace upon her features and

---

[1]*Procès*, Vol. IV, p. 205, *Chronique de la Pucelle: Y eut aucuns qui avoient
volonté d'y essayer; mais aussi tost qu'ils la voyoient ils étoient refroidis et ne leur en
prenoit volonté. Procès*, Vol. IV, p. 118, *Journal du siège d'Orléans: Si tost qu'ilz
la regardoient fort, ilz estoient tous reffroidiz de luxure.*

[2]*Procès*, Vol. I, p. 230: *Quant aux autres œuvres de femmes, il y a assés autres
femmes pour ce faire.*

found no answering reflection in her eyes. One does not begin at the age of twelve to spend four to five years in the daily company of saints, secretly nursing a mission of so alarming a gravity, without some corresponding change in one's expression, of exaltation, mystery, and awe. Even so short a time as four years, at her tender age, must have sufficed to leave their mark upon her. Nor can one be born with the aptitude to entertain such company, and to be charged by them with such a mission, without some indication of that temperament becoming discernible to the eye of the observant. Still, such inward beauty of expression as Jeanne may, and surely must, have possessed, was not of a nature to rouse the concupiscence of men-at-arms, or to endanger her chastity by increasing the appeal of her youth and sex. Rather, it must have been definitely discouraging to those who were sensitive enough to be aware of it, and, in a subtle subconscious way, eventually discouraging also for those cruder ones who otherwise might have seen in the healthy young body merely a temptation to mischief and natural play. It would take, of course, a little time for the chill to work. Those who had learned to know her might entertain for her nothing but the most platonically minded veneration; but what of her avowed enemies, and what of uninformed newcomers, to whom her sex and virginity would appear only as a ribald joke? Robert de Baudricourt himself, before she won him round to do what she wanted, had exercised his smutty wit at her expense, when only the disinclination of his soldiers, once they beheld her, saved her from further trouble.

It was, however, not enough for her to know that she had only to appear in person for these objectionable ideas to be dispersed. Something more drastic must be done about it: the practical inconvenience of belonging to the wrong sex must be faced and overcome; and Jeanne, with her usual common sense, took the obvious step of turning herself into the least outward semblance of a woman possible. Off came both her skirt and her hair. It was an indicated measure—it was, indeed, a measure necessary for a girl who proposed to ride in the company of six men for hundreds of miles over a countryside thick with soldiers—but it was a measure that must have required considerable moral courage. One wonders what her feelings were, when for the first time she surveyed her cropped head and moved her legs unencumbered by her red skirt—the coarse red skirt still worn by the peasant women of Lorraine within living memory? The unfamiliar masculine garments which she then assumed were not even her own: she had acquired them from her cousin, Durand Lassois, who recounts the circumstance philosophically and without comment, saying merely that she "had received" them from him, *Ipsa recepit vestis ipsius testis.*[1] What he really means, is that she took them. Before very long this arrangement evidently ceased to satisfy her, and one may hope that the long-suffering Lassois had his clothing returned to him when his arbitrary young relative induced the townsfolk of Vaucouleurs to buy her a man's complete outfit, including boots. By what means she or her friends induced them to do this is not related. Certainly Robert de Baudricourt had nothing to do with it, for later, when she was specifically asked if her change of costume had not taken place according to Baudricourt's orders, she denied the suggestion, admitting no other authority in this matter than that of God and His angels. However she managed it, it was done: she stood equipped as a man and a soldier. According to the *greffier* of the Hôtel de Ville of La Rochelle,[2] she arrived at Chinon dressed in a black doublet, a short dark-grey tunic (*robe courte de gros gris noir*), high boots, and a black cap. As she had travelled straight from Vaucouleurs to Chinon, we may fairly suppose this was the original equipment supplied to her by the people of Vaucouleurs, for she would hardly have wasted time stopping to buy anything else on the way; such delays as she permitted herself in towns were devoted to the services of the Church. The most interesting piece of

---

[1] *Procès,* Vol. II, p. 444: Deposition of Durand Lassois.

[2] *Revue historique,* IV, p. 332: *Relation du greffier de l'hôtel de ville de la Rochelle.*

information with which the *greffier* de La Rochelle provides us, is his remark about her hair. It was, he tells us, black and short. That settles once and for all a question which might otherwise have been a matter for dispute.

What happened to her own red gown is not clear: it would appear as though she had taken it with her, for at Châlons, on her way to Reims to crown the Dauphin, she met Jean Morel, her godfather from Greux, near Domremy, and gave him a red garment of her own.[1] Was this the one in which she had travelled from Domremy to Vaucouleurs? If so, the gift must have represented the last link with her old life; for her, no doubt, a brief significant moment—a moment carrying her back to her home at the height of her glory.

iv

It would be a mistake to represent Jeanne, although so prompt to abandon her feminine semblance, as lacking in appreciation of fine raiment and its suitable complements. For all her privately religious integrity, there was no inclination in favour of the hair-shirt about Jeanne in her public life. She regarded herself, I think, as the captain, never as the saint, though other people tended to regard her as the saint rather than as the captain; and as the captain she seems to have enjoyed a richly decorative taste for equipment and picturesque adjuncts. She seems rapidly to have acquired a nice approval of pageantry; one of the endearing inconsistencies of her simple, surprised nature. For all her severity, for all her single-mindedness, there was something of the woman in her make-up, undeveloped partly owing to her extreme youth; partly to the extraordinary and terrifying mission imposed so early upon her inexperience; partly to the plain peasant life she had seen around her and had herself led, lacking all grace or elegance. It is amusing to observe how the woman in Jeanne made the most of the chance provided by her sudden emergence from

[1] *Procès*, Vol. II, p. 391: Deposition of Jean Morel.

obscurity into a public personage. Cinderella turned into a princess could scarcely have been assailed by a greater bewilderment, and it remains very much to Jeanne's credit that she did not lose her head altogether—for her good sense always kept her head tightly screwed on—but indulged herself only in such harmless decorative extravagances as might have been expected from her years, her sex, and her opportunity. Consider what had happened. The dark little cellar-like room at Domremy had been replaced by the splendours of Chinon and the relative comforts of Poitiers and Tours. The rude company of peasants had been replaced by the company of princes, courtiers, and ladies. Instead of her father's farm-horses she had chargers of her own to ride; she broke lances with a royal duke; instead of a pitchfork she carried a banner and a sword; instead of doing menial work herself, she had pages attached to her service. From being a little girl, ordered hither and thither by her parents, she had blossomed suddenly into the envoy of God, browbeating a king into doing the bidding of the King of Kings. The change of worlds and of circumstances must have been, to say the least of it, difficult to grasp.

In this changed world Jeanne could have practically anything she liked to ask for—clothes, banners, horses, and accoutrements. To do her justice, it would appear that she did not have to ask for them, but merely accepted and used them with pleasure once they had been given. Contemporary records exist, describing tunics of cloth of gold and scarlet, lined with fur[1]; contemporary account-books record the purchase by the Duke of Orleans of crimson Brussels cloth, green cloth, and white satin; they dressed her in the colours of the house of Orleans—scarlet and green—embroidering the heraldic nettles of Orleans on her robes; the townsfolk of Orleans subscribed to send her such miscellaneous gifts as corn, wine, bread, partridges, pheasants, rabbits, and capons. Probably these tributes in kind appealed to her less than the gifts of apparel,

---

[1] *Chronique dite des Cordeliers,* in *La vraie Jeanne d'Arc,* Père Ayroles, Vol. III, p. 631; *Procès,* Vol. IV, p. 445: *Chronique de Georges Chastellain.*

for she was as abstemious as regards eating and drinking as she was natural in her love of finery. It has been suggested, and I think with truth, that Jeanne as a captain was shrewdly aware of the value of fine clothes, floating standards, and shining armour for the inspiration of her followers, but it detracts in no way from her ideals to recognise with a smile that in this matter the service of God was agreeably compatible with the tastes of her age and sex.

Two other feminine traits are chronicled by her contemporaries, surprising and endearing: her womanly voice and her ready tears. They soften the conception which might otherwise incline to harshness. Both Guy de Laval and Perceval de Boulainvilliers, the one in a letter to his mother, the other in his letter to the Duke of Milan, make reference to her voice: *Assez voix de femme*, says de Laval; her voice is womanly, says Boulainvilliers.[1] Yet the latter was not trying to make her out more feminine than she need be, for in the preceding sentence he says frankly that she had something virile in her bearing, and remarks also that, so great was her strength in the endurance of fatigue, she could spend six days and six nights without removing a single piece of her armour. This clear voice, proceeding from the sturdy peasant, evidently struck both these young men as something agreeably unexpected. Boulainvilliers, again, in the same letter, is responsible for a comment (though by no means our only authority) on her capacity for tears: her tears, he says, flow freely. She was, in fact, emotional, and wept copiously at every possible opportunity—as queer a mixture of feminine and masculine attributes as ever relentlessly assaulted the enemy and then wept to see him hurt.

[1] *Procès*, Vol. V, p. 108; *Procès*, Vol. V, p. 120.

Chapter II

THE HUNDRED YEARS' WAR

i

It will be assumed (perhaps unjustifiably, but I hope forgivably) for the purposes of this brief chapter, that the reader is possessed of no greater knowledge of conditions in France at the time of Jeanne's birth and during her subsequent career than he may have vaguely and confusedly remembered from the unpalatable books of his schooldays. I have observed that quite well-educated people retain no more than a vague impression that Jeanne d'Arc was a peasant girl who heard voices, saw visions, raised the siege of Orleans, and was burnt to death by the English at Rouen. Going a step further, you may be told that an English soldier made two pieces of wood into a cross, and gave it to her as the flames rose round her on the pyre. Such romantic facts and details have taken a hold on the general mind, kindly abetted by such brilliant and untrustworthy artists as Mr. Bernard Shaw and M. Anatole France. But if you ask what the English were doing in France, and why Jeanne's own countrymen connived with the English at her burning, they are unable to give any clear answer. I have observed, also, a tendency to believe that very little is known of Jeanne beyond the cardinal facts of her inspiration, achievement, and death. Nothing could be less true. We know practically every detail of her passive existence as a child and, as to the few months of her active career, they are so thoroughly documented that we know exactly where she spent each day, and in whose company; what she wore, what horse she rode, what arms she bore, what she ate and drank; and, more importantly still, what words she uttered. Scores of her friends, neighbours, followers, and companions-in-arms have left vivid testimony as to her appearance, manners, habits, character, and speech. The idea that there is any paucity of material for reconstructing her life and personality is fallacious in the last degree.

The initial difficulty, however, lies in disentangling the twisted strands of history before the pattern of Jeanne can stand out, clear-cut, simple, uncompromising. The state of political parties, the rich crowd of personages, the endless rivalries, battles, truces, treaties, assassinations, relationships, alliances, enmities, treacheries, produce an effect of maddening bewilderment upon the reader. It seems impossible, at first, that he can ever hope to sort them out. All those various kings and princes—they all seem to have been christened by the same name, or a name chosen out of a most unenterprising handful of names. They all seem to have been each other's uncles, nephews, cousins, sons-in-law, brothers-in-law, or sometimes merely fathers and sons. The difficulty one found as a child in arranging one's own relations, who at least were living people with recognisable features, personal characteristics, and known homes, is as nothing compared with the difficulty of distinguishing between these remote figures of history, whose faces are unknown and whose names for the most part are meaningless labels plus a Roman numeral. It is absurdly difficult to differentiate, without a conscious effort, between a Charles V, a Charles VI, and a Charles VII. How greatly do the victims of this system of nomenclature suffer from its levelling impersonality! Immediate and instinctive recognition refuses to leap into the mind. Nor can I believe that any honest reader would maintain that occasional epithets really assist him: John the Good, John the Fearless, Philip the Bold, Charles the Bad—such downright black-and-whiteness fails to convince and offers very little help towards instant identification. Then, again, historians, in an almost inevitable effort to avoid clumsy repetition, seek to vary their descriptive references to the prince in momentary occupation of their paragraphs: he becomes "the late king's son-in-law," or "the younger brother of the queen," or "the nephew of the cardinal," until the unfortunate reader holds his head in the effort to remember who the late king was, or who the queen is, or who the cardinal. In the case of the historians of Jeanne d'Arc, an extra confusion is introduced, for, since they are obliged constantly to allude to the young man whom Jeanne was trying to restore to his throne, they refer to him now as the Dauphin, now as the King, now as Charles VII, now as Charles *tout court*, now as "the son of the late mad King"—anything rather than choose one form of designation and, having chosen it, stick to it. All these traps lie in the way of the historian and, consequently, of his reader. I have suffered from them myself to such an extent that I have come to the conclusion that, even at the risk of monotonous repetition, it is better to say France, France; England, England; Burgundy, Burgundy; Dauphin, Dauphin; Orleans, Orleans; over and over again, rather than introduce a possibly elegant but certainly confusing variation. The difficulty of understanding the situation existing in France at the time when Jeanne d'Arc was a child is sufficiently great without the introduction of stylistic complications.

ii

In order to understand the task which confronted Jeanne, it is necessary to start with some knowledge of the back-history of France up to the time of her birth. Never had a country been so unhappily divided. Not only were Frenchmen divided amongst themselves, but the kingdom itself was disputed by two different thrones. War, both civil and foreign, had intermittently been raging for over seventy years. Stated briefly the position which had led up to the war was as follows:

Through their descent from William the Conqueror, the Kings of England had always claimed and enjoyed sovereignty over the greater part of France. Normandy, of course, was theirs, and through Matilda, William the Conqueror's granddaughter, who had married Geoffrey of Anjou, they also possessed Maine, Anjou, and Touraine. Matilda's son, Henry II of England, in addition to these inherited provinces, further acquired Gascony, the Limousin, Poitou, the Angoumois, and other territories through his marriage with Eleanor of Aquitaine. It will readily be seen that such a partition of the whole country of France was liable to give rise to serious trouble. Then there were other contributing factors, which need not be gone into in too much detail here, but among which must be mentioned the constant interference of the French in Scottish affairs, and French interference in the vassal county of Flanders. It was obviously impossible for Edward III of England to tolerate the presence of French troops in Scotland; it was equally impossible for him to allow English trade with the Flemings to be imperilled by the actions of France. The Flemings themselves, under the leadership of Jacob van Artevelde, appealed for help to the English King, going so far as to suggest that he should definitely lay claim to the French crown. It would have suited the Flemings admirably to become the vassals of England instead of France, for the English interests were their own, and although they could scarcely support the King of England against their lawful liege the King of France, they could quite well and logically, as the vassals of England, oppose the King of France, if he were to be declared a usurper, in favour of the English King.

This invitation of the Flemings gave Edward III a welcome pretext for laying his claims officially before his own Parliament and also before his princely equals on the Continent. It was, of course, an unjustifiable and, as it proved in the end, an exceedingly foolish step. However, he took it, backed by the support of the German Emperor, the Duke of Brabant, and other rulers. The Hundred Years' War between France and England had begun (1337.) (See map at end of book.)

The Hundred Years' War means, in brief, that for a hundred years the Kings of England attempted to unite France and England under one crown—their own. They tried hereditary justification, and they tried force of arms. Neither attempt, in the long run, was successful. A certain amount of blood was shed, and a considerable amount of suffering entailed, all to no purpose. The Hundred Years' War was one of the most foolish and ill-advised wars ever undertaken.

It is fortunately not in the least necessary to follow the ups and downs of the English cause throughout the first eighty-odd years of the war. The battles of Poitiers, Crécy, and Agincourt were only incidents in the general complication which obliged the reluctant Jeanne d'Arc to become the saviour of her country. The treaties of Tournai (1340), Brétigny (1360), Auxerre (1412), Arras (1414), the truces of Calais (1347), Bruges (1375), were no more than temporary interruptions in a conflict which must already have begun to seem interminable and insoluble. These battles and treaties and truces all preceded the day when Jeanne rode into Chinon to take control of the situation, and require no more than a passing mention. It is necessary, however, to explain in greater detail the vital Treaty of Troyes (May 1420). By the terms of this treaty, it was agreed that Henry V of England should:

(i) take the title of regent and heir of France;

(ii) marry Catherine, the daughter of the French King Charles VI, succeed to the throne of France, and thus unite France and England.

(iii) Furthermore it was agreed that no consideration should be accorded to Charles the "so-called" Dauphin, son of Charles VI, the then reigning King: no treaty of peace or concord was to be concluded with him, without the consent of "us three" (the Kings of France and England, and the Duke of Burgundy). This extraordinary clause in the Treaty of Troyes really meant that Charles the Dauphin could henceforward and legally have no say at all in the affairs of France. He was declared a bastard, if not in so many words, then at least by implication.[1]

The marriage of Henry V of England and Catherine of France duly took place (June 1420), but neither Henry nor Charles VI long survived it. Henry V died two years later

[1]There were, of course, other clauses, but for purposes of simplification I have picked out the three most important.

(August 1422), and Charles VI within two months of his son-in-law (October 1422). Men of very different types, they each left a son who, by reason respectively of his age and his nature, was quite incapable of dealing with the more than awkward position created by the Treaty of Troyes. There were now, in fact, two Kings of France, one of them a baby nine months old, the other a futile youth of nineteen. How could either the little Henry VI of England, or the ineffectual Charles VII of France, grapple with the problem his father had bequeathed to him? Henry VI, of course, was out of the running altogether. His rattle was still more important to him than his sceptre. Cutting his teeth troubled him more than the succession to the throne of France. Charles VII was out of the running also, though for a different reason. In his case, it was not his tender age which precluded him from playing his part in public affairs, but the inherent weakness of his character. For this he was perhaps no more to blame than was Henry VI to blame for having inherited the double crown of England and of France at an age when he could neither properly walk nor talk. Charles VII could not help being born a backboneless creature, any more than Henry VI could help being nine months old. Neither of them had any choice in the matter. Little people should not be called upon to become great kings. Such a demand of destiny is fair neither upon the sovereign nor the kingdom.

Charles VII had the further excuse of a bad heredity. We cannot know for certain who his father was, his mother, Isabeau de Bavière, according to that clause in the Treaty of Troyes, having implied that he was not the son of his official father Charles VI. Otherwise, she would scarcely have allowed him to be described as the "so called" Dauphin. Was he the son of Charles VI or was he not? Perhaps even his mother could not have answered this question by a yes or a no.[1] At any rate, she allowed it to be understood by all those who could read

[1] Scandal said that his true father was Louis Duke of Orleans, brother of Charles VI. See genealogical table on p. 138.

between the lines of the Treaty of Troyes that the parentage of her son was, to say the least of it, doubtful. Neither the first nor the last woman to entertain such doubts, she stands out in history as one of the few women so brazen as to declare those doubts in an official document.

Whether Charles VII was the son of the mad Charles VI or not, his heredity on his mother's side was sufficiently dangerous. Isabeau de Bavière was a woman of the dominating type which tends to produce weak sons. Whether he was the son of Charles VI or not, he was indubitably the son of Isabeau, a mother who had not only allowed it to be publicly insinuated that her child was a bastard, but had also allowed him to be described in terms surely as offensive as were ever applied to royal prince. He was excluded from all part in public affairs—*considéré les horribles et énormes crimes et débits perpétrés audit royaume de France par Charles, soi-disant dauphin viennois,* as it was expressed in the Treaty of Troyes. Although there is little to be said in favour of Charles VII, one cannot withhold all sympathy from the son of such a mother. The pressure of her personality on him in his early years must have been crushing, and, moreover, it was his misfortune to be born with a nature meekly resigned to accept insults. Both his mother and his enemies might insult him with impunity. *You, Charles of Valois, who used to call yourself Dauphin and now without reason call yourself King* . . . thus the Duke of Bedford addressed him in a letter inviting Charles to meet him in the open field. Charles offered no more retaliation to this piece of insolence than he had previously offered to the brutality of his mother. A poor creature—a poor warped weak creature—it is not surprising that he should have allowed his kingdom to remain split under the domination of other princes, who, whatever their faults, were at least more vigorous men than he.

iii

The above reference to the domination of other princes leads inevitably to some further exposition of the state of affairs in unhappy France on the deaths of Henry V and Charles VI in 1422. This state of affairs was by then so complicated that the only clear way of setting it forth must lie in numbered paragraphs:

(1) Henry VI of England, an infant nine months old, was recognised, according to the terms of the Treaty of Troyes, as King of France and England, with his uncle, the Duke of Bedford, as regent during his minority.

(2) Charles the Dauphin, nominally Charles VII of France, was excluded from his succession to the French throne by the terms of the Treaty of Troyes.

(3) The French themselves were divided into two parties, known as Burgundians and Armagnacs. The former party took its name from their head, the Duke of Burgundy; the latter from Bernard d'Armagnac, who had assumed the leadership on behalf of the three young sons of the murdered Duke of Orleans. The Armagnac party should thus more properly have become known later on as the Orleanist party, but, since Armagnac's name stuck to it, its adherents are always referred to as the Armagnacs. Roughly speaking, the west and south were Armagnac, the north and east Burgundian.

(4) These two parties were at bitter enmity. This enmity, which had originated in the old rivalry for power between the Dukes of Burgundy and Orleans, had been further increased by the assassination, in 1407, of Louis of Orleans by John of Burgundy. (This was the occasion when Bernard d'Armagnac had undertaken the conduct of the party for the young sons of the murdered duke.) So bitter was the hostility between the two parties, both personal and political, that all considerations of patriotism were swept aside in the struggle for supremacy. Naturally the French should have united to drive the English for ever out of France. Far from this, the Burgundians entered into a definite alliance with the English, for which reason their faction is often referred to as the Anglo-Burgundian party.

(5) A further incitement was given to their mutual hatred by the murder of John of Burgundy, himself the murderer of Louis of Orleans, in 1419, at Montereau, where he had gone for a meeting with Charles the Dauphin. It is not known for certain whether Charles himself was privy to the plot, but he was regarded by the Burgundians as guilty, and the new Duke of Burgundy, Philip, took an oath that his father's assassin should never assume the crown of France. In pursuit of this revenge, he acquired the support of Charles's mother, Isabeau de Bavière, and the Treaty of Troyes (1420) was the direct result, by which the English were more firmly than ever assured of their claim to France.

(6) The Armagnacs, on the other hand, may be regarded as the Nationalist party, since their opposition to the Anglo-Burgundians involved them logically in hostility with the English.

This extremely bald and simplified statement may help to explain the situation in France at the time when Jeanne d'Arc was receiving her first celestial commands at Domremy.

iv

It may help, also, to explain the magnitude of the task Jeanne regarded herself as summoned to undertake. A child in years, she was asked to solve a problem which the most experienced and violent men of two nations had been struggling to solve for nearly a century. On her own side, she was to meet with the poorest backing. Trying to make an impression on Charles VII was almost as unprofitable an occupation as trying to make a permanent dent in a pillow. On the other side, she had at least two men of outstanding personality and ability as her adversaries. What peasant girl could prove herself a match for Philip of Burgundy and John of Lancaster?

John of Lancaster, Duke of Bedford, son of Henry IV and Mary Bohun, brother of Henry V, uncle and godfather of Henry VI, had already lived for twenty-three years in this world when Jeanne d'Arc entered it, and thus had attained the age of forty when she arose to take arms against him. The difference in their ages was even less considerable than the difference in their upbringing. The King's son had been brought up in the magnificence of the Court; invested with the Order of the Bath at ten years old, with the Garter at eleven, with his dukedom at fifteen; by the time he was thirty-three he found himself the guardian of his nephew the infant King. It was not very long before he found himself Regent of France also. His soldier brother, Henry V, had on his death-bed (1422) directed him to offer this position to the Duke of Burgundy: the Duke of Burgundy had declined it. The mantle of regency descended upon Bedford himself. Two months after the death of Henry V, he was attending the funeral of Charles VI at St. Denis, and re-entered Paris with the naked sword of sovereign power carried before him.

Within a very few months (April 1423) he had concluded an alliance with the Dukes of Burgundy and Brittany, and had married the Duke of Burgundy's young sister, Anne, at Troyes, in June of the same year.

The Duke of Bedford, however unsympathetic a figure he may appear to the partisans of Jeanne d'Arc, was in fact no sinister character. His business, so far as we are concerned, was to look after the English interest in France, and in doing it he was only doing his duty. As an English prince, and a soldier, he could do no less. It must be recorded to his credit that when he could spare the time from his job of keeping the country in subjection, and of managing the turbulent elements he had to deal with, he did his utmost as an administrator to bring contentment and even prosperity to the people under his rule, encouraging their commerce, reorganising their debased coinage, suppressing so far as lay within his power such abuses as the ill-treatment of prisoners and the prevalent system of bribery. Hot-tempered and red-faced as he was, with a strong beaked nose and strong prominent chin, his humane qualities surprise us by their unexpectedness in that savage age. In war he was ever opposed to the rash act, although his courage was beyond question; in peace a dignified and sober servant of his country, he never allowed his personal ambitions to come between himself and the duty he owed to the crown. The blackest charge against his name is, of course, his treatment of Jeanne d'Arc when once she had fallen, by purchase, into his hands, but even here it is necessary to remember that he regarded her, not only as the most dangerous enemy of the English cause, but also as an evil thing acting under the guidance of some dark sorcery, which, to a devout son of the Church like Bedford, could be nothing but anathema. "That limb of the Fiend," he called her, and no doubt sincerely meant it. With soldierly generosity, however, he would not deny her the credit of the amazing services she had rendered to France.

Of his troubles at home, especially in connexion with his brother, Gloucester, it is not necessary to speak here. They have no direct bearing on the more immediate problem which confronted the daughter of Jacques d'Arc in the valley of the Meuse.

Chapter III

DOMREMY (1)

i

Domremy lay, a small village of the Meuse valley, relatively far removed from the troubles of a harried France. Relatively, but not wholly. Both politically and geographically its position was as absurdly complicated, on a small scale, as the position of its greater neighbour, the rest of France. It had the misfortune to be a border village, half of it situated in France and the other half in the duchy of Bar.[1] It is even a matter of dispute whether Jacques d'Arc's house was included in the French part or the Barrois part of the village. M. Siméon Luce tends to the opinion that it lay in the French part.[2] Without going into the question of which half could actually claim Jeanne's birthplace, the fact remains that the allegiance of the inhabitants of Domremy was difficult to decide. It meant that half the village belonged immediately, officially, and geographically to France, and the other half to a duchy committed to the Anglo-Burgundian party. It meant, moreover, that according

[1] As this reference to the duchy of Bar may naturally puzzle all those who have been accustomed to regard Jeanne d'Arc as a native of Lorraine, I had better explain the reason. It is simply that the duchy of Bar formed part of the duchy of Lorraine, although under a separate ruler. Such portion of Domremy as did not come immediately under the French crown, came under the Duke of Bar, and thus only indirectly under the Duke of Lorraine. Thus it is more accurate to speak of Jeanne's village as lying in the Barrois than as lying in Lorraine, though, less strictly, it is possible to include it under the geographical name Lorraine. In the popular version, the whole has proved greater than the part.

Jules Quicherat, the most authoritative of all Jeanne's historians, puts the geographical position clearly (*Aperçus nouveaux sur Jeanne d'Arc*, p. 2): "Domremy lies on the left bank of the Meuse, at the foot of a slope whose summit then belonged to the duchy of Bar; the heights above the opposite bank marked the boundaries of Lorraine; thus, only the valley with the river flowing through it was French territory."

[2] Siméon Luce, *Jeanne d'Arc à Domremy*, p. cxcvi, footnote.

to the terms of a treaty of capitulation concluded in 1428 between the Anglo-Burgundian party and the duchy of Bar, reinforced by an act of homage exacted from the Barrois by the Duke of Bedford, the semi-dependent village of Domremy ran a grave risk of falling entirely under the domination of English arms—a risk which Jeanne, her patriotism aroused, could never have tolerated. It was bad enough to hear of the whole of France threatened by the domination of the foreigner; it gave an extra twist, a more personal stab, to see her native village threatened in the same way. It brought the menace nearer home. Domremy, in spite of the position geographically imposed upon it, was not in the least inclined to submit to Anglo-Burgundian rule: according to Jeanne's own subsequent statement, it counted only one avowed Burgundian in the whole of its population, whose head she would gladly have seen cut off, if that had been God's pleasure.[1] Whether that one Burgundian was her own *compère* or not makes little difference. Jeanne's unusually vindictive comment shows what she thought of Burgundians in her village. Even admitting that her first resentments and her first perceptions of the danger were limited and local, she had only to extend her range a little, looking up and down the river, to realise that Domremy among the villages of the Meuse valley was not unique in its unfortunately divided situation. Badonvilliers, Burey-en-Vaux, Mauvages, Goussaincourt, Saint-Germain and others suffered from the same disadvantage. On the other hand, certain other of the neighbouring villages, such as Maxey-sur-Meuse, were whole-heartedly Anglo-Burgundian. The remarkable thing is that, in spite of these differences and difficulties, local feeling should not have run higher in the officially split villages themselves, or between such villages as Domremy and Maxey, which were entirely opposed as to their politics, both geographically and by conviction. Little boys and rowdy youths took part in rival fights, echoes of the larger quarrel in progress

[1]*Procès*, Vol. I, p. 65. This refers to Gérardin d'Epinal. *Compère* means that Jeanne and Gérardin were co-godparents to the same child.

DOMREMY AND THE VALLEY OF THE MEUSE TO-DAY

in greater France, but a certain Doctor Liétard, a native of Domremy, told M. Siméon Luce that he, as a boy, between 1840 and 1850, had taken part in these schoolboy squabbles which still went on between Domremy and Maxey. Now by 1840 the Hundred Years' War could scarcely still be held responsible, and it seems more likely that both Jeanne's contemporaries in 1420 and thereabouts, and the adolescents of 1840, squabbled for the sake of squabbling, as a healthy and normal outlet for their high spirits and hot young blood. In Jeanne's day, of course, the squabble arose out of a more immediate pretext. It was natural that the pugnacious youth of the Meuse valley should pretend to be violently Burgundian or Armagnac. It was suggested, even, that Jeanne herself might have joined in the fun with the boys, but on this point she replied, most unbelievably, that she could not remember; she remembered, however, that she had seen those of the village of Domremy who had fought against those of Maxey, when they returned badly hurt and mishandled (*bene læsi et cruentati*).[1] We may here suspect Jeanne of not answering her judges quite truthfully. Either she went out with the boys of Domremy to fight the boys of Maxey or else she did not. In either case, she could not have forgotten. Whatever the truth may be, and whatever her reasons for evading it, there seems to be no particular reason for imagining that she participated in these escapades. There seems to be no justification for imagining Jeanne as a tomboy. On the contrary, all the evidence points to her having been a serious and aloof little girl, even to the extent of being regarded as rather a prig by the other children. This point is perhaps worthy of consideration, remembering that her adoption of boy's clothes was later held against her as one of the principal articles of her accusation.

ii

In the village of Domremy, Jacques, or Jacquot, d'Arc held a respect-worthy position. He was not a native of Domremy,

[1] *Procès*, Vol. I, p. 66.

having been born at Ceffonds in Champagne, in the diocese of Troyes, in 1375, transferring himself to Domremy just before his marriage to Isabelle Romée of Vouthon, another village lying within five miles of Domremy. Oddly enough, his name was not really d'Arc at all, or, rather, it did not sound like that when pronounced by the people of Lorraine. It sounded like d'Ay. So strong, indeed, was (and still is) the local habit of suppressing the *r* and of pronouncing the *a* short, that it is actually and phonetically written d'Ay in a most pompous and important document, sealed with a Great Seal of green wax, and a double lacing of ribbons red and green, no less a document than the Act of Ennoblement conferred by Charles VII on Jeanne and her family.[1] The paradox thus arises that Jacques, as a native of Champagne, probably pronounced his name in one way, and his children, with their Lorraine accent, in another.

Jacques d'Arc has been represented both as very poor and as very prosperous. The truth, as usual, lies between the two. In actual fact, it appears that he was what we should now call a peasant-farmer, with certain official responsibilities suggested by his exemplary character and that of his wife, as much as by his social standing and solvency. An upright man in a small place, it was natural that he should be appointed to such functions as *adjudicataire* of the local château (1419), and subsequently as doyen or sergeant of Domremy (1423), ranking immediately after the mayor and sheriff, and being charged with the collection of the *tailles*, a tax levied on persons other than noble or ecclesiastical. He is to be found also among seven other worthies of his village, answerable for the tribute exacted by the *damoiseau* of Commercy (1423). Four years later (1427), he is to be found active as delegate of his neighbours in a dispute conducted before the governor of Vaucouleurs, Robert de Baudricourt, a captain who, however reluctantly, and much to his own surprise, was destined to

---

[1] *Procès*, Vol. V, p. 150. The *Chronique de la Pucelle* spells it Daix.

play an important rôle at the outset of the extraordinary career of Jacques d'Arc's daughter.

Taking all these facts together, it becomes apparent that Jacques d'Arc was a personage of some consideration in his adopted village. Not only did he officially rank third in its hierarchy, but he was charged with responsible offices in its little local affairs. This is no very glorious boast to advance on behalf of the father of the notorious Pucelle. The village was small and humble; Jacques d'Arc was small and humble too. He lived in a cottage. He married a girl from a neighbouring village. The records of his official life suggest no more than that he was locally respected; they suggest in no way that he played a part in anything more than local business. He made himself esteemed and trusted by his fellow-villagers. He represented them when representation was needed. He was a pious and decent man, and, by all showing, his wife was a pious and decent woman too. They were in no way remarkable, and are perhaps best described as being of a good, useful, and enduring type.

There is not much to be drawn, even by deduction, from what we know of Jacques d'Arc's character. Its lines are the simple ones of probity, piety, and perhaps also a certain severity—although Mr. Andrew Lang does suggest that there were "convivial elements in the character of this austere sire."[1] This suggestion he bases on the fact that when Jacques d'Arc went to Reims for the coronation, having received a present of money from the King, he remained two full months at the inn of the *Ane Rayé*, kept by the widow Alice Moriau, opposite to the Cathedral, instead of returning to Domremy after the ceremonies were over. Mr. Lang draws the inference that he could get more enjoyment in Reims, a town famous for its wines, than he could at home.

[1] *The Maid of France*, p. 164.

iii

From everything we can gather of his wife Isabelle, or, in the local patois, Zabillet, she belonged to exactly the same type as Jacques. There is a unanimity in the comments of their friends and neighbours which links this estimable couple in a well-matched conjunction. "They were good and faithful Catholics; good working-people (*laboratores*) of good repute, leading an honest life according to their condition."[1] "They were labourers, truly good Catholics, honest and worthy, according to their means, for they were not rich."[2] "They were good Catholics, of good repute, honest people, honest labourers."[3] "They were an honest couple, Catholics, of good repute, hard-working, honest in their poverty, for they were not rich."[4] "They were persons of good repute, good Catholics, and respectable people."[5] By the time one has read all this, and more to the same effect, one is convinced to the point of exasperation of the unassailable respectability of the d'Arc *ménage*. Isabelle was even said to have acquired her surname of Romée from having made a pilgrimage to Rome, but this is an uncertain point, and it is quite possible that she may have inherited the right to call herself Romée from some ancestor who made the pilgrimage in question. Whether she had been to Rome or not, she was certainly a woman of devout and irreproachable character. She brought up her children well, teaching them the Pater, the Ave, and the Credo[6]; she taught her daughter Jeanne to be a good housewife and to take a pride in the crafts considered suitable to her sex.[7] It was by no fault of Isabelle Romée, if, instead of a chicken, she had hatched an eagle.

[1]*Procès*, Vol. II, p. 388: Deposition of Jean Morel.
[2]*Procès*, Vol. II, p. 395: Deposition of Beatrice Estellin.
[3]*Procès*, Vol. II, p. 398: Deposition of Jeannette Thévenin.
[4]*Procès*, Vol. II, p. 403: Deposition of Jeannette Thiesselin.
[5]*Procès*, Vol. II, p. 422: Deposition of Gérardin d'Epinal.
[6]*Procès*, Vol. I, p. 47.
[7]*Procès*, Vol. I, p. 51.

She must have been a woman of proud spirit. It was she who, although *très fort malade* at the time, removed herself from Domremy to Orleans in 1440, at the age of sixty, some nine years after the deaths of her husband and her daughter, and, after a lapse of ten more years, instituted an appeal which worried the Pope into ordering a re-examination into that daughter's trial. By the time that re-examination started, she was *décrépite par l'âge*, and was asking to be excused from attending all the sittings. None but a woman of character could even have envisaged such an attempt, much less have carried it through. If one considers the circumstances of the parties concerned, it appears astounding that a woman, born a peasant of France in the fifteenth century, should have had the courage to tackle so supreme and mysterious a figure as the Pope in Rome—an achievement far more surprising than that of the injured mother of to-day, who sends a letter to the Home Office petitioning for the reprieve of her child. One cannot help feeling that such a mother, who, although ill, bothered the Pope to that extent, was a mother worthy to engender the daughter she did engender, and that perhaps justice has never been wholly done to her.

iv

Life in the little Domremy household, with two such parents at the head of it, cannot have been soft for its children. Isabelle could scold; Jacques could threaten; and, when Jacques threatened, he did it in no measured terms. His threats took the form of saying that, in given circumstances, he would drown his daughter himself, if her brothers refused to do so.[1] There spoke no sentimental, spoiling father, but a father who brought up his daughter in a proper, moral school, safeguarding her virtue as a father should. He would rather drown her than allow her to lose it. Poor Jacques d'Arc, he seems to have been endowed with his share of his daughter's gift of divination.

[1] *Procès*, Vol. I, p. 132.

He suffered from the most distressing dreams about her—dreams that she would go off with armed men instead of making the comfortable marriage he was devising for her.

They were decent, strong-minded, respectable people, and to them was born, in January 1412, their second daughter and fourth child, whom they named, not very inventively, Jeanne.[1]

V

Legends subsequently and inevitably sprang up, attendant upon the circumstances of that mid-winter day. One cannot start life as a mere squalling little ordinary Jeanne in a cottage somewhere in provincial France, and then turn oneself into a Maid of Orleans, a Pucelle of dreaded reputation, without some legend arising around the actual date of one's birth. But for once such legends, far from confusing the historian, help him to establish the exact date he wants. Jeanne, daughter of Jacques d'Arc, was born on January 6th; Epiphany; Twelfth Night; the day of the Three Kings. She would have chosen more suitably had she chosen the feast of Saint Michael, Saint Catherine, or Saint Margaret to make her first appearance in the world. The choice, however, had not been left to her. It seems destructive, in the face of several pretty fairy-tales, to suggest that the village at the moment took no more interest in the labour of Isabelle Romée than it took in the labour of any other villager's wife. A woman accepted her pain in her turn; she went through her necessary hours; and in the course of time was delivered. Country people take these things very much as a matter of course. But subsequently, needless to say, everybody remembered that Jeanne had been born on the feast of the Epiphany. Even the poultry of the village, according

[1]*Procès*, Vol. I, p. 46: She was always called Jeannette at home, and never Jeanne until she went to France. The other children were Jacquemin and Jean, her elder brothers; Catherine, a sister who is presumed to have died young; and Pierre, a younger brother.

to some accounts, seem to have noticed it. Perceval de Boulainvilliers, in that letter to the Duke of Milan, flings himself with
true mediæval fantasy into his version of the story: "It was
during the night of the Epiphany that she first saw the light
in this mortal life, and, wonderful to relate, the poor inhabitants of the place were seized with an inconceivable joy. Still
uninformed of the birth of the Maid, they ran one to the other,
enquiring what new thing had happened. For some, it was a
cause of fresh rejoicing. What can one add? The cocks, as
heralds of this happy news, crowed in a way that had never
been heard before, beating their bodies with their wings;
continuing for two hours to prophesy this new event."[1]

Andrew Lang, usually determined to romanticise as far as
his conscience would allow him, in this instance comments
with sober good sense.[2] He sees no reason why all this should
not have occurred, nor does he see why the facts should not be
regarded as highly probable instead of miraculous. Twelfth
Night would naturally be celebrated with noise and festivity;
the villagers "would run about in high spirits, and awaken
the poultry." Later on, of course, when Jeanne became famous,
the superstitious gleefully interpreted the facts to suit their
own purposes. That, for him, and for me also, is the long and
short of the matter. The important thing is that the legend
enables us to fix the exact date of her birthday.

vi

She was baptised in the little church at Domremy, by one
Jean Minet, or so she believed,[3] and her godfathers and god-
mothers were numerous. Her parents, after all, were well
known and much esteemed, counting many friends among
their neighbours. Considering that Jacques d'Arc and Isabelle

[1]*Procès*, Vol. V, p. 116: Letter of Perceval de Boulainvilliers to the Duke
of Milan.
[2]Andrew Lang, *The Maid of France*, p. 25.
[3]*Procès*, Vol. I, p. 46.

Romée already had three children, they still seem to have had plenty of friends to draw on in compliment at the birth of their fourth child. Moreover it was still the custom to give one's child a lot of godparents, the number not yet having been limited by the Council of Trent. It is odd to think that, but for the circumstance of these honest people having been invited to watch that particular baby at the font, they would by now be swallowed up into the blackness of death and obscurity, with no more record of their names and personalities than millions upon millions of their equals. As it is, they have been spared from ranking among the unnumbered and anonymous dead. We know them all by name, and several of them by their avocations. In some cases we have a report of their actual words, spoken some forty-four years later, when the representatives of the Pope—surely as alarmingly as once the soldiery from whom their small god-daughter had liberated France—descended upon them to ask them what they could remember of that god-daughter as a child. By one of the many freaks of history, that irresponsible infant conferred a relative immortality upon those humble peasants who happened to be friends of her family so long ago as fourteen hundred and twelve.

Jeanne herself displays a surprising vagueness about the names and number of her godparents. She mentions only the first six out of the ten, though she does add that her mother had told her there were others:

Jeanne, wife of Aubéry or Aubry, mayor of Domremy.
Agnès, surname unknown.
Jeanne, surname unknown, unless, as seems probable, she was referring
    to the wife of Thévenin the wheelwright, who is known to have
    been her godmother.
Sibylla, surname unknown.
Jean Lingué.
Jean Barrey.
Jean Morel, labourer, of Greux near Domremy.
Beatrice, wife of Estellin, a *cultivateur* of Domremy.

Jeannette, wife of Thiesselin, a clerk of Domremy, originally from Vittel.

Mention is made also of a Jean Rainguesson, but, as both he and Jean Lingué were dead by the time her sponsors were required to give evidence on her behalf, nothing, unluckily for them, is known of them beyond their names.

They varied in their ages: Beatrice Estellin was thirty-six; Jeanne Thévenin and Jean Morel were each twenty-six; Jeannette Thiesselin only sixteen. Thus by 1456, when called upon to testify, Beatrice Estellin was just eighty, Jeanne Thévenin and Jean Morel just seventy, and Jeannette Thiesselin sixty. They do not seem to have taken their early duties very seriously, for Jeanne remarks that no one but her mother taught her the articles of her faith.[1] They were all agreed, however, that she was an exceptionally pious child, and had been brought up as a good Catholic. They were very emphatic and unanimous on this point; just as emphatic and unanimous as they were on the point of her parents' outstanding honesty and virtue.

[1] *Procès*, Vol. I, p. 47.

D

Chapter IV

DOMREMY (2)

i

Jeanne d'Arc's early life at Domremy, for all the trouble, controversy, and legend to which it subsequently gave rise, was in fact one of the most simple and ordinary description. Life was hard; it is hard for the peasant at Domremy to-day. Passing down the streets of that poverty-stricken village, it is difficult to imagine much difference between conditions then and now. The houses are still little better than hovels, damp, ill-ventilated, and ill-repaired. Whole families live in rooms whose squalor we should scarcely tolerate in a farm stable. Thanks to the car-loads of tourists who come to spend a few hours visiting the birthplace of the national saint, and strolling about the sites once hallowed by her presence, the village street is kept a little cleaner than most village streets in that country district where men and their animals live in a truly Irish state of sociability; but go behind the houses, and you will find the hens scratching among the manure-heaps still lusciously and oozingly stacked beside the kitchen door. It is fair to presume that in Jeanne's day nobody bothered whether the manure-heap was within sight or out of it, any more than they bother to-day in the less distinguished villages of Lorraine; nor is it unfair to imagine that the condition of the dwellings was, if anything, more deplorable and more insanitary then than now. It is true that Jacques d'Arc was in a slightly superior position to the ordinary peasant, but the dark little rooms of his square grey house will convince anybody that Jeanne's days at home were spent in conditions of extreme harshness and discomfort —a harshness and discomfort which, of course, she took entirely for granted. She might almost as well have been sleeping in a cellar, and, in spite of Jacques d'Arc's superior position, there were certain features of Domremy life from which even the most prosperous could not escape. None, living in that valley, could escape the heavy morning mists which blanket the water-meadows and shut out the struggling sun. None could escape that cold and penetrating damp, least of all those who were obliged to rise early and to go out, huddled under a rough cloak, into the dripping pastures. It was a rheumatic rather than a gay existence. The peasants of Domremy, to this day, are not a pleasure-seeking race, and I doubt whether gaiety entered at any point into the life of Jeanne and her young companions, except in so far as they created it for themselves in certain innocent pastimes which later on were to figure so seriously amongst the other outrageous indictments of her trial. For the rest, a Domremy child found life a strict and businesslike affair. It was strict in a matter-of-fact way, scaling no romantic heights; strict in a plodding way, with its pleasant moments, its hours of sunshine as well as its hours of fog and rain. Perhaps for this very reason it seems all the more difficult to understand the sources of Jeanne's extraordinary inspiration. She was no Emily Brontë, denizen of wild moors. She was a perfectly ordinary little peasant girl, accustomed to take the rough with the smooth, born to a countryside which suggested no violent contrasts between reality as she lived it and reality as it might ideally be lived. True, there were certain features which might be said to excite the fancy of an imaginative child, but in the first place there is no reason to picture Jeanne, in her normal hours, as a particularly imaginative child, and in the second place the local traditions in themselves in no way superseded the customs of widespread country folk-lore. There were vast woods, big trees, and woodland springs; there were attendant tales of fairies; there were special days on which the children of the neighbourhood went out in a body to hang wreaths and garlands on the boughs—innocent festivals which, in one form or another, were being reproduced all over Europe with no greater significance than the survival of some local though ancient superstition. Everybody at Domremy had grown up with these customs, and everybody consequently took them as a matter of course. It was a little hard on Jacques d'Arc's daughter, who had gone out with the troop of other children ever since she was old enough to toddle the necessary distance, to be burnt some sixteen years later on a charge of idolatrous practices.

ii

If Jeanne were to return to Domremy to-day, she would notice but little change in the features of the landscape. She could stand at the top of the hill, and look across the valley at the hills opposite, with the same flat, characteristic, table-like top. She would notice that the forest no longer stretched right down to the river, but that the trees had been cleared to half-way up the slope, apparently in order to open the view from the steps of a new, enormous basilica, which she would soon, with consternation, discover to have been erected in her honour. Entering, she would discover with surprise that she, who had drawn her dying breath in torture, branded as a witch, was now regarded as a saint; and that the English, whose hands had hoisted her on to her funeral pyre, now hung up their flag in reverence to her name. Faintly puzzled by the mutability of human opinion, she might descend towards the village, passing on the way a crucifix erected at the very spot where the footpath she had followed to Neufchâteau had struck across the fields, and then she would come down between the houses and out into the village street, where the tiny church would present an almost familiar appearance, but on closer inspection would reveal itself as having turned the wrong way round. She would look in vain for the Château de l'Ile. Once outside the village, however, away from the works of man and among the works of God, she could very easily, and without being unduly disconcerted, pick her way to the sites and haunts she knew.

Domremy itself, a small grey village, lies, as has been said, in the valley of the Meuse. The valley of the Meuse fans out between the wooded hills of Lorraine. It is a green, large, gentle, and undramatic countryside. The Meuse at Domremy

THE MEUSE VALLEY AND THE BOIS CHENU
TO-DAY

is a slow and gentle stream. The water-meadows are lush and full of buttercups in spring. There are more cherry-trees in blossom than it is fair for any province to possess, and more cowslips and dandelions than are necessary to turn any grass from green to gold. In autumn the wooded hills are on fire with colour, ranging from the dark green of the fir-trees to the gold and red of the beeches. It is a lost, pleasant, rural land, with the little villages lying along the river as beads at intervals upon that silver string.

There is nothing sinister, or even suggestive, about Domremy or the Meuse valley. It lies rather out of the way, but that was all to its advantage in the unfortunate days when Englishmen, Burgundians, and Armagnacs snarled like quarrelsome dogs all over the rest of France. The repercussions of war which affected it really reduced themselves to occasional raids, and to brawls between the boys of neighbouring villages. For their broken heads the state of French and English politics was responsible, rather than anything inherent in the character of the Lorraine duchy. But for the distant war-like elements in French and English camps, the population of Lorraine, young and old, could have pursued its ordained course of life without disquiet or disturbance. There was nothing disquieting or disturbing about its fields and forests. Nothing in Nature suggested evil, violence, or mystery. All was calm and open; propitious, even, to the husbandman, thankful for his fertile soil and matter-of-factly resigned to such exigencies as were normally imposed by the seasons. There were neither mountains nor cliffs of fall; no ravines, chasms, or torrents; no melodramatic scenery; no haunt of giant, demon, spectre, or afreet. A pastoral rather than an agricultural region, when the sun breaks through the morning mists, it is as fair and smiling as many parts of rural France.

Then there are the woods: miles of beechwood, bright and shot with sun, translucently green as only young beech-trees can be green, carpeted with anemones, lily of the valley, wild strawberry; speared by the young fronds of Solomon's

Seal; crossed by many paths, and opened into clearings with newly cut cord-wood neatly stacked. So, at least, it is to-day: a richly wooded country on either side of the Meuse valley, and if there was any difference at the beginning of the fifteenth century it would be in favour of still deeper woods and paths with less danger of frequentation. In such a wood stood one of Jeanne d'Arc's favourite shrines (Notre Dame de Bermont), a couple of miles from her native village, so that her steps were often turned in that direction, and she must have known the way through the woods as well as the squirrel or the rabbit.

Another wood, more famous in history, lay nearer to the village, on the slope of a hill, and visible from the house of Jacques d'Arc. This was known as the Bois Chenu, or wood hoary with age, which may also be interpreted in the double sense of the word as meaning the wood of oak-trees. The Bois Chenu, on two counts, was regarded as a place to be avoided; it was the home of wild boars and wolves,[1] and it was also said to be the haunt of fairies. Jeanne herself later denied that she had heard this legend, but added that on her arrival at Chinon several people had asked her whether there was not a wood called the Bois Chenu in her country, because, apparently, certain prophecies were current, to the effect that a young girl who would work wonders should come from the neighbourhood of a wood of that name; "but," she added, "I never gave any credence."[2] From this statement it would appear that the Bois Chenu and its legends enjoyed not only a local but a more widespread reputation (unless, indeed, as is possible, Jeanne's own companions brought the first gossip about it to Chinon when they arrived there with her from Vaucouleurs?). Merlin and the Venerable Bede were both held responsible for these prophecies. Jeanne's own views on magic were flat,

---

[1] There are still some wild boars in the Bois Chenu to-day, but wolves are so rare that, when they do appear, they are thought to have strayed from other parts of France. *Ils sont égarés* (local information).

[2] *Procès*, Vol. I, p. 68.

sound, and contemptuous: "I hold all that," she said, "to be sorcery."[1] Similarly, when they asked her what she had done with her mandrake, she replied that she had not got a mandrake and had never possessed one; she had heard tell, she said, that there was a mandrake somewhere near the village, and that a nut-tree grew above it, though she did not know where; she had heard, also, that it was a dangerous thing, evil to possess; but she had never seen it, and was ignorant of the purposes to which it might be put. In short, although she had heard that it brought money, she did not believe it, and her voices had never told her anything about it.[2]

Nevertheless, her judges pursued her with questions as to other magical traditions of her native village, and on these questions she was ready to be more explicit. When they asked her about a certain tree, she replied frankly, without pretending not to know to which tree they alluded, that there was indeed a tree called the *Arbre des Dames* or, by others, the fairies' tree; or, again, *le Beau May*; a big tree, a beech, standing near a fountain. She had heard, and had seen with her own eyes, that persons attacked by fever went to drink of the waters of this fountain, but she did not know whether a cure was ever effected. She had heard, also, that the sufferers, when restored to health, had got up and walked to the tree in question. She had heard old people, though not her own contemporaries, say that the fairies held conversation there. Her own godmother, the wife of the mayor of Domremy, an honest woman, neither a soothsayer nor a witch, had said in her presence that she had seen fairies (*Dominas Fatales*) round that tree, but she, Jeanne, did not know whether that was true or not. For her own part, she had never, to her knowledge, seen the aforesaid fairies near that tree, though whether she had seen them elsewhere or not, she did not know. What she did know was, that the girls hung garlands on the branches, and that she herself had sometimes hung garlands there with her companions; sometimes they left them hanging, sometimes they brought them away.

[1] *Procès*, Vol. I, p. 187.   [2] *Procès*, Vol. I, pp. 88-9.

She added that since she had learned that she must go into France, she had taken as little part as possible in these games and amusements; since she had come to years of discretion (which in her case must be interpreted as twelve or thirteen), she could not recall having danced near the tree; it might be, she said, that she had danced there with children, but even then she sang rather than danced.[1] Why she thought it less offensive to sing than to dance, is not explained; perhaps because it brought her into no physical contact with other people, not even with children.

She could not, or would not, say whether Saint Catherine or Saint Margaret had ever spoken to her beside the tree. On the other hand, she replied, without hesitation, that they had spoken to her beside the neighbouring fountain, but could not remember what they had said to her there.[2]

All these stories of fatal women, mandrakes, and miraculous cures thus appear to have produced little but scorn or incredulity in Jeanne's mind. This is the more surprising, when we consider that she was, as an ignorant peasant, potentially as credulous and superstitious as the rest of her class. She seems, however, with her habitual gift of disregarding everything except the matter which directly and urgently concerned her, to have discounted her local traditions for what they were worth. "Yes," she says, in effect, "I heard about all that, but I never believed it." Whatever did succeed in convincing her, convinced her so unshakably that she was able to toss the rest aside.

All these stories, however silly and childish, were a part of rustic life. As such, they were innocent and inevitable. Such relaxations as the children's expeditions to the *Arbre des Dames* were only the natural escape from a daily existence which was always poor and sometimes harsh; they were treats away from the boring round. Children who had to scrub and dig and drive animals into the fields deserved a holiday every now and then, and if invented beings such as fairies were

[1]*Procès*, Vol. I, pp. 67–8.   [2]*Procès*, Vol. I, p. 87.

supposed to play a part in the day's outing, no sinister motive could be adduced, beyond the usual legends of folk-lore. Jeanne went for fun with the rest. In any case, the tree, in spite of the sinister suggestions attached to it by the judges at Rouen, seems to have been well patronised by the local gentry. Several of the Domremy witnesses[1] testified that the seigneurs of Bourlémont frequented it with their ladies and their daughters, sometimes going for a picnic under its branches, sometimes even joining the youth of the village there on a special Sunday—an arrangement which not only suggests a rather surprisingly democratic relationship between the village and the members of its lordly house, but also invests the poor maligned tree with a certain cachet of respectability.

Village romps to which the noble Bourlémonts could thus lend their sanction cannot have been too disreputable or discreditable. And if Jeanne, having come to years of discretion, decided to abstain as far as possible from the merrymaking of her companions, it was only because a truer sense of proportion had been secretly vouchsafed to her. When one believes oneself to hold visual, audible, and tactile communion with saints, one no longer cares much for such frivolities as hanging wreaths on boughs to please the fairies.

iii

Apart from the evil interpretation set later upon these venial superstitions and amusements of Domremy, the life of the peasants and their children in that village was as simple and hard-working as in any other place where a living depended upon the crops and the cattle. They had to use their hands and their muscles in order to keep their little concerns going. Besides, there was always the complication of politics and

[1] e.g. Jeannette Thévenin, Jeannette Thiesselin, Isabellette d'Epinal, Perrin le drapier, Jacquier de St. Amant, and Gérardin d'Epinal who described the tree in spring as being "beautiful as a lily."

factions in the background. France and England were at war; had been at war so long that no living Frenchman could remember the day when his country had been free from the claim across the Channel, or from the presence of foreign troops on his native soil; so long that Frenchmen themselves were divided, and now no longer knew clearly whether it was the French or the English party that they supported. Even a province so remote as Lorraine, a village so remote as Domremy, could not fail to be affected by the disturbance and insecurity of greater France. It all added, however intermittently, to the anxieties of an already strenuous existence. Flocks and herds were liable to be driven off, houses and churches burnt, without much warning. Nevertheless, looking back in retrospect at a state of affairs which sounds uncomfortable and uneasy when read in detail, one must try to preserve a sense of balance between the facts as they appear in print and the facts as they probably appeared to those who actually experienced them. Human standards adapt themselves most quickly and surprisingly, and a people who had grown up with the discomforts of vague though continuous war handed down to them by their very grandfathers, surely accepted those conditions in a spirit of acquiescence and philosophy as naturally as the vicissitudes of farming or the vagaries of the climate. Cows might inexplicably die; hay-ricks catch fire; crops be ruined by drought or hail; soldiers come and set fire to half the village—it was all in the day's work. Life was like that, and so it had to be. It had been like that ever since the oldest inhabitant, and his father before him, could remember.

Thus it is probably as well not to exaggerate, as some historians would seem to have exaggerated, the troubles suffered by the peasants of a little village like Domremy. Their life would not have been easy, even in times of peace. The times being times of war merely added another complication, in so far as they had to reckon with the caprices of men as well as with the caprices of Nature. But, on the whole, life seems to have flowed on its usual course, with its ups and downs, for the d'Arc family during the childhood of its daughter Jeanne. I am of course aware that M. Siméon Luce, that meticulous and conscientious biographer of Jeanne's early years before she left her home, has pointed out that Domremy was not so isolated a hamlet as one might imagine, lying, as it did, on the old Roman highway between Dijon, Langres, and Verdun.[1] I am aware also that when Antoine and Jean de Vergy, under English orders, marched on Vaucouleurs in July 1428, the inhabitants of Domremy thought it prudent to retire into the neighbouring market-town of Neufchâteau, seven miles away, driving their animals before them; returning a fortnight later to find their church burnt and their fields in pitiable ruin. I am aware also that news travelled far more quickly than we might suppose possible in an age of primitive means of communication, when every item of news arrived by word of mouth without the aid of the daily paper, the telegraph, telephone, or wireless, and that the peasants of Lorraine were consequently kept quite well informed of current events in the rest of France. Those events were certainly disturbing enough. Still, I believe that nearly a century of habit must have accustomed their minds to accept the state of affairs almost as a normal condition, the more immediate preoccupations of daily life bulking larger in the foreground of their consciousness than the distant whistle of arrows on the battlefields of France.

iv

An additional complication of course arose out of the politically ambiguous position of Domremy itself. It has already been suggested that Jeanne may have taken part with the boys and youths in the scrimmages between Domremy and Maxey, but there is no evidence that the grown men lent their hand to an increased disturbance of their common countryside.

[1]Siméon Luce, *Jeanne d'Arc à Domremy*, p. lv.; and P. Champion, *Jeanne d'Arc écuyère*, p. 8.

They realised, probably, that as they might at any moment have quite enough to suffer from the incursion of armed raids from the outside, it was to their interest to live at peace in their respective hamlets, allowing the incomprehensible politics of the noble factions to affect their daily life as little as possible.

There was another reason which, whatever the unexpressed anxiety in Jeanne's young, earnest, and awakening mind, must have impelled the farmer-peasants of Domremy to club together for mutual protection. This was the system by which each family took it in turn to watch their collected herds at pasture. M. Louis Bertrand, himself a Lorrainer, says that each family, according to a prearranged order, had to supply what was called in Lorraine a *pâtureau* or a *pâturelle*, a boy or girl to drive out the cattle in the morning, watch them during the day, and bring them home at night.[1] It seems probable from the subsequent testimony of the many witnesses, who had known Jeanne as a girl, that the men of the village as well as the children sometimes accompanied the procession of animals. I should imagine that this escort of adults was not the usual rule, but was provided only when some rumours of a possible raid had reached their ears, and that normally the children were left in sole charge, in very much the same way as the passing motorist in France to-day sees a little girl sitting by the roadside, her head tied up in a handkerchief, while three or four cows wander within call. Obviously it would have been injudicious and absurd for men, whatever their politics, to disagree too openly when next day their precious cattle would be entrusted to the charge of their opponent's son or daughter, or even to the supervision of the opponent himself. On the whole, it appears that the inhabitants of Domremy lived at peace amongst themselves, which is scarcely to be wondered at.

Occasionally, when the rumours of raids were particularly pressing, they would not take the collective beasts into the

[1] Louis Bertrand, in *Pour Jeanne d'Arc (Jeanne en Lorraine)*.

open pastures, but would drive them into the enceinte of a walled fortress known as the Château de l'Ile. This fortress has now disappeared, but for a few traces of foundations and some scattered stones which give a definite indication of its original site in the village opposite the church on the north side of the present bridge over the Meuse.[1] The island which gave the château its name has likewise disappeared, and the river, which in Jeanne's day divided itself into two branches, now flows in a single stream. But in Jeanne's day it provided a place of security and refuge. It was in the possession of a private family. Its owners, the family of Bourlémont, were the seigneurs of Domremy, and, judging by the will of Jean de Bourlémont in 1399,[2] were Christianly minded men. Not only was Jean de Bourlémont careful to arrange that all his squires and pages (*varlés*) should be paid according to their deserts, that the ashes of Saint Catherine should be restored to the church of Maxey (ashes which had been given to him by the *curé* of Maxey, and which would be found *en Bourgogne en mon écrin*), that prayers should be said for his soul and candles burned, but he also went into such details as that if his men of Domremy chose to say and could prove that he had done any injustice to them in respect of the twelve dozen goslings they yearly paid to him, those goslings should be restored (*rétablis et restitués*) by his son. Such a will and testament shows, I think, that a better understanding and a more democratic spirit could exist between the local lord and his dependants in the fifteenth century than is commonly supposed. It is commonly supposed that in mediæval days the great consistently oppressed the humble, the rich the poor. But there is certainly no evidence of oppression in Jean de Bourlémont's will. There is, on the other hand, a manifest desire to treat both his servants and his village-people decently. Bearing Jean de Bourlémont's conscience in mind, it ceases to surprise us that his men of Domremy should have been allowed to drive their cattle on occasion within the walls of his private property.

[1] Siméon Luce, *Jeanne d'Arc à Domremy*, p. 18, note.   [2] Ibid, pp. 16–21.

Great lords did not suffer from scruples about wages and goslings unless urged by some form of social responsibility.[1]

v

This system of *pâturage*, current at Domremy for mutual convenience, and innocent enough in itself, as one might think, since it saved busy farmers a lot of trouble to share out their children in the communal tending of their beasts, gave rise later on to some curious dissensions and contradictions when the daughter of one of those busy farmers had ceased to be merely his daughter and had turned into a personage so public and so important as to be condemned to death by the representatives of a great Church at the instigation of a great nation. It had its sequel twenty-four years after that, when the Pope himself intervened in the question of her posthumous reputation and decreed that his venerable brothers the Archbishop of Reims and the Bishops of Paris and Coutances should hear the testimony of all those concerned in the case (*intéressés dans la cause*), in order to see that justice might be done.[2] It has its sequel even to-day, in the legend of Jeanne the shepherdess which survives in the popular imagination side by side with the legend of Jeanne the captain and the martyr. How puzzled the friends and the playmates of Jeanne d'Arc must have been, when they were asked to answer, amongst other things, the question whether Jeanne had taken her part in looking after the cattle, or whether she had not. To them, it must have seemed so simple: of course she did. They all did. Jeanne, they thought, took her turn with the rest.

[1] F. J. S. Darwin, *Louis d'Orléans*, p. 106: That such consideration shown by a landlord to his peasants was not unusual, is attested by the Duke of Orleans' account-books of almost the same years (1398–1400), when he allows eight crowns to a farmer whose sheep had been worried by his dogs, and also compensation for damage done by himself or his people to a crop of oats.

[2] J. B. J. Ayroles, S.J., *La Pucelle devant l'Eglise de son temps* (Decree of Calixtus III), pp. 603–5.

Now the curious thing is, that Jeanne in the course of her trial had denied her share in this occupation, and, since Jeanne had been dead for twenty-four years, the representatives of the Pope were unable to confront her with her former acquaintances in order that she should explain the discrepancy between her answers and theirs. Why Jeanne should have denied this perfectly respectable and indeed praiseworthy pursuit, which her obedience as a daughter exacted of her and her duties as a citizen enjoined, is difficult to understand—unless M. Louis Bertrand has made a lucky hit in his suggestion that "the games played by the shepherds and shepherdesses in the fields were not always entirely innocent."[1] Some support is given to his theory by the fact that, in so far as her judges were then trying to prove the immorality of her life, she was being cautious to make no answer which might lend colour to their insinuations. Personally, I cannot wholly agree with this explanation. Jeanne, although frequently shrewd in her replies, was never so cautious as to grow sly. Almost invariably, she was forthright and sincere, even rash, giving the impression that she had nothing to hide, except, indeed, when she replied that her voices would not allow her to answer, and said *"Passez outre."* Nor was she ever intimidated to the extent of trying to placate her judges by untruths; indeed, she frequently answered their questions in a fashion better calculated to annoy than to placate. Besides, the untruth on this particular point could readily have been unmasked by a dozen witnesses, as she must herself have known. I believe the explanation to be much simpler than has been held by those who take a pleasure in looking for *midi à quatorze heures.* I believe that both Jeanne and the Domremy witnesses were speaking the truth according to the best of their recollection; only, Jeanne's recollection being more recent, she spoke it more accurately than they. There is no reason to suspect the Domremy witnesses of any desire to falsify their account of what they remembered of her youth; after all, they were appearing as witnesses for her

[1] Louis Bertrand, in *Pour Jeanne d'Arc.*

defence, for the guidance of judges determined to give her a favourable verdict if they possibly could. The Domremy witnesses, however, were all advanced in age when the twist of history caused their obscure hamlet to be invaded by the representatives of formidable prelates, armed with a *questionnaire* which should oblige them to search their memories on behalf of a little girl who had once been one of themselves. Jeanne herself, on the other hand, was young, very young, only nineteen, when hostile judges at Rouen asked her questions on the same subject, though in a very different spirit. The answers she gave them were drawn from a fresh memory, a memory obliged to look only nine or ten years back. The Domremy witnesses were obliged to look some thirty-four years back. Memory, with advancing age, might become a little confused, though not necessarily mendacious. Jeanne, when she appeared before her judges, had been at an age to answer presumably more accurately than her former friends; besides, it was her own personal life that she was remembering, and, as such, more vivid to her; whereas the Domremy witnesses in their old age were recalling only the life of one little girl out of many little girls in their village. It is reasonably arguable, I think, that Jeanne's answers give on the whole a more accurate account of her early life than the later depositions of her friends from Domremy, and that neither she nor her friends meant intentionally to mislead, despite the apparent contradiction of their statements.

Jeanne, in short, while admitting freely that she had helped in the domestic duties of her father's house, and even boasting that she feared no woman in Rouen as a rival at the needle or the spindle, denied that she had accompanied the cattle or other animals into the fields. Her words are quite clear: "And she added, that when she was in her father's house, she went about the familiar business of the house, and did not go into the fields with the sheep and other animals."[1] That was her first statement on the subject in response to her judges. Two

---

[1]*Procès*, Vol. I, p. 51: *Addens ulterius quod, dum esset in domo patris, vacabat circa negotia familiaria domus, nec ibat ad campos cum ovibus et alliis animalibus.*

days later, when they revived it, she contributed a qualifying clause. She had, she said, already answered the question, but added that when she had grown older, and had come to years of discretion, she did not watch the communal cattle, although she helped to lead them into the fields and to a castle called the Island, for fear of the armed men; she did not remember whether as a child she had watched them, or no.[1] Thus her two statements, at first sight contradictory, are really perfectly consistent: she was merely splitting hairs in the interest of a scrupulous accuracy. There were evidently two very important distinctions present in her mind, and, being a conscientious person (anxious, also, at the moment, not to be trapped into any unnecessary admission which might further endanger her life), she took trouble to make these distinctions as clear as possible. First she wanted it to be understood that although *as a girl* she had not been in the habit of remaining in the fields with the cows, she had occasionally helped to drive them there, or into the Château de l'Ile; secondly, she wanted it to be understood that she could not remember whether she had ever guarded them all day, even *as a child*, though she was not prepared to deny this suggestion as categorically as the other. She evidently distinguished very definitely between the comparative dignity of driving cows out in the morning and the comparative in-dignity of guarding them throughout the day; also between the difference in propriety of a girl or a child being employed in so ignoble a task. It may seem strange that Jeanne, the professed associate of saints, and, at the moment, in terror of her life, should have set so much value on so incommensurable a distinction. But it is precisely the kind of distinction which would assume a disproportionate importance to the peasant mind, and precisely the kind which is so difficult for the more elastic-minded to estimate. It is the same kind of false pride as is apt to make the domestic servant so inconveniently touchy about his or her obligations, expressing himself or herself in familiar phrases, difficult to understand because so difficult

[1] *Procès*, Vol. I, p. 66.

to sympathise with. One must just accept the fact that the shape of the mentality is different. And Jeanne, apart from her especial guidance, was, as I conceive her, a very simple person. Had she not been so simple a person it is in fact unlikely that she could have lain so readily open to the influence of that especial guidance. She shared both the simplicity and the inexplicability of the genius; only, in her case, the simplicity was paradoxically complicated by her peasant mind, which saw a real difference between driving cows to pasture and remaining to watch them while they ate.[1]

The replies of her Domremy friends were less confusingly scrupulous. They, evidently, saw very little difference between an occasional and a regular cowherd, between a child and a girl. What did it matter whether you were nine or thirteen? At thirteen you were still a child of the village, under the orders of your father, and his obligations were still yours. They were old themselves when called upon to give their evidence, and had forgotten the enormous and pathetic difference a few years can make in the eyes of the very young.

There is no ambiguity about their statements, nor is there a single one which disagrees with the others. They disagree only with Jeanne's own statements, and it is still difficult to make out why. Another point, which increases the difficulty, is this: had Jeanne flatly refused to take her turn with the rest, such a refusal would surely have been noticed in the village, and would have been remembered by her contemporaries even when they had reached old age. In a small village every circumstance is known and provides matter for current gossip: if Jacques d'Arc's young daughter had struck against her father's orders, Jacques d'Arc would certainly have boxed her

[1]On the other hand she is also reported as having said that she wished God would allow her to return to her father and mother, to keep their sheep and their cattle, and to do that which she had been accustomed to do (*et garder leur brebis et bestail, et faire ce que je soulois faire*). *Chronique de la Pucelle*, édition de Vallet de Viriville, chapter 59, p. 285. This passage, if authoritative, reads rather as though she regretted her quiet life and humble occupations, longing to go back to them.

ears, and the echo of that slap would have echoed all over Domremy. Either he or his wife would have confided to some crony the inexplicable rebelliousness of their daughter's behaviour. And the ancients would have remembered. Small events make an impression on small minds. Moreover the extraordinary subsequent career of Jeanne, the notoriety she had conferred on their humble village, the dramatic rush of her victories, capture, trial, and death, would naturally have singled her out in their recollection. Besides, several of the witnesses were her own godparents, intimate friends of her family, and, as such, would have been doubly distressed on hearing of the unusual insubordination of their spiritual daughter. The only possible inference, I think, is that Jeanne never openly rebelled. I think she merely evaded, without making an open fuss, because she already had more important matters on hand. She already wanted to be alone, in a solitude to be filled by a richer company than the company of materially and even dirtily minded youths and girls. In short, she played truant. It was her quiet way of getting what she wanted without saying anything about it to anybody. This is no fanciful explanation of the mistake made later on by the Domremy villagers: it is clear from the evidence of her godfather, Jean Morel, that sometimes when her parents believed her to be in the fields, she was somewhere quite different. She was at the shrine of Our Lady of Bermont (*quod, prout vidit, ipsa Johanneta libentur et sæpe ibat ad ecclesiam sive heremum Beatæ Mariæ de Bermont, dum sui parentes credebant ipsam fore in campis, ad aratrum, aut alias*).[1] Now it is quite a long walk from Domremy to Bermont, so Jeanne's absences must have been considerably prolonged. One wonders that she dared take the risk; one wonders why, at her trial, she did not give this very simple explanation, since, however much she may once have feared being punished for truancy, that childish dread must certainly have vanished, only to be replaced by far greater dreads; one wonders, also, why no one, noticing her absence or meeting

[1] *Procès*, Vol. II, pp. 389–90: Deposition of Jean Morel.

her on the way, ever got her into trouble with her unsuspecting parents. Judging by the evidence, her godfather was the only one to discover or to remember her truancies, although other witnesses remember accompanying her to Bermont on open occasions, and both Michel Lebuin and Perrin le drapier say that she sometimes took her sister with her.[1] She must have been either extremely wily or extremely lucky.

Bermont, when she got there, was, and still is, a lost little chapel in the heart of the woods. To reach it, and to avoid passing through the village or through the next village of Greux, she certainly took a short cut through the fields and woods, which was quicker than the road, as well as more secret. There is no road up to the chapel itself, nothing but a steep scrambling track, which first rushes down into a swampy little valley overhung by trees, overgrown by reeds, and then, after passing a spring where Jeanne must often have paused, rushes up the opposite hill, to emerge on an unexpected clearing and the white rough-cast building which is the hermitage. Poor, simple, deserted, and utterly countrified, it is a strangely moving place. In the tiny whitewashed chapel, above the altar, hangs a crucifix upon which her eyes may have rested; on a bracket stands a crude wooden statue of Notre Dame de Bermont herself, which is said to have been the object of her special veneration. It is perhaps at Bermont, on a still afternoon, with no other company than the rabbits nibbling beside the gorse, that one comes closest to the spirit of Jeanne d'Arc and of the influences that made her.

vi

The legend of the shepherdess, meanwhile, is destroyed by Jeanne herself. She cuts it down with her words as surely as she cut down the harlot with the slash of her sword. It is replaced by the red-skirted figure making off surreptitiously

---

[1] *Procès*, Vol. II, p. 413: Deposition of Perrin le drapier; ibid., p. 439: Deposition of Michel Lebuin.

towards the woods of Bermont; by the figure of the little girl whose companions teased her for being too pious[1]; by the figure of the little maid-of-all-work (not yet the Maid of Orleans), busy with her duster in her mother's house, then sitting down to her stitching and her spinning, unable to run away just then, since her mother had her within doors, under her eye. It is replaced, above all, by the figure of the little girl most astonishingly and terrifyingly addressed by a disembodied voice speaking to her in the open air, at the most dramatic and significant moment of her whole career.

Jeanne stated that she was in her thirteenth year when this event occurred.[2] On the other hand, when asked her age, at the beginning of her trial, she replied rather vaguely that, so far as she knew, she was about nineteen.[3] Interrogated again, she replied that she could not tell at what age she had left her father's house. Such uncertainty on the part of the person principally concerned diminishes, to say the least of it, the reliability of her statement. Her uncertainty, however, does not seem to have extended to the date when she first heard her voices: she says repeatedly that she was in her thirteenth year, i.e. twelve years old. She may have hesitated over her age on other occasions, but there was never any doubt in her mind that Saint Michael first visited her when she was twelve. Both Perceval de Boulainvilliers and Alain Chartier, her contemporaries, believed her to have been somewhere near that age (*tandem peractis ætatis suæ duodecim annis*[4]; and *ubi vero duodecimum annum attigit*),[5] so, taking one thing with another, we must calculate this extraordinary experience to have befallen her in the year 1424.

Two separate and slightly different accounts of it have come

---

[1]*Procès*, Vol. II, p. 420: Deposition of Jean Waterin; ibid., p. 430: Deposition of Mengette Joyart.
[2]*Procès*, Vol. I, p. 65. *In ætate tredicim annorum.*
[3]*Procès*, Vol. I, p. 46.
[4]*Procès*, Vol. V, p. 116: Perceval de Boulainvilliers.
[5]*Procès*, Vol. V, p. 132: Letter from Alain Chartier to a foreign prince.

down to us: Jeanne's own, which is one of the most moving and poetical paragraphs of autobiography it is possible to read anywhere, and that of Perceval de Boulainvilliers in his previously quoted letter to the Duke of Milan. Nobody could regard de Boulainvilliers as a very well-balanced or credible reporter—in fact more credulous than credible, remembering the wild fairy-tale he repeated in perfect good faith about her birth on Twelfth Night—but since the pretty story he recorded seems to have gained some popular credence, it can scarcely be omitted here. This is his account, transcribed almost textually from the words of his letter[1]:

"She was keeping her parents' sheep, with the other girls, some of whom were playing about in the meadows. They called to her, suggesting that she should join in their races, the prize being a handful of flowers, or something of that sort. She, having consented to accept their challenge, ran the course two or three times at such a speed that one of the girls cried out, 'Jeanne' (for that was her name), 'I see you flying above the ground' " (*video te volantem juxta terram*).

This curious remark, which seems to demand a literal rather than a metaphorical rendering, suggests an allusion, unconscious on the part of the speaker, to the puzzling phenomenon known as levitation. It is worth noting that Jeanne, among saints and visionaries, is by no means unique in having given this impression to onlookers. Her contemporary, Colette de Corbie and her predecessor, Guillemette de la Rochelle, were both credited with the same accomplishment. So was Saint Catherine of Siena. So was Saint Theresa. Jeanne herself never laid claim to it, unless we may read some hint into her words to Brother Richard as he came to meet her at Troyes[2]: "Approach boldly," she said. "I shall not fly away." But these words, I am sure, were innocently spoken, without any meaning that Jeanne believed herself to be possessed of these miraculous powers. They were spoken because Brother Richard, on seeing her, made the sign of the cross—the usual procedure when one

[1]*Procès*, Vol. V, pp. 116–17.   [2]*Procès*, Vol. I, p. 100.

believed oneself to be in the presence of a witch or other evil thing; now, witches, by common superstition, were supposed to levitate at will—in plain English, to fly. Jeanne's remark was therefore sarcastic rather than boastful.

Of course, if she were really independent of the laws of gravity, it would do everything to explain how she could jump off a tower seventy feet high without breaking any limbs.[1]

To return to the letter from Boulainvilliers:

"She then, the race over, retired to the edge of the meadow in order to rest her tired body and to regain her breath; she seemed as one rapt and deprived of her senses [*quasi rapta et a sensibus alienata*]. Then came a youth, who, approaching her, addressed her in this fashion: 'Jeanne, go home; your mother has need of your help.' She, believing it to be her brother or some other boy of the neighbourhood, hastened home. Her mother, meeting her, enquired the reason for her neglect of the sheep, and scolded her. The innocent child replied, 'Did you not send for me?' Her mother said 'No.'

"Thinking then that the boy had played a trick on her, she started back to rejoin her companions, when suddenly a luminous cloud [*nubes prælucida*] appeared before her eyes, and out of the cloud came a voice, saying, 'Jeanne, you are destined to lead a different kind of life and to accomplish miraculous things, for you are she who has been chosen by the King of Heaven to restore the Kingdom of France, and to aid and protect King Charles, who has been driven from his domains. You shall put on masculine clothes; you shall bear arms and become the head of the army; all things shall be guided by your counsel.' After these words had been spoken, the cloud vanished, and the girl, astounded by such a marvel, at first could not give credence to it, but, in her ignorant innocence, remained perplexed as to whether she should believe it or no. Night and day similar visions appeared to her, renewing and repeating their words. She kept her own counsel; to none, save to her

[1]The full account of this remarkable leap will be found in Chapter XIV, pp. 289–94.

priest, did she speak; and in this perplexity she continued for the space of five years."

Her own account, as reported at her trial, is briefer, less sentimentally pretty perhaps, but in its brevity far more poignant:

"I was in my thirteenth year when God sent a voice to guide me. At first, I was very much frightened. The voice came towards the hour of noon, in summer, in my father's garden. I had fasted the preceding day. I heard the voice on my right hand, in the direction of the church. I seldom hear it without [seeing] a light. That light always appears on the side from which I hear the voice."[1]

vii

But for the utter simplicity which invests this statement with a poetry of its own, it would be regrettable to have to destroy the picture suggested at the beginning of Boulainvilliers' letter. Boulainvilliers' picture has a fresh and rather Botticellesque charm: the sheep, the flowery grass, the happy children, their voices, their laughter, their innocent sports— in so care-free, vernal, and idyllic a scene, armed men and the troubles of France seem very far away. It would be regrettable to destroy it, were we not able to replace it by that other and simpler picture of Jeanne alone in her father's garden, in summer, at the hour of noon. I wonder, in fact, whether it is necessary to destroy it altogether? It is true that Jeanne herself never mentions the delusive boy who had sent her hurrying off to her mother. It is true, also, that Perceval de Boulainvilliers reports her as having mistaken that boy for her brother or for one of the village children; a statement which, on the face of it, is scarcely credible, for how could she have mistaken so familiar a figure as that of her own brother or even one of her daily playmates?—unless, indeed, we accept the perfectly logical contention that an

[1]*Procès,* Vol. I, pp. 51–2.

apparition could adopt the semblance of a brother or a play-
mate as easily as the semblance of an archangel or a saint.
Apart from this slight and easily dismissed difficulty, and
apart from the fact that Boulainvilliers entertained a romantic
though understandable cult for Jeanne, apart also from the fact
that he betrays his inaccuracy in some other particulars—
a great many "aparts," I admit—still I can see no reason to
query the plain nature of his account. I can see no reason for
supposing that Jeanne herself had not privately and personally
told him the story of the children's races and of the delusive
boy, even though she made no mention of them in her examination by her judges. Probably she came to regard the delusive
boy as unimportant. She may have come to regard him as a
mere freakish prelude to the far more important things which
subsequently happened. She may have told Boulainvilliers
about him, lightly, as a frivolous anecdote, not worth repeating
to her judges, and entirely superseded in her mind by the far
more impressive personages who succeeded him. She may
not ever have accorded him recognition as the messenger of
God: according to her view, as reported by Boulainvilliers,
he had tricked her. He was a fraud. He could not have come
from God, and, so far as we know, he never reappeared.[1]

Again, it is possible to dovetail the two stories, so that they
tally to a sufficient extent, by regarding one of them as the
prelude to the other. Jeanne says expressly that she was *in
her father's garden* when she first saw the cloud of light; now,
according to Boulainvilliers, she had run home to her mother,
had been scolded, and sent back to her sheep. The whole
apparent discrepancy may therefore be explained by supposing
that she saw the light on her way back through the garden.

---

[1]It is also worth considering that she may have told the story in its entirety
at her first examination, at Poitiers, the record of which has been lost or
perhaps destroyed. The date of Boulainvilliers' letter, June 21st, 1429, is nearly
three months later than the examination at Poitiers, which makes it possible
that he could have heard the story from somebody who had been present at
Poitiers.

Nor can I see any reason why Boulainvilliers should deliberately have invented the whole story of the delusive boy: it seems far more probable that he had it from Jeanne's own lips, or at any rate from the lips of someone to whom she had confided it. It does not sound like a story which, with all its detail, would come of its own accord into anybody's head, still less like a story which anybody would invent for fun in a serious letter to a foreign prince.

viii

Whatever the nature of the voices, and however they arrived, they had come to stay. Once they had begun, they never left her. She heard them with increasing frequency and clarity. At first she was frightened and doubtful, and could not understand what was happening to her; then after she had seen her first strange visitant several times, she decided that he was no other than Saint Michael. Asked how she had finally decided on his indentity, she replied that she recognised him at last because he spoke with the tongue of angels.[1]

How did she know, they asked, that he was speaking the language of angels? She replied that she had believed it quite early in the proceedings, and was very much inclined to believe it—a significant phrase, I think; *et eust ceste voulenté de le croire.* Anyway, she ended by being completely convinced. If she was not convinced at first, she said, it was because she was only a child and very much alarmed, but subsequently he, Saint Michael, taught her and showed her so many things, that she came to believe entirely in his identity.[2] She

[1]*Procès*, Vol. I, pp. 170–1: *Interroguée comment elle cogneust que c'estoit Saint Michiel, respond: "Par le parler et le langaige des angles," et le croist fermement. . . . Respond que à la première fois, elle fist grant doubte se c'estoit Saint Michiel. Et à la première fois oult grant paour; et si le vist maintes fois, avant qu'elle sceust que ce fust Saint Michiel.*

[2]*Procès*, Vol. I, p. 171: *Respond que à la première fois, elle estoit jeune enfant et oult paour de ce: depuis lui enseigna et monstra tant, qu'elle creust fermement que c'estoit il.*

was quite sure, she said, that it was not the Enemy, meaning the Devil, who had appeared to her in the guise of an angel, for she would know at once whether it was Saint Michael or a thing made in his semblance.[1] Poor little childish Jeanne, she had obviously been frightened and worried, with no idea of the comfort and guidance she was destined to obtain. The moment when she *creust fermement que c'estoit il* must have been a great moment in her life: a great moment, a great relief. At that moment she stopped being frightened and acquired, instead, a confidence and a trust which were never to desert her. Having ceased to wonder, she accepted her miraculous visitations as part of her daily life.

The archangel was not, at first, very precise in his instructions. He appears to have proceeded with more tact, caution, and consideration than are usually accredited to supernatural apparitions. He never attempted to rush Jeanne. He broke his message very gently. He started by telling her mildly that she must be a good girl, and that God would help her; and told her then, amongst other things, that she must come to the help of the King of France,[2] warning her also that Saint Catherine and Saint Margaret would presently appear to her, and that she must obey their instructions, since they would be sent by the ordinance of Our Lord.[3] Jeanne listened to all this without breathing a word to anybody.

The story, as it goes on, becomes more and more extraordinary. The wealth of detail which we possess about the

---

[1]*Procès*, Vol. I, p. 170: *Interroguée, se l'Annemy se mectoit en fourme ou signe d'angle, comme elle congnoistroit que ce fust bon angle ou mauvais angle: respond qu'elle congnoistroit bien se ce seroit Saint Michiel ou une chose contrefaicte comme luy.*

[2]*Procès*, Vol. I, p. 171: *Interroguée quelle doctrine il luy enseigna: respond, sur toutes choses il luy disoit qu'elle fust bon enfant, et que Dieu luy aideroit; et entre les autres choses qu'elle venist au secours du roy de France.*

[3]*Procès*, Vol. I, p. 170: *Et dit oultre que Saint Michiel, quant il vint à elle, luy dist que sainctes Katherine et Marguerite vendroient à elle, et qu'elle feist par leur conseil, et estoient ordonnées pour la conduire et conseiller en ce qu'elle avoit à faire; et qu'elle les creust de ce qu'elles luy diroient, et que c'estoit par le commandement de nostre Seigneur.*

voices and apparitions comes to us at first hand from Jeanne herself. There is no need to draw upon the imagination or to reconstruct events from scraps of evidence: Jeanne's own full, unshakable account given by herself to her judges at her trial tells us everything we want to know. It is true that every now and then she would refuse to answer a question, saying that her voices had not yet given her the necessary permission, but in spite of these occasional reticences her replies were frank and complete enough to allow us to form a brilliant picture of her experiences during those five strange secret years. Standing alone, a girl of nineteen, before the formidable array of judges of the Ecclesiastical Court and the Holy Inquisition, she spoke as her voices had told her to speak, *hardiment*, never deviating from either the basis or the detail of her conviction.

This is the account of her visitations, founded almost textually on her own replies:

The spirits who habitually appeared to her were three in number—the Archangel Michael, Saint Margaret, and Saint Catherine. She claimed also to have seen the Archangel Gabriel and several hundreds of other angels, but it was with her three familiars that she was chiefly concerned. She saw them with her bodily eyes, and wept when they left her, wishing that they could have carried her away with them. They came always accompanied by the cloud of heavenly light. She could touch them and embrace them. Asked whether she embraced them round the neck or round the lower parts of their bodies, she replied that it was more seemly to embrace them round the lower part, by which I presume that she meant round the knees, and that she herself was on her knees before them. Asked whether she felt their warmth when she embraced them, she replied that she could scarcely embrace them without feeling and touching them. They spoke to her in French, addressing her as *Jehanne la Pucelle, fille de Dieu*. Why should they speak in English, she asked, when they were not on the English side? They smelt good, and wore beautiful crowns, but she could not, or would not, describe their clothes. Asked whether Saint Michael was naked or not, she retaliated by enquiring scornfully whether they imagined that Our Lord had not the wherewithal to clothe him? Asked whether he had any hair or not, she enquired why it should have been cut off? Asked whether the two female saints had any hair (the judges seem to have insisted curiously on this question of hair, no doubt because Jeanne, amongst her other crimes, had cut hers short), she replied, "*C'est bon a savoir.*" Asked whether their hair was long, she replied that she did not know, and, more surprisingly, that she could not say whether they had arms or other limbs. Saint Michael had wings, she said, but she would not say anything about the bodies or limbs of Catherine and Margaret. When they asked her what she meant by this refusal, she replied that she had told them what she knew, and was not going to say anything further. Asked if she had seen their faces only, she lost her temper, and replied tartly that she would sooner have her throat cut than tell everything she knew; adding, more mildly, that she would willingly tell everything which concerned the trial. She had no hesitation, however, in saying that they spoke very well and beautifully (*tres bien et bellement*), with soft and humble voice. They appeared to her several times a day, especially if she were in a wood. Whenever they came, they brought guidance and comfort.[1]

She appears, also, to have been specially affected by the sound of bells. She herself answered freely and at first-hand that while in prison she had heard her voices three times in one day: once in the morning, once at vespers, and once in the evening when they were ringing for the Ave Maria.[2] It was reported of her after her death that she had claimed to hear her voices most distinctly when the bells were ringing for compline and matins,[3] though this is perhaps neither a reliable nor an unprejudiced testimony. The witnesses who had known her

[1]*Procès, passim.*   [2]*Procès,* Vol. I, pp. 61–2.

[3]*Procès,* Vol. I, p. 480: Pierre Maurice; and Jean Toutmouillé, ibid., p. 481.

in her early Domremy youth make, it is true, no allusion to any connexion between the bells and the voices, but their words do go to prove that church-bells meant something to her —as, to be sure, they would to any devout Catholic. Without insisting too much on any association between the bells and the voices, and bearing always in mind that the bells of the villages strung up and down that river valley must have echoed in the consciousness of any pious little inhabitant habitually within earshot, we can, without further comment, let the Domremy witnesses speak in their own words. One of them says, "When she was in the fields, and heard the bells ringing, she bent her knees"; another, "When the bells rang out, she made the sign of the cross and bent her knees."[1] Thomas Basin, afterwards Bishop of Lisieux, repeats the same story.[2]

ix

Nothing would move her from her convictions. Neither would anything induce her to say a word more about her saints than she meant to say. She was positive that she had heard, seen, touched, and even smelt them, not once or twice, but daily, totalling hundreds of times over a period of seven years. In the last resort, she preferred a frightful death to the re-cantation which would have saved her life. There can be no question as to the absolute sincerity of her belief. Our only problem—which in the present state of our knowledge seems insoluble—is, to what extent was her belief justified? Did the saints really appear to her, engaging four senses out of the five? Or was she merely the victim of her own delusions?

We had better pursue the story of her life, before discussing these difficult questions.

[1]*Procès*, Vol. II, p. 420: Deposition of Jean Waterin; Simon Musmier, ibid., p. 424.
[2]*Procès*, Vol. IV, p. 352.

i

In May 1428, Jeanne, being then sixteen, made her first tentative effort to get herself sent into France to find the Dauphin. The voices were becoming more and more urgent. She herself had reached the marriageable age, and one may reasonably assume in face of the evidence that her parents' projects of marriage for her were becoming more urgent too. Her father, uninformed though he was of his daughter's strange experiences, had begun to have disturbing dreams about her. On several occasions, while she was still living at home, in fact about two years after the voices had first started, Jacques d'Arc was visited by the nocturnal information that his daughter would go away with soldiers—information which appears, not unnaturally, to have upset him considerably. It upset him so much, indeed, that he did not mention it to Jeanne herself, but communicated his fears to his wife, who passed them on to the child.[1] One can scarcely blame Jacques d'Arc for interpreting the idea of his daughter going away with soldiers in the worst possible sense. An ordinary, sensible man, conversant with the ways of soldiers—as he had good cause to be—no idea of a religious mission could possibly have entered his head. Any respectable girl becoming aware of a religious mission wanted to join a convent, not an army. There was only one interpretation to be placed against the warning that one's daughter was about to go away with soldiers, and Jacques d'Arc placed it. He little knew the treatment that his daughter would later mete out to women who had joined the army for different purposes; he little knew that she would

---

[1]*Procès*, Vol. I, p. 131 and p. 219: *Interroguée des songes de son père: respond que, quand elle estoit encore avec ses père et mère, luy fut dit par plusieurs fois par sa mère, que son père disoit qu'il avoit songé que avec les gens d'armes s'en iroit ladicte Jehanne sa fille.*

break her sword across their backs. In consequence, parental supervision was tightened. Her father and mother were careful to keep her strictly and in great submission.[1] Moreover, Jacques talked to his sons about it—a conversation which, again, was repeated to Jeanne by her mother. She heard her mother say that her father had said to her brothers: "If I believed that the thing I have dreamed of her should come to pass, I should want you to drown her; and if you did not do so, I would drown her myself."[2] That was no equivocal pronouncement. There is an echo of the Old Testament in its stern and uncompromising grandeur.

Without undue fancifulness, one may imagine that the family breakfast-party at Domremy, after a night when Jacques d'Arc had been visited by such dreams, was not a very cheerful affair. There was the surly father; the worried mother; the puzzled sons. There was the silent little daughter, oppressed by her enormous secret, and in great doubt as to what her parents and her brothers were thinking. Without undue fancifulness, also, one may imagine the distressing conversations which must have taken place between mother and daughter after the men had gone out to their work in the fields. Jeanne respected her mother; it must, humanly speaking, have tortured her to listen to these accounts of dreams which, for her part, she knew to be only too well justified. Her conscience must have played queer tricks, and undergone strange perplexities. It is never easy to judge between right and wrong, especially when one is only fourteen.

Again, it may not be too fanciful to suggest that some curious sympathetic bond existed between Jeanne and her father, which increased the pain of her deception, and which can only be explained by assuming some telepathic communication between them. For, after all, what was he doing but dreaming

[1]*Procès*, Vol. I, pp. 131–2: *En avoient grant cure ses père et mère de la bien garder, et la tenoient en grant subjection.*

[2]*Procès*, Vol. I, p. 132: *Se je cuidoye que la chose advensist que j'ay songié d'elle, je vouldroye que la noyessiés; et se vous ne le faisiés, je la noieroye moymesmes.*

her unrevealed thoughts? I offer this suggestion for what it is worth; it is a point which, so far as I know, has not hitherto been remarked upon by any of her biographers.

However this may be, she stuck to her original plan of saying nothing. She let her mother tell her these stories, and never gave herself away.

ii

Rumours of a fresh English attack were spreading over France. Thus both private and public reasons spurred Jeanne to her first attempt. In pursuance of this attempt, she enlisted the help of a certain Durand Lassois or Laxart, who had married her first cousin,[1] but whom Jeanne, out of respect for his seniority of sixteen years, called, not cousin, but uncle. This seems to have been the principal, if not the only, mark of respect she ever accorded him: for the rest, she appears to have been able to do pretty well as she liked with him. She took his clothes from him when she wanted them, returned them when she had no further use for them, forced him to risk his credit with her parents, and to oblige her in almost incredible ways. Manifestly a man of patient, credulous, and amenable character, well known to his relatives Jacques and Isabelle, a suitable escort for their daughter owing to his affinity by marriage and to the blood-relationship of his wife, he was the very tool to suit Jeanne's purpose, and with subtlety and determination she made the most of his services.

Durand Lassois and his wife lived at Burey-le-Petit, only two miles short of Vaucouleurs, and to Vaucouleurs it was necessary that Jeanne should go. She had very wisely and obviously decided on Vaucouleurs because that was the nearest place held in the name of the Dauphin; a small garrison town on a hill, about twelve miles up the valley north of Domremy. It was commanded at the time by one Robert de Baudricourt,

[1] He married Jeanne, daughter of a labourer named le Vauseul, and of Aveline, a sister of Isabelle Romée.

who has been generally represented as an ordinary hearty soldier with an eye to the main chance. He had, for instance, contrived to marry two wealthy widows in succession—although, to be sure, he had been so incompetent, or, possibly, so easy-going, as to allow some shepherds to steal the cart conveying the provisions to his wedding-breakfast.[1] He came of a respectable family: his mother, Marguerite d'Aunoy, of Blaise in Bassigny; his father, Liebault de Baudricourt, chamberlain to a duke of Bar and governor of Pont-à-Mousson; his uncles had also held responsible positions, to which he had succeeded.[2] He was thus what one may call a gentleman, meaning that he came of gentle birth, without necessarily meaning that he was himself a man of refined character. The long and short of it seems to be that Robert de Baudricourt was neither better nor worse than other men of his type; that he was naturally rather bored, stuck away in his little provincial command at Vaucouleurs; that he was as ready as other men to make a bawdy joke when he saw the chance of it; that the arrival of an unknown Jeannette from Domremy provided him with just such a chance, relieving the monotony of his garrison days; that he was not a man sentimentally disposed to respect a woman, unless and until that woman gave him very good cause to do so—in short, a good-natured, practical, muscular, coarse-grained captain, neither more cynical nor more believing than the rest. Such was the man to whom Jeanne proposed to address herself as the first step to her wild adventure.

She may have heard accounts of him in the family circle of her own home, for it seems probable that her father had once met him in person at Vaucouleurs, in March 1427, owing to the following circumstances: the inhabitants of Domremy and of Greux were under the obligation of paying a yearly tax to the *damoiseau* of Commercy in return for his protection. Fourteen of the leading men of the two villages

[1] Anatole France, *Vie de Jeanne d'Arc*, Vol. I, p. 70.
[2] Siméon Luce, *Jeanne d'Arc à Domremy*, p. clxii.

had signed the agreement, amongst whom appears Jacques d'Arc under the designation of *doyen de Domremy*. In the winter of 1423, the contract having been entered into during the autumn of the same year, the villagers found themselves unable to pay their toll, and, aware that the *damoiseau* was not a man to overlook a debt, arranged that two wealthy individuals of the neighbourhood named Jean Aubert and Guyot Poingnant, to whom they habitually sold their surplus hay and their wood, should stand warrant on their behalf with their impatient creditor. The *damoiseau*, however, without waiting for the affair to be amicably settled, seized and sold some twenty waggon-loads of hay and eighty waggon-loads of wood, besides a number of horses belonging to Guyot Poingnant, the value of the goods thus sequestrated being assessed as rather more than half the total debt. A few days after this raid had taken place the debt was paid in full, and Guyot Poingnant, who meanwhile had been detained as hostage in Commercy, hurriedly left for Vaucouleurs to institute proceedings against the villagers of Greux and Domremy for the loss of property he had suffered owing to their temporary insolvency. These proceedings, which, of course, were laid before Robert de Baudricourt in his capacity of governor of Vaucouleurs, trailed on after the manner of such disputes until the spring of 1427, when Guyot Poingnant, at the end of his patience, refused to renew the powers of the two arbitrators who had previously been appointed by common consent of the parties. It thus appears that he decided to cut his loss, for the dispute was dropped, and the *acte de refus* was conveyed by the two arbitrators to the defendants. The interest of this small local quarrel lies for us in the fact that among the three representatives concerned in the *acte de refus* the second was Jean Morel, of Greux, one of Jeanne's numerous godparents; and the third, Jacquot d'Arc, of Domremy, her father.[1]

Thus, doubly, Jeanne had heard of Robert de Baudricourt from two men who had probably seen and spoken with him.

[1] Siméon Luce, *Jeanne d'Arc à Domremy*, pp. cliv–clvi.

He was, in a sense, no stranger to her. Deeply and rightly as one mistrusts the historian who draws too freely on his imagination to fill in the details of the cold outline provided by official documents, there are occasions when it becomes only reasonable for him to do so. The present occasion enters, I think, into this reasonable category. It is impossible not to imagine that Jacques d'Arc, on his return from Vaucouleurs, related his experiences at great and repetitive length to his friends and his family. After all, it had constituted quite an adventure for a small man. Robert de Baudricourt was a power in the little local world of the Meuse valley. He may not have approached royalty in their eyes, even as a representative of the Dauphin, but he did at least, putting it into modern terms, approach something more than the equivalent of the local J.P. Not only did he hold the sword of justice: he held also the sword of a royal lieutenant, combining the military with the civil. And Jacques d'Arc, although by that time described as doyen of Domremy, remained a simple villager to whom the governor of Vaucouleurs was a great man. Jean Morel, too, described as a labourer of Greux, must have been equally impressed by his introduction into the castle of Vaucouleurs and into the presence of its commander. They must both, one imagines, have been rather halting and intimidated and tongue-tied so long as they were within its precincts; they must both, equally, have let themselves go when they got home, boasting perhaps a little, certainly describing their visit in every detail over and over again, after the fashion of the countryman who has experienced an unusual interruption to his normal life—the kind of interruption which in the England of to-day would provide an endless topic of conversation in the local public house. In France of the fifteenth century, the family circle would replace the local public house. Such meeting-grounds scarcely exist, or, at any rate, enjoy no corresponding social importance, in countries where children learn to drink wine in their homes from the age of three onwards, and consequently do not grow up to regard drinking, be it wine or beer, as an incentive to social conviviality. In an English village, the pub is the club. In a French village, people are more domestically minded. When disposed to talk, they are quite ready to talk in their own homes. The children are not sent to bed earlier than their elders, even to-day when modern propaganda of child-welfare might well be presumed to have penetrated even into the most rural districts of England and the Continent; how much less, when no such theories had taken hold, but when everybody went to bed at the same time, grown-ups and children, at an hour dictated only by the going-down of the sun and by the necessity of getting up early on the following morning. Therefore, it is fair, I think, to assume that Jacques d'Arc would be inclined to sit talking about Robert de Baudricourt during the family supper and even after supper was over; and that Jean Morel, when he came from Greux to see his friends Jacquot and Zabillet, would join with Jacquot in recounting the experiences that Jacquot's long-suffering family had already heard a hundred times. One member of Jacquot's family, at any rate, kept her ears open, even though her mother may have yawned and wished she might be free to go about such household tasks as clearing away and washing-up. That one member, silent, non-committal, and receptive, must have registered every word relating to the representative of the Dauphin at Vaucouleurs. The conversation, however reiterative, however boring to others, must have been full of value and information to the one really interested member of the audience. To her, Robert de Baudricourt was an important, even a vital, figure. Her father and her godfather, so far as she was concerned, might discuss him as much as they pleased. They were doing nothing but contribute valuable information to one whom they little suspected of pigeon-holing every comment for her own purposes. Robert de Baudricourt was the man she must see before she could set off on her ultimate journey. He was the man from whom she must obtain a safe-conduct, horses, and an escort. Therefore no scrap of information about him was negligible: it was extremely lucky for Jeanne, in fact, that her father and her godfather should have been in a position to describe him so fully, being meanwhile unaware that the silent girl at the table intended within the year to make use of the redoubtable governor to send her on her rationally inconceivable mission into France. Jacquot described; Jeannette listened. Jean Morel joined the circle of his friends occasionally. The brothers were probably tired, and rather bored.

But the fun of the historian consists partly in destroying his own theories once he has built them up. The foregoing passage reads plausibly enough, and the gist of it has been indicated by practically every biographer of Jeanne d'Arc. In point of fact there is no actual evidence to prove that either Jacques or Jean Morel ever set eyes on Robert de Baudricourt at all. It is true that Jacques was once seen in Vaucouleurs[1]; it is true, also, that both he and Morel were concerned in the *acte de refus*. But it is equally true that Vaucouleurs was only twelve miles from Domremy, so that Jacques probably went there frequently during the course of his life; and it is equally true that being concerned in the *acte de refus* did not necessarily entail any personal contact with Baudricourt, any more than a mortgagee necessarily comes into personal contact with the mortgagor whose signature appears on the same document as his own. Insistence on this point may seem exaggerated and pernickety. But the point as to whether Jacques and Morel had really ever seen Baudricourt or not is interesting, not only for the amusement of first drawing a picture and then tearing it up, but because it also affects one of Jeanne's so-called miraculous inspirations. It is well known that, when she finally got to Chinon, she was able to pick the Dauphin out of the crowd of his courtiers, even though another man had been designated to her in the attempt to trick her as a test of her sincerity. She claims the same power of recognition as regards Robert de Baudricourt, although she had never yet seen him. "She recognised the said Robert through her voices,

[1] *Procès*, Vol. II, p. 460: Deposition of Jean le Fumeux.

the voice having told her who he was."[1] Now if she had heard her father describe Baudricourt, her recognition of him was not at all miraculous but quite natural; if, on the other hand, her father had neither spoken with nor, consequently, described him, her recognition may fairly take its place among such facts of her life as are difficult if not impossible to explain or to explain away. With a remnant of caution, however, one must take into consideration that, even failing her father, she may have heard the accounts of other people who had caught a glimpse of the local governor, even so distantly as to see him riding through the streets of Vaucouleurs. On the whole, I think we must take this particular miracle with a very large grain of salt; and prove, later on, that the analogous miracle of her recognition of the Dauphin may likewise be explained by perfectly normal means.

iii

However it may be, it was natural, and, indeed, necessary, that Jeanne should decide to make her way towards Robert de Baudricourt at Vaucouleurs. Her voices themselves had told her to do so. They assured her, moreover, that he would give her an escort to go into France. She, alarmed by these instructions, replied at first, rather piteously, that she was only a poor girl who knew neither how to ride nor how to conduct war.[2] The voice told her, also, that she should go to her uncle, a command which must have seemed as comforting and reassuring as the other command was frightening, for Durand Lassois, the "uncle" in question, was, as I have already pointed out, an amenable man.[3] Nothing was more natural than that Jeanne

[1]*Procès*, Vol. I, p. 53: *Ipsa cognovit Robertum de Baudricuria, cum tamen antea nunquam vidisset; et cognovit per illam vocem prædictum Robertum, nam vox dixit sibi quod ipse erat.*

[2]*Procès*, Vol. I, p. 53: *Ipsa Johanna tunc respondit quod erat una pauper filia quæ nesciret equitare, nec ducere guerram.*

[3]*Vie de Jeanne d'Arc*, Vol. I, p. 67. M. Anatole France, with his usual

should suggest going on a short visit to her relations. The visit was short indeed—only a week,[1] but during that week, if she did not succeed in accomplishing her main desire, she did at least make the most of her time and contrive to lay a trail due to prove very useful to her in the future.

iv

This first visit to Durand and Jeanne Lassois took place in 1428, towards the feast of the Ascension, which in that year fell on May 13th. According to M. Siméon Luce, Jeanne refrained, till her visit was drawing to a close, to tackle her "uncle" direct on the subject of her real purpose.[2] Probably she had spent the preceding days in preparing the way to gaining his help and sympathy. For Durand Lassois, although persuadable, was still a peasant, and therefore naturally slow and cautious, and the proposal which Jeanne had to lay before him was, to say the least of it, startling—no less a proposal than that he should escort her into the presence of the formidable governor of Vaucouleurs. When one reflects that she was a girl of sixteen, and her "uncle" a man of nearly forty who,

sagacity, indicates that on this occasion the voices were doing no more than express her own desires. He rather undermines our confidence in his reliability, and consequently in his judgment, by misquoting the passage in question, which he renders thus: *Fille de Dieu, lui dit-il, tu iras vers le capitaine Robert de Baudricourt, en la ville de Vaucouleurs, afin qu'il te donne des gens pour te conduire auprès du gentil dauphin.* Now there is no mention in the original passage of either *fille de Dieu* or *gentil dauphin*, although it is true that these expressions occur elsewhere. But not in that place. Jeanne's actual statement, shorn of M. France's decorations, runs as follows: (*Procès*, Vol. I, pp. 52–3) *Dixit etiam quod sibi videbatur esse digna vox, et . . . cognovit quod erat vox angeli. . . . Dixit ulterius vocem præfatum sibi dixisse, quod ipsa Johanna iret ad Robertum de Baudricuria . . . et ipse traderet sibi gentes secum ituras.* It will be seen from this quotation, in which the dots represent no essential omission, that neither the *fille de Dieu* nor the *gentil dauphin* appear on the scene at all.

[1] *Procès*, Vol. I, p. 53.

[2] Siméon Luce, *Jeanne d'Arc à Domremy*, pp. clxi-ii.

as such, must have regarded her as having only just emerged from childhood; when one reflects, furthermore, that the very idea of bearding the governor in his fortress must have appeared to him, a mere labourer, as an almost unthinkable piece of impertinence, one begins to realise how disturbing a visit that week's visit to the stolid, peaceful household at Burey-le-Petit must have proved to the head of that household. The pretext itself was a crazy one: that of introducing a young relative, female at that, arbitrarily demanding an authorisation to journey into France to bother no less a personage than the Dauphin with the wild scheme of restoring France when experienced soldiers and statesmen had for nearly a hundred years failed to do so. One puts it inevitably into modern terms, saying: What would an agricultural labourer in England to-day think, if his wife's sixteen-year-old cousin arrived on a week's visit to his cottage in a small village, and by gradual degrees broke to him that she wished him to conduct her before the Lord-Lieutenant of the county, with a view to despatching her to tell the King at Windsor not only what he ought to do for the salvation of his country, but undertaking to perform that duty on his behalf? Let us imagine, for the sake of emphasis, that such a proposal had been made at any time during the late European war (as, indeed, it was; see Appendix A, p. 389), for the Hundred Years' War in France, with its prolonged attrition and exasperation, must have appeared as distressful and endless to the French of the fourteenth and fifteenth centuries, events moving more slowly then, as the European war, in its more intensive form, appeared to us of the twentieth. It is hard to imagine that an agricultural labourer in, let us say, a village of Herefordshire, would have welcomed with any enthusiasm the proposal that he should introduce his wife's sixteen-year-old cousin to his Lord-Lieutenant, in order that she might make her way to Windsor or Downing Street, uniting in her own person the offices of Marshal Foch and the Archbishop of Canterbury. For that, in short, was what Jeanne proposed to do. She proposed, first, to vanquish the enemy, and then to crown the King. Certainly, she did not propose to set the crown upon his head with her own hands: her modesty and her respect for the Church would alike have precluded her from so arrogant a programme. But she did intend to vanquish the enemy, and fully believed herself to be the appointed saviour. She broke it gently to her poor puzzled cousin, supporting her intentions with references to current prophecies. Had he not heard, she asked, that France, having been lost through a woman, would be restored by a girl?[1] This was a prophecy uttered by one Marie d'Avignon, and had evidently taken a hold on Jeanne's mind, for she repeated it later in a more specific form to Baudricourt,[2] but in talking to Durand Lassois she left it as a mere generalisation. She did, however, end by telling him that she must go into France to get the Dauphin crowned, and that he must conduct her to Vaucouleurs with that object in view.

His consent may seem astonishing, but it becomes less astonishing when one takes two factors into consideration: first that Durand Lassois was, naturally, a Catholic, and second that the general standard of religious credulity was far more simple in the fifteenth century than it is now. On the first count, the analogy with the agricultural labourer of Herefordshire is thereby not quite accurate; on the second count, saints and miracles were taken far more as a matter of course by everyone, the ignorant and the educated alike. Visions, voices, and prophecies were matters of relatively common occurrence. Visionaries such as Jeanne abounded, the difference between them being one of degree rather than of kind; and, as later events were to prove, of accomplishment as opposed to bombast. Durand Lassois and his prototypes must have been quite well accustomed to hearing gossip and rumours about such

---

[1]*Procès*, Vol. II, p. 444: Deposition of Durand Lassois: "*Nonne alias dictum fuit quod Francia per mulierem desolararetur, et postea per virginem restaurari debebat?*" The reference to the woman who had desolated France is to Isabeau de Bavière, mother of the Dauphin.

[2]*Procès*, Vol. II, p. 447: Deposition of Catherine le Royer.

people. Therefore, when Durand Lassois discovered that his young cousin imagined herself to have joined their ranks, the surprise and incredulity cannot have been so great as we, in our more rational age, might suppose. Whatever the explanation, he gave way and did as she demanded.

v

Most fortunately, two eye-witness accounts remain to us of the first interview between Jeanne and Baudricourt, apart from Jeanne's own account, which is brief and exceptionally uncommunicative. The first eye-witness is, of course, Durand Lassois himself. His evidence is muddled and incomplete; he does not, for instance, differentiate at all clearly between the first time Jeanne persuaded him to take her to Vaucouleurs and the second. Similarly, when he tells us that at one moment she made up her mind to start out independently on her journey in search of the Dauphin, and borrowed his clothes for that purpose, he is evidently confusing the two visits. Here, however, is his account, which appears to apply to the first visit: "She asked me to go to Robert de Baudricourt, who would cause her to be conducted to the place where the Dauphin was. The said Robert told me several times that I should take her back to the house of her father, and should give her a smacking."[1] The second eye-witness gives more details, and is a certain Bertrand de Poulengy, then a man of thirty-six, who afterwards became one of Jeanne's most loyal adherents. He had known her home at Domremy, for he had often been to her parents' house; he was present at her interview with Robert de Baudricourt. He heard her telling Robert that she had approached him in the name of her Lord, in order that the said Robert should send a message to the Dauphin to conduct

[1]*Procès*, Vol. II, p. 444: Deposition of Durand Lassois. *Et hoc ipsa dixit eidem testi, quod iret dictum Roberto de Baudricuria quod facerat eam ducere ad locum ubi erat dominus Dalphinus. Qui Robertus pluries eidem testi dixit, quod reduceret eam ad domum sui patris et daret ei alapas.*

himself with discretion, and not to engage in battle with his enemies, because her Lord would give him help after mid-Lent. The reason she gave for these rather arbitrary commands enjoined on the Dauphin, was that the kingdom was no concern of his, but was the concern of her Lord. Nevertheless, she said, her Lord intended the Dauphin to become king, and to hold the kingdom in fief; and added that the Dauphin should become king despite his enemies, and that she herself would lead him to his coronation. When Baudricourt, not unnaturally, enquired whom she meant by her Lord, she replied, "The King of Heaven."[1]

This remarkable interview, thus recorded by Bertrand de Poulengy, ended abortively for Jeanne. Baudricourt simply laughed at her, and not only told Lassois to take her back to her home after a sound correction, but jested coarsely that he might hand her over to the pleasure of his soldiers.[2] Abortive though the interview turned out to be, it gives rise to one or two curious speculations. For instance, Jeanne's allusion to mid-Lent of the following year (1429) suggests that she never intended to accomplish her mission as an immediate result of this first visit to Vaucouleurs, but regarded it rather as a preliminary skirmish, almost as a warning to Baudricourt of the real attack he might expect from her later on. There is this further point, to which, so far as I know, attention has never hitherto been drawn. Jeanne's first visit took place in the middle of May 1428. Her second visit lasted from the beginning of January till the middle of February 1429.[3] Jeanne's pretext on this occasion was that Lassois' wife was about to have a baby, and that she, Jeanne, by going to stay with her relations, would be able to lend a helping hand. Now Jeanne Lassois, if she were going to have a baby in January 1429, would just have begun to suspect the fact in May 1428. In any case, Burey-le-Petit and Domremy were

[1] *Procès*, Vol. II, p. 456: Deposition of Bertrand de Poulengy.
[2] *Procès*, Vol. IV, p. 205: *Chronique de la Pucelle.*
[3] Siméon Luce, *Jeanne d'Arc à Domremy*, p. clxxxiv.

so close that this anticipated event would have come to Jeanne's ears some time during the ensuing months. I think it is therefore likely that she laid her plans accordingly, more especially as Lent always meant a great deal to her, and would have appeared a most propitious moment for embarking on her enterprise. It is worth noting, also, that Saint Margaret, one of the saints who habitually appeared to Jeanne, was the especial protector of women in childbirth, and of peasants.

vi

We have no record of how Jacques d'Arc received his daughter on her return, or of whether the correction recommended by Baudricourt was ever administered or not. It is a mere, though perhaps not an unfair, assumption to imagine that Jeanne's home life during the succeeding months of 1428 was not made too easy for her. She may have counted herself lucky that outside events should have occurred to distract her father's attention from the speculation as to whether his daughter was merely eccentric or actually going off her head. For the position at Domremy was becoming serious. Vaucouleurs itself was threatened by the Burgundians under Antoine de Vergy, and by the second half of July it was clear that the inhabitants of both Domremy and Greux would have to seek a temporary refuge[1] within the walls of the neighbouring town of Neuf-château. It is not necessary to enter into too many details; what concerns us is to note that Jeanne and her parents, taking their cattle with them, shared in the general exodus which left their village abandoned to the enemy. There can be no doubt that she accompanied her parents on this occasion, or that, more importantly, she was accompanied by them. She was, in fact, seen at Neufchâteau by one Jacquier de Saint-Amant, who observed her driving her father's cattle into the fields.[2]

[1]Siméon Luce, *Jeanne d'Arc à Domremy*, p. clxxix; and *Procès*, Vol. I, p. 51.
[2]*Procès*, Vol. II, p. 409: Deposition of Jacquier de Saint-Amant, or Amance.

This flight to Neufchâteau had one disagreeable consequence for poor Jeanne at her trial. She and her parents having found a lodging with a certain Madame la Rousse, it was charged against her that she had spent some time in an inn which was in reality a house of ill fame. The accusation is absurd. Not only does La Rousse appear to have been a perfectly respectable woman, but Jeanne's parents were scarcely the type of people to find their lodging in a brothel, much less to allow their daughter to accompany them there, and certainly not the type to countenance their daughter contributing to the amusements of such an establishment. The accusation was apparently based on a supposition that Jeanne had been employed as a servant in the inn,[1] a supposition which probably arose because Jeanne, a hefty girl, accustomed to helping her mother with the household duties at home, extended her good nature to helping her hostess with the work involved in looking after her sudden influx of guests. As M. Siméon Luce suggests, the refugees from Domremy must have found some difficulty in filling up their time in their unfamiliar surroundings, so it was natural that Jeanne should carry on with her habitual ploys.

vii

It also seems likely that she had other things to occupy her mind during this enforced and unpleasant sojourn at Neufchâteau. A shadowy suitor enters her life at this period, and it is suggested that, during her fortnight's exile at Neufchâteau, he dragged her off to Toul, the centre of the diocese, to answer in a breach-of-promise action before the episcopal court.[2] He is a young man without a name, but with the breach-of-promise action behind him to give him a worldly solidity; a young man whose existence would never have been known to us at all but for Jeanne's judges having chosen to mention him, in the ninth article of their accusation, as an

[1] *Procès*, Vol. I, p. 214.
[2] Siméon Luce, *Jeanne d'Arc à Domremy*, p. clxxi.

additional example of how badly she had always behaved. Poor Jeanne defended herself over this as best she might. She had never, she said, brought an action against him; it was he, on the contrary, who had brought one against her, but she had never given him any promise, and had vowed her virginity to God from the first time of hearing her voices.[1] It was not true, she said, that he had refused to marry her because she had lived in a house at Neufchâteau with women of ill fame, nor that he had died while the case was pending, nor that she, Jeanne, in despite, had abandoned her employment for that reason. She mentioned, also, that her voices had assured her that she would win her case. This was perhaps not a very well-chosen assurance to quote, since it meant mixing up the secular with the heavenly. Still, it was allowed to pass without comment.[2]

The shadowy suitor presumably added to Jeanne's worries during the second half of 1428, both at Neufchâteau and at home. It was trying enough to have to cope with importunate saints, distressed parents, an indignant lover, and a future full of menace, but, on the top of all that, to hear smug matrimonial plans discussed for oneself must have been irritating in the extreme. It must have been exceedingly difficult to respond in any way save by a flat refusal; and parents of well-brought-up girls were not, at that time, inclined to accept flat refusals in good part.

If Jeanne's suitor really forced her to go to Toul during this period, she must have spent a busy as well as a disturbed fortnight.

However it may be, she and her parents returned to Domremy to find most of the village burnt and the church in ruins.

viii

War had been brought very close—in fact, to their very home. Jeanne could no longer attend Mass in her accustomed place,

[1] *Procès*, Vol. I, pp. 215 and 127–8.

[2] For a further discussion of the Toul affair, see Appendix B, p. 390.

but must perforce walk, or perhaps ride, to Greux, where the church had been spared.[1] Apart from these sorrows and inconveniences, there was still actual danger from armed raids, if we may judge by the restrictions placed upon the villagers of the district for their greater safety. Thus, they were not allowed out into the country beyond the refuge of fortified places. These restrictions evidently continued in force for several months. We have the example of a labourer at Foug, called Jean Bauldet le Vieux, who, so late as November 1428, was fined twenty sous for having gone to look at his plough which had been left abandoned in a field.[2] These sidelights do make history less dry and more human: one sees Jean Bauldet le Vieux creeping out to examine his precious plough rusting in the damp November grass—an offence all the more serious, he having been appointed to guard the gates of Foug while a number of its citizens had gone to Sorcey by the order of the Cardinal of Bar. Far from setting a good example to his fellow-villagers—in whose interest, as in his own, the regulation of guarding the gates had been made—he deserted his post the moment their backs were turned. One wonders what *Haultchappel, sergent de Foug,* said to him when he found his orders disregarded. Probably he did not spare his words, when Jean le Vieux came back, having dared enough to go out into the fields himself, but not having dared to take a horse with him, to drag his plough back into safety.

Life under these conditions must have been alarming and irksome to all. More especially to Jeanne, the appointed and impatient saviour of unhappy France. The suspicions of her father, the importunities of the young man making such a fuss about her refusal to marry him, must indeed have appeared tiresome and contemptible, in view of the charge laid upon her, as it became more urgent and more urgent. Still, she waited.

[1]*Procès,* Vol. II, p. 396: Deposition of Beatrice Estellin: *Quando villa de dicto Dompno Remigio fuit combusta, ipsa Johanneta diebus festivis semper ibat auditum missam ad villam de Greu.*

[2]Archives de la Meuse, B. 2213, folio 91.

Nevertheless, it appears from the evidence that her discretion began to break down a little. She began to reveal her impatience by hints and allusions. She had already told her friend Michel Lebuin, on the eve of Saint John Baptist, that a young girl living between Coussey and Vaucouleurs would cause the King of France to be crowned before the year was out.[1] She told another young man, Jean Waterin, that she would restore France and the blood royal.[2] More mysteriously, she said to Gérardin d'Epinal, "*Compère*, if you were not a Burgundian, I would tell you certain things." He, very naturally, thought she was alluding to some man she wanted to marry.[3] What, indeed, could be more obvious to Gérardin's mind? Marriage projects were in the air, as is proved by the Neufchâteau-Toul affair. Jeanne was of marriageable age, and marriage the only alternative to a convent, unless she wished to become the family drudge for the rest of her life. From Jeanne's point of view, however, it was equally obvious that she must remove herself as speedily as possible from such a threatened fate. She knew she was destined for more important things. What more comprehensible than that she should have said nothing definite about her intended departure, an announcement which would only have had the effect of speeding up her parents' desire to see her safely clamped in matrimony? Once married, she was doubly caught: she would have not only a father but a husband to evade.

The remark she made to Gérardin d'Epinal was obviously made just before her final departure, and referred to something very different from any young man she might have in mind. The dark allusions made by her to Michel Lebuin and Jean Waterin about the young girl, living between Coussey and Vaucouleurs, who should restore the kingdom of France, equally obviously referred to herself. By the time she left

---

[1] *Procès*, Vol. II, p. 440: Deposition of Michel Lebuin.
[2] *Procès*, Vol. II, p. 421: Deposition of Jean Waterin.
[3] *Procès*, Vol. II, p. 423: Deposition of Gérardin d'Epinal: *Dum ipsa voluit recedere, dixit sibi: "Compator, nisi essetis Burgundus, ego dicerum vobis aliqua." Credebat enim dictus testis quod fuisset pro aliquo socio quem vellet desponsare.*

Domremy for ever, her friends and her family must all have at least suspected her intentions, even though they may have ignored the exact date she had fixed for her final departure. It seems inexplicable, in the circumstances, that her parents should so easily have allowed her to escape them a second time. Forewarned, in this case, was not forearmed. Perhaps, even up to the last moment, they never took her quite seriously. It seems the more inexplicable when one remembers that she had already paid her first visit to Robert de Baudricourt, a visit which must certainly have given rise to common talk, even supposing that Durand Lassois kept silence out of loyalty and conviction.

Chapter VI

DOMREMY AND VAUCOULEURS (2)

i

In January of 1429, Jeanne, then aged just seventeen, left Domremy for ever. She left, on this second occasion, ostensibly to stay again with Durand Lassois and his wife at Burey-le-Petit, when Jeanne Lassois' baby was about to be born. The first visit was child's play compared with this, the first really decisive step that she took in her strange and brief career. For nearly five years she had kept her private instructions to herself; now the moment had arrived when she must turn those private instructions into a public declaration of a nature to startle two nations out of their wits. Without saying a word to her parents, and with very few words to her friends, she set out on the first stage of her earthly voyage. The distance from Domremy to Burey was not great—under ten miles—but measured figuratively it was enormous. It represented the whole difference between her private and her public life. It required a tremendous effort of courage and conviction.

It must, also, have been attended by a mental suffering which only a corresponding state of mental exaltation could have rendered tolerable. A virtuous, helpful, and obedient daughter, the small deceptions she had hitherto practised on her parents in the form of minor truancies while she was supposed to be looking after the cattle, even the escapade to Vaucouleurs eight months earlier, were as nothing compared with the major truancy she now contemplated. Nothing but the commands of God Himself could have superseded the authority of her parents in her dutiful mind, and it is clear from her own words that the recognition of this divided authority involved her in a final anguish as to the right decision. She said that sooner than go to France without God's permission she would be torn to pieces by horses.[1] She

1*Procès*, Vol. I, p. 74.

recorded, also, that her parents nearly went out of their minds when she left them.[1] It is impossible not to dwell with passionate sympathy on the struggles which must have taken place in that childish soul, so ill-informed on the one hand, so miraculously informed on the other. All her training, all her traditions, pointed to her parents' word as absolute law; all her inner experience persuaded her to follow the higher dictate. One must take into consideration, however, that she had been following it in a quiet way, without open demonstration, for the past five years, a training and self-discipline which cannot have been without its value when the moment came to put it to the first real test. Indeed, when one considers the power of reticence displayed by the child of twelve in concealing revelations of so terrifying a magnitude from her natural confidants, the decisive action of the girl of seventeen becomes less surprising. Less surprising, but quite as painful to contemplate sympathetically in retrospect.

At any rate, it is abundantly evident that Jeanne was, and had been from the first, possessed of a strength of will and a self-control beyond rational explanation. It may be argued that the average child, confronted by a luminous cloud from which emerged an unknown voice, would have rushed screaming to its mother; that the average child, even if it had kept its head in the first moment, would have relapsed into confidences about it later, since there are certain hours of daily life in which a child's confidence may be easily and almost inevitably won. That argument, however, clatters to the ground in face of the fact that no average child would have been confronted by a luminous cloud, or would have heard a voice speaking out of it. The very fact that she did find herself confronted by such a cloud, and did hear herself addressed by such a voice, marked her out as in some essential way different from other children. Her reticence, her self-control, even though maintained over so long a period as nearly five years, prove nothing more than that she was normally abnormal. They go, also, a long way

[1]*Procès*, Vol. I, p. 132: "*à bien peu qu'ilz ne perdirent le sens.*"

towards helping to prove her own unquestionable conviction. It is a great, though simple, point in favour of her sincerity that she never prattled about her experiences during the years when she might have been expected to prattle. Visionaries, generally speaking, shrink from communicating their experiences to others; either the fear of ridicule, or, more probably, an inner sense of self-preservation, shuts them into themselves during the initial period of probation, until such time as the filling reservoir overflows its dams, and the barriers of reticence give way before the compelling flood of demonstration. One may, at first sight, wonder greatly over this apparently extraordinary reticence displayed by a child; one wonders less when, on second thoughts, one considers the natural secrecy of most children on matters affecting their private innermost life, and then extends one's imagination to the comprehension of a child altogether removed, for some inexplicable reason, to a private innermost life almost unimaginable in its mystery, inspiration, and awe. It is not surprising that Jeanne should have abstained from the children's revels round the Fairies' Tree, when once she had begun to live so astounding a fairy-story of her own. It is not surprising that she should have kept her secret even from the mother who, apart from the local *curé*, had been the only guide to her religious life. Boulainvilliers, indeed, says that she told it to her priest, but Jeanne, surely a more reliable authority, says that she told it to no one. Assuming, for the sake of argument, that she did tell it to her priest (which, on the face of Jeanne's evidence, is impossible to believe),[1] what would his counsel have been? He would certainly have advised her to keep it to herself, not because he disbelieved her, but because his instinct and tradition would have warned him that such a secret should be preserved at all costs from outward comment and contact, lest it should vanish like a web of

---

[1]*Procès*, Vol. I, p. 128: *Interroguée se de ces visions elle a point parlé à son curé ou autre homme d'église: respond que non, mais seullement à Robert de Baudricourt et à son roy.* In the margin is written: *Celavit visiones curato, patri et matrie et cuicumque.*

gossamer at the touch of an earthly hand. He would, in his own simplicity, have recognised that a simplicity such as Jeanne's must be safeguarded in its virgin state. He would, quite justifiably, have encouraged her in the belief that this was God's business, to the exclusion even of her parents. It would have been no more than his duty to do so. But it must have been one of the strangest confessions he ever heard, if he did hear it; and, poor man, we can feel for him whenever he met Jacques d'Arc or Isabelle Romée, either in the village street or in the confessional, and remembered the secret he had encouraged their daughter to keep from them. For, after all, he was a neighbour as well as a priest: they were all friends together.

How queerly life turns out! How impossible that Jeanne, in spite of all her prescience, could have foreseen that I, trying in 1935 to interpret the facts of her existence from 1412 to 1428, should receive a visiting-card from the *Curé-Doyen de Domremy-la-Pucelle, Chanoine honoraire de Saint Dié et d'Orléans, Chapelain d'honneur de Jeanne d'Arc, téléphone Greux 7.*

We need not, however, waste our sympathies over a *curé* who almost certainly has no reason to deserve them. We had far better accept Jeanne's statement that she confided in no one. Quite apart from any possible priestly influence, and quite apart from any warning personal instinct, she had ample cause for keeping her own counsel. Her father's dreams alone would have sufficed to make her hold her tongue. Jeanne was sagacious always; the sagacity of the peasant was hers, as well as the inspiration of the mystic. Therein lay, I think, her real strength.

ii

In January, then, she departed quietly to stay with the Lassois at Burey, giving as her pretext that Jeanne Lassois was about to have a baby.[1] She might help Jeanne Lassois over her trouble, lending a useful hand in the house, even as

[1]*Procès,* Vol. II, p. 434: Deposition of Colin Colin.

she had helped Madame la Rousse at Neufchâteau. Helping Jeanne Lassois over her trouble would naturally provide an excuse likely to appeal to Jacques d'Arc and Isabelle Romée. Neighbours and relatives in country districts, or, indeed, anywhere amongst the unaided poor, are accustomed to come to each other's assistance in moments of emergency. If Jeanne took advantage of a pretext of this sort, who shall blame her? She may be blamed for having acted rather slyly towards her parents, but by that time she was convinced that a greater law than her parents' word was enjoined upon her; she had no choice but to obey. When her judges asked her whether she thought she had done right in leaving without the permission of either her father or her mother, she replied that she had obeyed them in all things, save on this matter of her departure, but since then she had written to them, and they had forgiven her. Asked, again, whether she had no thought of sinning in thus leaving them, she replied that, since God ordered it, she was right to obey. She added, in the magnificent manner she could at times command, that, since God ordered it, she would have gone, even if she had had a hundred fathers and a hundred mothers, even had she been the daughter of a king.[1]

It is impossible not to recall another answer: "Wist ye not that I must be about My Father's business?"

When they asked her whether she had enquired of her voices if she should speak of her departure to her father and mother, she replied that the voices would quite gladly have allowed her to do so, so far as her father and mother were concerned, but for the grief they would bring upon her in the telling. The voices left it to her whether to tell them or not, but made it clear that she might tell it either to her father or to her

[1]*Procès*, Vol. I, p. 129: *Interroguée s'elle cuidoit bien faire de partir sans le congié de père ou mère, comme il soit ainsi que on doit honnourer père et mère: respond que en toutes autres choses elle a bien obey à eulx, excepté de ce partement: mais depuis leur en a escript, et luy ont pardonné.*

Interroguée se, quant elle partit de ses père et mère, elle cuidoit point péchier: respond, puis que Dieu le commandoit . . . s'elle eust C pères et C mères, et s'il [sic] eust été fille de roy, si fust-elle partie.

mother, otherwise she must keep silent. The responsibility thus having been thrown on Jeanne, she decided that on no account would she tell them. Here, as always, her worldly wisdom shows itself, for although she said frankly that her voices had never constrained her to entire secrecy, she had hesitated to reveal them, lest the Burgundians should prevent her journey, and, more especially, lest her father should prevent it also.[1] It is thus made clear that although Jeanne obeyed her voices in essentials, even to the extent of going against her natural affections and against her traditions of filial obedience, she could still reserve her own judgment when the decision was left to her. Her voices would have authorised her to confide in her parents: her own judgment restrained her from doing so. Her native prudence was, I think, mixed up with her kindly feeling towards her parents. She was reluctant to hurt them unduly. Nor did she want them to hurt her. Her voices themselves had warned her that they might do so. Nor did she want to provoke the parental authority which might prevent her from going to stay with her relatives at Burey-le-Petit—the stepping-stone to Vaucouleurs, to Robert de Baudricourt, and, eventually, to Chinon. She wanted to slip away without impediment or fuss. Did she act rightly or wrongly? The decision is less difficult for us to settle to-day, in retrospect, than for the very young Jeanne in January of 1429. We know now that the end justified the means, so who are we, with our advantage of getting history into its more or less correct perspective, to criticise the girl for having taken the safer, though perhaps more surreptitious,

[1] *Procès*, Vol. I, p. 129: *Interroguée s'elle demanda à ses voix qu'elle deist à son père et à sa mère son partement: respond que, quant est de père et de mère, ilz estoient assés contens qu'elle leur dist, se n'eust esté la paine qu'ilz luy eussent fait, s'elle leur eust dit; et quant est d'elle, elle ne leur eust dit pour chose quelconque. Item dit que ses voix se raportoient à elle de le dire à père ou mère, ou de s'en taire.*

Procès, Vol. I, p. 128: *Et dit oultre qu'elle ne fust point contraincte de ses voix à le céler; mais doubtoit moult le révéler, pour doubte des Bourguegnons, qu'ilz ne la empeschassent de son voyage; et par espécial doubtoit moult son père, qu'il ne la empeschast de son véage faire.*

course at that crisis of her life, under the terrifying compulsion of what she sincerely believed to be God's orders? It is clear that she thought she was doing right; it is clear, also, that she suffered humanly while she did it.

iii

The accounts of Jeanne's departure from Domremy prove her distress. Not only did she not dare to say good-bye to her parents for practical reasons (*et par espécial doubtoit moult son père, qu'il ne la empeschast de son véage faire*), but for sentimental reasons she avoided saying good-bye to her personal friends.

Naturally, she had many such friends in the village. She had known them all her life. They had all, so to speak, grown up together. They had shared the same experiences always, such as the fun of the picnics at the Arbre des Dames, in safe and happy days, and also the scares of the dangerous days which drove them and their parents and their cows away into refuge while the Burgundians burnt their village and their church. They had shared their games, their pleasures, their frights, and their disasters. It cannot have been easy for Jeanne to go away from such intimate companions without even telling them that she was going; without giving them any indication of what she was going to do, knowing that in all likelihood she would never see them again. Their accounts of her farewells to them make pathetic reading.

To some she threw a word, not very explicit perhaps, but, all the same, a word by which they might, as indeed they did, remember her. She called out to Mengette Joyart, for instance, saying "Good-bye!" and recommending her to God, as she left for Vaucouleurs.[1] Jean Waterin heard her saying "Good-bye!" to various people as, in her patched red dress, she passed

[1]*Procès*, Vol. II, p. 431: Deposition of Mengette Joyart: . . . *recedendo ipsa dixit eidem testi "Ad Deum!" et tunc recessit, et eam testem commandavit Deo, et ivit ad Vallis-Colorem.*

through Greux on her way.[1] Gérard Guillemette, equally, the youngest among her witnesses, who can have been no more than fourteen years old at the time, remembered having seen her pass in front of his father's house in company of Durand Lassois, when she bade his father "Good-bye! I am off to Vaucouleurs."[2]

To Hauviette, however, her most intimate friend from childhood upwards, she spoke no farewell at all. Hauviette was often with Jeanne, and even slept with her in her father's house. This was a common custom, especially between girls who had made their first communion together,[3] though in this case Hauviette uses the rather curious expression *jacuit amorose*. Jeanne evidently avoided any form of farewell to Hauviette, who "wept bitterly on learning of her departure, because she loved Jeanne greatly for her goodness, and because she had been her friend."[4]

iv

It is difficult to disentangle Jeanne's exact movements during the six weeks which elapsed between her second visit to her Lassois relations at Burey in the beginning of January 1429, and her final departure for Chinon on February 23rd of the same year. They are confused by variously conflicting evidence. But do such things matter very much, except to scholars, each anxious to catch the other out on a point of accuracy? It seems to me, perhaps wrongly, that the question of a disputed day

[1]*Procès*, Vol. II, p. 421: Deposition of Jean Waterin: . . . *quod vidit eam recedere a villa de Greu, et dicebat gentibus: "Ad Deum!"*

[2]*Procès*, Vol. II, p. 416: Deposition of Gérard Guillemette: . . . *vidit ipsam Johannam transire ante domum patris sui cum quodam avunculo suo, nuncupato Durando Laxart, et tunc ipsa Johanneta dixit suo patri: "Ad Deum, ego vado ad Vallis-Colorem."*

[3] Siméon Luce, *Jeanne d'Arc à Domremy*, p. clxxxiii.

[4]*Procès*, Vol. II, p. 419: Deposition of Hauviette, wife of Gérard de Sionne: . . . *hoc multum flevit, quia eam multum propter suam bonitatem diligebat, et quod sua socia erat.*

or so, or even of a week or so, adds nothing except a too scrupulously pedantic interest to an ultimate estimate of the phenomenon represented by Jeanne d'Arc.[1]

The confusion arises largely because Durand Lassois, obliging as he proved himself towards Jeanne, does not appear to have possessed the most lucid and orderly of memories, nor the gift of arranging his facts in their unmistakably chronological order. Without entering into too many details, we must consider the evidence of a certain Catherine le Royer, in whose house, at Vaucouleurs, Jeanne stayed as a guest for three weeks. Lassois states that Jeanne stayed in his house, at Burey, for *six* weeks; therefore, if Jeanne left Domremy for Burey at the beginning of January 1429, and subsequently left Vaucouleurs for Chinon on February 23rd, as is certain, the three weeks she spent with Catherine le Royer must be included in the six weeks spent under the wing of the Lassois from early January to mid-February. Even the suggestion that Lassois may have muddled up Jeanne's first visit to his house in May of 1428, with her second visit in 1429, does not get us out of the difficulty.[2] When we remember, however, that Jeanne not only went backwards and forwards between Burey and Vaucouleurs, but also made a separate journey to Nancy during this period, and that Lassois was testifying twenty-six years later and was probably frightened, a simple peasant then aged sixty, his confusion becomes quite comprehensible.

These details of where, exactly, she spent her time during those critical six weeks, and of how she divided them between the Lassois' home and that of Catherine and Henri le Royer, are not, in themselves, of very great importance. We can take it for granted that she was staying either in one house or the other. She must, incidentally, have had plenty to occupy her

---

[1] It has even been advanced by some authorities that Jeanne paid only one visit to Lassois, not two. It is a moot point, but on the whole I incline to the view that she went twice to Burey-le-Petit—once in May 1428, and once in January 1429.

[2] Siméon Luce, *Jeanne d'Arc à Domremy*, pp. clxxxiii–iv.

mind: there was Jeanne Lassois' baby—that convenient infant who never reappears in Jeanne's history—and, above all, there was the task of coaxing Robert de Baudricourt round to her own point of view.

That task had become considerably simplified since the previous May 1428. For one thing, the position in France was becoming more and more desperate. Orleans had been besieged since October 1428 by the English. Baudricourt himself had his troubles and dangers in his own little governorship of Vaucouleurs. The local lord, René Duke of Bar, his friend and ally, was even then resisting the efforts of the Duke of Bedford to turn him into a vassal of the English King. It no longer seemed so natural to Baudricourt to receive any possible saviour with derision, even when that saviour announced herself under such fantastic colours. As M. Siméon Luce caustically remarks, *quand on n'attend plus rien de la terre, on est moins prompt à dédaigner un secours annoncé au nom du ciel.*

Besides, Jeanne by now had acquired, so to speak, friends at Court. One of these, Bertrand de Poulengy, has already made his appearance on the scene (see *supra*, Chapter V, p. 77). The other one, Jean de Nouvilonpont, or Novelompont, or Nouillompont, more commonly known as Jean de Metz, now walks out from the wings on to the stage for the first, but not for the last, time. Although neither Bertrand de Poulengy nor Jean de Metz may claim to rank as deep or dominating influences in Jeanne's life, and although they were later to be superseded by far more consequential and vivid personages, they must still retain a place of honour as among the first to believe in her startling mission, and, more importantly, as ready to give her their practical support at a time when she was most in need of it. Young adventurous soldiers as they were, they would appear as the very last people likely to award their credence to a village girl having no experience either of the arts of war or of the leadership of men. Yet, somehow, very early in her career, they turned themselves into the pioneers, almost the impresarios, of Jeanne d'Arc, recognising a quality in her: the quality which has enrolled her not only among the saints, but also among the captains of history.

Very little is known about either of them, apart from the rôle they played at the outset of her public career. They both appear to have been men of relatively gentle birth—that is to say, not of the same class as Jeanne's own parents, friends, and relations, who belonged mostly to the class of labourers and wheelwrights and suchlike simple rustic people. Bertrand de Poulengy and Jean de Metz were both a cut above that. They were men of the sword. Poulengy is the one of whom we know least. We know, in fact, very little about him save that he is described as *écuyer de l'écurie royale de France*; and that he was born noble, whereas Jean de Metz was not. Of Jean de Metz we know a little more, but still not much. He may, or may not, have inherited the *seigneurie* of Nouillompont from his father; he had been attached to another captain before taking service under Baudricourt, and was ennobled in 1449.[1] Poulengy was in the middle thirties, de Metz between twenty-eight and thirty-one, when they met Jeanne at Vaucouleurs. They had both got themselves into slight and insignificant trouble with the authorities before she arrived to upset their lives—very much the same sort of trouble as a lively young man of to-day might get himself into, whatever one may choose as the modern equivalent— Bertrand de Poulengy for helping someone to escape from prison, Jean de Metz for swearing a *vilain serment* and for flinging an award of money on the ground.[2] In short, they seem to have belonged to a very usual type of young men of good family, and to have comported themselves very much as one would expect such young men to do. Where they differed from ordinary young men—ordinary rough young soldiers—was in their early recognition of Jeanne and the possibilities of her mission. It does not appear that either of

[1] De Bouteiller et de Braux: *Nouvelles recherches sur la famille de Jeanne d'Arc*.
[2] Archives de la Meuse, B. 1431; and ibid., folio 100.

them had known her personally before she came to Vaucouleurs, though Poulengy was acquainted with her parents, perhaps only later on, as he never appears to have seen Jeanne in their house, but only to have heard of her good repute. He, as already related, was present at her first interview with Baudricourt. Jean de Metz, as his own deposition makes clear, had heard of her and of her ambitions, for, on first meeting her in the house of Catherine and Henri le Royer, dressed in her poor red dress (*pauperibus vestibus, rubeis, muliebribus*), he went up to her, saying, "*Ma mie,* what are you doing here? Must the King be driven from his kingdom and must we all become English?" Jeanne's reply to him was either much longer than she was accustomed to make or else his memory served him better than that of other witnesses; that he invented it or any part of it I do not believe, for it bears the authentic stamp of Jeanne's utterances, much as Queen Elizabeth's always bear the stamp of hers. "I have come to this royal town," she said, meaning Vaucouleurs, "to ask Robert de Baudricourt either to lead or to send me under escort to the King. He takes no notice of me or of my words; nevertheless, before mid-Lent, I must be on my way to the King, even if I must wear out my legs to the knees. There is no one in the world, neither king, nor duke, nor daughter of the King of Scotland,[1] nor any other, who can regain the kingdom of France; there is no help for the kingdom but in me. I should prefer to be spinning beside my poor mother, for these things do not belong to my station; yet it is necessary that I should go, and do these things, since God wishes that I should do them." Jean de Metz then took her hand and swore on his faith that, God helping them, he would lead her to the King. He asked her when she wanted to start. "Now, rather than to-morrow," she replied, "and to-morrow rather than the day after."[2]

[1]Jeanne was referring to the recent betrothal of Margaret of Scotland to the son of Charles VII, the future Louis XI.

[2]*Procès,* Vol. II, p. 436: . . . *ipse testis loquens vidit dictam Johannam indutam pauperibus vestibus, rubeis, muliebribus; et erat locata in domo cujusdam Henrici le*

How unconsciously complete is the picture thus created! Henri le Royer being only a wheelwright in humble circumstances, the house in the little mediæval town must have been small, and the room dark. As in a Rembrandt, one can see the group of three, uncertainly lit: Catherine le Royer watching apart; Jeanne in her red dress, quiet and earnest; the puzzled soldier standing over her, then going up to her and taking her hand—but such games of imagination are too easy, and the temptation must be resisted. It is better to come back soberly to the actual words of Jean de Metz, which will carry us a step further in the narrative.

v

Having taken his oath of alliance, almost of allegiance, he appears to have turned immediately to the practical aspects of the question. Did Jeanne, he asked, want to go on her journey dressed in her own clothes? To this she replied that she would gladly adopt masculine garments, whereupon he fitted her out with both clothes and boots belonging to his servants.[1] This

Royer, dictæ villæ de Vallis-Colore; qui locutus fuit sibi, dicendo: "Amica mea, quid hic facitis? Oportetne quod rex expellatur a regno, et quod simus Anglici?" Quæ Puella tunc sibi respondit: "Ego veni huc ad cameram Regis, locutum Roberto de Baudricuria, ut me velit ducere aut duci facere ad Regem; qui non curat de me neque de verbis meis; attamen, antequam sit media quadragesima, oportet quod ego sim versus Regem, si ego deberem perdere pedes usque ad genua. Nullus enim in mundo, nec reges, nec duces, nec filia regis Scotiæ, aut alii, possunt recuperare regnum Franciæ, nec est ei succursus nisi de memet, quamvis ego mallem nere juxta meam pauperam matrem, quia non est status meus; sed opportet ut ego vadam, et hoc faciam, quia Dominus meus vult ut ita faciam." Et dum idem testis quæreret ab ea quis esset ejus Dominus, dicebat ipsa Puella quod erat Deus. Et tunc idem Johannes, testis promisit eidem Puellæ, per fidem suam in sua manu tactam, quod eam, Deo duce, duceret versus Regem; et tunc idem testis loquens petiit sibi quando vellet recedere; quæ dicebat: "Citius nunc quam cras, et cras quam post."

[1]*Procès*, Vol. II, pp. 436–7: Deposition of Jean de Metz: *Et petiit sibi idem testis iterato si cum suis vestibus vellet ire; quæ respondit quod libenter haberet vestes hominis. Et tunc idem testis de famulis suis tradidit sibi vestes et calceamenta, ad induendum.*

seems rather odd, in view of the respect in which he so evidently held her. It may be asking too much of a needy soldier to suggest that he might well have bought her a new outfit, all to herself, but one would at least expect him to have given her some clothes from his own wardrobe, rather than such menial equipment as he could borrow from his servants. There may have been reasons which, at this distance of time, we cannot estimate. Perhaps he was too tall for his clothes to fit her. In any case, he certainly meant her no disrespect; nor was it long before he, in conjunction with Poulengy, arranged for a complete masculine equipment to be provided for her by the people of Vaucouleurs.[1] He must therefore have regarded the borrowing from the servants as a temporary measure.

I fear that Jeanne cannot have been very fastidious. One could scarcely expect it of a fifteenth-century peasant. But that she should have been ready to wear either Lassois' clothes or those of common soldiers was perhaps going a little too far. We must, however, consider that habits of personal cleanliness appealed but mildly to the mediæval mind. If the more civilised Italians were shocked by the unsavoury habits of the French aristocracy, even towards the end of Jeanne's century, so that French guests in Italian palaces had to be requested not to blow their noses in the bed-curtains, what must the habits of the French proletariat have been at its beginning! To use Jeanne's favourite expression, *"Passons ouetre."*

---

[1]*Procès*, Vol. II, p. 437: ibid.: . . . *et hoc facto, habitatores dictæ villæ de Vallis-Colore fecerunt sibi fieri vestis hominis et calceamenta.*

Procès, Vol. II, p. 457: Deposition of Bertrand de Poulengy: . . . *ipse Bertrandus, testis loquens, et Johannes de Metis tantum fecerunt, cum adjutorio aliarum gentium de Vallis-Colore, quod ipsa dimisit suas vestes mulieris, rubei coloris et fecerunt sibi fieri tunicam et vestimenta hominis, calcaria, ocreas, ensem et similia.*

vi

The red dress was threatened—faithful red dress, so often mentioned, so soon to be discarded. It is noteworthy, I think, that Jean de Metz should so quickly have turned to tackle the problem of her outward appearance, whether it should remain feminine or become masculine. Was it because, having committed himself to conduct her across France, his practical mind rushed at once to the possible, and, indeed, probable, hazards which would be incurred by a woman on so perilous a journey—a journey perilous for anybody, but doubly so for a woman? It is fair to assume that he would have felt his responsibility lightened if his charge would consent to travel under the guise of a boy instead of a girl. His normal soldierly experience would certainly have suggested the very necessary expedient of this apparent change of sex, in view of the ride they were proposing to undertake over some two hundred and fifty miles of a country in a state of war.[1]

vii

It is not stated whether Jeanne was still wearing her own clothes when she saw Robert de Baudricourt for the second time, or whether she had already acquired the servant's garb. In either case, he must have been considerably surprised by her reappearance. At first he was still unwilling to agree to her requests.[2] Then some leaven seems to have worked in his mind. This insistent visionary, who kept on turning up with

[1] Of course, in calling his apparently instant pre-occupation with her dress "noteworthy," one must always bear in mind that witnesses such as Jean de Metz were answering definite questions relative to definite accusations previously brought against Jeanne at the time of her trial, amongst which the accusation of adopting men's clothes bulked very importantly.

[2] *Procès*, Vol. II, p. 446: Deposition of Catherine le Royer. The wording of Catherine le Royer's deposition suggests that Jeanne sent him a message before approaching him in person: *tunc fecit loqui domino Roberto de Baudricuria, ut eam duceret ad locum ubi erat Dalphinus; qui dominus Robertus noluit.* Did she perhaps send Poulengy or Jean de Metz as her envoy?

H

her fantastic schemes; this visionary whom neither derision nor rebuffs nor coarse levity had succeeded in discouraging—might it perhaps be worth while to investigate her claims after all? It could do no harm; at the worst, the girl might get raped or even killed; that was her look-out, not his. Besides, the state of France was so really precarious that any promise offered at least a hope. Miracles had been known to happen before; they might happen again. His own men, Poulengy and Jean de Metz, solid soldiers, no sentimentalists, had fallen under her spell, a spell in which, oddly enough, no question of sex could possibly be mixed up. No doubt the conviction of his two young captains went far towards persuading him to reconsider his own ideas. There must have been something in Robert de Baudricourt beyond the hearty soldier with his eye to the main chance: something of the same element that Jeanne had succeeded in touching in Poulengy and Jean de Metz. It was a credulous, frightened, groping age, where life and death, Church and State, mystery and brutality, were all very much mixed together, and Baudricourt was of his age. Still, although no longer completely scornful, he was determined to proceed with caution. Evidently he had no intention of despatching a charlatan, or, worse, a witch, under his ægis to incur the Dauphin's sneers and possible displeasure. So a second scene took place in Catherine le Royer's dark little room.

Catherine relates it in her own words: "She [Jeanne] liked spinning, and span well; we span together in my home. . . . During this time [i.e. while Jeanne was staying with her] I saw Robert de Baudricourt, governor of the town, enter my house, with M. Jean Fournier, of whom I have already spoken."[1] At this point it seems likely that Catherine was sent out of the room, for she continues as though she were no longer an eye-witness. "Jeanne told me that the priest was wearing his stole, and that he adjured her to keep away from them, if she were an evil thing; but that if, on the other hand, she should

[1] M. Jean Fournier was then the *curé* of Vaucouleurs, to whom Jeanne went to confession while staying in that town.

be good, she should approach them. Jeanne told me that she
had crept towards the priest, even to his knees; she added that
the priest had not acted properly towards her, because he had
already heard her in confession."[1]

At this point, it would appear that Catherine was allowed
back into the room, or, as seems even more likely, eaves-
dropped. She was a good and honest woman, appreciative of
the young guest who helped her with her spinning; but, like
many other good and honest women, she may reasonably be
supposed to have been born with her fair share of curiosity, and
a guest such as Jeanne from Domremy—a guest whose family
she knew only by hearsay—foisted on her by her neighbour
Durand Lassois of Burey, may as reasonably be supposed to
have aroused that curiosity to its highest pitch. After all, it
was not an everyday occurrence for the governor of the town
to arrive at the house of a mere wheelwright, accompanied by
the *curé*, in order to interview an obscure young stranger from
a neighbouring village. Never before had her house been thus
honoured. Something very especial and exciting must be afoot.
Who shall blame Catherine le Royer, if, having been dismissed
from the scene of this very unusual interview, she returned to
listen behind the door?

At any rate, she heard, or overheard, the rest of the conversation:

"When Jeanne saw that the said Robert would not send her,
I heard her say that it was imperative that she should go to the
place where the Dauphin was, saying, 'Have you not heard the
prophecy, that France shall be lost through a woman,[2] and
shall be redeemed by a virgin from the frontiers of Lorraine?'

---

[1]*Procès*, Vol. II, p. 446: Deposition of Catherine le Royer: . . . *vidit intrare
Robertum de Baudricuria, tunc capitaneum dictæ villæ de Vallis-Colore et dictum
dominum Johannem Furnerii in domo sua, et audivit dici eidem Johannæ quod ipse
presbyter apporteverat stolam, et coram dicto capitaneo eam adjuraverat, dicendo sic,
quod si esset mala res, quod recederet ab eis, et si bona, veniret juxta ipsos. Quæ
dicebat quod Johanna se traxit juxta ipsum sacerdotem et erga sua genua; dicebat etiam
ipsa Johanna quod presbyter non bene fecerat, quia suam audierat confessionem.* . . .

[2]Here, again, the reference is to Isabeau de Bavière, mother of Charles VII.

I remembered then that I had heard this said, and was much astonished. Jeannette's impatience was so urgent that the time seemed to her as long as to a woman great with child."[1]

Perhaps the comparison with the woman on the eve of her delivery was drawn from her recent experience in the house of Jeanne Lassois?

viii

The unforeseen ordeal of confrontation with the priest and his stole turned out as a success for Jeanne. She had neither howled nor writhed, nor foamed at the mouth, nor tried to escape, nor given way to any of the hysterical demonstrations expected of persons supposed to be possessed of devils; and, as for flinging herself on the floor, she had done no more than fall on her knees in order to approach the man of God in that most humble of attitudes. She had certainly evinced no terror of him. Robert de Baudricourt could not fail to be impressed. Moreover, his insistent visionary was obviously bothering him beyond resistance, and was on the high road to persuading him in her favour against his better judgment. One cannot help feeling sorry for the poor man when one reads an account such as that of an anonymous author who relates that: . . . *fut moult ennuyeusement prié, requis et pressé ce capitaine par la dessus dicte Pucelle.*[2] We may well believe it. *La dessus dicte Pucelle* was not the person to let her conviction go, once it had taken a hold on her, to whatever extent it meant bothering *ce capitaine.* Fanatics are made of that stuff, and cannot stop to consider the nuisance they are making of themselves to

---

[1]*Procès*, Vol. II, p. 446: . . . *et dum ipsa Johanna vidit quod dictus Robertus nolebat eam ducere, dixit ipsa testis quod audivit eidem Johannæ dici quod oportebat quod iret ad dictum locum ubi erat Dalphinus, dicendo: "Nonne audistis quod prophetizatum fuit quod Francia per mulierem deperderetur, et per unam virginem de marchiis Lotharingiæ restauraretur?" Et tunc ipsa testis hæc audisse recordata est, et stupefacta fuit. Dixit etiam ipsa testis quod ipsa Johanneta bene desiderabat, et erat tempus sibi grave ac si esset mulier prægnans, eo quod non ducebatur ad Dalphinum.*

[2]*Procès*, Vol. IV, p. 268: *Le miroir des femmes vertueuses.*

other more soberly minded people, otherwise they could never accomplish the things they set out to accomplish. Besides, Robert de Baudricourt was not entirely unwilling to be convinced. The same chronicler, after giving his little tribute of implied sympathy to the *capitaine moult ennuyeusement prié*, adds, *lequel capitaine adjouxta quelque foy*.

We are not at all clear as to how often Jeanne bothered the governor of Vaucouleurs, or as to what passed between them during their various interviews. She was later accused of having told him on one occasion that she would have three sons: the first should become Pope, the second Emperor, and the third a king. Baudricourt is represented as having replied gallantly to this announcement, that he would willingly father one of the three sons himself, since they were destined to be so powerful, and he would profit. To which she is represented as having replied that the time had not yet come, but that the Holy Ghost would see to it. This conversation, according to the accusation, had been repeated by Baudricourt in various places and in the presence of prelates and other notable people.[1]

Several queer stories, not exactly legends, crop up in connexion with Jeanne, and this one certainly deserves to rank amongst them. It is one of the puzzling articles in the Act of Accusation later brought against her. Did she really make this boast to Baudricourt, or did she not? Was she falsely accused of having made it, and, if so, why? What gave rise to it? Was it compatible with what we know of her character? We know that she had vowed herself to virginity, but was that vow necessarily incompatible with the idea that the Holy Ghost might collaborate in the conception of her sons? Finally, if she

[1]*Procès*, Vol. I, pp. 219-20: . . . *ipsa habitura erat tres filios, quorum primus esset Papa, secundus imperator, et tertius rex. Qui quidem capitaneus hoc audiens, dixit: "Ergo ego vellem tibi facere unum, ex quo erunt viri tantæ auctoritatis, ut ex inde melius valerem." Cui ipsa respondit: "Gentil Robert, nennil, nennil, il n'est pas temps; le Saint-Esperit y ouvrera"; prout dictus Robertus præmissa in diversis locis, in præsentia prælatorum, magnorum dominorum et notabilium personarum, asseruit, dixit et publicavit.*

had really boasted thus to Baudricourt, would it have led him to a greater belief in her, or the reverse? Would the claim have appeared any more extravagant to his mediæval credulity than the claim that she could redeem France? It is difficult to decide. Certainly the opening words of the article of accusation, with their implication that she had beome his mistress (*habita familiaritate dicti Roberti*), are nothing but an empty outrageous insult.

Anatole France, who, according to his usual practice whenever he sees the chance of a page of picturesque writing, accepts the story after casting only the most perfunctory doubt, in a footnote, upon its authenticity, and then provides an ingenious theory to account for Jeanne's remark, to the effect that she was speaking allegorically. By her prophecy concerning her three children, he says, she meant that the peace of Christ should be the outcome of her task, and that, having once accomplished her mission, the Pope, the Emperor, and the King should establish love and concord in the Church of Christ. The captain, he adds, was incapable of understanding this subtlety, and, being a plain and jolly man, took her words at their literal value, and answered accordingly.[1]

It is not impossible. Jeanne was quite capable of inventing allegories when they would serve her purpose. She invented another one, far more extensive and elaborate than this, which will be dealt with in its place. But what seems to me far more important as an agent contributing to Baudricourt's final conversion is that on her own showing she told him about her voices, the first man to whom she had ever revealed her secret. Now this interview, or interviews, must have taken place in private, since she herself said she told no one but Baudricourt and her King.[2] No one else can have been present. And she must have convinced him, or, at any rate, disturbed him, to the extent of actually despatching a messenger to the Dauphin on Jeanne's behalf.[3] This was a great advance for Jeanne—the first

---

[1] Anatole France, *Vie de Jeanne d'Arc*, Vol. I, pp. 90–1.
[2] *Procès*, Vol. I, p. 128.
[3] *Procès*, Vol. III, p. 115: Deposition of Simon Charles, *maître des requêtes*.

real advance she had been able to make. Now, at least, she was in touch with her Dauphin. A messenger from Vaucouleurs was really on his way to the Dauphin at last. The references to the reception of Baudricourt's letter at Chinon are neither contemporary nor, consequently, very reliable. Still, they have an air of probability which carries conviction; they report, in fact, precisely the attitude which one would expect them to report. They report that some people amongst the great personages surrounding the Dauphin received Baudricourt's letter in a spirit of scepticism, saying that it was all a fantasy to which no attention should be paid; others, on the contrary, held that God intended to redeem the unhappy country of France through the good sense and commands of one whom, alone, He would inspire beyond the dictates of human understanding.[1] This version may read as rather too romantical to be wholly believed; yet I suspect that there is a good residue of truth in it. Even if wildly misleading on certain points (e.g. the statement that Jacques d'Arc and Isabelle Romée were fetched to Chinon, which they certainly never were), it represents in essence the effect that Baudricourt's letter must have produced at Chinon. Baudricourt, after all, was no irresponsible man. No, but even responsible men were apt to be misled by witchcraft and superstition. Thus did the opposite camps argue. The sceptics lost. Jeanne was finally to be allowed to leave for Chinon.

ix

Before receiving the long-desired permission, however, she had had a long interval of waiting, and a great deal of time to fill in. It is easy to believe that her by then restive and straining spirit found the feminine occupation of spinning at the side of Catherine le Royer scarcely adequate as a pastime. She was, it must be remembered, impatient as a woman great with child. Any diversion, especially an active diversion, must have been

[1]*Procès*, Vol. IV, p. 268: *Le miroir des femmes vertueuses.*

welcome. Otherwise, her expedition to the Court of the Duke of Lorraine at Nancy, which she undertook in the midst of her stay at Vaucouleurs, accompanied as far as Toul by Jean de Metz, and all the way to Nancy by the faithful Lassois, would surely have to rank as one of the oddest incidents in the whole of her odd career. Except in view of her impatience, it seems not only odd, but meaningless; a waste of time, leading to nothing. Why did she agree to go to Nancy to be interviewed by the Duke of Lorraine at precisely the moment when she ought to have remained on the spot at Vaucouleurs, keeping Robert de Baudricourt up to the mark? What could she hope to gain from this inopportune journey? The Duke, as she must have known, was avowedly attached to the Anglo-Burgundian party—in other words, an enemy, one of those who, abiding by the Treaty of Troyes, schemed to give her country over to the English rule. Therefore she could hope for nothing from him in support of the French cause. Her agreement to this interruption in her arguments for immediate departure for Chinon would be more comprehensible had she aspired to enlist the services of a great feudal vassal in the interest of her King. In the case of the Duke of Lorraine, she could, reasonably speaking, entertain no such aspiration. He was an Anglo-Burgundian out and out. Yet she went. She was wasting valuable and urgent time. Why? There seems to be no valid answer to this question, unless, perhaps, the answer is to be found not only in her fretting impatience, but also, quite simply, in the fact that when a great feudatory prince summoned her she obeyed the summons. Perhaps she did not dare refuse. She had not yet acquired the habit of earthly princes, having had as yet no communion with any princes save those of the sky. Earthly princes may still have inspired her with respect, so that, when Charles II of Lorraine sent for her, she obeyed the summons.

So much for Jeanne's part in the expedition to Nancy. But why did he, a great noble in his capital, ever think of sending for her? What rumours had he heard which could make him think of sending for the peasant girl who had but recently made her appearance at Vaucouleurs, disarranging the ideas of that solid, cautious, and sceptical soldier Robert de Baudricourt to such an extent that he had despatched a messenger to the Dauphin across half of France? The curiosity of the Duke was doubtless tickled. As a prince living a life of pleasure, as well as of duty, on his estates, he may well be supposed to have welcomed any extra diversion from the monotonous round of pleasure and government. The virgin of Domremy was a novelty from the outside; and, as such, something to be attracted to his Court. Besides, he was frightened about his health. Perhaps the virgin of Domremy could give him some useful, or, indeed, miraculous, advice? In any case, he sent for her. She came.

But when she arrived she found that he was less interested in politics than in himself. Her own words may speak for their interview. "I told him that I wanted to go into France. He asked me how he might regain his health, and I answered him, that I knew nothing about that, and said little to him about my journey [into France]. I told him nevertheless that if he would give me his son and some men [*filium suum et gentes*] to conduct me into France I would pray to God for his health."[1]

This terse statement of Jeanne's is full of matter. Taken phrase by phrase, it shows first that she had come into his presence full of her own idea: *I told him that I wanted to go into France*. Then, seeing that he was not interested, she grows reserved on the subject of her own desires and intentions: *I said little to him about my journey;* nevertheless, though shrewd enough not to bore and perhaps even to irritate him by insisting on an unwelcome topic, she is also shrewd enough to use it in order to strike a bargain, and tells him that she will pray to God for the restoration of his health if he will give her his son and some men to conduct her into France. He gave her neither, but he did give her four francs towards the expenses of her journey, which she dutifully handed over to Durand

[1] *Procès*, Vol. I, p. 54.

Lassois,[1] and he did give her a black horse.[2] The four francs may not have been lavish, but it does seem strange that his other gift should have been one which could but facilitate a venture of which, as a supporter of the Anglo-Burgundians, he could only disapprove. He gave her, in fact, a horse which she could ride into France—the last thing which he could have wanted her to do. Was it her compelling personality which persuaded him? Or was it in the nature of a bribe to obtain her prayers? History and Jeanne are silent on the subject.

It seems all the stranger that the Duke should have treated her so favourably when we learn, later on, from the words of another witness, that Jeanne had taken it upon herself to rate him soundly on what she considered as his wicked ways. This witness was Marguerite La Touroulde, wife of the treasurer of Charles VII, in whose house Jeanne had stayed for three weeks at Bourges, sleeping in the same bed as her hostess, and, as her hostess later implied, on terms of considerable intimacy. The two women had all the hours of the night or day in which to exchange their confidences. It appears that Jeanne told her that she had warned the Duke of Lorraine, *atteint d'une certaine infirmité*, that, unless he abandoned his evil life and returned to his virtuous spouse, he would never be cured.[3] This seems rather hard on the virtuous spouse (Margaret of Bavaria), but perhaps Jeanne was inadequately informed on the question of infection in contagious diseases.

It is sufficiently remarkable that a great and powerful noble should have accepted so frank a criticism from a peasant, little more than a child. He was more accustomed to see such people tremble in his presence. Such impertinence must have taken his breath away. Besides, it attacked him in his most private feelings. For, at his somewhat advanced age of sixty-three, he was still passionately attached to a certain Alison Dumay, the daughter of a vegetable-seller of Nancy who

[1]*Procès*, Vol. II, p. 444: Deposition of Durand Lassois.
[2]*Procès*, Vol. II, p. 391: Deposition of Jean Morel.
[3]*Procès*, Vol. III, p. 87: Deposition of Marguerite La Touroulde.

kept her shop at the doors of the ducal palace. He had had five children by this Alison Dumay, a bastard herself, the natural daughter of a priest,[1] and, not content with establishing her in a house complete with furniture and gold and silver plate, he had made provision also for her children and for her mother and sisters. The citizens of Nancy took their revenge upon her after his death, forcing her first to walk through the streets of Nancy while they pelted her with human excrement, and then putting her secretly to death.

Poor Alison Dumay. She came to a certainly humiliating and probably painful end, which she had deserved no more and no less than many of the mistresses of kings and princes. It was perhaps hard on her to have been so severely punished at the last. Harlot though she was, our sympathy goes out as we imagine her losing her house, her furniture, her gold and silver plate, her security, at one sweep. These things must have meant so much to her—quite as much, in her own limited way, as the salvation of France meant to Jeanne. The harlot and the saint; the material and the spiritual. Judging each according to the capacity of each, there is very little difference in values. The difference is of kind, not of degree. Yet I suppose we should not waste our sympathy unduly. She had had her good time while it lasted. It was not given to every vegetable-seller's daughter to become the mistress of the reigning duke. Like others of her sort, she was both fortunate and unfortunate. Unbelievably fortunate so long as her princely lover survived, tragically unfortunate the moment he was dead. She had, at any rate, enjoyed her day. Her children, her mother, and her sisters were well provided for. We can only hope that the terms of her lover's will—terms which would have brought some consolation to the French bourgeois mind—were known to her before the citizens of his capital, her fellow-townsmen, her aforetime friends and neighbours, caught her and filthily paraded her through their streets, finally to an unrecorded death.

[1]Arch. Nat., K.K. 1124, folios 216 and 217: *Nonobstant qu'elle soit bâtarde, fille naturelle et illégitime de prêtre.*

x

This attack upon the Duke's private morals by no means exhausts the sum of Jeanne's impertinence towards him. In the first place it was impertinent to a degree for her, the avowed prospective servant of France, to venture at all into that Anglo-Burgundian stronghold. It was even more impertinent to suggest that he might send one of his sons to accompany her in her quest after the Dauphin at Chinon. On this point a query arises—Was it for one of his sons that she asked, or was it for his son-in-law, the young Duke of Bar? Historians have taken it for granted that she meant his son-in-law. Yet Jeanne herself explicitly says that she asked for *his son* (*filium suum*). Now, Charles of Lorraine had no legitimate sons. Did she thereby mean that she wanted one of the illegitimate sons of Alison Dumay, who were then living, it appears, in the ducal palace, or did she mean that she wanted his legitimate son-in-law, René d'Anjou, Duke of Bar? Again, the question is confused and unanswered. On the whole, it is quite likely that she meant his son-in-law, since the reigning Duke of Bar would naturally be a far more valuable asset to her in her forthcoming expedition to Chinon than one of the illegitimate sons of the vegetable-seller's daughter. There were several reasons why Jeanne should thus boldly and impertinently demand the services of the young Duke of Bar. In the first place, the duchy of Bar depended on the duchy of Lorraine in so far as Charles II of Lorraine (Jeanne's duke), had given his daughter Isabelle, heiress of his own duchy, in marriage to René d'Anjou when the boy was only eleven, and his bride still younger. During his minority, the Duke of Lorraine, as regent for René's duchy of Bar, had committed his son-in-law to the English cause. But as soon as René took over the government for himself, his French sympathies became apparent, encouraged and influenced by his friendship with Robert de Baudricourt. Thus it would have been a real triumph for Jeanne to have taken René d'Anjou openly away from the convictions and obligations of his father-in-law. It was a high-handed attempt—the sort of gamble that would have appealed to her—but in this attempt she failed.

In the second place, René d'Anjou seems to have been a fantastically minded young man, who might readily have allowed himself to be enlisted in a mad venture such as the virgin of Domremy proposed to undertake. The younger son of Yolande, Queen of Sicily and Jerusalem, Duchess of Anjou, he was just twenty at the time when Jeanne went to Nancy. He had already acquired a dwarf jester (*petit fou*), called Didier, attached to his Court, and a negro from Morocco, who, poor wretch, provoked the pleasantries of the citizens of Metz on an occasion when he was attempting to carry two hats and some rabbits to his master. The citizens released the hats, but ate the rabbits at a banquet to which they invited the gay ladies of Metz. Apart from these uncommon servitors whom he attached to his person, the young man gave evidence of other tastes which marked him out from the run of ordinary young men. A fine horseman, skilled in the use of the lance, he nevertheless wrote poetry, drew illustrations in books, and took pleasure in the woven gardens of tapestry. Evidently a prince of many facets; just the kind of young man who would have been amused by this village girl from Domremy. It was unfortunate for Jeanne that she could not immediately enrol him among her followers—if, indeed, it was he whom she had in mind when she asked Charles II of Lorraine to give her his son to conduct her into France. She had not long to wait, as it turned out, for he threw in his lot with her and her Dauphin at Provins six months later (August 3rd, 1429.)[1]

It was perhaps not so very strange that he should thus have decided eventually to give his support to the Pucelle and to her newly crowned Charles VII. It is true that his mother, in conjunction with his uncle Louis, her brother, Bishop of

[1]*Procès*, Vol. IV, p. 23: Perceval de Cagny. The *Journal du siège d'Orléans*, however, mentions him as having been present at the coronation at Reims, July 17th, 1429 (*Procès*, Vol. IV, p. 185).

Châlons, a cardinal-prince of the Church, and hereditary Duke of Bar, had arranged his marriage with the heiress of the Duke of Lorraine, thereby committing him, irrevocably as it seemed, to the Anglo-Burgundian party. At the same time as the marriage was arranged (Treaty of Foug, March 20th, 1419) the cardinal-bishop agreed to hand over his duchy to his then ten-year-old nephew. A boy of ten cannot have had much say in the matter. A private schoolboy of ten years old to-day would not have any very definite ideas were he suddenly presented with a large duchy, a bride still in the nursery, and attendant commitments to a dangerously involved political party. What did poor little René d'Anjou, aged ten, know of duchies, of Anglo-Burgundians or of Armagnacs? He was probably more interested in playing with wooden soldiers. It was only when he reached adult age that he could seriously take a decision for himself. Having reached that age, he decided that his real interests and those of France lay vested in Jeanne and her crowned King. The English usurpers must be driven at all costs beyond the shores of France, despite the Treaty of Troyes, despite personal family commitments. Thus did René d'Anjou decide finally, and thus, finally, did he join Jeanne and Charles VII some five or six months after she had made that vain appeal to his father-in-law at Nancy, for he was a young man of independent decisions; a remarkable young man, familiarly known to history as *le bon roi René*.

Chapter VII

VAUCOULEURS TO CHINON

i

It would appear that Jeanne returned to Vaucouleurs from Nancy on February the 12th, sought out Baudricourt again, and startled him with the information that the Dauphin's arms had that day suffered a great reverse near Orleans, and would suffer still others if she were not soon sent to him.[1] Mr. Andrew Lang suggests, with some plausibility, that this may have been the occasion which prompted him to take the *curé* to see her at the Le Royers' house. For, indeed, when the news of the battle of Rouvray reached Vaucouleurs, several days later, and Jeanne's declaration was astonishingly found to be correct, he must in all seriousness have begun to wonder whether the girl was a witch or not. That she had second-sight could no longer be denied, and second-sight, in Baudricourt's belief, could proceed only from God or the Devil. If from the Devil, then she was a witch and would betray herself to the man of God. But if not . . .?

She did not betray herself to the man of God, and Baudricourt sent her off to Chinon on February 23rd.

ii

A messenger from the Dauphin was in Vaucouleurs at the moment, and was detailed to accompany her on her journey. It is permissible to suppose that this man, named Colet de Vienne, was quite possibly the bearer of the Dauphin's reply to Baudricourt's letter, authorising him to send his young visionary to the Court. Colet de Vienne was not to be her only escort. Jean de Metz and Bertrand de Poulengy were also

[1] *Procès*, Vol. IV, p. 125; *Journal du siège d'Orléans;* ibid., p. 206: *Chronique de la Pucelle.*

to go with her, their servants Julian and Jean de Honnecourt, and
a dim figure of whom we know only the name, Richard the
Archer. Before they could set out, it was necessary to equip
their charge. Baudricourt seems to have thought he had done
enough, for De Metz and Poulengy bore most of the expense
out of their own pockets,[1] assisted by Lassois and by some
citizens of Vaucouleurs, notably Jeanne's host Le Royer and a
man named Jacques Alain who had been her companion on the
expedition to Nancy. Poulengy leaves a brief description of
what they provided in the way of apparel: a man's tunic, spurs,
a sword, and boots,[2] but for greater detail we are indebted to
that other eye-witness who has already been quoted (Chapter I,
p. 10), the *greffier* of the Hôtel de Ville of La Rochelle—he
who gives us a picture of Jeanne with her short black hair,
arriving at Chinon dressed in black and grey. They also provided
her with a horse, which cost them sixteen francs. It is not
very clear what happened to the horse already presented to her
by the Duke of Lorraine. Perhaps, as M. Siméon Luce suggests,
her supporters did not think it fitting that the maid of
Domremy should ride to the Court of the Dauphin on a
mount provided by the liberality of an Anglo-Burgundian
leader. Perhaps, also, it was not a very good horse. Jeanne, in
spite of her protestations to Saint Michael about her inability
to ride, was rather particular as to the quality of her horses:
later on she rejected the *haquenée* of the Bishop of Senlis, as
being not good enough for her purposes, and said the bishop
might have the horse back if he wanted it—a rejection which
got her into considerable trouble at her trial before the
Ecclesiastical and Inquisitorial Court of Rouen.[3] Anyway, the
Duke of Lorraine's present disappears very quickly from
Jeanne's history and is replaced by the gift of the citizens of
Vaucouleurs. Robert de Baudricourt solemnly recommended

---

[1] They were refunded later out of the royal treasury.

[2] *Procès*, Vol. II, p. 457: Deposition of Bertrand de Poulengy.

[3] *Procès*, Vol. I, pp. 104–5. *Lui rescrist que il la reairoit, s'il vouloit, et qu'elle
ne la vouloit point, et qu'elle ne valoit rien pour souffrir paine.*

her to the care of her escort, gave her a sword, and bade her farewell. *"Va!"* he said to her. *"Va, et advienne que pourra."*[1]

Durand Lassois, her first convert, was left behind to resume his dull life at Burey-le-Petit—the dull life which Jeanne briefly, brilliantly, had on two occasions disturbed. How often he must have wondered what was happening to the young cousin who called him uncle because he was sixteen years her senior; who had dragged him before the governor of Vaucouleurs, only to get snubbed and ridiculed for his pains; who had returned six months later to the charge; obliged him to arrange for her to stay with his friends into whose humble household she attracted so terrifying a visitant as a priest bent on exorcism; borrowed his clothes; dragged him to the ducal Court at Nancy; made him take care of her money; and finally departed, equipped as a man, on that mad mission of whose success she seemed so firmly convinced. Jeanne went to Chinon. Durand Lassois remained at Burey. Perhaps his cousin from Domremy had upset his life more than he had bargained for. Perhaps he felt some natural relief at being allowed to resume his ordinary life. Nevertheless some curiosity drew him once more into her orbit, for the next time he saw her she was in full armour, holding her standard in the cathedral of Reims, beside the King.

iii

They rode out from Vaucouleurs through the Porte de France, late in the afternoon of Wednesday, February 23rd, 1429, on their journey of three hundred and fifty miles across France. Catherine le Royer saw them off, and it may be presumed that an interested concourse of other people were also present. They set forth in no very favourable conditions. The rains that winter had been exceptionally heavy, and the rivers were overflowing their banks. The Duke of Bar himself had had to forgo the fish for his table, by reason of the floods.[2]

[1] *Procès,* Vol. I, p. 55.   [2] Siméon Luce, *Jeanne d'Arc à Domremy,* p. ccxiv, footnote.

I

It is thought that for greater safety they muffled their horses' hooves,[1] and it is known that they sometimes travelled by night. Poulengy, riding beside Jeanne, asked her whether she would indeed accomplish what she had promised, and she always answered in the same way: that they should be without fear; that she had orders to do what she was doing; that her brothers in Paradise advised her as to what she was to do; and that four or five of her brothers in Paradise, and God Himself, had already told her that she must go to war in order to recover the kingdom.[2] They were evidently nervous—and, indeed, who can blame them? for it was no light responsibility they had undertaken, to conduct a heaven-sent virgin across a country infested by warring bands—and all at their own expense, too—but Jeanne's unwavering replies encouraged and heartened them. She never found it difficult to restore the confidence of her own men. Sometimes, in a more light-hearted mood, they teased her. Perhaps they were less teasing than testing her. They would pretend to be on the English side. They would pretend to run away, as though they feared an attack. None of these jokes in poor taste affected Jeanne. Whether she took them seriously or not, she exhibited no alarm, merely remarking, "Do not run away. By God's name, they will do you no harm."[3] In other ways, however, she worried them with suggestions to which their practical, masculine experience could not always accede. She was quite willing to travel by day or by night, as they judged best; she gave them no trouble as to her health, her endurance proving equal to theirs—unexpectedly in a woman; but she did bother them considerably by her constant desire to hear Mass. "If only we could hear Mass," she said to them, "all would be well." But they were afraid she might be recognised, and only on two occasions

---

[1] Marquis de Pimodan, *La première étape de Jeanne d'Arc*, p. 36.

[2] *Procès*, Vol. II, p. 437: Deposition of Jean de Metz.

[3] *Procès*, Vol. III, p. 199: Deposition of Ausson Lemaistre.

during the eleven days of the journey did they feel justified in allowing her to gratify her wish.

This fear of theirs, that she should be recognised, is suggestive. It can only mean that the reputation of the virgin of Domremy was already widely spread. We can take it only as indicative of the fact that she was already being talked about, and that the news of her progress through France was known.[1] Yet she had, so far, accomplished nothing very dramatic. She had merely succeeded in gaining the attention of the governor of Vaucouleurs and the confidence of two of his captains. She had gained the attention of the governor of Vaucouleurs to the extent of allowing her to proceed to Chinon. She had gained the confidence of his two captains to such an extent that they proved themselves not only ready to accept all risks, but also to bear the expenses of the journey out of their private pockets; a gesture which, as all those who intimately know the French will appreciate, represents a very definite tribute. It is true that they recovered their expenses later on from the Dauphin's treasury, but they could not have counted on that reimbursement with any certain reliance when they set out. So far, she had accomplished nothing save by the sheer pressure of her own personality. She had not yet, miraculously, recognised the Dauphin. She had not yet relieved Orleans. She had not yet recovered the kingdom of France. She had only affirmed her confidence in her powers to do so. Those few men believed in her; and it seems likely that other people had heard of her, and that her tiny, credulous escort, aware of the curiosity she was arousing, took especial precautions to safeguard her. Jean de Metz was regarded as the leader of the little troop; he believed absolutely in Jeanne, whose words inspired him with a love of God equivalent to her own; he believed her to be sent by God, for she never swore, liked going to church, was in the habit of making the sign of the cross when taking an oath, and frequently took his money in order to give it away

[1] We know for a fact, for instance, that the Bastard of Orleans had heard of her long before she reached Chinon. See Chapter VIII, p. 150, *infra*.

in charity.[1] Poulengy felt much the same, adding, though he little knew the prophetic nature of his words, that she was as good as were she a saint.

Their respect for her virtue was as profound as their conviction of her heavenly mission. Men in the prime of life—soldiers; rough-livers—they were travelling in the company of a solitary woman, a healthy peasant girl; opportunity was theirs, over and over again, yet no idea of taking advantage of her unprotected condition ever seems to have entered their heads. When they were not travelling by night, she slept beside them. Yet Jean de Metz could say of her that "each night during the journey, Bertrand, myself, and *la Pucelle*, we lay side by side, *la Pucelle* next to me, with her upper and nether garments closely shut; I felt such respect for her that I would never have dared to make her an unseemly proposal, and I declare under oath that I never felt an evil desire towards her, nor was aware of any sensual thought."[2] And Poulengy, in corroboration, says: "Each night Jeanne lay with us, I mean with Jean de Metz and with me who am making this statement. . . . I was young then, nevertheless I felt no desire for women nor stirring of the flesh (*attamen non habebat voluntatem, nec aliquem motum carnalem cognoscendi mulierem*); and I would never have dared to make her an evil proposal, by reason of the virtue I divined in her."[3]

It is difficult to make any comment. One may take it either way. Either it means that Jeanne was unusually devoid of any sexual attraction—which, given her robust youth and the equally robust youth and presumable lack of fastidiousness of her companions, who would normally have taken their fun anywhere they could get it, seems inadmissible as an explanation—or else it means that, on closer acquaintance, they really sensed some special quality in her which, for that exceptional moment, exalted their character above its natural plane. All

---

[1] *Procès*, Vol. II, p. 438: Deposition of Jean de Metz.
[2] Ibid.
[3] *Procès*, Vol. II, p. 457: Deposition of Bertrand de Poulengy.

evidence, not only concerning Jean de Metz and Poulengy, points overwhelmingly to the second interpretation.[1]

Michelet observes, with unconsciously humorless patriotism, that neither an English nor a German girl would have taken the risk: the indelicacy of such a proceeding, he says, would have horrified her—a point of view which tallies perfectly with the French theory that the word "shocking" plays a preponderant part in the vocabulary of the English, but nevertheless a point of view which one would scarcely expect to find adopted by a serious though too flamboyant, sentimental, and inaccurate an historian.

iv

Jeanne, then, still *virgo intacta*, proved herself right: they arrived without hindrance at Chinon. She had been right in saying that, although she must pass through a country full of enemies on every road, she could not fear them, since the way lay open before and God her Lord would see to it, she having been born, as she claimed, for that purpose.[2] It seems strange that the little band of six men and a woman should nowhere have been attacked. Travellers were liable to be attacked, if only for the advantage of highway robbery; but in this case there would have been, from the Anglo-Burgundian point of view, an additional reason for interfering with a small packet of people bent on coming to the succour of the Dauphin. Yet they got through without any trouble. The first stage of their journey has been worked out in detail by a gentleman who owned a château on the route they presumably followed, and who wished he might claim, but prudently refrained from claiming, that the little party paused for shelter within his walls of Echènay.[3] It seems certain, however, that they paused nowhere during that first night, but pressed forward as quickly

[1] J. Michelet, *Histoire de France au Moyen Age.*
[2] *Procès*, Vol. II, p. 449: Deposition of Henri le Royer.
[3] Marquis de Pimodan, *La première étape de Jeanne d'Arc*, p. 39.

as they could over the hilly miles that lay between Vaucouleurs and their first stopping-place, St. Urbain. The roads were dangerous, the enemy abounded, the season was unfavourable, the rivers were in flood, and the moon was on the wane. There was no time to stop, if they wanted to reach St. Urbain before the break of day. They knew they would be well-advised to avoid the sinister and windy forest known as La Saulxnoire. At St. Urbain they were certain of a hospitable welcome from the Abbot Arnould d'Aulnoy, himself a kinsman of Robert de Baudricourt. The abbey of St. Urbain constituted in itself a kind of sanctuary, having been recognised by the lords of Joinville as a refuge for ill-doers so far back as 1132, so that Jeanne and her little escort, under threat of pursuit, might have remained there indefinitely in case of need. Small wonder that Jean de Metz and Poulengy, who knew the whole of that countryside well from the frequent campaigns that they had followed backwards and forwards across it, had fixed on the hospitable monastery as their first destination and were anxious to reach it without delay. They reached it at dawn, and rode in under the pointed archway which is still standing, and which to-day leads into a farm-like courtyard with ducks and hens scuttling away at the approach of the stranger. For, to-day, St. Urbain is a lost little village, rather hard to find among all the lanes and by-ways of that remote part of France. The big church and the remains of the monastery, including a surprisingly inaccurate *plaque* on the front of the church, are all that are left to remind us of the first pause of those travellers, as dawn was breaking on February 24th, 1429.

After this, we lose any detailed track of them, but know only that they travelled on to Auxerre, where they heard Mass in the great cathedral with its magnificently jewelled windows. Then, having made their way safely to Gien, they came for the first time into territory owing allegiance to the French cause. From now onwards, their anxiety arose no longer from the hostility of Anglo-Burgundians, but only from the ordinary dangers of marauders who might fall upon them unawares,

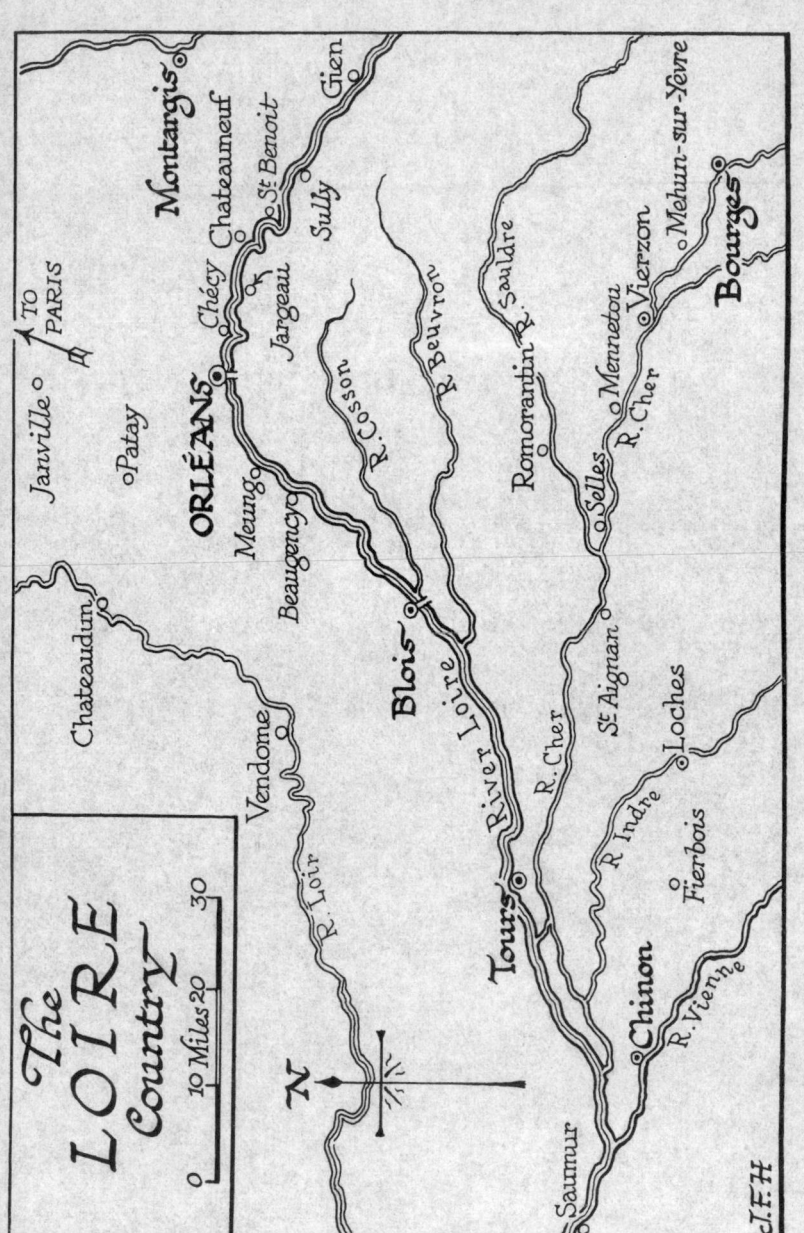

The LOIRE Country

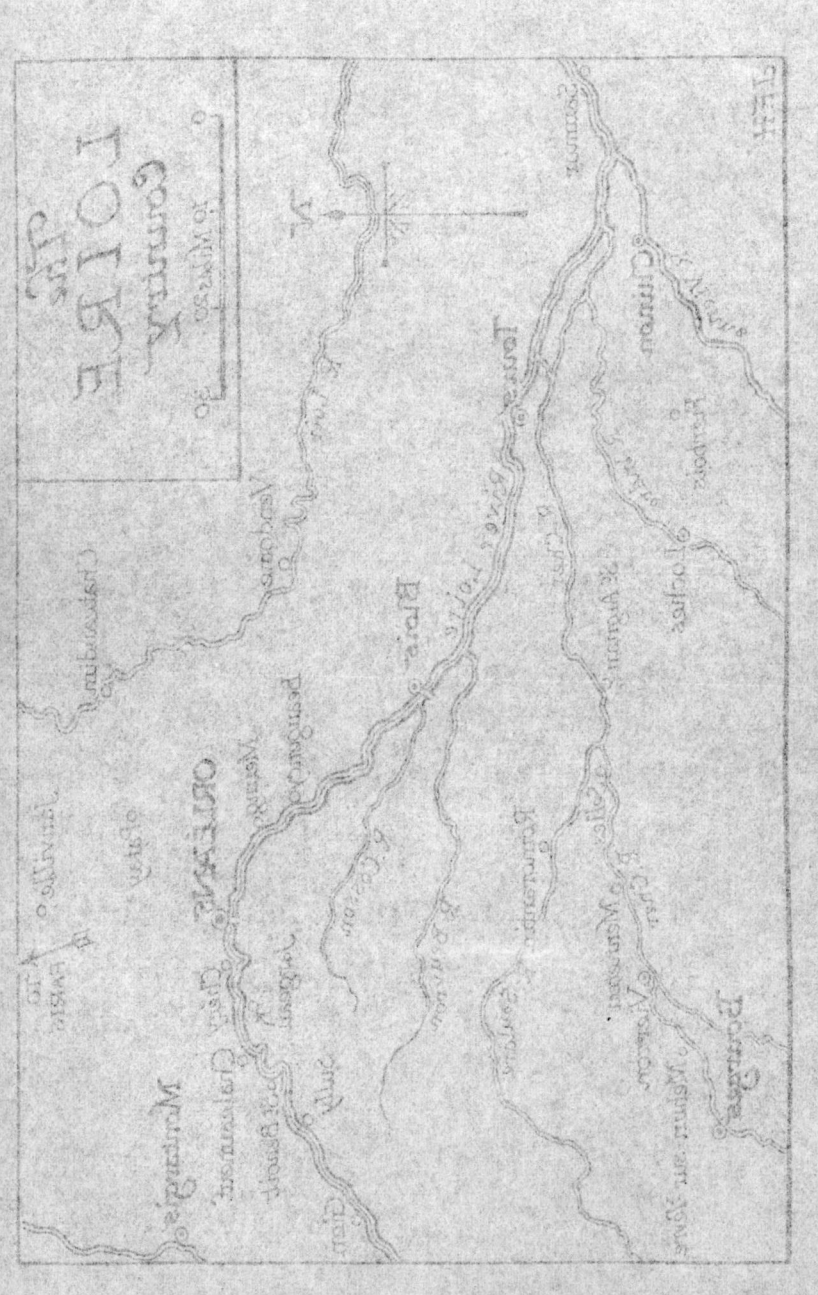

rob them, ill-treat them, and even hold them to ransom. And, oddly enough, according to Anatole France, although they might now consider themselves to have entered friendly country, it was in this very region that Jeanne had her narrowest escape. The underpaid, sometimes unpaid, soldiers of the Dauphin had less regard for the political convictions of their victims than for the possibility of extorting money. Here, they argued, comes a miraculous virgin who has been sent for by the Dauphin; if we throw her into a ditch, and leave her there with a huge stone to keep her down, the Dauphin will pay a large sum for her release. I fear that this is but one of M. France's outrageously embellished inventions. There is certainly a story that some soldiers had posted themselves in ambush on the road, with the intention of seizing and robbing her—not that she had anything to lose, poor girl, except the two treasured rings which she wore on her fingers—and that when the moment arrived for putting their intention into execution they found themselves unable to move from the spot where they lay waiting.[1] But I question whether this story is any more credible than M. France's interpretation of it.

What is sure and certain is that, after Gien, they went to Fierbois, a little village lying half-way between Loches and Chinon. Fierbois was to play a very important part in Jeanne's history; in the meantime, as a shrine of Saint Catherine, it was probably the most significant place to her on the whole route. There she was able to worship before the statue of Saint Catherine,[2] which, as anybody who chooses to visit both the hermitage of Bermont and the church of Fierbois can see for himself, bears a curious resemblance to the statue of Our Lady at Bermont. There she was able to hear Mass three times in one

[1] *Procès*, Vol. III, p. 203: Deposition of Frère Seguin. There is also the evidence of Marguerite la Touroulde, who says that her companions had begun by thinking her mad and wanting to throw her into a ditch (see Chapter XIII, p. 258).

[2] Chanoine Henri Bas et l'abbé Charles Pichon, *Sainte Catherine de Fierbois*, p. 115.

day. There she also dictated a letter to the Dauphin, informing him that she had travelled a hundred and fifty leagues to come to his help, that she knew a great many things for his good, and that she would be able to recognise him amongst many others.[1]

They were now quite near to the end of their journey. They arrived at Chinon, in fact, on Sunday, March 6th, 1429. It was the fourth Sunday of Lent, the Sunday called *Lætare*, the very Sunday on which the children of Domremy had been in the habit of taking their innocent picnics out to the miraculous fountain, a habit which later led poor Jeanne into such dangerous trouble.

v

The castle of Chinon stands magnificently rounded and embattled above the grey roofs of the little eponymous town stretched narrowly along the banks of the wide, dark Vienne. A grey and massive pile, it overlooks the river and the pleasant country beyond. More or less of a ruin to-day, with the wild snapdragon and yellow wallflower growing between the cracks of the stones, Jeanne saw it then in the full grandeur of its imposing bastions, deep *fosses*, and lordly towers, with formal gardens laid out inside the enceinte, the towers at their full unruined height, commanding broad views over the woods and vineyards of Touraine. It is not surprising that the indolent Dauphin should have preferred the life of Court and castle to the nobler and more arduous life of camps and battlefields. As one of his historians remarks, "*Vraisemblablement il aurait préféré d'être un particulier heureux.*"[2] The eleventh child and fifth son of his mother, though perhaps not of his father, it did not seem as though destiny had ever intended him for any higher or more responsible station than that of a younger prince, holding his little Court in some delectable corner of a brother's kingdom. The care and luxury lavished on him in his very early days were only too prophetic of the tastes which were to develop in his adult years. Known as the comte de Ponthieu, he had three

[1] *Procès*, Vol. I, pp. 75–6.   [2] Anquetil, *Histoire de France* (1805).

CHINON TO-DAY

cradles and three screens to shelter him from the draught. The windows of his nursery were padded with felt as well, to stop any cold air entering from the outside. He was further provided with a harp, *délivré aux gens de Monseigneur de Ponthieu pour en jouer devant ledit seigneur;* and also with *un petit chaudron de laiton, pour faire jouer et esbattre ledit seigneur, lequel estoit mal disposé.*[1] Now if Monseigneur de Ponthieu had been allowed to remain Monseigneur de Ponthieu all his days, or possibly even Duke of Touraine, as he at one moment became, he might have lived happy in the enjoyment of such secondary titles, with all their advantages and none of their responsibilities. Cradles, screens, amusements, were really all that he wanted. Unfortunately, fate turned him into Charles VII of France, and, as Charles VII of France, his character emerges with so little honour from his association with Jeanne d'Arc that one can scarcely restrain a smile of amusement at the ironical contrast between such protagonists as the weak, knock-kneed, pious little cad and the avenging virgin descending on him from the confines of his kingdom, bent not only upon forcing him to do all kinds of things he had no inclination whatsoever to do, but convinced, in a way which allowed of no open contradiction, of his ardent, if latent, willingness to do them. It would be interesting to know what Jeanne really thought of Charles; it would be equally interesting to know what Charles really thought of Jeanne. Outwardly she never expressed anything but the utmost loyalty and respectful affection. To her, he was, of course, the Appointed of God, who, as such, although she might pester him to any extent into the reluctant performance of his duty, must remain above criticism. I think we may discern, however, the slightest shade of difference between the manner she addressed Charles and the manner she addressed, say, the Duke of Alençon. Charles was always her *gentil Dauphin* (though it is true that she occasionally called him the *oriflamme*, a title more heraldic than appropriate), Alençon always *mon beau duc*. Is there an inflection of tender patronage in

[1] Du Fresne de Beaucourt, *Histoire de Charles VII*, Vol. I, pp. 6–7.

the one, and of appreciation for a gallant gentleman in the other—an inflection sufficient to set us wondering whether there were not moments when she privately shook her fists in exasperation and disheartenment at Charles' laggard ways, much as a more feminine woman might sigh over the inertia of an adored but lamentable lover; Jeanne fanatically inspired, Charles secretly desiring only to be left in peace; Jeanne determined to save France and believing herself to be celestially appointed to do so, Charles not caring much about France so long as he might retain a few agreeable provinces and palaces in which to lead a life of pleasure and retirement? He must have found it exceedingly troublesome to be metaphorically picked up and shaken until his big knees knocked together and his courage rattled like the teeth in his head. With half his mind he could not help being impressed, the more especially as he was a good Catholic, not evil at all, but just feebly amiable; with the other half of his mind he can scarcely have failed to regard Jeanne as a truly redoubtable nuisance. Tepid people always do regard passionate people as nuisances. Evasive people always do regard dynamic people who tell them to do what they know they ought to do, but do not want to do, as nuisances: the righter and more inescapable the nuisance, the greater. And Jeanne was as certainly right as she was inescapable. She found her way into his presence, recognised him when he tried to play a buffoon's trick on her, and, having once caught him, refused to let him go.

Poor Charles. He is not an impressive figure. Jeanne might give him the symbolic title of *oriflamme*, with its suggestion of heraldic scarlet and gold; actually, his limbs were so thin and frail that it gave people a shock to see him without his ennobling cloak, dressed only in his usual short tunic of green cloth.[1]

---

[1]Amelgard, quoted by Michelet, *Histoire de France au Moyen Age: Il avait une physionomie agréable mais il n'était pas grand, il avait les jambes minces et grèles. Il paraissait à son avantage quand il était revêtu de son manteau, le plus souvent, il n'avait qu'une veste courte de drap vert, et l'on était choqué de lui voir des jambes si menues, avec de gros genoux.*

And although one chronicler says that his face was pleasing enough, M. Anatole France, probably more truthful than polite, represents him as "very ugly, with small grey wandering eyes, his nose thick and bulbous."[1] Jeanne might call him *gentil Dauphin*, and, more superbly and defiantly, *oriflamme*, but other people, again more truthful than polite, called him *le Falot*, which, being interpreted, means clown, droll, grotesque— not a very dignified description for a King of France. He was poor; he was sometimes reduced to borrowing money from his cook; he had to pawn the crown jewels; he got his old tunics repaired with new sleeves.[2] His poverty lent itself to the wit of the epigrammatists:

> Un jour que La Hire et Poton
> Le vindrent veoir, pour festoyement,
> N'avoient qu'une queue de mouton
> Et deux poulets tant seulement.[3]

His miserable physique, his shifty eyes, his languor, his piety, his self-indulgence, his weakness towards his favourites, his envy of people more definite and successful than himself (which, I fancy, included not only his fellow-princes and counsellors, but also that dominating woman, his mother), might to-day receive a more sympathetic tolerance in the light of our increased psychological knowledge. Humanly speaking, we cannot withhold all sympathy from his mother who, apart from being married to a madman, had spent twenty-one years of her life either pregnant or mourning the death of one of her children,[4] and who, moreover, suffered from excessive

---

[1] Anatole France, *Vie de Jeanne d'Arc*, Vol. I, p. 195.
[2] G. du Fresne de Beaucourt, *Histoire de Charles VII*, Vol. II, pp. 194–5.
[3] Martial d'Auvergne, 1440-1508, *Les Vigilles du Roy Charles VII*, Vol. I, p. 56.
[4] Isabeau de Bavière, once reputed a beautiful woman, gave birth to twelve children between the years 1386 and 1407: Charles, who died aged three months; Jeanne, died aged two; Isabelle, who lived to be twenty; Jeanne, who attained the age of forty; Charles, died aged nine; Marie, lived to forty-five; Michelle, died aged twenty-seven; Louis, died aged seventeen; Jean, died aged seventeen; Catherine, died aged thirty-seven; Charles VII, who surpassed

stoutness and gout to such an extent that she had to spend most of her time in a wheeled chair. These misfortunes, however, had increased neither her tenderness nor her wisdom in her dealings with her unfortunate son. He was physically weak. He was mentally twisted. His own mother had, in so many words, declared him a bastard. To be declared a bastard by your own mother can never prove very conducive to a normal view of life when you grow up and realise what being a bastard means. It is as bad as, perhaps worse than, being a step-child—in either case you are put into a false and difficult position. But if, in addition, you have been brought up to regard yourself as the rightful heir to France, or, at any rate, to some part of it, then to find yourself stigmatised by your own mother with illegitimacy, must, to say the least of it, be an exceedingly trying experience to overcome. It would take a strong character to triumph over such a test. The Dauphin possessed no such strong character. He was doubly unfortunate. He had the question of his illegitimacy to worry him; he had the fact of his kingdom being claimed and partially occupied by a foreign power to worry him still more, a burden altogether too heavy for his inadequate sinews to support. He took refuge in being merely pious, hard-working at moments and pleasure-loving at others. Not only were his knees weak and knock, but his whole nature. To-day, we might extend a greater tolerance to his disability. As it is, we see him as a perplexed little man, contemptibly pathetic, shamed and terrorised by his alarming saviour into exercising the muscles which he frankly did not possess, to carry the load of so difficult a kingship. Jeanne and Charles, the one with her simplicity, the other with his neuroses, do indeed present themselves as the most ironical of protagonists.

He allowed himself to be insulted by his subjects. Jean Jouvenal des Ursins could write to him saying, in an untranslatable passage: *Vous voulez toujours être caché en châteaux,*

them all by living till he was fifty-seven; and Philippe, who died on the day of his birth.

méchantes places et manières de petites chambrettes, sans vous montrer et ouir les plaintes de votre pauvre peuple.[1] These are scarcely the terms in which a self-respecting sovereign should suffer a subject to address him with impunity. He allowed himself also to be insulted by his enemies, the Duke of Bedford writing to him in terms which no man of spirit or honour could have allowed to pass ignored. More seriously, at the time of Jeanne's arrival, he had allowed himself to fall under the influence of a quartet of advisers, two of them unscrupulous and despicable, one of them merely a cat's-paw, and the fourth an obstinate short-sighted old soldier. Neither Georges de la Trémoïlle, Regnault de Chartres, Archbishop of Reims, Robert Lemaçon, or Raoul de Gaucourt figures at all admirably in the history of Charles VII. Perhaps they are scarcely to be blamed. It was asking much of them to accept without opposition so preposterously young and unqualified an interloper as Jeannette from Domremy.

Charles himself received Jeanne in no very welcoming spirit. It is rather surprising that he should have consented to receive her at all. What, and who, he may well have asked, is this lunatical virgin whom one of my provincial governors is sending to me from the other side of France? Still, the very fact that so steady and solid a soldier as Robert de Baudricourt thought it worth while to despatch the girl, escorted by two of his own lieutenants and by a royal messenger, postulated that she must in some way be worthy of the despatching; also, it was an age when visionaries were common, though not usually very effective; it was an age when superstition was rife, faith paramount, and Charles himself a devoted son of the Church. It is also possible that his mother-in-law, Yolande, Queen of Sicily, used her influence on Jeanne's behalf. Other people, however, opposed her. The Dauphin, torn between his courtiers, his counsellors, and his relations, hesitated. Jeanne meanwhile found lodgings with a respectable woman near the castle of Chinon (*mon lougeis, qui est cheiux une bonne femme près du*

[1]MS. Saint Germain français, No. 352, folio 77, Bibliothèque nationale.

chastel).[1] It was Lent, and she was fasting according to her habit, although fasting was not obligatory on her at the age of seventeen; abstinence only would have been obligatory.[2] During these two days' delay, it is reported that Charles sent messengers to interview her and to ask her why she had come. At first she refused to reply, saying that she would speak only to the Dauphin, but, when they explained that they had come to her in the Dauphin's name, she condescended to say that the King of Heaven had sent her with a double mission, first to raise the siege of Orleans, and second to lead the Dauphin to Reims for his coronation.[3] It is reported, also, that during this time the Dauphin sent for *les gentilshommes* who had escorted her, by whom are presumably meant Jean de Metz and Poulengy, and questioned them, for they had been talking all over the town of rivers marvellously forded and dangers marvellously escaped.[4] Finally, after much hesitation (*grand doubte si ladicte Jeanne parleroit au roy ou non, et si il la feroit venir devers lui, sur quoy y eut diverses opinions et imaginations*),[5] it was decided that she should be admitted into his presence (*et fut conclud qu'elle verroit le roy*). But even after taking this decision, Charles did not play fair by Jeanne. Perhaps he was well advised. Perhaps he really wanted to test her. Perhaps he really wanted to find out whether this inspired virgin could support her claims, which were, to say the least of it, extravagant and excessive. Looking back, in the light of her subsequent accomplishment, it is easy to criticise Charles for his waste of her precious time. Looking at it from his point of view, it is equally easy to understand his

[1] *Procès*, Vol. I, p. 143.

[2] For the information of non-Catholic readers, *fasting* means that you may eat only one full meal a day, of course excluding meat; *abstinence*, that you merely refrain from eating meat. No one under twenty-one or over sixty is bound to fast, nor any invalid; children under seven are likewise exempted from abstinence.

[3] *Procès*, Vol. III, p. 115: Deposition of Simon Charles.

[4] *Procès*, Vol. IV, pp. 126-7: *Journal du siège d'Orléans*; and *Procès*, Vol. IV, p. 207: *Chronique de la Pucelle*.

[5] *Procès*, Vol. IV, p. 207: *Chronique de la Pucelle*.

caution. Visionaries were going cheap in those days, and only a very small percentage of them turned out to be of any practical use at all. Why should he, who was, after all, the potential King of France, have consented to give an audience to her, who was, after all, an unknown peasant from a remote part of his precarious domains? Why should he have done this in opposition to half his Court—in opposition, moreover, to his dominating counsellors? I think it may be explained in human, if historically unorthodox, terms. In Charles, though pious and in some ways conscientious, the frivolous side generously exceeded the serious side of his character. He was bored, and any diversion afforded a relief. More creditably, he was probably rather conscience-stricken, deep down inside himself, about the state of France. Then the religious-superstitious side of him was struck by this obscure virgin advertising herself as the saviour predicted by Merlin and other prophets. I think that all these things mixed themselves up in the Dauphin's muddled and cowardly mind. It is very difficult to enter into the mind of Charles VII. One has to sort out the differences between his indolence and his seriousness; between his natural weakness and the practical difficulties with which he had to contend. But there, again, how difficult it is to sort out those differences in the make-up of one's own personal friends, or even in one's own make-up. Who really knows himself? And who can really know another? So, logically, if we fail to know ourselves or our contemporaries, how can we hope to know a person who lived five hundred years ago, and whose character we can reconstruct only from very inadequate and polite contemporary records? Chroniclers are almost always polite to kings. Kings, even feeble kings, hold a certain glamour which prevents their chroniclers from telling the whole truth about them. It takes a brave man to call a monarch contemptible, especially when that monarch is still alive: it would be a rude, and, indeed, a rash thing to do. It is thus very difficult to arrive at a just estimate of the character and motives of Charles VII. It is especially difficult to organise one's ideas as to the spirit in which he received Jeanne. Was he credulous? Was he sceptical? It is one of the problems of history. The solid fact remains that he did eventually, after two days' delay, grant her an audience. The Dauphin and the virgin of Domremy were at last brought face to face.

vi

It was, as I see it, one of the most remarkable meetings ever consummated. Jeanne had to make her way up the steep hill, across the main drawbridge, and to pass under the Tour de l'Horloge, before she could reach the Château du Milieu where the Dauphin was accustomed to give audience. As she was about to enter the castle, a man on horseback drew rein to stare at her and to say, "*Jarnidieu!* is that not the Pucelle? If I could have her for one night, I would not return her in like condition." Jeanne heard his words. "Ha!" she said to him, "*en nom Dieu*, you deny Him, and you so near to your death!" Within an hour he had fallen into water and was drowned.[1]

Jeanne meanwhile had passed on. She crossed the drawbridge. She was to be received in the Grande Salle, a splendid apartment on the upper floor of the Château du Milieu, some seventy feet long by twenty-five feet wide, with a vast hooded fireplace at one end, three large windows overlooking the gardens of the inner court, and one smaller window overlooking the town, the river, and the landscape beyond. Curiosity had filled the *salle* into which Jeanne was introduced by the Comte de Vendôme. But even then the Dauphin did not play fair by her. He attempted to deceive her by concealing himself among the crowd,[2] less magnificently dressed than some of his lords.[3]

[1]*Procès*, Vol. III, p. 102: Deposition of Jean Paquerel. The translation of the words, *negando Deum*, by the old oath, *Jarnidieu*, meaning *je renie Dieu*, is, I think, justifiable, especially in view of what Jeanne then said to him. Jeanne's own words are given in French in the text: "*Ha! en nom Dieu, tu le renyes, et tu es si près de ta mort.*"

[2]*Procès*, Vol. III, p. 116: Deposition of Simon Charles; *Procès*, Vol. IV p. 207: *Chronique de la Pucelle.*

[3]*Procès*, Vol. IV, p. 52: Jean Chartier.

Yet, having first asked rather piteously that they should not seek to mislead her, she picked him out. She went straight up to him, disguised as he was, dropped a curtsey (which must have struck the onlookers as most incongruous with her boyish appearance), and thus addressed him: "*Gentil Dauphin, j'ay nom Jehanne la Pucelle.*[1] The King of Heaven sends me to you with the message that you shall be anointed [*sacré*] and crowned in the city of Reims, and that you shall be the lieutenant of the King of Heaven, who is the King of France."[2]

The recognition evidently created something of a sensation. The hall was lit by fifty torches and packed with over three hundred people,[3] a brilliant crowd of soldiers, courtiers, and prelates, some of them hostile, some of them frivolously amused, but all of them curious to see this new exhibit who might for an hour at least enliven the farce of their existence in a Court which was a Court only in name. A dancing bear, a juggler, a troupe of mountebanks, would have tickled their childish curiosity in much the same way. Jeanne's personal appearance alone must have produced a ripple of amusement. Not only was she breeched, but her cropped black hair must have struck an odd note among men accustomed to fashionable women who allowed no single lock to peep out from beneath their strange pointed head-dresses and floating veils. Yet this small, queer, solitary figure, this *paupercula bergereta,* showed no sign of hesitation, distress, shyness, or embarrassment, addressing the Dauphin familiarly and without awe, in terms of a firm arrogance which could not be called boastful in view of its sincerity and simplicity. One wonders especially what the Archbishop of Reims thought, being present, on hearing these arrangements made for his own cathedral; to which, in

[1] See Appendix C, p. 393.

[2] *Procès,* Vol. III, p. 103: Deposition of Jean Paquerel. There are several slight variants of Jeanne's first words; e.g. ibid., Vol. III, p. 17: Deposition of Raoul de Gaucourt; ibid., Vol. III, p. 92: Deposition of the Duke of Alençon; ibid., Vol. III, p. 115: Deposition of Simon Charles; but they all amount to very much the same.

[3] *Procès,* Vol. I, p. 75.

K

spite of having been Archbishop of Reims for over twenty years, he had never yet paid a visit.[1] Prelates of that standing were not accustomed to hearing of coronations arranged for them by unknown peasants; coronations either came, or did not come, according to the great traditional hierarchy of France. Still the Dauphin held firm and prolonged the test. "It is not I who am the King, Jehanne. *There* is the King," he said, pointing to one of his lords. She was not to be taken in. "In God's name, noble prince, it is you and none other."[2]

After this he gave way and took her aside for a private conversation out of earshot,[3] a procedure most tantalising for the rest of the Court. It was then, apparently, that she revealed something to him which sent him far along the road towards belief in the authenticity of her claims. "Sire," she said, "if I tell you things so secret that you and God alone are privy to them, will you believe that I am sent by God?" And then, being encouraged by him to continue, "Sire," she said, "do you not remember that on last All Saints' Day,[4] being alone in your oratory in the chapel of the castle of Loches, you requested three things of God?" He answered that he remembered it well. Had he, she asked, ever spoken of these things to his confessor or any other? He had not. Then she said, "The first request was that it should be God's pleasure to remove your courage in the matter of recovering France, *if you were not the true heir* [italics mine], so that you should no longer be the cause of prolonging a war bringing so much suffering in its train. The second request was that you alone should be punished, either through death or any other penance, if the adversities and tribulations which the poor people of France had endured for so long were due to your own sins. The third request was that the people should be forgiven and God's anger appeased, if the sins of the people were the cause of

---

[1] *Procès*, Vol. IV, p. 185: *Journal du siège d'Orléans.*
[2] *Procès*, Vol. IV, pp. 52-3: Jean Chartier.
[3] *Procès*, Vol. III, p. 103: Deposition of Jean Paquerel.
[4] This would have fallen on November 1st, 1428.

their troubles." The Dauphin admitted that she had spoken the truth.[1] He was duly impressed. Those who were present noticed the change in his face when he returned.[2]

vii

What Jeanne had really done, was to voice his own suspicion that the blood of the Kings of France did not run in his veins. It is easy to understand his suspicion and his anxiety. The possibility that he might be a bastard, with no real claim to the crown of France, must have haunted him ever since the signing of the Treaty of Troyes, nine years before (Chapter II, p. 18). By the terms of that treaty, his probable illegitimacy had been indicated with the widest publicity by his own mother, who, after all, was the person in possession of the best available information. She had done it in terms just sufficiently and decently veiled as to leave her son in doubt. In that doubt he had lived ever since. To him it was a vital, personal question. His mother, true, was the Queen of France, but was his father the King? No, almost certainly not. To everybody else in France and England it was an accepted fact that the Dauphin might not be the Dauphin at all; might be nothing more than one of the many illegitimate sons of the Duke of Orleans, whose mistress his mother may have been, at the appropriate time.[3] To most people it did not matter very much,

[1]Slightly abbreviated from the account of the anonymous author known as "l'Abbréviateur du Procès": *Procès*, Vol. IV, pp. 258–9.

[2]*Procès*, Vol. III, p. 116: Deposition of Simon Charles.

[3]This theory that he was the son of Louis d'Orléans is open to dispute; it is even denied by recent historians that Isabeau de Bavière had ever been anything more to d'Orléans than merely his sister-in-law. But was he the son of Charles VI? A consideration of the following dates is not irrelevant to this enquiry: Charles VII was born on February 22nd, 1403. Therefore he must have been conceived some time towards the middle of the preceding month of May. Now, his official father, Charles VI, is known to have entered into one of his periods of madness just before Whitsunday, May 14th, although up to that date he seems to have been in normal health, as is attested by his taking part in a tournament which began on May 10th, and

since for one thing he was officially the son of Charles VI, born in wedlock; and for another he seemed so disinclined to assert his claims to the throne, that he had not even attempted the preliminary step of getting himself crowned. But to Charles as an uneasy person it mattered very much, and when Jeanne arrived with her reassurances he naturally opened his ears.

There can, I think, be no doubt that the famous "King's secret" revealed by Jeanne referred to the question of his legitimacy. Why it should ever have been regarded as a secret at all is what I cannot understand, and, without wishing to be or to appear unduly cynical over this example of Jeanne's reputedly supernatural powers of divination, I find it hard to see why the revelation of the King's secret should be considered so miraculous as is commonly supposed. It seems to me much more like an example of the common sense which was one of Jeanne's leading characteristics—her common sense assisted by her feminine instinct. What more obvious than that Charles should dwell morbidly upon this problem of common gossip? What more obvious than that comfort was the one thing he desired? Besides, it must be remembered that Jeanne herself was absolutely and sincerely convinced that he was the true King. She was not humbugging him by her assurances. She was only saying that which she herself believed, and which she rightly guessed he most wanted to hear. Paquerel, her confessor, tells us that she said: "I tell you in the name of Our Lord that you are the true heir of France and the son of

lasted for two days. We must therefore conclude that the attack of madness began on May 12th or 13th—possibly brought on by the exertion and excitement of the jousting—and we know, further, that it lasted until the beginning of June. It is only fair to add that the Queen spent practically the whole of the month of May in his palace of Saint Paul in Paris; but it is also fair, in the interests of truth, to reflect that the madness of her husband must have left her a considerable degree of liberty during that important fortnight in the latter half of May.

The dates, of course, are not conclusive evidence, but they are at least suggestive. The legitimacy of Charles VII is just possible, but only just.

the King" (*que tu es vray héritier de France et filz du roy*), but implies that she uttered these words to Charles after he had taken her aside; therefore, in private, not in public. Why, then, if the question of his legitimacy was so widely discussed, did she wait until he had taken her aside? Why did she not declare him the true King at once, and publicly, when she was first brought into his presence? And why, again, was he so startled during their private conversation that his countenance was not only irradiated by joy,[1] but that it looked also as though he had been visited by the Holy Ghost?[2] We can understand Jeanne's reticence by no more subtle an explanation than her passionate loyalty to the Crown and her natural tact in alluding to so delicate a subject with three hundred people listening; Charles' surprise is more difficult to explain away. It is inconceivable that he should not have realised the extent of the common talk about his birth. Why, then, should he have been so startled when this peasant, suddenly emerging out of the mass of his unknown subjects, put her finger on his sorest wound? We can explain it only by suggesting that he must have been more of an ostrich than is reasonably likely, if he could imagine that the King's secret had ever been a secret at all.

But, of course, if we once admit the report of the "Abbréviateur du Procès," with all that story about the Dauphin's private prayers, alone in his oratory on a certain stated day, then, indeed, it becomes easy to understand why he looked as though he had been visited by the Holy Ghost— or, at any rate, by something altogether outside any rational explanation—but if we limit our credulity to the belief that Jeanne merely told him that he was not the bastard he had always suspected himself to be, then the miraculous element in her revelation comes to grief. In view of the Dauphin's extreme astonishment, I am almost persuaded to believe in the "Abbréviateur's" report. I am, in fact, almost persuaded to

---

[1]*Procès*, Vol. III, p. 116: Deposition of Simon Charles.
[2]*Procès*, Vol. V, p. 133: Letter attributed to Alain Chartier, the Dauphin's secretary, to a foreign prince.

believe that her revelation consisted in something more than was concerned in the obvious assertion that he was no bastard even though his mother had half declared him to be one. I am almost persuaded to believe in that story about Jeanne's divination of his private prayers. Nothing but a revelation of such intimate detail could have made such an impression on him. To be told that he was no bastard was reassuring enough to his uneasy mind, yet it was no more than the reassurance he might have received from any fanatical patriot acquainted with the current gossip. I am sure that Jeanne, with her common sense and feminine intuition, made the best use of current gossip and the Dauphin's uneasiness. Yet I am almost equally sure that she must have said something to convince him, beyond her knowledge of a secret which was, after all, *a secret de polichinelle* and not the King's secret at all. That is why I am disposed to accept the report of the "Abbréviateur du Procès" as authentic, and not as a mere elaboration of the story of what actually happened during that private interview between Charles and Jeanne.

viii

Whether my interpretation is right or wrong, some time elapsed before the Dauphin put his trust in Jeanne into any very practical form. He was, by nature and experience, a cautious rather than a reckless man. We may sympathise with him over this, even while despising him for the timidity which always held him back from making the generous gesture. He had had a difficult life. His childhood and boyhood had been punctuated by scenes of distress and drama with which his easy-going nature was entirely unsuited to deal. His character had prevented him from coping with his difficulties in the way that a bigger man would have coped with them. He was a small man, faced with big issues, an unfortunate situation which may enlist our sympathy, but cannot command the respect we accord only to tragedy on big lines. Jeanne worked always along the big lines, peasant though she was; Charles, prince though he was, always along the small, the mean. Jeanne, in consequence, emerges always as the largely generous spirit, Charles as the niggardly and withholding. Yet let us be fair. Jeanne was a fanatic, inspired, as she believed, by the commands of God or His representatives. Charles was a prince beset by personal doubts and worldly difficulties. Jeanne was a simple person making straight for her goal. Charles was a complex person, not at all sure of what his goal ought to be. Jeanne's position was therefore, in a sense, easier than his. She had no doubts of herself under her heavenly guidance; Charles was made up of doubts from first to last. He was not the man to accede impetuously to Jeanne's demand for an army wherewith she might proceed immediately to the relief of Orleans.

Here again we cannot blame him. Stronger men than he would have hesitated before putting the lives of thousands into peril under the guidance of an inexperienced girl. We cannot blame him for this. We cannot even call him vacillating or weak in this particular. On the contrary we ought to give him credit for his discernment in taking her seriously at all.

ix

In lighter mood, Jeanne, meanwhile, must have got a certain amount of pleasure out of her stay at Chinon. It is impossible to regard her as an entirely grim and exclusively serious person. She would be the less lovable were we so to regard her. After all, she was only seventeen; and at seventeen one wants one's moments of relaxation; one wants to enjoy oneself; one wants to play and laugh; one wants the company of one's contemporaries. Jeanne certainly found her best playfellow in the Duke of Alençon—*mon beau duc,* as she called him. This gay, handsome, and attractive young prince of twenty-three was away at Saint Florent, shooting quails, when she arrived at

Chinon, but, on learning from one of his servants that his cousin the Dauphin had received a girl claiming to be sent by God to raise the siege of Orleans, his curiosity was so much aroused that he decided to return the next day to Chinon. Here he found Jeanne and the Dauphin together. Jeanne, after enquiring from Charles who the young man might be, greeted him with a graciousness that makes one smile: "You are very welcome [*Vous soyez le très bien-venu*]. The more that are gathered together of the royal blood of France, the better."[1]

She had a special reason for welcoming him, since he had recently married the daughter of the Duke of Orleans; and the Duke of Orleans, at that time a captive in England, held for some reason a very high place in Jeanne's affections.[2] She had, of course, never seen him, but declared him to be under her especial charge, saying that she knew God loved him, and that if necessary she would cross the Channel to fetch him back to France.[3] There were, in fact, three men whom Jeanne loved: the Dauphin, the Duke of Orleans, and the Duke of Alençon.

[1]*Procès*, Vol. III, p. 91. Deposition of the Duke of Alençon.

[2]This is Charles d'Orleans, the poet. Among the many legends which have sprung up about Jeanne is one to the effect that she was Charles d'Orléans' illegitimate daughter. There is nothing to be said for this theory, but it is amusing to reflect *en passant* that if Jeanne was Charles d'Orléans' daughter, and the Dauphin Louis d'Orléans' son, then the Dauphin and Jeanne were uncle and niece!

Perhaps this genealogical table will make the pretended relationship clear:

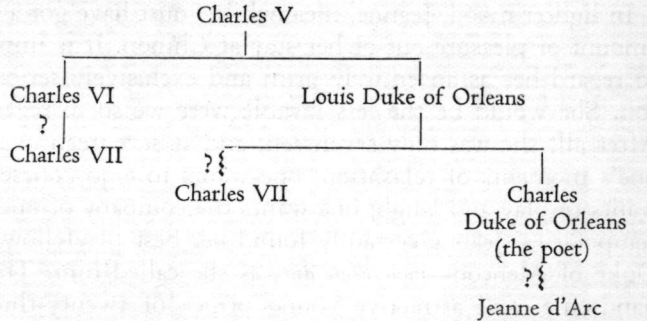

[3]*Procès*, Vol. IV, p. 10: Perceval de Cagny; and *Procès*, Vol. I, p. 254.

The first two she loved for the sake of an idea rather than for any personal reason, almost comparable to the way she loved her saints; d'Alençon alone was the one who personally caught her fancy, *et tousjours depuis se tint plus prouchaine et acointe du duc d'Alençon que de nul autre, et tousjours en parlant de lui l'appeloit Mon beau duc et non autrement.*[1]

He seems to have accepted her without hesitation; he was in fact the only one of the princes who did so. They became friends at once. He saw her again the next day, when they both heard Mass with the Dauphin, after which Charles sent everybody away except d'Alençon, the duc de la Trémoïlle, and Jeanne. These four had a long conversation, lasting until dinner. It is then that we get the little picture which shows us that life at Chinon was not altogether grim. After dinner, the Dauphin, no doubt tired of hearing from Jeanne that he must submit his kingdom to the King of Heaven, went out into the meadows; Jeanne also went out, lance in hand; and d'Alençon, admiring the grace and skill which she displayed in tilting, made her the present of a horse.[2]

Jeanne must have been a born rider, for she can have had but little experience save with the heavy farm-horses at Domremy. True, she had ridden to Nancy, and she had ridden from Vaucouleurs to Chinon, but on neither journey do we find any of her companions referring to any difficulty encountered by her in this unaccustomed exercise. And even this long ride must have been accomplished at a sober pace. Not only was it necessary to spare the horses, but a simple calculation will show that the six-hundred kilometres (estimated) of the journey could easily be covered in the allotted eleven days without ever going out of a walk—i.e. if a horse walks a kilometre in nine or ten minutes, and six kilometres in an hour,[3] they could have covered the whole distance travelling

[1] *Procès*, Vol. IV, p. 11, Perceval de Cagny.
[2] *Procès*, Vol. III, p. 92, Deposition of the Duke of Alençon.
[3] I accept the figures given by the Marquis de Pimodan, himself a cavalry officer, and the distance estimated by L. Champion, *Jeanne d'Arc écuyère*.

nine hours a day; though we must of course allow them a margin for rest and food. This quiet progress was a very different thing from tilting at a gallop with a long lance in one's hand; a proper charger was a very different thing from a cart-horse, or even from a travelling hack; and it is not surprising that Jeanne should have won d'Alençon's respect to cement their growing friendship.[1]

A few days later he took her to stay with his wife and his mother for three or four days at Saint Florent. The young duchess received Jeanne very warmly, but confided to her the fears she entertained for his safety. He had only just, she said, been released from captivity,[2] and his ransom had cost them so much money that she wished he would now remain quietly at home. Jeanne reassured her: "Madame, fear nothing. I will bring him back to you as safe and well as he is now, or even better."[3] She kept her word, and, indeed, on one occasion saved his life.

It is easy to contrast his ready acceptance of Jeanne with the Dauphin's hesitations, but the blame which attaches to Charles comes much later, when Jeanne had proved her value and when he so shamefully abandoned her to her enemies. No blame or shame attaches, so far as I can see, to his behaviour

---

[1] A story of Jeanne's visit to Nancy is given in the *Chronique de Lorraine*, that curious saga which credits her with the capture of Paris, Bordeaux, Bayonne, Dieppe, Harfleur, Honfleur, Caen, and all the towns of Normandy except Rouen. I append the story here, partly to give an example of the sing-song style of the chronicler, whose inversions and assonances throughout suggest that his chronicle is in reality nothing but a long poem broken up into prose: *Comment! dit le duc, tu ne portas jamais armes, ne à cheval ne fus! La fille respondit que, quant elle auroit un arnois et un cheval, dessus je monteray; la verra on si je ne le scay guider. Le duc luy donna un arnois et cheval, et la fit armer. Elle estoit legère; on amena le cheval et des meilleurs, tout sellez, bridez; en présence de tous, sans mettre le pied en l'estrier, dedans la selle se rua. On luy donna une lance; elle veint en la place du chasteau; elle la couru. Jamais hommes d'armes mieux ne la couru. Toute la noblesse esbahy estoient.*

[2] He had been taken prisoner at Verneuil by the English.

[3] *Procès*, Vol. IV, pp. 10–11: Perceval de Cagny; and *Procès*, Vol. III, p. 96: Deposition of the Duke of Alençon.

when she first arrived at Chinon or to his behaviour during the ensuing weeks.

Jeanne, of course, not having our advantage of seeing the situation retrospectively, fretted at the delay. She told Jean Paquerel how much she had suffered from the endless enquiries which prevented her from accomplishing her task. The time had come, she said, for her to begin her work. Weeks, however, were to elapse before she was allowed to do so. In the meantime, although subjected to the most rigorous examinations of every kind,[1] including an examination conducted by Madame de Trèves and Madame de Gaucourt to determine which sex she belonged to,[2] she was honourably entertained, and her humble lodging changed for rooms in the Tour du Coudray. In her circular bastion, with corkscrew staircase and a single circular room on every floor, she was living within the precincts of the castle itself, within an arrow-shot of her beloved Dauphin. She had a chapel attached to the tower, where she could retire to pray. She was put under the charge of the Dauphin's majordomo, Guillaume Bellier, and of his wife, reputed a virtuous and pious woman[3]; she had the services of a page specially assigned to her; and, most important of all, was allowed free access to the Dauphin. This little page, Louis de Contes, familiarly known as Minguet, spent all his days with her while she lived in the tower, remained as one of her most faithful servants in the more exciting days which were to follow, and has left an account of her during this exasperating period. He had been lent for her service by his master, the seigneur de Gaucourt, governor of Chinon. At that time he was between fourteen and fifteen years old, which to our modern ears sounds very young, until we realise with a start that Jeanne herself was only three years older than he. It is he who tells us that he often saw her coming from or going to see the Dauphin. Anybody who knows Chinon can

[1]*Procès*, Vol. III, p. 103: Deposition of Jean Paquerel.
[2]*Procès*, Vol. III, p. 102: Deposition of Jean Paquerel.
[3]*Procès*, Vol. III, p. 17: Deposition of Raoul de Gaucourt.

see that it was of course quite easy for him to observe her movements: he had only to climb to the top of the tower to command a view over the whole enclosure of the castle, especially over the bridge spanning the deep *fosse* which Jeanne must cross in order to reach the Dauphin's apartments. The rest of her time, when she was neither with Charles nor being examined by important men (*homines magni status*) nor snubbing the Duke of Alençon for using strong language, he often saw her on her knees, in prayer as it seemed to him; he could never hear what she was saying, but sometimes saw her in tears.[1]

It is easy to read between the lines of this deposition, made by the man who had once been Jeanne's page, the then little Minguet de Contes. The naïf admission, made in retrospect, that he could never overhear what she was saying as she knelt in prayer, brings a boy's natural curiosity vividly before us. So, also, it is permissible to discern a rueful tone when he speaks of the important men who visited her, but whose conversation he could not report, since he was obliged to withdraw whenever they arrived. He must have longed to stay in the room, and listen. It must have been an exciting experience for a boy of fourteen to be thus attached to the personal service of so controversial a figure as the virgin of Domremy. She was at that time the most discussed person in the whole little world of Chinon: and Minguet de Contes, had he expressed himself in the idiom of an English schoolboy of the same age to-day, would have described himself as "jolly lucky." It was lucky for him to be singled out as the page of this queer girl who had the Dauphin's ear, and who was visited in her lodging by men so formidably grand that he could not even record their names. (Incidentally, I think, Minguet must have been rather a stupid little boy. He certainly grew up into a man with the most confused memory for events. Chronology was not his forte. Let that pass. He was an honest and devoted soul.)

These two young creatures, then, shared their tower between

[1] *Procès*, Vol. III, pp. 65–7: Deposition of Louis de Contes.

them. He spent the whole day with her, but at night his place was taken by women. She was, in fact, although the Dauphin's guest, under guard all the time. She was under constant surveillance. Either the page was there, a friendly, inquisitive, devoted little page; or else the important men were there, asking her questions; or else the women were there, keeping an eye on her nightly morals. Then, having undergone these preliminary examinations at Chinon, she was taken away to the neighbouring town of Poitiers to undergo examinations of an even more searching kind. The Dauphin went to Poitiers too. Apparently Jeanne had no idea where she was being taken, if she was really already half-way to Poitiers when she bethought herself to make enquiries. "*En nom Dieu,*" she said then, "I know I shall have a lot of trouble at Poitiers, but *messires* will help me; so let us go."[1] She was still in her boy's suit, having refused to put on any other.

[1]*Procès*, Vol. IV, p. 209: *Chronique de la Pucelle;* ibid., p. 128: *Journal du siège d'Orleans.* The *Journal* differs slightly from the *Chronique,* in making Jeanne guess her destination by divine inspiration, but in substance the story is the same. Judging by what we know of Jeanne's character, it seems highly unlikely that she would have allowed herself to be conducted half-way to Poitiers before asking where she was going; she probably asked before she started; her remark, however, reads with her authentic accent; and, indeed, as the *Journal* adds, *c'estoit sa manière de parler.*

Chapter VIII

POITIERS TO ORLEANS

i

At Poitiers they lodged her in the house of one Jean Rabateau, *qui avoit espousé une bonne femme*.[1] The Rabateaux had a little oratory in their house, to which Jeanne would often retire in prayer.[2] But in spite of the gravity of her frequent prayers, she was in a gay and high-spirited mood, rising rapidly with the rising wave. Since leaving Domremy, she had certainly met with checks and delays: she had met with no definite reverse. She had convinced the Dauphin; she had no reason to believe that she would not equally succeed in convincing the doctors at Poitiers. Her replies to them were racy and almost cheeky. "I see you have come to ask me questions," she said to them; "I know neither A nor B." And, meeting a young man called Gobert Thibault, she clapped him on the shoulder, saying that she wished she had several men of such goodwill as he[3]—a remark which drew from Mr. Andrew Lang the surprising comment that "her ways were those of a clean honest public-school boy."[4] She was full of hope and thought she had nothing to fear. The record of her examination at Poitiers unfortunately no longer exists. It had already ceased to exist by the time she was brought to trial for her life at Rouen. If it were ever to be found, it would quite certainly supplement the already sufficiently extraordinary historical document of her trial; it would, in short, provide the justification to which Jeanne, during the course of that trial, was constantly making appeal. She repeatedly appealed to her judges to refer to the Book of Poitiers. They never did. It had either been suppressed, lost, or destroyed. It seems more

[1]*Procès*, Vol. IV, p. 209: *Chronique de la Pucelle*.
[2]*Procès*, Vol. III, p. 82: Deposition of Jean Barbin.
[3]*Procès*, Vol. III, p. 74: Deposition of Gobert Thibault.
[4]Andrew Lang, *The Maid of France*, p. 94.

likely that it had been suppressed or destroyed than lost. Its loss would argue a degree of carelessness scarcely credible. It seems far more likely that it would have proved too highly inconvenient a document for Jeanne's judges to have dared to produce at Rouen. It must be remembered, also, that she was being tried at Rouen by an ecclesiastical court, and that ecclesiastical courts were not to be credited with any greater degree of scrupulousness than secular. It was one of the most serious losses that poor Jeanne ever sustained, and would constitute one of the most interesting finds that the scholar or the historian could ever make, were they to bring it to light from some forgotten archives. Even the barest notes taken during the course of the investigation at Poitiers would prove of the utmost value. Jeanne herself evidently set great store by it. Her constant appeals to her judges to have it produced make pitiable reading. As it is, we are left to guess at what revelations the Book of Poitiers may have contained. We do know, however, that the President of the Board of Examiners at Poitiers was no less a personage than the Archbishop of Reims, Chancellor of France,[1] although he does not appear to have interrogated Jeanne in person; and we do possess one document of supreme interest, taken down from the lips of one Frère Seguin who was not only present at, but took part in, rather disastrously for himself, the examination of Jeanne at Poitiers.

She came in, sat down on the end of a bench, and asked them what they wanted of her.[2]

Frère Seguin, a Carmelite, Professor of Theology at the University of Poitiers, was said to be a disagreeable man— *bien aigre homme*.[3] I think Frère Seguin has been rather misjudged by his commentator. I think, on the contrary, that he was a man with a certain sense of humour, even though it may have been of the bitter sort. Otherwise, he would never have reported, twenty-five years later, the exchange

---

[1] *Procès*, Vol. III, p. 203: Deposition of Frère Seguin.
[2] *Procès*, Vol. IV, p. 209: *Chronique de la Pucelle*.
[3] *Procès*, Vol. IV, p. 210: *Chronique de la Pucelle*.

of question and answer which passed between him and Jeanne, in which he definitely got the worst of it. He had been so misguided as to ask her what language her voices spoke. He got his answer sharp and slick: "A better language than yours." Now, as Frère Seguin, according to his own admissions, spoke French in the patois of the Limousin, which is much the same as saying that an Englishman spoke broad Yorkshire, I suspect that Jeanne's reply provoked smiles, if not a titter, in the assembly. But Frère Seguin was not yet prudent enough to remove himself beyond the reach of Jeanne's tart peasant tongue. He pursued his questions. Did she, he asked, believe in God? Again he got his answer: "Yes, and better than you." Still undeterred, he then informed her that God was not willing that they should believe her on her mere word, and that they would not advise the Dauphin to supply her with men-at-arms unless she could give them some proof that she was deserving of their trust. At this point, Jeanne seems to have lost her temper. "By God's name," she said, "I have not come to Poitiers to perform signs. Lead me to Orleans, and I will show you the signs for which I am sent."[1]

This silenced Frère Seguin for the moment, but Jeanne went on to sketch her programme to him and to the rest of the assembly. It was a programme whose insolence took their breath away (*ils estoient grandement ébahis*). She made four cardinal points: the English would be destroyed after Orleans had been relieved and freed of their presence; the Dauphin would be crowned at Reims; Paris would be restored to its allegiance; and the Duke of Orleans would return to France out of captivity.[2]

[1]*Procès*, Vol. III, pp. 204–5: Deposition of Frère Seguin: *En nom Dieu, je ne suis pas venue à Poitiers pour faire signes.* (In French in the original.)

[2]*Procès*, Vol. III, p. 205: Deposition of Frère Seguin. It should be noted that Jeanne's claims had grown from two to four in number since she had first arrived at Chinon. Then, she claimed only that she would relieve Orleans and crown the Dauphin. It is worth noting, also, that these two prophecies only were fulfilled during her lifetime; the subjection of Paris and the release of the Duke of Orleans took place only after her death.

Thinking to catch her out, Guillaume Aymerie said to her, "You say your voices tell you that God wishes to free the people of France from their present calamities. But if He wishes to free them, it is not necessary to have an army." "*En nom Dieu,*" Jeanne said again, "*les gens d'armes batailleront et Dieu donnera victoire.*"[1]

The superb audacity of such announcements was not without its effect upon that assembly of learned men. They must, indeed, have been astonished on hearing themselves addressed in such confident terms by the boyish figure sitting on the bench, alone and unadvised, before them. Far from being hesitant, alarmed, or overawed, as in their pomp and solemnity they might have expected, it was evidently with difficulty that she restrained her impatience or remembered her manners just enough to prevent her from being actually rude—a child and a peasant confronting many doctors in theology under the presidency, even in the background, of so great a lord of the Church as the Archbishop of Reims himself. It was a good preparation for confronting a very differently minded assembly of learned men, under the presidency of another lord of the Church, the Bishop of Beauvais. Frère Seguin, our only first-hand authority for what happened at Poitiers, omits to tell us anything about the deliberations which finally induced them to change their minds; he bounces us straight into the fact that they had done so: "We decided that, in view of the imminent necessity and of the danger of Orleans, the King might allow the girl to help him and might send her to Orleans."[2] This slightly patronising phrase is corrected by another chronicler who was obviously founding his remarks on the evidence of Frère Seguin. According to this other chronicler, the things which she told them seemed very strange (*les choses dictes par ladicte Jeanne leur sembloient bien estranges*). So strange did these things seem, that the court

---

[1] *Procès*, Vol. III, p. 204: Deposition of Frère Seguin.
[2] *Procès*, Vol. III, p. 205: Deposition of Frère Seguin.

of enquiry eventually came to the decision that the Dauphin might be recommended to put his trust in her.[1]

ii

But, before that could happen, there were still other delays. They were still not certain of her. From Poitiers she was sent to Tours and to Blois—another maddening delay while precious time was being lost. What Jeanne wanted, and wanted urgently, was to go to the relief of Orleans. She wanted to get down to business; she wanted to be given an army; she had no wish whatsoever to be delayed by archbishops, bishops, doctors in theology, or by women appointed to examine her to find out whether she was a boy or a girl; and, if a girl, a virgin or not. The ladies at Chinon had already been deputed to determine her sex. Now, at Tours, the Queen of Sicily, the Dauphin's mother-in-law, in person, was put in charge of this second examination, with other ladies, and they reported their findings in the crude phraseology of their age.[2] They attested to the indubitable fact of her virginity. The coarse frankness of their report shocks us. It cannot fail to shock us when we consider the modesty that Jeanne consistently observed in her personal behaviour, as we are specifically assured by those who had every opportunity to watch her in her daily life. It cannot fail to shock us if we take it in terms of twentieth-century fastidiousness. Taken in those terms, we can feel nothing but a horrified sympathy for the girl exposed to so indelicate and repeated an examination. Yet perhaps we go wrong over this. Perhaps Jeanne did not resent the examination of the women so much as we might expect her to resent it.

---

[1]*Procès*, Vol. IV, p. 210: *Chronique de la Pucelle.*

[2]*Procès*, Vol. III, p. 209: Deposition of Jean d'Aulon. *Par lesquelles icelle Pucelle fut vue, visitée, et secrètement regardée et examinée es secrètes parties de son corps; mais après qu'elles eurent vu et regardé tout ce que faisoit à regarder en ce cas, ladicte dame dist et relata au roy qu'elle et sesdictes dames trouvoient certainement que c'estoit une vraye et entière pucelle.*

Perhaps we ought to bear more presently in mind that we are trying to reconstruct the mentality of people living in the fifteenth century, not in the twentieth. We most certainly ought to remember that the question of virginity was a vital question, since if she were a virgin the Devil could have no possible dealings with her. The examinations were thus no gratuitous insult. Perhaps we ought also to remember that Jeanne was a peasant, accustomed from her earliest years to the crudest facts of life, and, therefore, not so readily offended as we might imagine when those facts of life were applied in practice to the factual truths of her own body. She probably took these unpleasant tests in her stride. She was probably less offended by them than we might imagine. Yet, at the same time, how is it possible to refrain from picturing to oneself the effect upon a peasant girl, so intimately examined by no less a person than a queen? Jeanne's situation at this time (March–April 1429) was surely one of the most extraordinary. She, an insignificant peasant, had succeeded in forcing herself into the presence of her King. She had succeeded in impressing her personality on him to such an extent that he had appointed a court to enquire into her credentials, and had set such high-born ladies to enquire so indiscreetly into her private morals. Jeanne could scarcely have been blamed had she lost her head; she could scarcely have been blamed had she allowed her head to be turned. She allowed neither of these things to happen. She admitted to Pierre de Versailles that, without God's help, she would not have known how to protect herself against such idolatry as was manifested by the populace catching at her horse's legs in order to kiss her feet and hands.[1] She kept straight to her appointed path. She had made her way to the Dauphin; had told him what she intended to do; had submitted herself to the enquiry of the doctors at Poitiers; had submitted herself also to the more personal enquiry of the women at Tours. Morally and physically she had allowed herself to be thoroughly tested. She had accepted

[1] *Procès*, Vol. III, p. 84: Deposition of Jean Barbin.

everything which could be asked of her with all the patience at her command. And she was winning. Messages asking for help kept on arriving from Orleans; the people of Poitiers were clamantly on her side; the group of her friends was increasing daily, with the addition of powerful recruits. The Duke of Alençon was firmly her *beau duc*. The famous Bastard of Orleans had been taking so deep an interest in her for some time past as to send two gentlemen to Chinon to make enquiries about her.[1] It is quite clear that she made a profound impression on all who came into contact with her. It is equally clear that she made an impression on people even before she came into personal contact with them. Otherwise, why should the Bastard of Orleans have troubled to send his two gentlemen to Chinon to make enquiries about the virgin of Domremy when the said virgin was only on her way to Chinon, and had, in fact, got no further on her way than Gien? Why should the population of Orleans have assembled, as they did, to hear the report of the two gentlemen? She had accomplished nothing. She had not even achieved the honour of an audience with the Dauphin. How can we explain the Bastard's interest in her at so early a stage in her career? What reports had reached him? We cannot tell. We can only say, putting it into the terms of modern journalism, that Jeanne possessed news-value from the first. From the moment she left Vaucouleurs she was front-page news. It is an inexplicable quality, but Jeanne certainly possessed it.

And now, at last, she was seeing daylight; the obstacles were clearing away; things were really beginning to move. Preparations were made for her to join the army. She was given a regular household; Louis de Contes was now definitely made over to her as her page, with another boy called Raymond; the faithful Jean d'Aulon, "the most honest man in the French army," according to the Bastard, was detailed for her service by the Dauphin's orders; she was given two heralds

[1] *Procès*, Vol. III, p. 3: Deposition of the comte de Dunois (the Bastard of Orleans).

and two servants; her brother Pierre, and possibly also her brother Jean, came from Domremy to join her—which must surely have struck her as an odd twist of fortune when she remembered her rather surreptitious and disgraced departure from her father's house. She had played the supreme truant then; now she was in the position to receive her brother as a prince receives a suppliant. And, what must have seemed more important to her than all the rest, she was given Jean Paquerel as her own confessor. They brought him to her at the house of Jean Dupuy, where she was lodging in Tours, saying "Jeanne, we are bringing you this good father, whom you will grow to love as you know him better."[1] The days were over when she found difficulty in hearing Mass as often as she wished; she now could, and often did, hear it more than once a day, and confessed as often as the desire seized her. Moreover, again by the Dauphin's orders, she was given a complete equipment of armour, banners, and a horse. Most significant of all, she was allowed to despatch a letter to the English. That letter had been dictated at Poitiers, and constitutes one of the most arrogant incidents in the whole of her arrogant career.

iii

It started with her losing her patience with her examiners. "I cannot tell A from B," she had said to them, "but God has sent me to raise the siege of Orleans and to get the Dauphin crowned at Reims. Have you paper and ink? Write! I will dictate to you."[2] She then obliged them to take down the letter at her dictation. It is dated Tuesday in Holy Week, i.e. March 22nd, 1429.

"Jhesus Maria. King of England, and you, Duke of Bedford, calling yourself Regent of France; William de la Pole, Earl of Suffolk; John Lord Talbot, and you, Thomas Lord Scales, calling yourselves lieutenants of the said Bedford . . . deliver the keys of all the good towns you have taken and violated

[1] *Procès*, Vol. III, p. 101: Deposition of Jean Paquerel.
[2] *Procès*, Vol. III, p. 74: Deposition of Gobert Thibault.

in France to the Maid (*Pucelle*) who has been sent by God the King of Heaven. . . . Go away, for God's sake, back to your own country; otherwise, await news of the Maid, who will soon visit you to your great detriment " (*Alès vous en, en vos païs, de par Dieu, et se ainssi ne le faictes, attendés les nouvelles de la Pucelle qui vous ira veoir briefment à vostre bien grant domaige*).[1]

After this truly Elizabethan opening—save that even Elizabeth would scarcely have called a fellow-sovereign to account in such terms—Jeanne introduced a somewhat more kindly note. She appealed to the Duke of Bedford not to oblige her to destroy him (*Duc de Bethfort, la Pucelle vous prie et vous requiert que vous ne vous faictes pas destruire*). If only he would be reasonable, she said, the French might possibly give proof of the noblest act ever performed for the sake of Christianity[2] (*Se vous faictes rayson, y pouverra venir lieu que les Francois feront le plus biau fait que oncques fut fait pour la crestienté*). "But," she added immediately, if "you refuse, remember the great detriment which will overtake you " (*Se ainssi ne le faictes, de voz bien grans doumaiges vous souviegne briefment*). She was willing, in other words, to give him his chance, and also to give the French their chance of exhibiting a truly Christian spirit, but if he would not accept the offer, then let him look out for himself.

Some confusion exists as to the immediate fate of this letter. Some authorities, both ancient and modern, take it for granted that it was despatched from Blois before Jeanne started for Orleans, and that it was in the hands of the English before she ever arrived at Orleans at all. Others declare that it was not presented until the day after her entry into the town; implying, in other words, that she carried it there with her.

[1]*Procès*, Vol. V, p. 96. I have, of course, greatly abbreviated the letter. The spelling of the old French is erratic and inconsistent, but I have reproduced it exactly, and the discrepancies are not due to misprints. The full text will be found in Appendix D, p. 395.

[2]This refers to Jeanne's hopes of a Crusade. Christine de Pisan wrote:
"Des Sarrasins fera essart
En conquérant la Sainte Terre.
La menra Charles, que Dieu gard."

It seems to me that the evidence is in favour of the latter view, principally because that evidence is derived from contemporary witnesses, whereas the evidence in favour of the letter having been despatched from Blois is derived from chronicles only more or less contemporary, whose accuracy is in any case erratic and suspect. An alternative explanation of the confusion, which, so far as I know, has never been suggested, is that there may have been two copies of the letter, one of which was despatched from Blois to the Duke of Bedford in person and the other carried to Orleans by Jeanne, to be delivered straight into the hands of Lord Talbot, the English commander at Orleans. We know for certain that a definite summons was delivered to Talbot by Jeanne's heralds the day after she had reached Orleans. But had a similar communication been despatched previously to the Duke of Bedford? The letter which we possess constitutes, after all, an appeal to Bedford exhorting him to leave France, without any specific reference to the siege of Orleans, except to require an answer in that city (*et faites reponse, se vous voulés faire paix, en la cité d'Orléans*). Now, Jeanne knew perfectly well that Talbot, not Bedford, was in command at Orleans: why, therefore, should she have addressed her demands to Bedford if the letter was really meant for Talbot? On the other hand, it must be admitted that the letter was superscribed: *To the Duke of Bedford, so-called Regent of the Kingdom of France, or to his lieutenants before the city of Orleans.* It could therefore be equally logically argued that she did not mind very much whether the letter came into Bedford's hands, or into Talbot's.[1]

I offer the suggestion for what it is worth, and entirely without documentary backing. But let us for a moment suppose that the original letter did reach Bedford. How would it have struck him? In his way a fine and intelligent man, he was not of the type to whom such a letter was likely to appeal. Being an Englishman, he could scarcely have done otherwise

[1]It is true also that Henry VI, then aged seven, was included in the text of the letter. His name, however, does not appear in the superscription.

than put it down as the most outrageous piece of impertinence. As, indeed, it was. Being an Englishman, he could not have failed to overlook certain factors with which he had not reckoned. The English, apart from their poetry, are not an imaginative race: in the region of practical politics they are apt to rely on force rather than on imagination, a system which works ninety-nine times out of a hundred. Jeanne was the hundredth time. The Duke of Bedford could not have accepted the threat that Jeanne was bringing against him. How could he have been expected to accept it? Who was this Jehanne, this Pucelle whom the credulous French were proposing to pit against him? Solid English sense could say nothing but "Rubbish."

Whether Bedford ever got the letter or not, the siege of Orleans was not raised, nor did the English obediently pack up to retire to their own country.

iv

Jeanne, however, had by now got the management of affairs entirely into her own hands. What she said, went. The most remarkable change had taken place during the six weeks which had elapsed since her arrival at Chinon. She had been doubtfully received; treated with perhaps understandable caution; now, six weeks later, she had got the whole thing under her control. She had, in some extraordinary way, become the hope of France; a shrunken France. That shrunken France acclaimed her; wanted her; armed her; mounted her; and unfurled her flags above her boyish head. She had definitely ceased to be Jeanette from Domremy, and had become officially Jeanne la Pucelle, the hope, the saviour. The hour had come when she could impose her will. She accepted the armour and the banners; the sword she declined, having ideas of her own. She knew exactly which sword she wanted, and would have none other. They must go and fetch it for her. They would find it, she said, buried in the ground behind the altar in the church of Saint Catherine at Fierbois. This puzzled everybody, for no one had ever heard of the existence of this sword, but such was their belief in Jeanne by now that an armourer was sent from Tours, with a letter from Jeanne addressed to the priests of Saint Catherine asking them to be good enough to find the sword and to send it. To everybody's astonishment it all fell out as she had predicted. The sword was indeed there, engraved with five crosses; it was very rusty, but, as soon as the church people started to clean it, the rust fell off it with unusual readiness. Here was a miracle indeed, and Jeanne's prestige increased a hundredfold. The church people at Fierbois were so much impressed that they gave her a sheath for the sword, and so did the people of Tours, so that she had two sheaths, one of crimson velvet and the other of cloth of gold, but she herself caused yet a third sheath to be made, of stout serviceable leather.[1]

The story is undoubtedly a strange one, even if we discount the miraculous disappearance of the rust, and is scarcely covered by the suggestion that she might have heard of the sword when she passed through Fierbois on her way to Chinon. For if Jeanne had been told about it by one of the church people at Fierbois, why had others not heard of it also; and why did she have to write to the church people, describing so exactly where it would be found? All she need have said was, "Please dig up the sword you told me about, and send it to me." Her own explanation, of course, was her usual one: her voices had told her where it lay. The sceptical suggestion that Jeanne had hidden the sword there herself may be dismissed: it in no way accords with anything that we know of her character. I confess that I fail to see how the story can rationally be explained. At any rate, Jeanne's contemporaries made no attempt to explain it rationally, and legends grew up round the sword, including one to the effect that it had originally been used by Charles Martel against the Saracens

[1] *Procès*, Vol. I, p. 235.

at Poitiers in 732.[1] Jeanne's judges, later on, made no attempt to explain it rationally either: it was far too convenient an additional proof that she was, in very fact, a witch.

v

Altogether, the equipment assembled for her at Tours, picturesque, becoming, and romantic though it was, was destined to lead her into very serious trouble. The armour, apart from the fact that she had no business to wear men's clothes, was safe enough: they could find nothing to say against her armour, except to ask searching questions as to why she had offered it to Saint Denis—was it, they suggested, because she wanted it to be worshipped?—but the white standard fringed with silk was found reprehensible in the extreme. Blasphemy and sacrilege had quite obviously been intended. Why, otherwise, should she have caused a representation of the world, supported by two angels, with a portrait of Our Lord and the words *Jhesus Maria*, to be painted upon it? She did not improve matters by replying that Our Lord had commanded her to do so, through the medium of Saint Catherine and Saint Margaret. Her instructions had been very precise, both as to the symbols and as to the colours. Why, they asked, had she not included the light which accompanied her saints and voices when they appeared to her? That, she said, patiently, had not been commanded. They badgered her further. Which did she love most, they asked, her standard or her sword? Her standard, she said, forty times better—although previously she had admitted that she loved her sword, because it had been found in the church of Saint Catherine, whom she loved. Why did she carry her standard, they asked, when she went into battle? And she gave the very simple answer that it was in order to avoid killing anybody

[1]Chanoine Henri Bas et l'abbé Charles Pichon, *Sainte Catherine de Fierbois*, p. 23.

with her own hands. She had never, she added, killed any man.[1]

Her answers were frequently apt to be so simple that nobody could believe in them.

vi

Her few possessions became the subject of the most sinister interpretations. Those words J H E S U S   M A R I A, which she used as a heading to her letters[2] and also caused to be inscribed on her standard, reappeared most unfortunately for her on one of her rings. She had two rings. One of them had been given to her by her brother, the other by either her father or her mother; she does not appear to have been very certain which. In fact, she betrayed a rather pathetic vagueness about the ring when they questioned her about it at her trial: she could not say whether it was made of gold or of some alloy (*laiton*), modestly adding, as a peasant would add, that if it was made of gold at all, it was not of very fine gold. It had no stone in it. So far as she could make out, a cross and the words *Jhesus Maria* were engraved on it, but she did not know who had caused them to be engraved. She had never used it to effect cures. In spite of her vagueness about this ring, a vagueness which is to be attributed partly to her natural ignorance of precious metals and partly to her inability to read, she certainly treasured it. She treasured it so much that she was in the habit of looking down at it on her finger whenever she was about to enter into battle, thinking meanwhile of her father and mother, and of Saint Catherine whom she had touched with the hand that was wearing it. By an additional

[1]*Procès*, Vol. I, pp. 181 and 300–4. See also Appendix E, p. 397, for a note on the standard.

[2]e.g. in two letters to the English, dated March 22nd and May 5th, 1429; a letter to the citizens of Tournay, June 25th, 1429; a letter to the Duke of Burgundy, July 17th, 1429; a letter to the Comte d'Armagnac, August 22nd, 1429; a letter to the Hussites, March 3rd, 1430.

little twist of cruelty her enemies took both her rings away from her when she was captured, one of them being handed over to the Burgundians and the other retained by the Bishop of Beauvais. At her trial she begged that one of them might be returned to her, and the other given to the Church. There is no record of either request having been granted.[1]

vii

We can thus compose a fairly complete inventory of Jeanne's personal possessions at the time she set out for the deliverance of Orleans. She had her suit of armour, humbly made without any blazon whatsoever. She had her horse. She had her standard —a proud standard, bearing the image of Christ, the world, two angels, and the lilies of France. She had a lance. She had a pennon. She had a small battle-axe, which she sometimes carried in her hand. She had her two rings, one of which might be made of gold or might not, but which reproduced, as in a tiny mirror, the words written on the standard floating above her head: JHESUS MARIA.

A letter addressed, about five weeks later (June 8th, 1429), by the young Gui de Laval to his mother and grandmother, describes her with a freshness which has lost nothing after the lapse of five centuries:

"I saw her mount a great black charger, a little axe in her hand, armed entirely *en blanc*,[2] but for her head. The horse, which was making a great fuss before the door of her lodging, would not allow her to mount, so she said, 'Lead him to the cross,' which was in front of the neighbouring church. And then she mounted, and he stirred no more than if he had been bound. And then she turned towards the door of the church, saying in a fairly feminine voice, 'You, priests, and people of the Church, form yourselves into a procession and offer

---

[1]*Procès*, Vol. I, pp. 86 and 185.

[2]*En blanc*, or *à blanc*, does not mean *in white*, as might be supposed, but in armour which bore no gilding or coat of arms.

prayers to God.' And then, having returned to her road, she said, 'Go on! go on!' her little axe in her hand, her standard furled and carried by a graceful page."[1]

Among the many vivid and personal touches which make the figure of Jeanne not only legendary but human, one must record the pride of a citizen of Poitiers, one Christofle du Peirat, who in 1495, then being nearly a hundred years old, told Jean Bouchet, a boy of nineteen, that he had seen Jeanne mount her horse when she left for Orleans. *"Et me monstra une petite pierre qui est au coin de la rue Sainct Estienne, ou elle print avantage pour monter sur son cheval."*[2]

[1]*Procès*, Vol. V, pp. 107–8. Gui de Laval was no stylist, and his syntax is so confused that for the sake of clarity I have not attempted to reproduce it exactly. Here, however, is the text of the original French: *La veis monter à cheval, armée tout en blanc, sauf la teste, unne petite hache en sa main sur un grand coursier noir, qui à l'huis de son logis se demenoit très fort, et ne souffroit qu'elle montast; et lors elle dit: "Menés-le à la croix," qui estoit devant l'eglise auprès, au chemin. Et lors elle monta, sans ce qu'il se meust, comme s'il fust lié. Et lors se tourna vers l'huis de l'eglise, qui estoit bien prochain, et dit en assés voix de femme: "Vous, les prestres et gens d'eglise, faites procession et prières à Dieu." Et lors se retourna à son chemin, en disant: "Tirés avant, tirés avant," son estendart ployé que portoit un gracieux paige, et avoit sa hache petite en la main.*

[2]*Procès*, Vol. IV, p. 537. Jean Bouchet, *Annales d'Aquitaine.*

Chapter IX

ORLEANS (1)

i

It would be tedious and unnecessary to go into too many details relating to the siege of Orleans previous to Jeanne's arrival. It has been described many times elsewhere, and this is no military handbook. It must suffice to say here that by April 29th, 1429, Orleans had been besieged for about six months, i.e. since October 12th, 1428, in, as I read the story, a rather half-hearted and ineffectual way. Lord Salisbury had been killed by a cannon-ball shortly after the siege had begun, thus depriving the English of their first commander. The Duke of Bedford had never thrown himself with any conviction into the siege. "And all things there prospered for you," he wrote, "till the time of the siege of Orleans taken in hand, God knoweth by what advice."[1] His government in London either would not or could not send him the reinforcements he needed, and indeed he scarcely encouraged them to do so. He asked for men and money, as was his duty, but was careful to point out that, without "great expense of money the siege cannot be maintained," which was almost tantamount to saying that they had better allow him to cut his loss and retire. By April, large numbers of the English had deserted; the Duke of Burgundy, after a dispute with the Duke of Bedford, had withdrawn his troops; a contingent of Norman vassals had gone crossly back to Normandy. The English, although they could hinder and hamper, could not entirely prevent the entry of food, men, and money into the town. Either one holds a very exaggerated idea of the closeness of mediæval sieges, or else the English were unusually lax in the way they permitted the enemy and his convoys to pass freely in and out. It must be remembered that the English had not drawn a *complete* circle round the town, as a glance at the map will show: only three

[1] *Procès*, Vol. V, p. 136.

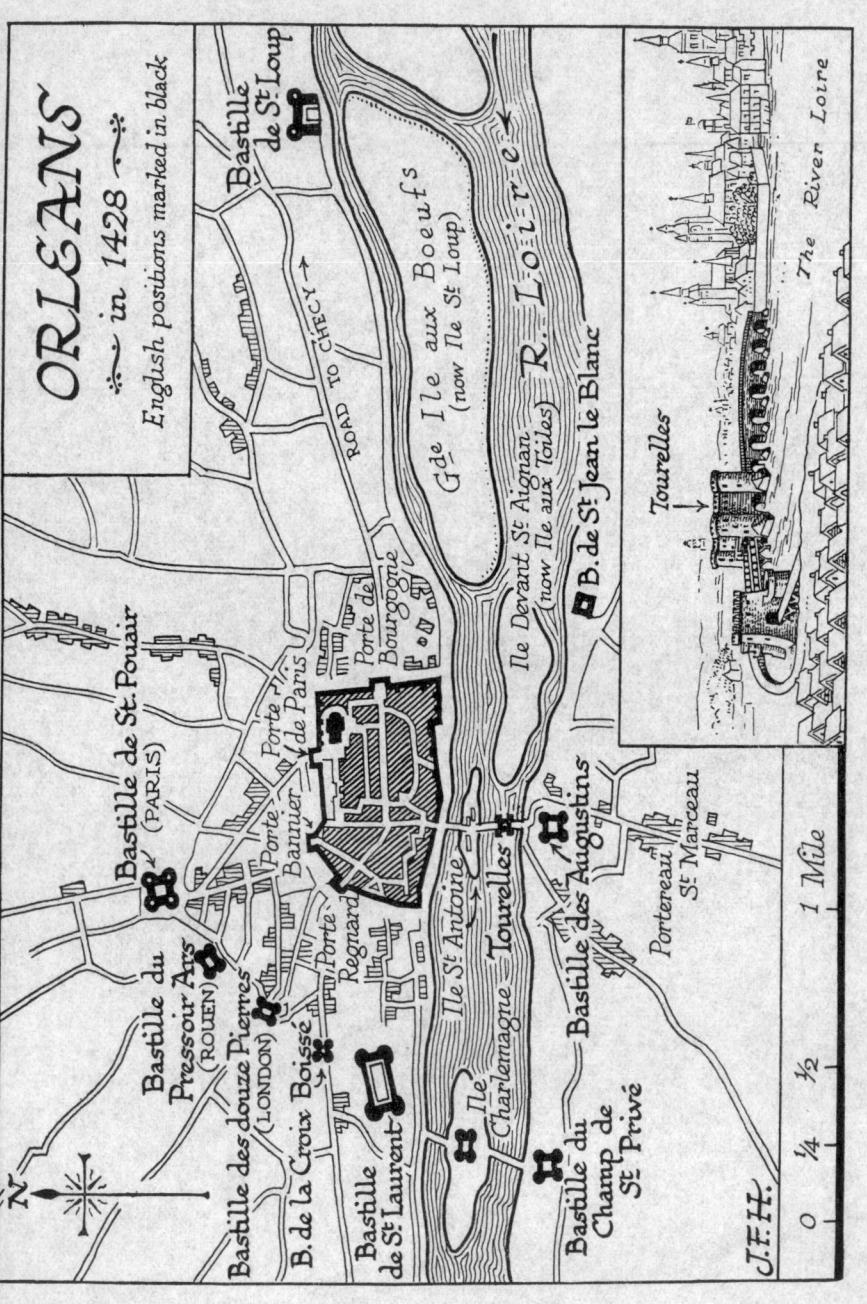

ORLÉANS in 1428

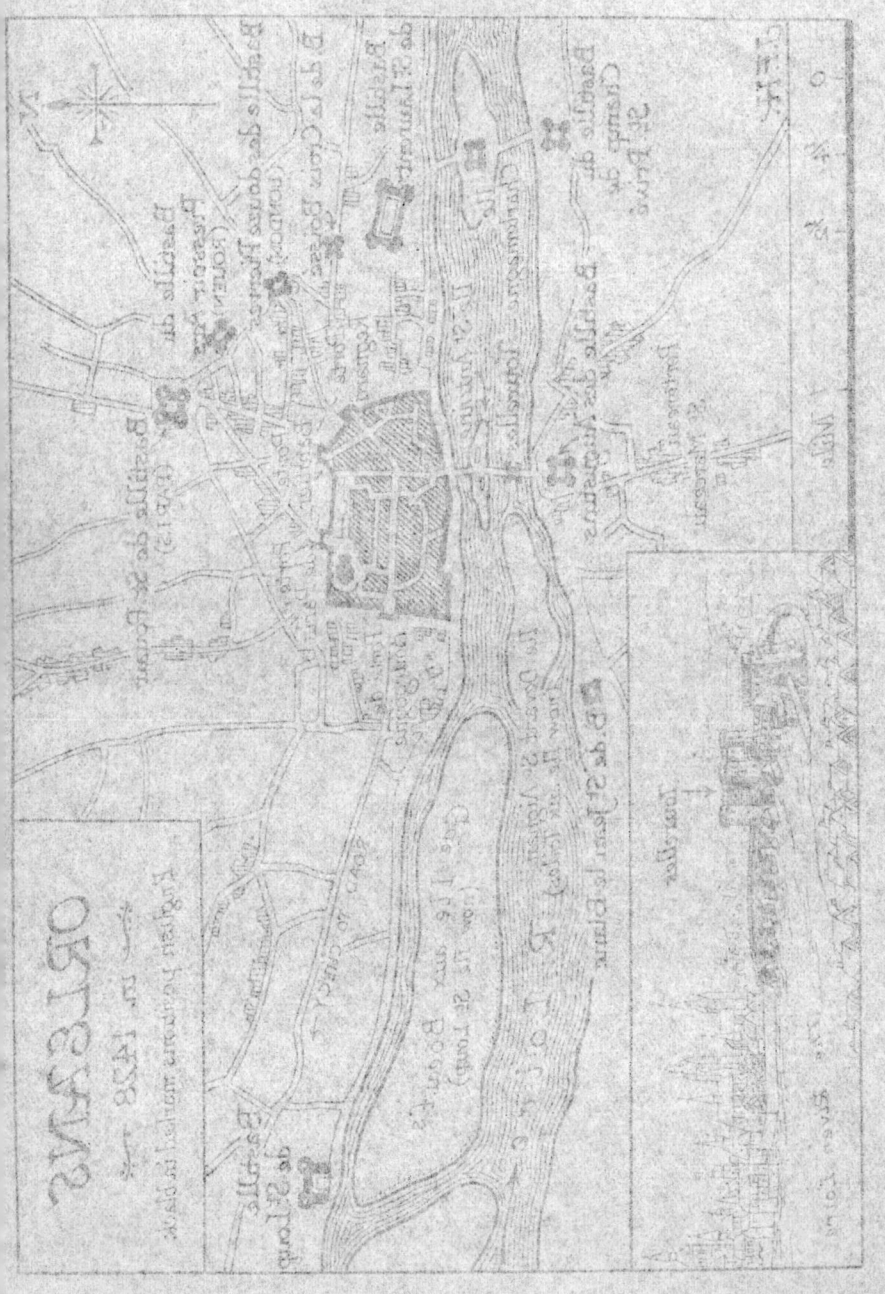

quarters of the circle, on the north, west, and south, were complete. As M. Jollois, the historian of the siege, points out, it is easy to see that all roads of approach were not intercepted, and that between the Bastille of Saint Loup and that of Saint Pouair, nearly three miles apart, no obstacle existed to prevent the entry of provisions and munitions into the town. Of course, they were relatively short of supplies, but there was no imminent question of their giving in through starvation. The mere statistics of the supplies which kept on arriving are enough to show that whatever their friends outside could send, the besieged population could smuggle in. Thus, on April 2nd, nine fat beasts arrived, and two horses laden with kids and other provisions; on April 5th, a hundred and eighteen pigs, six fat beasts, and two horses laden with cheese and butter; on April 6th, twenty-six horned beasts; on April 7th, seventeen pigs and eight horses, six of them laden with wheat. That is no bad record for four almost consecutive days, and the Orléanais, although anxious, cannot have been desperate. Everybody, in fact, had arrived at a sort of stalemate; neither the besieged nor the besiegers could move. It was not a position for good morale on either side. It was a discouraging position for both parties. But it was a serious position. Orleans was a key place, not lightly to be abandoned. It must have been quite obvious by April 1429, after six dilatory months of failure, that the English must make a determining attempt or else withdraw. In spite of the Duke of Bedford's lack of enthusiasm, they were not likely to withdraw after so prolonged an expenditure of men, money, and prestige. Nor were the besieged likely to give in, so long as starvation did not absolutely compel them to do so. That was, roughly, the position when Jeanne took matters in hand. What Jeanne did was to settle in a few days a dispute which had been going on for six months. And this she did, I believe, by her personal influence entirely. At the same time, I also believe that she arrived at what is now called the psychological moment. She arrived at the moment when the English no longer had the heart or the means to stage the conclusive attack. Without wishing to denigrate her tactical achievement at Orleans, I think we must recognise that achievement to have been largely psychological; psychological rather than military. Her personal example and confidence were worth ten thousand men. There is no denigration in saying that Jeanne was probably the only person then capable of inspiring the French troops and citizens to rid Orleans of an enemy who had held them in a snake-rabbit fascination for half a year. The particular inspiration which she brought to them at Orleans after six months' siege reflects, as a sort of symbol, the general inspiration which she brought to the whole of France after nearly a hundred years of war.

The relief of Orleans was not Jeanne's real achievement. Her exploit here has been much exaggerated, and Orleans is for ever historically associated with her name. History does always, for some odd reason, give rise to such disproportionate associations; on examination, they seldom prove to be wholly justified; on examination, one usually finds that they stand as the symbol of a wider truth.

Jeanne's real achievement was not the relief of Orleans, but the regeneration of the soul of a flagging France.

ii

In the meantime, however, to those concerned in the struggle in April 1429, the siege of Orleans was important. The French were more or less shut up inside the town, which was entirely surrounded by walls, reinforced at intervals by strong towers, and pierced by four gates, the Porte de Bourgogne, the Porte de Paris, the Porte Bannier, and the Porte Regnard. The river protected them on the south, spanned by a single bridge, which was commanded by two strong English positions, one at the Bastille des Augustins and the other at a fort on the bridge itself, known as les Tourelles. Apart from these two important forts, the English held strategical positions almost, though not quite, all round the walled town. They held forts and towers—*bastilles*. Thus the usual idea of a besieged town completely ringed by a strong and unbroken line of the enemy is, at any rate in the case of Orleans, misleading in the extreme. The only true picture to draw is a picture of fortifications at stated though irregularly spaced intervals, with undefended gaps in between. They gave nicknames to these fortifications in very much the same way as other English soldiers gave nicknames during a much grimmer war. Thus the *Bastille des Douze Pierres* at Orleans was familiarly known as London, the *Bastille du Pressoir Ars* as Rouen, and the *Bastille de Saint Pouair* as Paris. The French, too, in a kind of prophecy of *la grosse Bertha*, had their pet names for both their own cannon and that of their enemies: when the great English *Passevolant* flung its primitive ammunition, in the shape of one-hundred-pound balls of stone into the city, the French *Rifflard* replied. Another detail oddly recalls that other war. Much as the English and the German troops called an unofficial truce and played football in No Man's Land, so on Christmas Day, 1428, did the English send to the French commander to borrow a troupe of musicians. The Bastard of Orleans courteously responded, despatching *une note de haulx ménestriers, trompettes, et clarons*, who came and played to them for several hours, *faisans grant mélodie*. This truce, however, was of definite and brief duration, lasting only from nine in the morning till three o'clock in the afternoon, after which both parties *gecterent très fort et horriblement de bombardes et canons*.[1] The crash of stone balls again replaced the clear notes of the English carols.

It seems, at moments, to have been quite a friendly sort of siege. Perhaps war, then as now, was too serious a thing to be taken seriously all the time. Men had to have their jokes, in order to be able to endure it at all. Perhaps international hatred is never so deep-rooted as the love of the dangerous game. Anyhow, we find not only the English borrowing an orchestra

[1] *Procès*, Vol. IV, p. 105: *Journal du siège d'Orléans*.

from their enemies on Christmas Day, but the Bastard himself sending a warm fur to the Earl of Suffolk in exchange for a plate of figs.

One wonders how the Bastard addressed his fur coat to Lord Suffolk, for English names bothered the French considerably. Suffolk himself appears as Chuffort in the Bastard's own deposition, and his family name de la Pole rather naturally becomes La Poule. But even these were more fortunate attempts than some others. Sir Robert Willoughby is scarcely recognisable or pronounceable as de Wlbi, or Lord Poynings, who could take his choice of names between the seigneur de Bumus or de Pougnis. Falconbridge becomes Fouquembergue; Hungerford gets transformed into Hougue Foie. Gethyn defeated them completely, and Mathew Gough appeared to them more acceptable as Matago.

iii

The readjustment of our ideas as to the closeness and efficiency of the siege must be supplemented by a constant recollection of the small scale and clumsy conditions of mediæval war. Thus when Jeanne arrived at Orleans on April 29th the garrison, according to a careful computation, probably consisted of some three thousand men. By the time her reinforcements were complete, she could dispose of perhaps five or six thousand. The civil population of Orleans amounted to something like thirty thousand souls, of whom perhaps five thousand were men capable of taking part in the defence. We thus get ten to eleven thousand men under arms. The English, on their side, could throw about the same number into the field.[1] Hand-to-hand fighting being inevitable where no long-distance weapons existed, other than stones or arrows, personal protection became a matter of the greatest importance, and contributes enormously to our impression of an inelegant, bulky, and spear-streaked *mêlée* in which each man was struggling for himself. The weapons both of defence and offence were

[1] Jollois, *Histoire du siège d'Orléans*, pp. 42–6.

correspondingly primitive. On the one hand you had the defenders relying principally upon their towers, their high walls, their deep moats or *fosses* both dry and wet; commanding any path of approach not only by archers and cross-bow men sheltering behind the battlements, but also by enormous pieces of complicated machinery capable of launching great balls of stone to crash down on the heads of the attacking party. The size of these machines and their ammunition of course varied; but some formidable details are on record; thus, the account-books of Orleans prove that when the cannon mounted on the Tour St. Paul was demolished, twenty-six waggons were necessary to remove its wooden framework, and when the town of Montargis lent the cannon known as the *Rifflard* to Orleans, twenty-two horses were required to drag it up to the Hôtel de Ville. The missiles projected by these monsters were of accordant size. The *Rifflard* itself could throw a stone weighing a hundred and twenty pounds; and other cannon balls, presumed to have been flung against the city by the English, are now peacefully resting on the paving-stones of Orleans with estimated weights varying from seventy to ninety-four kilogrammes, and a circumference of a metre to nearly a metre and a half. They were all of stone, for it was only in the succeeding reign that iron balls were substituted. An especially hard stone was chosen for projectiles to be used against walls or masonry; a softer stone could be used for projectiles intended only to crack the human skull.[1] Although Orleans boasted of seventy-one cannon and *bombardes*, they seem to have been singularly ill-served, for only twelve master-gunners were provided, some of them, but not all, with an assistant. It thus seems fair to presume that all the *bouches à feu* could not be in action at the same time, but only those stationed on the threatened section of the defences, wherever that happened to be. The gunners could move round although their engines could not. We must

---

[1]This softer stone appears to have sometimes been too soft to achieve its purpose; witness the one which broke to pieces on Jeanne's helmet (see p. 221, *infra*).

not, however, forget the more mobile culverins or miniature cannon which (it is thought) were of very recent invention and which were employed almost for the first time at the siege of Orleans. As they weighed only ten to twelve pounds, they could readily be carried from place to place.

The French had a wag amongst them, in charge of a culverin; he was called Maître Jehan, and was a compatriot of Jeanne, whom he followed faithfully until the Burgundians took her prisoner at Compiègne. This wag, who had made a "hide" for himself and his weapon inside one of the piers of a bridge over the Loire, was in the habit of shooting his projectiles with great accuracy to the equally great detriment of the English. Every now and again, in order to make fun of the English, who were watching him with apprehension from their towers of fortification, he would emerge to throw himself down on the ground in the pretence of being either dead or wounded, and would even get himself carried back into the city, presumably on a stretcher, only to return later to his culverin in order to teach the English that he was still alive and active, to their great harm and displeasure,[1] a piece of Gallic wit which the English were unable to appreciate.

iv

The rude equipment of those ensconced behind their walls finds its counterpart in the equipment of the attacking party. Armed with lances, swords, leaden maces, and that particularly damaging weapon the *guisarme* or battle-axe, which could first smash through armour with its hatchet-blade and then turn itself round to dig into the flesh with its sharp iron spike, they advanced to the assault under cover of large wooden shields known as *pavas* or *pavois*.[2] One's usual idea of a shield is of a buckler held before the chest and body. The French

---

[1] *Procès*, Vol. IV, p. 105: *Journal du siège d'Orléans*.

[2] *Histoire du siège d'Orléans*, p. 12 and footnote. M. Jollois suggests that the *pavois* was an invention of the period of the siege of Orleans, and is obliged to go back to ancient Thebes before meeting with any similar device.

pavois was not like that at all. Far from being carried before the chest, it was worn upon the back, so that its wearer might creep or run forward in a stooping position, relatively safe-guarded from any shower of stones, arrows, or boiling oil which the enemy might see fit to send down upon him from above. Its construction was as simple as that of an ordinary barrel; and indeed if we can imagine a barrel sawn perpendicularly in half, covered over with stout leather, reinforced by two hoops, and fitted with two leather straps nailed on the inside, through which the arms were slipped to the shoulder, and can further imagine that this contrivance must be large enough to cover not only the buttocks and back but also the head of its wearer, we shall form some idea of what a mediæval attacking party looked like. It must have looked like a battalion of giant tortoises advancing under their shells. Ladders or lances must have looked very queer, sloping, and thin, sticking out from under the cover of such horizontal and convex forms. The *pavois* had the advantage of leaving both hands free, whether to carry scaling-ladders or to cling to the rungs of those ladders once they had been set against the walls. It left the hands free, in-deed, for any use; even for the final desperate use of scattering *chausse-trappes* in the path of a pursuant enemy in cases of repulse. These *chausse-trappes* or calthrops were always carried: four-spiked iron balls which, flung behind one, would lame a horse in the soft frog of his foot, or cause the running feet of dismounted men to stumble in avoidance and thus delay their chase—an elementary device, but efficacious; so efficacious as on one occasion to catch the miraculous Pucelle in person.

The register of warlike engines, both large and small, is sufficiently impressive, and the smallness of their execution correspondingly surprising. Our modern ideas of warfare must, in fact, be looked at through the wrong end of the telescope before we can get things into their proper proportion. This applies to the casualties as well as to the general effective. It seems strange that large lumps of stone hurtling through the air, massive enough to knock a breach through a solid wall, not to speak of showers of bolts and arrows, should have done as little damage as they did, even allowing for the armour or mail or leather which protected the combatants. Yet the chroniclers are frequently at pains to record such insignificant losses as *un seigneur d'Angleterre*, or a woman killed by mistake, or an English soldier who had tumbled into a well, where he was despatched by the French; this on a day of *grosse escarmouche*. Such statistics and details tend somewhat to diminish our respect for mediæval battles and even for Jeanne's achievement. Compared with modern warfare, heavy artillery, shells, barrage, gas, mines, tanks, and all the ingenious resources of progress and civilisation, the poor cumbersome contraptions of the fifteenth century—the huge wooden shields, scaling-ladders, faggots, culverins, bows and arrows, cross-bows—suggest a picture by Mr. Heath Robinson rather than an engagement in which desperate men intended to fight to the death. Yet it must be remembered that the personal element was much more dominant for each man concerned. He was in no danger of being suddenly blown to bits by an unseen gun a couple of miles away. He could dodge the stone; if he was very quick, he could even dodge the arrow. The men who ordered his fate were not vague tiny figures sticking pins into a map at a distant G.H.Q. On the other hand he was quite likely to be tumbled backwards off a ladder by the fist of an enemy thrust against his face, and the men in the highest positions of command were equally likely to be fighting by his side, as sweaty, gasping, and exhausted as he. In such conditions, where half the battle was hand-to-hand, concentrated into a small space, the spirit and example of the leader counted for much. When we remember this, it becomes easier to understand the astonishing effect of Jeanne's presence upon the French troops. Her position as a leader was a unique one. She was not a professional soldier; she was not really a soldier at all; she was not even a man. She was ignorant of war. She was a girl dressed up. But she believed, and had made others willing to believe, that she was the mouthpiece of God.

v

On Friday, April 29th, 1429, the news spread in Orleans that a force, led by the Pucelle of Domremy, was on its way to the relief of the city, a piece of news which, as the chronicler remarks, comforted them greatly.

The army had, in fact, left Blois on the 27th, the priests going ahead intoning the *Veni Creator Spiritus*,[1] the long train of horsemen, men-at-arms, waggons, and four hundred head of cattle stringing out along the road behind them. It was a great moment for Jeanne. She had got her forces at last—three to four thousand men following her. Jean de Metz and Poulengy were still with her; they were familiar companions; they had believed in her from the first—they had accompanied her on that precarious journey from Vaucouleurs to Chinon. On that journey, they had ridden on either side of her horse in the desire to escort and protect her; then, she was nothing but a girl dependent upon their chivalry; now, she was officially the envoy of the Dauphin, as well as the self-appointed envoy of the Lord. Her brothers had joined her too: Pierre and Jean, those same brothers who had been told by their father to drown their sister rather than allow her to "go with soldiers." Besides these, she had some of the most distinguished names of France in her company; she was riding in the midst of famous captains: the maréchal de Sainte-Sévère; the maréchal de Rais[2]; Louis de Culen, Admiral of France; Ambroise de Loré, and the formidable Gascon, Etienne de Vignolles, known as La Hire.[3]

Although she was not actually in command of the army, as is frequently and erroneously supposed, but was merely under the escort of these men, she conducted herself from the first in her usual high-handed manner. She interfered with them, not on military but on personal grounds. First she made them all go to confession, and then decreed that all their loose women should be left behind, two edicts which must have

[1]*Procès*, Vol. III, p. 105: Deposition of Jean Paquerel.
[2]This is Gilles de Rais, of infamous memory.
[3]*Procès*, Vol. III, p. 4: Deposition of Dunois.

astonished them considerably, but which they nevertheless obeyed. She had them all under her control, the only woman now left riding with those thousands of rough men, not even officially their leader. La Hire, least tractable of soldiers, was forced to forgo his habit of violent swearing, though as a concession he was allowed to use Jeanne's own two favourite exclamations: *en nom Dieu* and *par mon martin!*—which must, to him, have seemed very like a cup of milk to a man pining for strong drink. La Hire emerges out of the crowd as a definite personality. Whatever we know of him is all very much of a piece. His oaths and his prayers fit together. He swore and he prayed. When he prayed, his prayer was almost in the nature of an oath, it was almost in the nature of a threat to God: *"Sire Dieu, je te prie de faire pour La Hire ce que La Hire ferait pour toi si tu étais capitaine et si La Hire était Dieu."*

Even his jokes have their personal flavour. It was he who nicknamed Aymert de Puiseux, a French page, *Capdorat,* partly because he was very brave and alert and partly because his hair was so golden.[1] It was he, again, who made the bold and memorable answer to Charles VII: *"Je pense,"* he said to the King, *"que l'on ne sçauroit perdre son royaume plus gaiment,"* on one occasion when he had come to ask the King for some important decision, and had been put off by Charles consulting him as to the preparations for a fête.[2] La Hire evidently had no patience with the frivolities of a Charles VII, when a Jeanne d'Arc was in the offing.

vi

They slept in the fields, the first night on the way from Blois. Jeanne, unaccustomed to the weight of the armour which she refused to remove, awoke bruised and weary.[3] But they were drawing nearer to Orleans and the spirit counted for more than the body. The second night, that is, Thursday 28th, they

[1] *Procès,* Vol. IV, p. 143: *Journal du siège d'Orléans.*
[2] *Nouvel abrégé chronologique de l'histoire de France.*
[3] *Procès,* Vol. III, p. 67: Deposition of Louis de Contes.

encamped opposite the Ile Saint Loup, little more than a mile beyond Orleans, on the south bank of the Loire. It was then that Jeanne discovered that she had been, as she thought, tricked. A great deal of ink has been spilt in trying to decide how far and how intentionally the captains had tricked her; for my own part I do not believe that they had intended to trick her at all.

This was the position (if the reader will refer to the map facing p. 160, I think it will readily become clear):

Blois and Orleans both lie on the Loire with a distance of thirty-four miles between them. Orleans, however, lay entirely on the north bank; therefore in order to arrive there from Blois, the army had two alternative routes: the one on the north side, which would have allowed them to approach the city without having to cross the river; the other on the south side, which would entail the use of boats and bridges. On the face of it, it seems inexplicable that the captains should have chosen the south side, with the dangerous necessity of transporting a large force and all their supplies by a water-way involving slow sailing-boats or pontoon-bridges linking the opposite shores with the help of sandy islets. Still, choose it they did, and on her arrival Jeanne to her great disgust found herself with the river between herself and her enemies. There were reasons, of course, for a choice which otherwise seems so inexplicable, and those reasons may be very briefly stated by saying that the English positions were far stronger and more numerous on the north, west, and south sides than on the east, and that in the neighbourhood of the Ile Saint Loup, where the army was brought to a halt, the English positions were especially weak. What strikes us as odd is that they should not have explained their reasons quite simply to Jeanne when they saw her beginning to get into one of her tempers. Why, after all, should they have wanted to trick her, once having accepted her as their hope and their salvation? If she had really expected to be led through la Beauce (that is to say, on the north side), instead of through la Sologne (on the south), why on earth should they not have trusted her with the reasons for their decision? Was it because they regarded her as a religious inspiration rather than as a military commander? She held, after all, no official command. Was it because, haughtily but not unnaturally, these experienced captains saw no obligation to admit this totally inexperienced girl into their councils, although they were quite prepared to indulge her whims by going to confession on her demand and even by dismissing the disreputable women from their ranks? Was it because they regarded her as a sort of mascot rather than as a soldier like themselves? Was it merely because they already knew the danger of entering into argument with so intransigent a personality and thought the only chance of keeping her quiet was to keep her in the dark? Or was it that Jeanne herself had displayed no interest whatsoever in her route, being by now confident that she was being led straight towards Talbot and his English? Was it, finally, because they regarded themselves less as a relieving force than as an armed escort to the valuable provisions they were taking to the necessitous Orleans? They were, undeniably, so much encumbered that they could scarcely have risked a sudden swoop from the English on the road through la Beauce. The road through la Sologne, though less heroic, was much safer. I think any, or several, of these explanations may be true. But that they deliberately tricked her with malicious intent I find hard to believe.

Jeanne, however, was very angry indeed. It was pouring with rain; it was a stormy day; it was late; she was tired; her armour hurt her; and she was disappointed. She had expected to find herself under the very walls of Orleans, with nothing but the English between her and the accomplishment of her dream, instead of which these men whom she had trusted had landed her on the wrong side of a large river, with, so far as she could see, nothing but further delays and difficulties in her way. The Bastard of Orleans, hastily crossing the river in a small boat to greet her on her arrival—for he was as anxious to see her as were the people of Orleans—met with a very poor reception. Jeanne was no respecter of persons. It did not affect her in the least that the Bastard should be in command of the very city she had come to relieve; that his goodwill should be of such vital importance to her; that he should be of royal blood, the first cousin of her own Dauphin, the half-brother of her especial charge the captive Duke of Orleans, and the half-uncle by marriage of her beloved Alençon; that he should already be the Bastard of Orleans, whereas she was not yet its Pucelle. Nor did she stop to reflect that it was very gracious of him to come in person to receive her. Her opening words to him were anything but gracious. He himself has left a report of them. "Jeanne spoke in the following terms: 'Is it you who are the Bastard of Orleans?' 'I am, and I rejoice in your arrival.' Then she said, 'Is it you who advised them to bring me here by this bank of the river, instead of sending me straight to Talbot and his English?' I replied that I, and others wiser than myself, had given this advice, believing it to be the best and wisest. Then Jeanne spoke in these terms, '*En nom Dieu!* the counsel of Our Lord is wiser and better than yours. You thought to deceive me, but you have deceived yourselves, for I bring you the finest help that ever was brought to knight or to city, since it is the help of the King of Heaven.' "[1]

The poor Bastard must have been in great perplexity. The whole of Orleans was feverishly awaiting the Maid, and he

---

[1] *Procès*, Vol. III, p. 5: Deposition of Dunois. The Bastard of Orleans was later known as comte de Dunois, but as he did not come into possession of this title until later, he will not be referred to as Dunois here except in footnote references. Bastardy was regarded as no disgrace to such scions of royal or noble houses: the Bastard of Orleans himself, at the age of twelve, had rejected his official father, a certain wealthy Aubert le Flamenc, seigneur de Chauny or Canny; had voluntarily forgone his inheritance, and had declared that he would henceforth be known only as Bastard of Orleans. He had, in fact, been adopted by Valentina Visconti, widow of his true father, Louis Duke of Orleans, and brought up with her own children. Of course, for the Dauphin the case of illegitimacy was different, involving, as it did, the question of succession to the throne.

could not afford to alienate her. Besides, he himself believed in her; was it not largely due to his efforts that she had arrived at Orleans at all? And, now that she had arrived, he confronted no soft saintly girl, but a stern and angry young captain with very definite ideas of her own. Luckily, as soon appears from subsequent events, he was possessed of a certain instinctive skill in managing her. He needed all the skill he possessed, for there were complications which Jeanne had not taken into consideration; which nobody, indeed, could have taken into consideration unless they had been familiar with the place, or furnished with excellent maps, or in close and constant touch with those upon the spot. Jeanne had enjoyed none of these advantages; it is far more probable that she had formed no practical idea of Orleans at all before arriving there, and had thought of it in her simple faith as a second Jericho whose walls would fall before the trumpet-blast of her Lord. She had made some such declaration at Poitiers, saying that the siege would be raised and the city liberated after she had made her demand in the name of God. The Bastard took a more practical view. He had formed a plan which in appearance was a sound and simple one. He had intended to borrow boats from the citizens and to sail them up-stream as far as Chécy, a village on the north bank about five miles distant from Orleans. The cattle and provisions were meanwhile to await the arrival of the boats opposite Chécy, and were to be fetched by them on the following morning, when they were to be transported across the river and driven down towards Orleans, entering the town by the east gate or Porte de Bourgogne. This side of the town was the least strongly defended, as can readily be seen by another reference to the map. The English held only one fort on that side, the Bastille de Saint Loup, and it had been calculated that the French garrison, issuing from the Porte de Bourgogne with the support of the citizens, would suffice to hold the garrison of Saint Loup in check while the train of cattle passed into the town. It reads almost from the Bastard's account, as though he had no thought of

attempting actually to relieve the town by force of arms until
he had been able to re-victual it, a sensible and prudent course
which, at best, could not have accorded at all with Jeanne's
ideas. Unfortunately for the Bastard, even this sensible and
prudent course went wrong. It went wrong for two reasons.

For one thing, he and his fellow-commanders were forced
to the conclusion that the relieving force which had just
arrived was wholly inadequate to oppose to the English resistance. For another thing, and far more importantly, it
proved impossible to take the boats up the river. The wind
was blowing in the wrong direction. That was a factor beyond
all human calculation or control.

They tried to explain this to Jeanne. She would only reply by
telling them to wait a little, all would be well.[1] And suddenly,
inexplicably, the wind changed.

vii

In spite of this dramatic event, which enabled them to pass
the English fort and up the river in safety, Jeanne's difficulties
were not yet at an end. True, her reputation had gone up at a
bound, for her prophecy about the wind had very naturally
impressed the Bastard and his friends, but there still remained
the practical obstacle that the army was not considered
sufficient to encounter the English in battle. Indeed, it seems
unlikely that either the Bastard or the captains had ever
regarded it otherwise than as a convoy for the cattle and the
waggons. Having accomplished its mission, the Bastard wanted
it to return to Blois. At the same time, he wanted Jeanne to
stay behind and to accompany him into Orleans. Orleans was
very anxious to see Jeanne. Now that the sails were filled
with wind, he begged her to cross the Loire with him and
the Grand-Prior of France, Nicolas de Giresme. This
suggestion seems to have distressed her considerably, and for
the most unexpected reason. It was not that she resented

[1]*Procès*, Vol. IV, p. 218: *Chronique de la Pucelle;* and *Procés*, Vol. III, p. 6:
Deposition of Dunois.

the dismissal of her army; it was not that she feared that their disappearance would diminish her chance of relieving Orleans; no, she seems to have forgotten all about Orleans at the moment, and to have thought only of her own reluctance to separate herself from her troops, who were all confessed, repentant, and animated by good feelings. Really, what a strange character the Bastard must have thought her! Here she was within reach of Orleans at last; having worried Baudricourt, the Dauphin, and the Court of Poitiers into allowing her to go there; having spoken in and out of season of her divine mission to relieve the town; having even induced the elements to alter their arrangements in order to oblige her, and now she only wanted to go away again, all because she refused to be separated from an army which she had persuaded into a state of grace! What could the Bastard have made of such a girl? Certainly his opinion of her religious convictions may have grown, but he cannot have thought any better of her as a military authority. Curiously enough, the captains who had brought her all that way seemed equally reluctant to part with her; the Bastard had to beg and require of them that they should allow her to enter Orleans, while they themselves returned to Blois, crossed the river by the bridge there,[1] and made their way back to Orleans by the northern road. His diplomacy succeeded; he got the captains to add their persuasion to his—"Jeanne," they said, "go in surety, for we promise to return to you before long,"[2] and Jeanne finally also relented, coming towards him with her standard in her hand.[3] They crossed and spent the night at Chécy. It was his first experience of managing his saint, but not the last; a few days later she was telling him that she would have his head off if he did not do as she demanded.

A queer little experience seems to have befallen Jeanne at

[1]The bridge at Blois was the nearest by which they could have crossed, all the others being in the hands of the English.
[2]*Procès*, Vol. IV, p. 219: *Chronique de la Pucelle.*
[3]*Procès*, Vol. III, p. 7: Deposition of Dunois.

Chécy or at Reuilly near Chécy, the night before she entered Orleans. She spent the night, it appears,[1] in the house of a certain Gui de Cailly, a local seigneur whose name would scarcely deserve to be rescued from oblivion, save that he has been mentioned as the only person who ever shared in the visions of Jeanne d'Arc. Some verisimilitude is given to the story by the fact that Charles VII ennobled the said Gui de Cailly a few months later (June 1429) in a document couched in the strangest language of fantasy and heraldry combined.

Jeanne entered Orleans on a white horse, in full armour, her standard borne before her. She rode at the Bastard's right hand. They were followed by many knights, squires, captains, and soldiers, a crowd of citizens bringing up the rear. Other soldiers and citizens came to meet her, both men, women, and children, carrying a great number of torches—for it was already eight o'clock in the evening—and rejoicing as though God had come amongst them. It seemed to them as though the siege were already raised; and such was the press round her, as they tried to touch her or her horse, that a torch set fire to her pennant. At this, Jeanne struck spurs into her horse, turning it with great skill and herself extinguishing the flame. Their admiration knew no bounds, and they escorted her with acclamation right across the city from east to west, from the Porte de Bourgogne to the Porte Regnart, where a lodging had been arranged for her in the house of the treasurer of the Duke of Orleans.[2]

---

[1]Mathieu de Goussancourt, *Martyrologe des chevaliers de St. Jean de Jerusalem;* Le Brun des Charmettes, *Histoire de Jeanne d'Arc,* Vol. II, p. 18.

[2]*Procès,* Vol. IV, pp. 152–3: *Journal du siège.* Lest this account of Jeanne's entry into Orleans should be suspected of being fanciful, I append the original French: *A huyct heures au soir, malgré tous les Angloys, qui oncques n'y mirent empeschement aucun, elle y entra armée de toutes pièces, montée sur ung cheval blanc; et faisoit porter devant elle son estandart, qui estoit pareillement blanc, ouquel avoit deux anges tenans chacun une fleur de liz en leur main; et ou panon estoit paincte comme une Annonciacion (c'est l'image de Nostre-Dame avant devant elle ung ange luy presentant ung liz).*

Elle ainsi entrant dedans Orléans, avoit à son cousté senestre le bastart d'Orléans,

Once the door had shut behind her, she made them disarm her, and indeed she must have been longing for that moment, for, apart from the emotions she had undergone, it is related that she had spent the day without either eating or drinking. Supper had been prepared for her, but she accepted only a little wine in a silver cup, which she filled up with water and into which she dipped five or six sops of bread. After which she went to bed, where she had for company Charlotte, the daughter of the treasurer, a child of nine.[1]

One hopes that this much-honoured child observed the rules that children were then taught to observe when sharing a bed; to keep to their own side, not to fidget, and to sleep with their mouths shut.[2]

viii

It is tempting to pause at this point and to survey the position and frame of mind of the various parties concerned. Jeanne, the Bastard, the townsfolk of Orleans, and the English commanders, all held their different points of view as they went to their beds on that night of April 29th when the jubilation had died down and the torches had been extinguished. Jeanne, as we know, was tired, but at any rate she was in the place where she had most ardently desired to be. True, she had met with an irritating check on her arrival, but God had come to

armé et monté moult richement. Et aprez venoyent plusieurs autres nobles et vaillans seigneurs, escuyers, cappitaines et gens de guerre, sans aucuns de la garnison, et aussy des bourgoys d'Orléans, qui luy estoyent allez au devant. D'autre part, la vindrent recevoir les autres gens de guerre, bourgoys et bourgoyses d'Orléans, portans grant nombre de torches, at faisans autel joye comme se ilz veissent Dieu descendre entre eulx.

[1] *Procès*, Vol. IV, p. 219: *Chronique de la Pucelle*. The *Chronique* also states that she had spent the whole day on horseback without dismounting, but this must be an inaccuracy, as it cannot have taken her more than two hours to ride from Chécy. On the other hand, the statement that she dipped sops of bread in wine mixed with a great deal of water as her only refreshment during a whole day is supported by the Bastard, although on a different day (*Procès*, Vol. III, p. 9: Deposition of Dunois).

[2] Franklin, *La vie privée d'autrefois*, Vols. II and XIX, *passim*.

her rescue, and had sent a sign from Heaven at the most opportune moment. She could not help knowing that she was established in the minds of thousands as something inspired from above; as the true envoy of God. No personal vanity entered into this knowledge, for she had never doubted it herself; her only difficulty had lain in getting her fellow-countrymen to accept so manifest and undeniable a fact. Her own faith in her mission and in the support of her great Ally had never wavered for an instant; the change of wind had come to her as no surprise, but simply as a thing which was bound to happen, God being on her side. It was convenient, partly because it enabled the boats to get across, partly because it startled the Bastard and his companions and reinforced their belief; it was convenient certainly, but it was no more than might have been expected. God meant her to carry out His divine pleasure; God was omnipotent; God had changed the wind.

With this childlike trust in her heart, she was almost equally confident that next day the English also would listen to the voice of God as represented by the letter she had so carefully brought with her. She would send that letter to them, giving them every opportunity for a peaceful withdrawal before she set about chasing them away by force of arms. Some remnant of her native common sense suggested to her that possibly the English would not be quite so amenable as the wind to the voice of God; the wind was an element under the direct rule of God; the English were a reasoning people, endowed by God Himself with the quality of free will; they might refuse to turn and scamper; they might refuse to go away into their own country, as she was requesting them to do. In that eventuality she was ready to fight. But even her idea of fighting was closely mixed up with her religion. She had been extremely reluctant to allow her chastened and well-confessed army to depart towards Blois, and nothing but their assurance that they would soon return to her had induced her to let them out of her sight; as it was, she had sent her own

N

confessor, Jean Paquerel, to accompany them. It was a sacrifice to let him go, for she depended on him greatly for Masses and frequent confession, but the needs of the army must come first. Perhaps it was some consolation to her as she lay in the dark in the unfamiliar room at Orleans, with the child's small body discreetly stretched beside her, to reflect that that man of God would watch over those three thousand men whom she had persuaded into a state of grace, and who were even then retracing their steps along the road she had just travelled.

As for what she thought of the prospect of possible battle for herself, she already knew that she would suffer. She had predicted her wound to the Dauphin; she had predicted it to her confessor, Paquerel. The prophecy is beyond doubt and seems to have been a matter of fairly common knowledge, for on the 12th of April,[1] nearly a month before the event, a Flemish envoy living at Lyon wrote a letter home to Brussels describing in detail the occasion on which Jeanne knew she would be wounded. Prophecies thus recorded in advance cannot be disputed. They depend neither on hearsay, nor on falsified memory, nor on subsequent legend, but on the blunt testimony of the written, dated word. Legends sprouting like tropical growths quickly hung themselves in garlands round Jeanne's neck, almost strangling her, and making it very difficult for her to distinguish between what she knew to be false and what she believed to be true. Lying in bed at Orleans on the night of April 29th, she knew some things for certain. She knew she would relieve the siege; she knew she would be hurt; she knew she would not die. She knew she would lead her Dauphin to Reims for the supreme ceremony of his coronation, a consummation overdue for seven years, since Charles VII had succeeded his father in 1422. She knew all

[1]J. Quicherat, *Aperçus nouveaux sur Jeanne d'Arc,* and *Procès,* Vol. IV, p. 426. Quicherat, contrary to his usual scholarly habit, contradicts himself as to the date of the letter. In the *Aperçus nouveaux* he says April 12th; in the *Procès* he says April 22nd. In either case, the letter was written some time before Jeanne received her wound.

these things, because her voices had told her about them, and her voices were not to be discounted or disbelieved. Lying in bed at Orleans that night, she must have reviewed these future things quite simply as things ordained and consequently inevitable. Probably the idea of being wounded in her physical body was no more alarming to her than the idea of the great responsibility of pushing a weak and reluctant Dauphin into an overwhelmingly historical cathedral. These things lay before her. She had been told about them by her voices. They were part of the future. To people like Jeanne, there is not very much difference between the future and the past. One thing melts into the other. The ordinary rules cease to apply.

The Bastard, a practical man for all his gallantry and charm, must have felt somewhat appalled if he lay awake in bed reviewing the events of the day. True, he was partly responsible for bringing Jeanne to Orleans, but, having brought her there, he must have realised within the space of a few hours that she was going to prove something of a handful. She had shown no respect for him, either as a semi-royal prince or as a commander. She had no respect for military strategy or obligations. She had horrified him both by her unorthodoxy and her obstinacy. To the assumptions of a man she had added the unreasonableness of a woman. Yet it could not be denied that the weather itself had obeyed her, and that the common people in their worship had almost allowed themselves to be trampled underfoot by her horse. She had exhibited all the signs of an inspired being, certainly, but what was she going to prove like as a companion in arms? How was she going to be managed as a military collaborator? One might be prepared to believe in the voice of God speaking, but there were also other considerations, such as the lives of men for whom one was responsible. There were also one's colleagues, intemperate men who would not at all relish having their opinions over-ridden. I cannot believe that the Bastard went to sleep early that night.

The townsfolk of course were in a state of exaltation, produced partly by religious fervour and partly by mass-hysteria. Their deliverer was at last amongst them, and the end of their troubles in sight. Like sparks on stubble, the fire of enthusiasm had run across the crowd. They blazed; but with a blaze that could not be put out with blood. The fire kindled in Orleans that night was not to be extinguished during the week that followed, nor were the red embers of gratitude and veneration to cool for many years.

The English within their fortifications alone remain inscrutable, undiscernible, and taciturn.

Chapter X

ORLEANS (2)

i

When they all awoke on the morning of Saturday, April 30th, the paramount question in everybody's mind was, What was to happen next? We might well expect to find that Jeanne's arrival would prove the signal for a renewed and desperate attempt on the part of the French to drive away their besiegers: after all, both the garrison and the citizens were whipped up into a readiness for any effort, and the Bastard might well have taken advantage of their inspired excitement to fling them in full force against the English forts. Quite on the contrary, the presence of the Pucelle produced a lull lasting for four days. There were several excellent reasons for this. In the first place, the Pucelle herself—who, to put it mildly, had to be reckoned with—was determined to deliver her summons to the English before embarking on hostilities.[1] In the second place, the Bastard, having sent the army back to Blois, now began to feel anxious lest it should return to Orleans insufficiently reinforced. He had therefore come to the conclusion that he must ride to Blois in person to supervise this all-important matter; perhaps there was even a sneaking and quite justifiable fear at the back of his mind that the army might not, if he were not there to ensure it, return to Orleans at all. In any case, he very wisely hesitated to attack: no man in his senses would have gone to the supreme assault when a paltry delay of four days offered him a very good chance of obtaining reinforcements enough to tip the balance. La Hire and Florent d'Illiers were all for an immediate attack, but the wiser and more prudent Bastard put a brake on these Hotspurs. He had a very ticklish situation to deal with, as ticklish a situation as any man might be called upon to deal with. Reading the various accounts, our sympathy

[1] *Procès*, Vol. III, p. 7: Deposition of Dunois.

goes out to the Bastard. Not only had he to deal with that inexplicable character, the girl-boy-captain—La Pucelle—but he had to cope with such incidentally troublesome people as the sieur de Gamaches. The sieur de Gamaches lost his temper over the high tone taken by the Pucelle, and, as the sieur de Gamaches was one of the Bastard's recognised colleagues, the situation for the Bastard must have been extremely awkward. He was in the unenviable position of having to manage both the incalculable Pucelle and the calculable captains. The sieur de Gamaches took a perfectly understandable line. "Since you pay more heed," he said, "to the advice of a little saucebox (*péronelle*) of low birth than to a knight such as myself, I will no longer protest; when the time and the place come, my good sword will speak; I may meet my end in the doing, but the King and my honour demand it. Henceforth I lower my banner and am no longer anything more than a simple squire. I prefer to have a noble man as my master, rather than a hussy (*fille*) who may once have been God knows what." So saying, he furled his banner and handed it to the Bastard.[1] The captains, however, intervening, succeeded in calming him down and in persuading him and Jeanne to kiss one another on the cheek, which they both did with extreme reluctance.

It must have been very difficult for the Bastard to decide where he was most urgently needed, whether in Orleans to keep Jeanne in order or at Blois to encourage the army. Moreover, Jeanne was as disinclined to let him go as she had been disinclined to let her purified army disappear. The day of April 30th seems to have been spent largely in arguments between the Pucelle and the Bastard, arguments in which the Bastard's tact again prevailed, for we find him leaving for Blois on the following day. No account has come down to us of their discussions; we can judge only by the result.

[1] *Vie de Guillaume de Gamaches*. Jollois, *Histoire du siège d'Orléans*, p. 77, and *Procès*, Vol. IV, pp. 358-9. M. Quicherat, however, has the poorest opinion of the accuracy of this story.

In the meantime, the day of April 30th had not been solely occupied by the two principal protagonists sitting together in conference. La Hire and Florent d'Illiers with other officers of the garrison, and some of the townsfolk, went out to worry the English, and succeeded in driving them back into the fort they called Paris (Saint Pouair)—an engagement typical of what had been taking place for weeks and months past. Whether this was done with Jeanne's approval or not, we do not know. She took no part in it. She was probably talking to the Bastard while all this scrapping went on between the English fort and the city walls. The scrap threatened at one moment to develop into a serious affair, for they shouted loudly all through the city that everyone should bring straw and faggots to set fire to the English in their retreat; luckily for the English, they set up their war-cry of Hurrah! which had never failed to strike terror into the French, so neither faggot nor straw was brought, and the French retired under a salvo of cannon and culverins, after a skirmish in which several were killed, wounded, or made prisoner, both on one side and the other.[1]

There is no record of whether Jeanne knew what was going on while she was closeted with the Bastard. The moment had come when her ultimatum was to be delivered to Talbot. As I have already explained (Chapter VIII, pp. 152-4), some confusion exists as to what had actually happened to the letter to the English which she had dictated at Poitiers on March 22nd. Was it already in Talbot's hands when she arrived at Orleans, or was it not? We shall probably never know, nor shall we ever be able to disentangle satisfactorily the complex story of what happened to her various heralds. The only thing which seems certain is that on April 30th she did summon the English to depart in peace if they wished to avoid the *grans doumaiges* she would bring upon them in battle. The Bastard himself depones to this: "She wanted to summon the English to retire, before forcing them to raise the siege or going so far as to attack them.

[1] *Procès*, Vol. IV, p. 154: *Journal du siège d'Orléans.*

This, in effect, is what she did. She summoned them by means of a letter written in the maternal idiom, in very plain terms, informing them in substance that they should give up the siege and withdraw to England, otherwise she would deliver such an assault upon them that they would be constrained to depart. The letter was given to Talbot."[1]

That statement is clear and unequivocal; moreover, it tallies perfectly with the terms of the letter dictated at Poitiers. I think we may accept the Bastard's evidence in preference to that of the *Journal du siège*, which relates that she merely sent two heralds demanding the return of the herald she had sent with the letter from Blois, supported by a message from the Bastard that, failing the herald's safe return, he would put to death all those English whom he held as prisoners in Orleans. This would give a total of three heralds, whereas only two seem to have been concerned: Ambleville and Guienne, both of whom were sent out from Orleans with the letter on April 30th. Guienne was detained, thrown into irons, and a stake prepared to burn him. Ambleville, who was allowed to return, charged with rude messages to the effect that Jeanne had better go home and mind the cows, otherwise she would be caught and burnt, did not at all relish his mission when Jeanne told him to go back again and rescue his companion,[2] for the English captains had read Jeanne's letter with surprise and rage, calling her by every uncomplimentary name they could think of, notably *ribaude* and *vachère*, though we may well believe that their vocabulary was not limited to that.[3] Fortunately for her poor envoy, Guienne, they did, however, hesitate before putting their threat of burning him into practice. They knew that that was not the way to treat a

[1]*Procès*, Vol. III, p. 7: Deposition of Dunois. See also *Procès*, Vol. III, p. 126: Deposition of Pierre Millet.

[2]*Procès*, Vol. IV, p. 221: *Chronique de la Pucelle*, and *Procès*, Vol. III, pp. 26-7: Deposition of Jacques Lesbahi. The *Chronique* adds erroneously that Ambleville brought Guienne back with him.

[3]*Procès*, Vol. IV, p. 141: *Journal du siège d'Orléans*.

herald and despatched a messenger to the University of Paris, asking for authorisation. The delay saved his life, for before the answer could be received the English were in flight, leaving the waiting stake and the fettered Guienne to be rescued by the French as they poured victoriously into the abandoned fort.[1]

Still, Jeanne, although much annoyed (*fort yrée*), was not satisfied that she had done her utmost to avoid hostilities if she possibly could. So that evening she went in person on to the bridge, and from there shouted to Sir William Glasdale, the commander of the English fort called les Tourelles (see map, p. 160), that in God's name he should give himself and his companions up, and save their lives. The English shouted back. "Cowgirl!" they called her, as before; shouting loudly that they would burn her if they could catch her. On this occasion she was not annoyed at all; she simply replied that they were liars, and, having said that, withdrew into the city.[2]

It seems extraordinary that, in spite of all their threats of catching her, the English made no attempt whatsoever to do so. They had allowed her to enter Orleans unopposed. They allowed her to come right on to the bridge and shout at them across the river. It is true that when she went on to the bridge she had the protection of a French fort behind her and that a gap in the bridge separated her from the Tourelles, but all the same it seems inexplicable that they should have contented themselves with a flight of insults instead of a flight of arrows. Was it because, in their English arrogance and stupidity, they did not take her seriously? She was good enough to burn, but not good enough to bother much about. They

---

[1] *Procès*, Vol. IV, p. 42: Deposition of Jacques le Bouvier (le hérault Berri).

[2] *Procès*, Vol. IV, p. 155: *Journal du siège: Quant vint sur le soir, elle s'en ala au boulevert de la Belle Croix, sur le pont, et de là parla à Glacidas et autres Anglois estans ès Tourelles, et leur dist qu'ils se rendissent de par Dieu, leurs vies sauves seullement. Mais Glacidas et ceulx de sa rote respondirent villainement, l'injuriant et appelant vachère, comme devant, crians moult haut qu'ilz la feroient ardoir, s'ilz la povoient tenir. De quoy elle fut aucunement yrée, et leur respondit qu'ilz mentoyent; et ce dit, s'en retira dedans la cyté.*

made a mistake. Although in the end they caught and burnt her, they had by then paid dearly for their procrastination.

Their conduct during the three following days continues to be equally inexplicable. Not only did they allow the Bastard, accompanied by Jean d'Aulon, to set out for Blois on his recruiting mission (May 1st), but they allowed Jeanne and La Hire, with some troops, to ride out a certain distance with them to cover and protect their departure.[1] Why on earth the English did not attack the Bastard and the Pucelle on that occasion, passes my comprehension. They might have caught them both, and what a prize that would have been! Still further does it pass my comprehension to understand why they refrained from delivering a decisive assault on Orleans during the three succeeding days. They must have known that the Bastard was away. They must have known, if they had spies worth the name, that he had gone to Blois for the express purpose of fetching as large an army as he could possibly raise, with which he intended to return as quickly as possible. What an opportunity was theirs, had they only chosen to take it! Orleans, deprived of its commander, lay practically at their mercy. The Bastard, indeed, must have felt some qualms on leaving the problematical Pucelle and the reckless La Hire in virtual control of his carefully guarded city; still, it seemed more urgent to him to take the risk and to go and throw his weight in at Blois. He made his financial arrangements before taking his departure, signing a receipt for six hundred *livres tournois* that he had borrowed from the citizens to pay the wages of the garrison during his absence.

Jeanne and La Hire, having seen him off, returned into Orleans unmolested by the English. Jeanne, if she hoped for a quiet day in the retirement of the treasurer's house, did not get it. The people of Orleans were still in so great a state of excitement about her that they almost broke down the door of her lodging in their desire to see her. So she spent the rest of that Sunday riding through the streets of the city,

[1] *Procès*, Vol. III, p. 211: Deposition of Jean d'Aulon.

but could scarcely make any progress owing to the crowd of people insatiable for her presence. All the same, she managed her horse so well, and carried herself in so grand a manner, that they all marvelled at her, as though she had made a profession of arms and war from her youth upwards.[1]

Not content with this, she went once more to argue with the English. It was her third challenge; her fourth was to take a very different form. History does not relate whether the Bastard, plodding on his way to Blois, knew anything of her intention. He had left her behind and she was her own mistress. Neither Paquerel nor d'Aulon was there to restrain her. Paquerel had been sent off to look after the morals of the army; d'Aulon had been sent to look after the Bastard. La Hire, left more or less in charge, must have been puzzled and amused. Jeanne harangued the English in much the same terms as before, and, receiving much the same answer, retired as before, back into Orleans.[2] Thus, in this curious lull, passed Sunday.

On Monday, May 2nd, the English were still quiet within their fortifications. Jeanne rode out in a leisurely way to survey their positions. A crowd of people followed her, happy if they might see and surround their idol. When she had inspected the English defences to her heart's content, she went to hear vespers at the cathedral. That is all that we know of the events of May 2nd.

On May 3rd the garrisons of Gien, Montargis, Château Reynard, and Châteaudun began coming into Orleans, with

[1]*Procès*, Vol. IV, p. 155: *Journal du siège: Chevaucha par la cité Jehanne la Pucelle, accompaignée de plusieurs chevaliers et escuyers, parce que ceulx d'Orléans avoient si grant voulenté de la veoir, qu'ilz rompoient presque l'uys de l'ostel où elle estoit logée; pour laquelle veoir avait tant grant gent de la cité par les rues où elle passoit, que à grant peine y povoit on passer, car le peuple ne se povoit saouller de la veoir. Et moult sembloit à tous estre grant merveille comment elle se povoit tenir si gentement à cheval, comme elle faisoit. Et à la vérité aussi elle se maintenoit aussi haultement en toutes manières, comme eust sceu faire ung homme d'armes, suivant la guerre dès sa jonnesse.*

[2]*Procès*, Vol. IV, pp. 155–6: *Journal du siège d'Orléans.*

many men on foot, and towards evening the news was received that the army from Blois was on the way, under the command of the maréchal de Sainte-Sévère, the maréchal de Rais, the Norman baron de Coulonces, and monseigneur de Bueil. They were coming by the northern road, through la Beauce, though it is usually supposed that the convoy of supplies, under a separate escort, was making its way by the southern route, as previously on April 28th.[1] In order to guard against any surprise attack, a sentry mounted guard night and day in the belfry of Saint Pierre Empont; when the danger was especially pressing, as now, a second sentry kept watch on the tower of Saint Paul. It was thus possible for a message to be sent down into the town that the banners and lances of an army could be seen advancing from far away.[2] At that moment the excitement in Orleans must have been great. No one knew what the English would do. Would they attack, or would they remain tamely within their forts, allowing the Dauphin's men to stream through the city gates without opposition? Jeanne was taking no risks. At dawn on the following morning, May 4th, the eve of Ascension, the army then being only a league away, she rode out *à estendart desployé*, with five hundred men, to meet them.

It is a little difficult to discover who was where on this occasion. In fact, the accounts of the different witnesses and chroniclers of Jeanne's history are sometimes so much at variance in their details that it turns into a sort of picture puzzle whose pieces refuse to fit. Where, for instance, was La Hire? The *Chronique de la Pucelle* says that he was with the army, which in any case is difficult to reconcile with the statement that he had been left in Orleans with Jeanne— unless, indeed, as is possible, he had ridden ahead to meet

[1] Jean Paquerel, however, says that the French were allowed to introduce the supplies into the town *sous les yeux des Anglais*. This, as the army entered by the northern gate, would indicate that they were escorting the supplies by the same route.

[2] Jollois, *Histoire du siège d'Orléans*, p. 78, note.

them. Jean d'Aulon also says that La Hire entered Orleans with them, but does not make it clear whether he had joined them earlier on their march or had come out with Jeanne. The *Journal du siège* and Jean Chartier both definitely say that he came out with Jeanne. More importantly, where was the Bastard? We know that he had gone to Blois on May 1st, meaning to return with the army, yet we find no mention of his name among the leaders of the army registered by the *Chronique*, which states, on the contrary, that he rode out with Jeanne to meet them, thus implying that he had hurried back to Orleans ahead of their slowly moving train. The *Chronique*, quoting the *Geste des Nobles*, must be in error. The *Journal* and Jean Chartier both agree that the Bastard was with the army.

We may take it, then, that Jeanne, at the head of her five hundred men, accompanied by the seigneur de Villars, Florent d'Illiers, Alain Giron, Jamet de Tilloy, and possibly also by La Hire,[1] left Orleans very early in the morning to meet the Bastard and the train that followed him. The English still took no notice whatsoever. They contented themselves with watching from afar, instead of falling in full force upon this relatively small company trailing across the open, undefended by wall, trenches, or fortifications. If they had had an ounce of sense in their stupid heads, they would first have fallen upon Jeanne and her five hundred; then upon the Bastard and his men. Instead of this, they allowed them to wend their way unmolested, with the priests chanting and Jean Paquerel bearing in their midst the banner which Jeanne had caused especially to be made for them.[2]

I fail entirely to understand what the English were about. The French, of course, explained it by saying that Jeanne had terrorised them; almost that she had cast a spell upon them.

[1]*Procès*, Vol. IV, p. 156: *Journal du siège d'Orléans.*
[2]*Procès*, Vol. III, p. 106: Deposition of Jean Paquerel.

ii

The day of May 4th was only just begun. They had entered Orleans *environ prime,* which means between six and seven in the morning. The day was young, and Orleans full of new troops, new food, and new hope. The morning seems to have been passed quietly. One may suppose that the new troops were finding their billets, and that the new supplies were being distributed—everybody, in short, too busy to think of fighting. Jeanne herself dined quietly with d'Aulon in the treasurer's house.

After dinner the Bastard came in. He had had information that Sir John Fastolf was on his way with support for the English and was already at Janville, a day's march from Orleans. Jeanne appeared delighted at this piece of news, though it is difficult to see why: perhaps by that time, tired of being insulted and treated with contempt, her blood was up and the more enemies she could rout, the better. She was at any rate determined that Fastolf should not slip through her fingers. "Bastard, Bastard," she said, "in God's name I order you to let me know as soon as you hear of Fastolf's coming, for if he passes without my knowledge, I promise you that I will have your head off." The Bastard, who from the first had known how to treat her, and had never taken offence at her blunt words, answered reassuringly: she need have no anxiety on that point, for he would surely let her know.[1] He then went away. I imagine that he knew what was going on just outside the town, although Jeanne and d'Aulon did not.

Jeanne, who had got up early, was tired, and so, according to his own confession, was d'Aulon. They both went upstairs to rest,[2] d'Aulon lying down on a couch in Jeanne's room, Jeanne lying down on another bed with her hostess in order to rest and sleep. Poor d'Aulon, however, had only just settled down to rest, and was already half asleep, when Jeanne sprang up from

[1]*Procès,* Vol. III, p. 212: Deposition of Jean d'Aulon.

[2]That Jeanne's room was upstairs is apparent from the account given by Louis de Contes.

her bed and woke him. He asked her what she wanted; and perhaps it is not too fanciful to imagine that he was rubbing his eyes. From every account it is clear that she was in a state of great agitation. *"En nom Dieu,"* she replied, "my counsel has told me to go against the English, but I do not know whether I am to go against their forts or against Fastolf, who is on his way with supplies."[1]

At this point, the reading of the various accounts produces a kind of uproar in the head, much as the actual occasion must have produced an uproar in the treasurer's house. Jeanne was no peaceful guest. The witnesses become confused, and we are left with an impression of scared people running hither and thither, with Jeanne raging and storming in the midst of them. D'Aulon says that he got up at once, and armed her as quickly as he could. Louis de Contes, her little page, says that her hostess and the child Charlotte armed her. Jean Paquerel says that, as he arrived with some other priests, she was shouting, "Where are they, whose business it is to arm me? The blood of our people is reddening the ground." Meanwhile, there were shouts in the street below, saying that the enemy was doing great harm to the French. Jean d'Aulon, who was already hurrying into his armour as Jeanne ran downstairs, never noticed that she had left him.[2] Here she found Louis de Contes, who still believed her to be asleep in her room. *"Ha, sanglant garçon,"* she said to him, "you never told me the blood of France was being spilt," and sent him off post-haste to fetch her horse.[3]

When he returned she was waiting downstairs. She sent him

---

[1] *Procès*, Vol. III, p. 212: Deposition of Jean d'Aulon.

[2] *Procès*, Vol. III, p. 212: Deposition of Jean d'Aulon.

[3] *Procès*, Vol. III, p. 68: Deposition of Louis de Contes. Here, again, there is a slight confusion, for Louis de Contes says she came down to him *before* she had put on her armour, but was armed by the time he returned with her horse. Simon Beaucroix, Aignan Viole, a lawyer of Orleans, and Colette Millet, the wife of a clerk, all endorse the story of Jeanne's sudden uprising. Their versions differ very little from those of d'Aulon and Louis de Contes. According to Viole (*Procès*, Vol. III, p. 127), she exclaimed: *"En nom Dé, nos gens ont bien à besoigner.* Bring my arms and fetch my horse." Colette

up to fetch her banner, which for some unexplained reason he handed down to her through the window. One can only suppose that she was shouting impatiently for it in the street. Impatient she certainly was, and nobody moved quickly enough to please her; she was gone before d'Aulon could follow her,[1] and those who saw her go testified that she went at such a pace that her horse's hooves struck sparks from the pavement.[2]

Louis de Contes, who was evidently rather bewildered by all this flurry, was sent after her by her hostess. D'Aulon caught her up at the Porte de Bourgogne. Here they met a badly wounded man who was being carried in. Jeanne was much upset. After all, it was her first taste of real fighting. She stopped to ask who he was, and, on hearing that he was a Frenchman, exclaimed that she could never see French blood spilt without her hair rising on her head.[3] But she could not afford to wait, for a battle was taking place at the English stronghold of Saint Loup and she must be there. (Refer to the map facing p. 160.)

Again, it is difficult to determine whether the attack on Saint Loup had been delivered with or without her knowledge. The probability is that it had been delivered earlier than she expected.[4] Otherwise, she would scarcely have gone to rest,

---

Millet (*Procès*, Vol. III, p. 124) says that she called her page and said to him, "*En nom Dé*, this is ill done. Why was I not awakened earlier? Our people have much to do."

It must further be noted that Louis de Contes makes a mistake as to the date, placing these events on April 30th. It is quite obvious, however, that he is making a mere slip, and that he is really referring to May 4th. After a lapse of twenty-six years, such errors are understandable.

[1]*Procès*, Vol. III, pp. 212–13: Deposition of Jean d'Aulon.

[2]*Procès*, Vol. III, p. 124: Deposition of Colette Millet.

[3]*Procès*, Vol. III, p. 213: Deposition of Jean d'Aulon. Paquerel likewise testifies to the horror she experienced.

[4]On the other hand, Paquerel says that they went out at Jeanne's insistence to assail the English in the Bastille de Saint Loup. One wishes that these witnesses could agree better. It makes it terribly confusing for anybody who wants to discover what actually happened.

nor have sprung from her bed in such indignation and surprise. She may have agreed with the Bastard on the advisability of making such an attack, especially in view of the rapid advance of Fastolf, but she certainly did not expect it to take place so soon. When she got there, she found the affair in full swing. D'Aulon says that he had never yet seen so many French troops gathered together as on that occasion. Louis de Contes says that the English were preparing to defend themselves, but that the French, on seeing Jeanne, shouted in triumph and carried the fort.

This was the first time that the French had succeeded in capturing an English work. It was an important one, too, for it was the only one on that side of Orleans, protecting the road between Orleans and Jargeau, at that time occupied by an English garrison. There was now nothing to hinder the French from pouring supplies and reinforcements into Orleans by the eastern gate. They burnt and demolished the fort, killed a hundred and fourteen English soldiers, and carried off another forty as prisoners into the city. How absurdly small these numbers seem!—yet, if we compare them with other statistics of the siege, we see that the taking of the Bastille de Saint Loup ranked as an unusually serious engagement. Talbot himself seems to have recognised, either that his troops were demoralised, or that they were outnumbered, for having attempted a *sortie* from the Bastille de Saint Pouair, in order to come to the assistance of the garrison at Saint Loup, he very quickly withdrew on observing a force of six hundred Frenchmen advancing against him. Perhaps, by the time Talbot sat down that evening to think it over, he had begun to wonder whether the cowgirl was not to be taken seriously after all.

The cowgirl, characteristically, was more distressed by the death and discomfiture of her enemies than elated by the success of her friends. The religious aspect, again, was dominant in her mind. It distressed her to think that so many of the English should have died without going first to confession, especially on the eve of Ascension. She deplored their fate (*eos multum plangebat*), and, as though she held herself responsible, summoned Jean Paquerel to confess her there and then. Moreover, she ordered him to see to it that all the men-at-arms should also confess their sins and should render thanks to God for their victory. Otherwise, she said, she would leave them and would not remain in their company.[1] She further issued a proclamation, with trumpets, to the effect that no plundering was to take place in the church of Saint Loup.[2] It looks as though the English were already acquainted with her weakness, for it is related in the not very reliable *Chronique* that some of them climbed into the belfry and dressed themselves up in the priests' vestments, hoping, rightly as it proved, to escape with their lives. Jeanne intervened when her compatriots, less gullible than she, wanted to put them all to the sword: one should ask nothing of church people, she said, and caused them all to be brought safely into Orleans.[3]

All the church-bells of Orleans rang out to celebrate the victory, and Jeanne and the captains went to give thanks.[4]

iii

The next day being Ascension Day (Thursday, May 5th), Jeanne decreed that there should be no fighting. She confessed again, and received the Sacraments, and also issued a proclamation that no one should dare to emerge from the city next day to take part in an assault or to engage in battle, without having previously presented himself for confession; also that women of ill repute should be rigorously dismissed from the army; otherwise, she said, God would bring defeat on them by reason of their sins. Again she was obeyed.[5]

Apart from these religious and moral observances of the

[1] *Procès*, Vol. III, p. 107: Deposition of Jean Paquerel.
[2] *Procès*, Vol. III, pp. 124–6: Depositions of Colette and Pierre Millet.
[3] *Procès*, Vol. IV, p. 224: *Chronique de la Pucelle*.
[4] *Procès*, Vol. IV, p. 224: *Chronique de la Pucelle*.
[5] *Procès*, Vol. III, p. 107: Deposition of Jean Paquerel.

holy day, she also felt justified in turning their attention to more practical and war-like matters. These matters, on that day, did not go very happily for Jeanne. It is a curious and illuminating story; illuminating in so far as it illustrates the degree to which the French captains disregarded her as a member of their military council. That she should inspire their men by her presence was well enough, but it obviously never entered their heads that she should be admitted to their secret plans. Their behaviour on this and on other occasions disposes finally of the notion that she had in any way been put in command of the army. We cannot blame them. Her knowledge of military tactics was necessarily nil, and they were all hardened men. It is not very surprising to find that while the Bastard held a council of war in the very house where Jeanne had her lodging, she was excluded from their deliberations.

The Bastard, the maréchal de Rais, the maréchal de Sainte-Sévère, the chancellor, Cousinot, the sire de Graville, the sire de Gaucourt, Ambroise de Loré, the baron de Coulonces, the seigneur de Villars, Poton de Saintrailles, Denis de Chailly, Thibaut de Termes, Jamet de Tilloy, La Hire, and a Scotch captain whom the French called Canède, but whose name was really Sir Hugh Kennedy, were all present. There were also some leading burgesses of Orleans. At this secret session they arranged to deliver a violent attack next day on the English fort of Saint Laurent, hoping thereby to entice the English, who were on the southern bank across the river, to the help of their friends on the city side (please refer to the map). This attack, however, was to be more in the nature of a feint than of a genuine battle. The true battle was to take place on the southern bank, against the reduced English forces which had remained behind. Having come to this decision, they sent Ambroise de Loré to fetch Jeanne, being agreed amongst themselves that they should tell her only of the proposed attack on Saint Laurent and should say nothing of the true battle which they wished to engage across the water. When she appeared in answer to their summons, this information was accordingly imparted to her by the chancellor, Cousinot. They had reckoned without Jeanne's intuition. She waited until the chancellor had finished, then, becoming exceedingly irate, refused the seat they offered her and walked up and down the room, saying, "Tell me what you have really decided and appointed. I should know how to keep a far greater secret than that."

At this, they seem to have been very much taken aback, and the Bastard, with his gentle tactful ways, again came to the rescue. He saw that it was idle to try and conceal the truth. "Jeanne," he said, "do not get angry. We cannot tell you everything at once. What the chancellor has told you has indeed been decided and appointed, but we have also decided that if those who are on the Sologne side of the river come to the assistance of those who are in the fort, we shall cross the river to do whatever we can against them there. We consider this plan good and profitable." This satisfied her, and she said that all was to be carried out as they had decided.[1]

Every day they were discovering more and more that Jeanne was not easy to deal with. The comment made by Jean Chartier after describing this scene has a rueful note which makes one smile: "And very often the said Bastard and other captains met together to discuss what had best be done; but whatsoever conclusion they came to, when they sent for Jeanne la Pucelle she decided something else quite to the contrary."[2] If Jean Chartier is to be believed, it was even against their wishes that she went personally into battle, *de quoy les gens de guerre estoient courouciez et moult esbahiz.*

iv

Jeanne's activities on Ascension Day were not limited to ordering the troops to confession, issuing edicts against the

[1]*Procès*, Vol. IV, pp. 57–9: Jean Chartier.
[2]*Procès*, Vol. IV, p. 59: Jean Chartier.

women, and disconcerting the assembly of the captains.
The English still remained to be dealt with. Since she could
not fight them on a holy day, she would at least write them
another letter. It was couched in even less conciliatory terms
than the previous message: "You, men of England, who have
no right to be in this kingdom of France, the King of Heaven
commands you through me, Jeanne la Pucelle, to abandon
your forts and to go back where you belong; which if you fail
to do, I will make such a *ha-hai* as will be eternally remembered.
I am writing to you for the third and last time. I shall not write
any more.—JHESUS MARIA. JEHANNE LA PUCELLE."

She added a postscript: "I would have sent you my letter
in a more honourable manner, but you detain my heralds, you
have detained my herald called Guienne. Please send him back
to me, and I will send back some of your people captured at
Saint Loup, for they are not all dead."

As she did not want to risk another herald, she then took
an arrow, fastened the letter to it with a piece of thread,
and ordered a cross-bow man to shoot it into the English camp,
shouting meanwhile, "Read, here is news." That particular
news, by then, must have been growing a little stale. The
English evidently thought so, for, when they had picked up
the arrow and read the attached letter, they replied by derisive
shouts of "Ah! news from the harlot of the Armagnacs!"
On hearing this, Jeanne appealed to God and burst into floods
of tears (*flere cum abundantia lacrymarum*). A little later she
declared that God had consoled her, and commanded Paquerel
to get up even earlier on the following day, in order to receive
her confession again.[1]

v

There was fighting next day (Friday, May 6th), in which
Jeanne took part. Contradictory accounts exist of what the
captains had decided to do, and of what actually took place,

[1] *Procès*, Vol. III, pp. 107–8: Deposition of Jean Paquerel.

but it seems unnecessary to go into them here. It is a matter of only the slightest importance whether the Bastard and his council had agreed upon making a feint or not, or whether their intention was defeated by the action of Jeanne followed by the mass of the town-people. The account given by Jean d'Aulon, who himself took part in the battle, is probably the most reliable that we can follow. Briefly, then, as soon as the English perceived the French advancing in force towards the Bastille of Saint Jean de Blanc, having crossed the river by means of a bridge of boats linking the Ile devant Saint Aignan (or Ile aux Toiles) with the shore, they evacuated Saint Jean le Blanc, falling back on the stronger and bigger Bastille des Augustins. The French, who had not yet been rejoined by Jeanne,[1] finding Saint Jean le Blanc empty and judging that they could not attempt to capture les Augustins, were about to return to Orleans, under the orders of the sieurs de Gaucourt and de Villars, and of d'Aulon himself, when Jeanne and La Hire galloped up together. By this time the English had begun to stream out of les Augustins, with the intention of falling upon the rear of the retreating French. La Hire and Jeanne incontinently couched their lances and charged against them. This example was too much for the French, who despite the order to retreat turned round and flung themselves forward to chase the English back into the *bastille*; more especially was it too much for d'Aulon and a certain brave Spaniard, who had been left behind to guard the rear. In a somewhat free translation, d'Aulon relates it thus: "I, who was staying behind . . . with some others including a very valiant soldier of Spain named Alfonso de Partada, saw one of our company outstripping us, a fine man, tall, and well armed, to whom I called out that he should wait behind with the others in order to offer resistance to the enemy if necessary, but he answered instantly that he would do nothing of the sort. Then Alfonso said that since as brave men as he could obey orders, he could

[1] Her delay appears to have arisen owing to the necessity of getting her horse across the river, whereas the troops had crossed on foot.

obey them also and stay behind. But he answered Alfonso saying that he would not. So they had high words (*eurent entre eulx certaines arrogantes paroles*) and ended by taking each other by the hand, and ran to the foot of the palisade, in order to see which would prove to be the better man."

D'Aulon, however, who was watching, discerned a great strong Englishman (*ung grant, fort, et puissant Anglois*), opposing their passage, and called to the famous Jean with his culverin, that he should shoot down the Englishman who was creating far too much damage.[1] Such details, which are of frequent occurrence in contemporary records, all go to prove how vivid the personal element was then in war. D'Aulon might forget or muddle far more important things in his recital, but the incident of the big Englishman who was getting in the way of Partada and his companion, until tumbled over by the skilful Jean, remained impressed upon his memory.

The day ended with the French in possession of Saint Jean le Blanc and of les Augustins. The English had been obliged to abandon the latter position and to take refuge within the strong and vitally important fort of les Tourelles. Jeanne limped home, for she had been wounded in the foot by a *chausse-trappe*.[2]

After the exhaustion of the day, she forwent her usual custom of fasting on a Friday, but was still at supper when one of the captains, whose name the witness forgets, came to her with a displeasing message. It was to the effect that the French leaders sitting in council had come to the conclusion that their troops were too few in number in comparison with the English, and that it was advisable to wait for further reinforcements from the Dauphin. The town was well

---

[1] *Procès*, Vol. III, pp. 213–15: Deposition of Jean d'Aulon.

[2] The fact that she had thus been wounded makes it apparent that she had dismounted at some given moment, in spite of d'Aulon's picture of her charging on horseback, lance in hand. She probably dismounted to enter les Augustins with the victorious French, as the English were leaving it by its other gate.

provisioned and could afford the delay. On the following day, therefore, no *sortie* would take place. Jeanne turned on him: "You have been with your council, and I have been with mine. Believe me, my council will hold good and will be accomplished; yours will come to naught." Then in her imperious way she turned to her confessor Paquerel, who was sitting with her: "Get up early to-morrow morning, even earlier than you did to-day [a command which she seems to have enjoined almost daily upon this hard-worked man], and do the best you can. You must stay near me all the time, for to-morrow I shall have much to do, more than I ever had yet, and the blood will flow from my body above my breast."[1]

vi

She had now been in Orleans for a week, and in spite of these various affrays nothing really decisive had happened. The siege was not yet raised. Troops had arrived; *escarmouches* had taken place; three English forts and some prisoners had been captured; the Bastard and his colleagues had improved their acquaintance with Jeanne; the English had, apparently, learnt nothing. The week's delay had not taught them that their fatal day was at hand, the fatal day which now, five hundred years later, is still commemorated with flags, processions, celebrations, and fireworks. The English, still secure in the possession of some of the forts they had held for over six months, apparently had formed no idea of the demon which was about to be let loose against them. Yet their losses, although not decisive, had been considerable. They had lost Saint Loup, les Augustins, and Saint Jean le Blanc. Their defences, thus reduced, left them in a weaker position than they had ever occupied since the inception of the siege in October of the previous year.

Nobody knows how many men were engaged on either side. The French reinforcements from Blois may have numbered

[1] *Procès*, Vol. III, p. 109: Deposition of Jean Paquerel.

three thousand men. Of course the usual garrison was in Orleans already. The English are variously estimated at anything between three thousand five hundred and ten thousand.

The moment had come which was to demonstrate the extent of Jeanne's personal influence on so small and concentrated an army. It came on May 7th, and is known as the *journée des Tourelles*.

vii

The Tourelles was the name given to the English fort consisting of two stone towers near the head of the broken bridge across the river. These towers were protected on the Orleans side by the gap in the bridge, the gap itself being further protected by an outwork; on the other, or southern, side they were protected by the usual outwork with high walls, known by the to us rather misleading name of *boulevard*; between this *boulevard* and the Tourelles flowed a branch of the river, which could, however, be crossed by a drawbridge; "the defenders of the *boulevard*, if too hard pressed," as Andrew Lang succinctly puts it, "could rush across, retire into the Tourelles, raise the drawbridge, and defy the enemy." The *boulevard* was further defended by a deep *fosse* or ditch. These details are necessary if we are to understand clearly what happened later in the day.[1]

Some six hundred English soldiers manned the Tourelles, and the names of some of them have come down to us. Among the commanders, we know of Sir William Glasdale, whom the French called Classidas, Sir William de Moleyns, Gifford, and a gentleman whom Jean Chartier calls by the improbable name of the sire de Bumus, but whose name was in reality Lord Poynings. Among the yeomen we know of John Reid from Redesdale, Bill Martin, Matthew Thornton, Thomas Jolly, Geoffrey Blackwell, Walter Parker, William Vaughan,

[1] I must again refer the reader to the map facing p. 160, and especially to the little separate sketch of the Tourelles.

William Arnold, John Burford, George Ludlow, Patrick Hall, Thomas Sand, John Langham, Dick Hawke, Davy Johnson, and Black Henry.[1] Reading these so English names is rather like sweeping a searchlight over a mob in the dark, and seeing a few weather-beaten faces leap into the beam.

The French are less democratically recorded, for we have only the names of the leaders and not of the rank and file: The Bastard, the maréchal de Rais, the sieur de Gaucourt, the sieur de Graville, Guillaume de Chaumont, sieur de Guitry, Raimon Arnaut, sieur de Coarraze en Béarn, Denis de Chailly, Louis de Culen, La Hire, Poton de Saintrailles, Florent d'Illiers, Le Bourg de Masquaren, Thibaut de Termes, and Archambault de Villars, a hardened old knight who had made his reputation in a combat between seven Frenchmen and seven Englishmen nearly thirty years before.

The struggle for the Tourelles lasted all day, from seven o'clock in the morning till eight o'clock at night. The French captains were prudently opposed to the attack, but Jeanne, supported by the populace of Orleans, overrode their objections.[2] How right her judgment was, they were to learn before the day was over. That she was confident of victory is proved by a curious little incident which took place before she had set out from her lodging. Someone brought a fish into the house. Jacques Boucher, the treasurer, her host, said to her, "Jeanne, let us eat this fish before you go out." "En nom Dieu," she replied, "we will not eat it until supper, when we have recrossed the bridge and have brought back a godon who will eat his share."[3] Then, having confessed and heard Mass, she

[1] Molandon et Beaucorps: L'Armée anglaise vaincue par Jeanne d'Arc, pp. 134–43.
[2] Procès, Vol. III, p. 70: Louis de Contes; Procès, Vol. IV, p. 227: Chronique de la Pucelle.
[3] Procès, Vol. IV, p. 227: Chronique de la Pucelle; Procès, Vol. III. pp. 124–5: Deposition of Colette Millet. The two versions vary slightly, but are in substance the same. The fish in question was an alose or sea-trout, which goes up rivers in spring. A godon, of course, is a corruption of Goddam, which the French supposed to be the favourite oath of the English soldier.
It is just possible that the fish incident may have occurred earlier, for, on

rode out of the town towards the victory which was to entitle her to the proud name of Maid of Orleans.

A slight hitch occurred as she tried to leave the town, for the sieur de Gaucourt, who had been charged with the duty of seeing that the gates were kept closed, came into a clash with Jeanne, who wished to go out by the Porte de Bourgogne followed by both citizens and men-at-arms. It was not in Jeanne's nature to find a gate shut against her and to retire meekly. Backed by her following, she stormed against de Gaucourt: "You are a bad man" (*malus homo*), she said. "Whether you like it or not, the soldiers will come and will win as they have won hitherto." The sieur de Gaucourt admitted to the *maître des requêtes* that he had found himself then in great danger[1]; it was evidently not safe to expose oneself to a tumultuous populace led by a Joan of Arc. People who meant to fight would fight, and neither a shut gate nor a sieur de Gaucourt would deter them. Nevertheless, the sieur de Gaucourt can scarcely have failed to remember the day when he first kindly gave up one of his pages to Jeanne's service. Things had changed very much since then.

viii

The various accounts of the battle tally to a satisfactory degree. Four of the principal ones come from the lips of men who were present: the Bastard, Jean d'Aulon, Jean Paquerel, and young Louis de Contes.[2] The first three are especially

May 3rd, Raoulet de Recourt received "twenty *sols* for an *alose* presented to the Pucelle" (*Procès*, Vol. V, p. 259: *Comptes de forteresse*). But Colette Millet says May 7th, and there is no reason why Jeanne should not have been offered a trout more than once.

[1]*Procès*, Vol. III, pp. 116–17. Deposition of Simon Charles, *maître des requêtes*, who, although not present, claims to have the information from de Gaucourt himself.

[2]In order to avoid the irritation of constant and repetitive footnotes, it may be assumed that all details about the battle are taken either from these four accounts or from the *Journal du siège d'Orléans*, or from Jollois' *Histoire du siège d'Orléans*.

detailed and circumstantial. From them we learn that the attack on the Tourelles was concentrated in the great *fosse* or moat below the *boulevard*, the French assaulting the highest places of the fortifications with such valour that they appeared to think themselves immortal, rearing their ladders against the walls and being flung back many times by the English from the height of the walls into the *fosse* below, beaten down with hatchets, lances, battle-axes (*guisarmes*), leaden maces, and even with their fists, amidst the smoke and flare of guns. For all their valour, the place remained untaken when evening came. The French began to despair; the Bastard decided upon a general retirement.

In the meantime, towards mid-day, Jeanne's most authentic prophecy had been fulfilled: she was hit by an arrow just above the left breast. It penetrated into her flesh to a depth of six inches. The pain frightened her, and she wept. The sieur de Gamaches—he who had previously given up his banner sooner than serve under her command—rode up hastily to defend her with his axe, seeing that the English were about to descend from their walls to surround her. "Take my horse," he said, and added a generous apology.[1] She allowed herself to be led away from the battle, and it is said that she pulled out the arrow with her own hands.[2] Some soldiers, seeing her wounded, came up, wanting to recite charms to cure her. This remedy she rejected, saying that she would rather die than do anything that she believed to be a crime or contrary to God's will. Nevertheless, she said, with her usual common sense, that she was quite ready to let them apply a proper remedy to her wound, for, although she knew she must die some day, she was willing to be cured now if she could do so without sin. They staunched the blood, and dressed the wound with olive oil and lard. It seems that she then consented to rest for a little, and confessed again with tears.[3]

[1]Jollois, *Histoire du siège d'Orléans:* Vie de Guillaume de Gamaches.
[2]*Procès,* Vol. IV, p. 228: *Chronique de la Pucelle.*
[3]It must be remembered that this evidence was given by her confessor,

Meanwhile the battle was going on without her, no doubt to the great encouragement of the English who from the commanding height of their walls had observed her disappearance from the tumult of the attacking forces. It is not easy to determine how long she remained absent, but it is at least certain that she returned to her place during the course of the afternoon—no small proof of courage for one who had been pierced by an iron-tipped arrow a few hours before. She was in the thick of the fight when the Bastard and his fellow-captains finally abandoned all hope of carrying the Tourelles that day. It was then eight o'clock in the evening; the assailants, who had striven for thirteen hours in all that din and danger, were exhausted; the Bastard, however reluctantly, gave orders that the trumpeters should proclaim the retreat.

Fortunately for Orleans, this was one of the occasions on which Jeanne chose to disagree with the commanders' advice. Before the trumpets could sound, she went to the Bastard and begged him for a little more time.[1] Then, mounting a horse, she rode off alone into a neighbouring vineyard, where she remained in prayer for about a quarter of an hour. Nobody makes any comment as to what the Bastard thought as he saw her ride off or as he was awaiting her return. On the other hand, the author of the *Journal du siège* gives us a very definite account of the sensible instructions she left behind her. "Rest a little," she said, "drink and eat," *ce qu'ilz feirent, car à merveilles luy obeissoyent.*

After this the accounts become slightly confused. The Bastard says that she seized her standard and stood with it on the parapet of the *fosse*, at which sight the English trembled and the French, recovering their courage, returned to the assault on the walls, meeting with no resistance whatsoever.

Paquerel, who was naturally doing his utmost to disprove the charge of witchcraft brought against her at her trial.

[1] This is the Bastard's own account. Jean d'Aulon says that the order had actually been published. The Bastard's memory or his enthusiasm seems to have misled him on this point, as they did on many.

This sounds rather too good to be true. The English, after holding out all day, were scarcely likely to let an exhausted enemy swarm over their walls without attempting to beat them back once more. It is elsewhere stated that Jeanne had left the standard behind her when she went off to pray, which bears the stamp of probability, and is further endorsed by d'Aulon's remark that on her return she believed it to be lost. All things considered, it seems very unlikely that the Bastard's heroic picture of the Maid standing on the parapet brandishing her flag is as accurate as he would like us to believe. Jean d'Aulon's story is far more exciting and far more credible, in spite of being conceived in a spirit of boastfulness about his own prowess which relegates Jeanne's part in the *journée des Tourelles* quite to the background.

According to him, Jeanne was not carrying her standard herself. It was borne by an anonymous soldier, who, being extremely weary, handed it over to a follower of Archambault de Villars, a certain Basque whom d'Aulon knew to be a valiant man. D'Aulon, still according to his own showing, greatly feared that a retreat would mean leaving the *boulevard* and the forts in the possession of the enemy. He probably thought that the triumphant English would fall upon the retreating force and hack them to pieces. Even more to his credit, he also perceived that if the standard were carried forward, a chance remained of inspiring the men to a final and victorious assault. He therefore asked the Basque if he would follow him across the *fosse* to the foot of the walls. On receiving the Basque's promise, he leapt down into the *fosse*, covering himself with his shield as he ran, believing himself to be closely followed by the Basque. The Basque, however, had meanwhile been intercepted by someone far more redoubtable than d'Aulon—the Pucelle herself, who had caught sight of her flag, which she had believed to be lost. She tried to pull it away from the Basque, crying, "*Haa! mon étendart! mon étendart!*" and, in trying to get it from him, shook it in such a way that d'Aulon thought everyone would believe her to be giving them a signal. What that signal was supposed to be he does not relate, but evidently he disapproved of it, for he called out, "Ha, Basque! Is this what you promised me?" At that, the Basque pulled so hard that he tore the standard from her grasp, ran across the *fosse* and joined d'Aulon with it at the foot of the wall. Then, says d'Aulon proudly, the whole army of the Pucelle assembled and returned to the attack, assailing the walls so bitterly (*par si grant aspresse*) that both the *boulevard* and the fort were taken.[1]

It is a good story, and must have proved to d'Aulon's complete satisfaction that he had played a dominant part in raising the siege of Orleans.

ix

The *journée des Tourelles* was almost, but not quite, over. Jeanne had not yet spoken her last word. She, who eight days previously had shouted to Glasdale in that same fort, and who had shot him her letter attached to an arrow, only to be greeted with insults and derision, now summoned him once more in very different circumstances. The English by this time were in complete rout. On the one side the French were pouring over the walls on to the *boulevard*; on the other side reinforcements were streaming out of the city on to the bridge before the Tourelles. The English had imagined that they were safe from attack on this side, thanks to the gap in the broken bridge. The French had thought so too. But now, in their excitement and exhilaration, they attempted and achieved the seemingly impossible. They brought carpenters with ladders and gutter-pipes, and, throwing them across, endeavoured to span the gap. When they found that their improvised bridge fell short, they nailed a piece of wood to the longest gutter, so firmly that it

---

[1]*Procès*, Vol. III, pp. 216–17: Deposition of Jean d'Aulon. *Procès*, Vol. IV, p. 161: The *Journal du siège* adds a detail omitted by d'Aulon. Turning to a knight at her side, she said, "Hold yourself in readiness for when the tail of my standard touches the wall." A few moments later he said, "Jeanne, it touches." "Then all is yours," she replied; "enter!"

held. The Grand Prior, Nicolas de Giresme, was the first to cross this narrow and insecure foothold (*merveilleusement longue et estroite, et haute en l'air, sans avoir aucun appuy*); others followed him. The English were appalled to find their enemies both in the front and in the rear. So much appalled were they that some of them observed the Archangel Michael and Saint Aignan, patron saint of Orleans, riding on horseback in mid-air, and coming to the aid of the French troops.[1] Panic overcoming them, they rushed wildly to the other bridge—the drawbridge which connected the *boulevard* to the Tourelles. A cry went up from Jeanne. "Clasdas! Clasdas! *renti, renti* [*rends-toi, rends-toi*], to the King of Heaven. You called me harlot, but I have great pity on your soul and the souls of your men." It was too late. A fire-boat had already been moored and lit under the drawbridge, and, as Glasdale and de Moleyns, with other knights, dashed on to the bridge in their heavy armour, it gave way beneath them. Of all those who fell, not one escaped death by drowning; and of those who remained on land, every single one was either killed or taken prisoner.

Jeanne, of course, wept at once for the soul of Glasdale and his companions. The French, in the midst of their triumph, found time to regret the loss of the richest ransoms. Still, they could not deny that the enemy was beaten, the siege raised, and the impregnable Tourelles in flames. Neither could they deny that Jeanne's prophecy, made that morning, that they would return at nightfall into the city "across the bridge," had been nobly fulfilled. While the Tourelles flamed, reddening the waters of the Loire, all the bells of Orleans rang out, and priests and people united in singing the *Te Deum laudamus*, giving thanks to God, to Saint Aignan and Saint Euverte, to their valiant defenders, and, more especially and above all, to Jeanne la Pucelle.[2]

---

[1]Jollois, *Histoire du siège d'Orléans*, p. 87.
[2]*Procès*, Vol. IV, p. 163: *Journal du siège*.

x

The shouting dies away; the flames die down; night falls; the quiet aftermath succeeds the strenuous and noisy day. A tiny picture of Jeanne remains to complete the story. "She was taken back to her lodging, to have her wound dressed. The dressing over, she refreshed herself with four or five slices of bread dipped in wine mixed with a great deal of water: it was all that she had eaten or drunk during the whole day."[1]

As for Sir William Glasdale, called Classidas, his body was fished up, cut into pieces, boiled, and embalmed; his remains lay for a week in a chapel, with four candles burning day and night, and then were transported to his own country for burial.[2]

Some other little echoes of that famous encounter come down to us. They are to be found in the account-books of the city of Orleans for the year 1429. Here are five of them:

"Paid: forty sous for a heavy piece of wood obtained from Jean Bazin when the Tourelles were won from the English, to put across one of the broken arches of the bridge."

"To Jean Poitevin, a fisherman, eight sous for having beached a *chaland* which was put under the bridge of the Tourelles to fire them when they should be taken."

"To Boudon, nine sous for two S-shaped irons weighing four pounds and a half, attached to the *chaland* which was kindled under the bridge of the Tourelles."

"Lard and resin bought to grease the flags for the firing of the Tourelles."

"Given to Champeaux and other carpenters, sixteen sous to go and drink on the day the Tourelles were won."[3]

[1] *Procès*, Vol. III, p. 9: Deposition of Dunois.
[2] *Procès*, Vol. IV, p. 463: *Le bourgeois de Paris.*
[3] *Procès*, Vol. IV, p. 161–2; and Jollois, p. 84.

Chapter XI

REIMS

i

Champeaux and the other carpenters may have enjoyed their drink, but the Duke of Bedford, reviewing the position, was far less happy. He expounded his views presently in a letter to those at home: "There fell, by the hand of God, as it seemeth, a great stroke upon your people that was assembled there [at Orleans] in great number, caused in great part, as I trow, of lack of sad belief and unlawful doubt that they had of a disciple and limb of the Fiend, called the Pucelle, that used false enchantments and sorcery. The which stroke and discomfiture not only lessened in great part the number of your people there, but as well withdrew the courage from the remnant in marvellous wise. . . ."[1]

The Duke of Bedford states the position dramatically, but dramatic events were in the air. Explain it as we may, the English appear to have been completely disconcerted, disorganised, and at fault. We have already seen how, inexplicably, they failed to attack Jeanne at her first entry into Orleans, and, subsequently, how they again failed to attack her or the French army coming to her support. The whole attitude of the English throughout is so odd and laggard as to be unexplainable save on supernatural grounds—grounds which we, in the light of our twentieth-century knowledge—or should we say in the darkness of our twentieth-century ignorance?—find difficult to accept. Bedford perhaps was wiser, except in so far as he attributed Jeanne's powers to the Fiend rather than to Jeanne's own King of Heaven. It was a superstitious age, and conclusions depended very much on whether one's commands proceeded from God or from the Devil. Jeanne thought her commands

[1] *Procès*, Vol. V, pp. 136–7: Fragment of a letter from the Duke of Bedford. M. Quicherat places, with a query, the date of this letter at the end of July 1429.

proceeded from God; the Duke of Bedford thought they
proceeded from the Devil. It was, in a sense, all very much the
same thing. Bedford and the English were, in their different
ways, as credulous as Jeanne. The net result was that Bedford,
for good or evil, laid stress upon her other-worldly inspiration.
In his letter he testifies to it, and Bedford was not by nature
an emotional man. He was not the sort of man who would
emotionally testify to the influence of a country-girl, unless that
country-girl had proved herself capable of exercising a very
definite and practical influence over the behaviour of her own
troops and over the effect of those troops on the war-hardened
English who had terrorised France for nearly a century, and
who, more immediately, had held Orleans in a state of siege for
half a year. Bedford himself could not deny that Jeanne had
turned the English out of Orleans in the space of thirteen hours.
Nor could he explain the sudden discomfiture of his English
troops, save by ascribing it to some supernatural power on the
part of "that disciple and limb of the Fiend, that used false
enchantments and sorcery." Bedford could conveniently, and
perhaps genuinely, overlook the fact that the English spirit
was no longer at all the same thing as it had been under the
gay and dashing leadership of Henry V, and that Jeanne's
arrival on the scene was, for the French, most fortunately
opportune.

In spite of Bedford, the disciple and limb of the Fiend
proceeded on her victorious career. She had inspired her
followers to capture the fort of the Tourelles on May the
seventh; on May the eighth the remaining English offered
battle, but she declined it, preferring to let the enemy retire
upon Meung. The story, like most stories about Jeanne, is an
odd one, and shows her in her most Quixotic, least vindictive,
light. Early, at dawn in fact, the English issued from their
tents, and ranged themselves in order of battle. Jeanne,
awakened to hear this news, arose from her bed, and, arrayed
only in a coat of mail (*jasseran*), by reason of the wound she had
received the previous day, forbade any attack to be made on

them, so that they might be allowed to retire without pursuit.[1] Nevertheless, she went out of the city with her usual escort of captains, La Hire, Sainte-Sévère, Gilles de Rais, Poton de Saintrailles, Florent d'Illiers, and others, and the French and English forces drew up and looked at each other for an hour without coming to blows.[2] It must have been an odd confrontation of the two armies. The French were obviously and wisely longing to follow up their victory of the previous day.

Jeanne forbade it. She held back the whole army, as a trainer holds back a pack of eager dogs. It was Sunday, a day on which one might not fight—unless, indeed, one was attacked, in which case it might be permissible to defend oneself. Here, again, Jeanne's mixture of religion and common sense comes into play: on a Sunday one should not be the aggressor, but, in the event of an attack, one might be allowed to defend oneself. Her colleagues could scarcely understand this point of view, although they obeyed it: *Les Francois souffryrent très envis, obtempérans au vouloir de la Pucelle, qui leur commanda et deffendit dès le commancement que pour l'amour et honneur du sainct dimanche ne commanchassent point la bataille n'assaillissent les Angloys, mais se les Angloys les assailloyent, qu'ils se deffendissent fort et hardiment et qu'ilz n'eussent nulle paour.*[3]

The *Chronique de la Pucelle* gives an exact account of how she proceeded. Sending for a portable altar, composed of a table and a block of marble, she caused two Masses to be said in the open field, with the whole army for congregation. This ceremony over, she told them to look and see whether the English were turning their faces or their backs. On hearing that they were turning their backs, she said, "Let them go, it is not the Lord's pleasure that we should fight them to-day; you will get them another time."[4]

---

[1] *Procès*, Vol. III, p. 9: Deposition of Dunois.
[2] *Procès*, Vol. IV, p. 164: *Journal du siège d'Orléans*.
[3] *Procès*, Vol. IV, p. 164: *Journal du siège d'Orléans*.
[4] *Procès*, Vol. IV, p. 232: *Chronique de la Pucelle*; and *Procès*, Vol. III, p. 29: Deposition of Jean Champeaux.

So Jeanne reined in the vindictive French by the sheer force of her personality—a real tribute, I think, to her personal influence, but also a great error, since she could easily have fallen then upon the disheartened English and wiped them out instead of letting them retire safely upon Meung. Jeanne, here, made as great a blunder as the English had made in allowing her to enter Orleans without opposition. They had both missed their chance—the English for a reason which can never be explained; Jeanne for a reason entirely due to her sentimental regard for Sunday. She has been frequently represented as a great military commander. Such episodes as her having allowed the English army to retreat after the defeat at Orleans must be reckoned among the mistakes she made. The fact that the day was Sunday was more important to her than the fact that she then held the English in her power. Because the day was Sunday, she allowed them to escape. One can only draw the conclusion that, on this occasion at least, she was no great military commander, but an inspired sentimentalist.

The French, less sentimental than she, pursued the English in their retreat, and took from them a number of cannon and other instruments of war.[1]

ii

Sentimentalist or not, Jeanne chased the Dauphin with more determination than she had shown towards the half-beaten enemy. On leaving Orleans, she tracked that reluctant and unhappy man down to Tours. She was determined at all costs to get him crowned at Reims. The coronation at Reims was, to her, more important than even the reduction of Paris. He should no longer be the Dauphin, but the King. She had achieved wonders on his behalf: she had cleared the English out of Orleans. He ought to be grateful to her. In spite of all the delays and tests he had imposed upon her, leaving her little more than a week to

[1] *Procès*, Vol. IV, p. 164: *Journal du siège d'Orléans*.

accomplish her first task, she had already made good the first part of her promise. She had delivered Orleans without any trouble to Charles himself. He had merely sat back in his comfortable seat at Chinon, while Jeanne went to do the necessary work. Now Jeanne, having done the work, having got herself wounded, having inspired the citizens of his own town of Orleans, having rid that important city of its protracted siege, Jeanne, having turned herself into the popular heroine of France, Jeanne, that bother, that nuisance, was coming back to ask him to go and get himself crowned at Reims.

He received her graciously enough, meeting her as, standard in hand, she rode into Tours (May 10th, 1429). She bowed low to him, but he told her to sit erect, and the onlookers thought he was on the point of kissing her, so great was his delight.[1] He was generous enough also to pay her a special tribute in a letter which he addressed to the citizens of Narbonne, apprising them of the recent events at Orleans.[2] But letters were easy to dictate, and these acknowledgments, however public and official, were not at all the same thing as putting himself out to the extent of hurrying off in person to Reims.

Jeanne, however, was importunate. She consented to go with him to his castle at Loches, but, having accompanied him there, she would not leave him in peace. She came to knock on the door of his private apartment, where he had retired with his confessor Christophe d'Harcourt, Bishop of Castres and the seigneur de Trèves, and, kneeling before him, clasping him round the knees, she addressed him once more as her *gentil Dauphin*. "*Gentil Dauphin*, do not hold such long and wordy councils, but come to your coronation at Reims. I am most eager that you should go there."[3] Neither the Dauphin nor his counsellors seem to have known what to make of

---

[1] *Procès*, Vol. IV, p. 497: Eberhard von Windecken.
[2] *Procès*, Vol. V, p. 103.
[3] *Procès*, Vol. III, p. 12: Deposition of Dunois.

this request. One would imagine that the course proposed by Jeanne was the obvious course to adopt, since a victory not followed up is only half a victory, yet they hesitated. Some of them were of the opinion that the English should first be driven out of Normandy. Others were of the opinion that all the principal towns along the Loire should first be brought into subjection. Others, again, the Dauphin amongst them, were of the opinion that Jeanne should be asked to say what her voices had told her, yet they hesitated to put the question, for fear of annoying her. She herself guessed what was in their minds, and, coming forward of her own accord, addressed the Dauphin: "*En nom de Dieu,* I know what you are thinking and what you would like to know about the voice I have heard, as concerns your coronation, and I will tell you that I entered into prayer after my usual manner. When I complained that no one would believe what I said, the voice replied, '*Fille de Dieu, va, va, va; ie seray en ton aide, va.*' "[1]

Eventually they arrived at a compromise. Charles would consent to go to Reims, but the Loire towns should be taken on the way. The army under the command of the Bastard, Poton de Saintrailles, and the maréchal de Sainte-Sévère had already been engaged on an unsuccessful attack upon Jargeau (May 10th or 11th),[2] Jeanne remaining in Charles' company, following him from Tours to Loches, while May passed into June. Once more she was being compelled to waste precious time—she who knew by her voices that her time on earth was limited. Charles, the supreme procrastinator, the forerunner of the Hamlet who could never make up his mind to action, dawdled in his pleasant province of Touraine, with Jeanne fretting at his heels. She ought, of course, failing Reims, to

---

[1]*Procès*, Vol. IV, pp. 168–9: *Journal du siège d'Orléans*. The Bastard, on the other hand, says that the Bishop of Castres asked her the questions straight away; and the Bastard ought to know, for he was with her when she rapped on the door of the Dauphin's room.

[2]*Procès*, Vol. IV, p. 167: *Journal du siège d'Orléans*.

have forced him to march direct on Paris; but so uncompromising an alternative could scarcely commend itself to the timorous and wavering soul of Charles VII. He contented himself by writing polite letters about her to his few faithful subjects, and by appointing her young friend and supporter, d'Alençon, her *beau duc,* as lieutenant-general of his armies.[1] This meant, at any rate, that her most loyal friend was a friend in the field, which perhaps was just as important as having friends at Court.

She was very much mixed up, by then, with friends in the field. The Bastard of Orleans had been at her side when she knocked at the Dauphin's private door at Loches, and it was in the company of d'Alençon that she took leave of the Dauphin and again entered the rejoicing portals of Orleans (June 9th, 1429).[2] Jeanne, I think, must thoroughly have enjoyed the several returns she made to Orleans, identified as she now was with that city, and more than *persona grata* with its inhabitants, who *de laquelle veoir ne se povoyent saouler.* It must indeed have been a moving experience for her to ride fearlessly now through those once-threatened gates. She knew her way about the city, which by that time had grown as familiar to her as her remote and native Domremy. She had her private friends there as well as the adoring anonymous populace. The friendly house of Jacques Boucher was well known to her. It must have seemed strange to her to look upon the charred ruins of the once formidable Tourelles, strange to look once more at the broken bridge which had precipitated Glasdale and his companions into the fire-lit river, strange to look once more at the deserted forts where she had shouted in challenge at the English. Fortunately for her, the geographical situation of Orleans allowed her to use it to some extent as her headquarters during the dazzling fortnight which follows.

For a week (June 10th to 18th) Jeanne, apparently grown irresistible, was engaged almost daily in a series of victories.

[1] *Procès,* Vol. IV, p. 169: *Journal du siège d'Orléans.*
[2] *Procès,* Vol. IV, p. 169: *Journal du siège d'Orléans.*

With d'Alençon in command of the army, and the Bastard, Florent d'Illiers, and La Hire supporting her, her hands were fairly free. Of course she was never officially the leader. Of course there were the customary disagreements among the captains, and the customary divisions of opinion on matters of military policy, but on the whole she was usually able to carry them along by the almost physical force of her inner convictions. Moreover they knew that she had the popular backing of the army, whose superstitious trust made them ready to follow her anywhere. The sight of that strange small figure in her gleaming armour, the famous standard floating wherever the turmoil was thickest, was enough to rally them over and over again. The Dauphin's friends at Court might whisper jealously against the adventuress from Lorraine, inspired less probably by God than by the Devil: in the field and in the eyes of the populace she was a leader to die for, a saint whose clothing was reverently to be touched.

And now, one by one, the English strongholds were falling before her. On June 10th she left Orleans, and, with her *beau duc*, spent the night in a wood.[1] In the morning they were joined by the Bastard and Florent d'Illiers, when a discussion ensued as to whether they should attack Jargeau or not. It was occupied by the Earl of Suffolk and his two brothers, the de la Poles; Sir John Fastolf, also, was known to be on his way from Paris with a large force for the reinforcement of Suffolk and his men. Some of the French captains gave the advice that Fastolf should be intercepted before the assault was launched against Jargeau; Jeanne, however, would hear nothing of this counsel. God, she said, was on their side; she was assured of success; otherwise, she would prefer to keep sheep than expose herself to such great perils. They listened to her, and took the road to Jargeau, in the hope of capturing the suburbs at least that day. At first they met with a reverse, for the English sallied out of the town to meet them, but Jeanne—the repetition of such incidents grows monotonous—threw herself into

[1] *Procès*, Vol. III, p. 94: Deposition of the Duke of Alençon.

the mêlée, and the troops, following her, carried the outlying portions of the town. D'Alençon was convinced that the hand of God was in it, and adds, rather naïvely, as an additional proof of the hand of God, that, owing to the small number of French sentries posted that night, the English could quite easily have fallen upon the army by surprise and put them into the greatest danger. The negligence of the French on this occasion is as inexplicable as the English failure to take advantage of their opportunity. The story of these military campaigns is full of such curious lapses on either side.

Jeanne, according to her custom, that evening advised the English to retire and to leave the place to God and the Dauphin; the English, according to theirs, ignored the suggestion.[1]

Next day the town fell. D'Alençon tried to hold back, judging it inadvisable to attack further; La Hire, unknown to his colleagues, started negotiations with Suffolk on his own account. Luckily this enterprise, which seems to accord ill with La Hire's robust and outspoken character, and especially with the respect he felt for Jeanne, came in time to the ears of the French captains then sitting in council; they were naturally angry, sent for La Hire to come back, and listened once more to Jeanne's persuasions—"*Avant, gentil duc, à l'assault.*" Still d'Alençon hesitated. Jeanne taunted him. Was he afraid, she asked? Did he not remember that she had promised his wife to bring him home safe and sound? Stung by these words, d'Alençon, who for all his caution was a gallant man, gave the order to attack. In the thick of the battle, he saw Jeanne at his side. "Move from this place," she said to him, "or that piece of ordnance on the rampart will kill you." A few moments later the sieur de Ludes was indeed struck and killed by the same gun on that very spot.[2]

D'Alençon was filled with fear at this apparent miracle, and followed Jeanne as she flung herself forward to the attack. Reading between the lines both of his own deposition and of

[1] *Procès*, Vol. IV, p. 12: Perceval de Cagny.
[2] *Procès*, Vol. III, p. 96: Deposition of the Duke of Alençon.

the accounts of other chroniclers, it is easy to perceive that the *beau duc* was inspired by an unusual excitement and confidence, for not only did he reject Suffolk's attempts to parley with him as the French were scaling the walls, but, in what can only be described as a boyish mood, he summoned the notorious Jean with his culverin—he who had hidden himself beneath the bridge at Orleans and had teased the English with his pretence of a mortal wound. To this Jean, d'Alençon pointed out a huge Englishman (*moult grant et groux*) who was hurling great lumps of iron from the height of the walls down upon the ladders and men below him. Jean, only too glad to obey the duke's instructions, shot the Englishman full in the chest, so that he fell dead, backwards, into the town.[1]

Jeanne herself was on a scaling-ladder, the inevitable standard in her hand, when a stone struck the flag, rebounded on to her helmet, broke into pieces, and knocked her to the ground. It can have been no pleasant experience to fall backwards from a ladder in heavy armour, but she was on her feet again in an instant, crying, "*Amis, amis, sus, sus!* Our Lord has condemned the English; they will be ours within the hour; be of good heart." The town was almost immediately carried, Suffolk taken prisoner, and more than eleven hundred English put to death.[2]

Suffolk is said to have surrendered himself to an Auvergnat squire named Guillaume Regnault, after first knighting him so that, according to the traditions of mediæval chivalry, it might be said that he had been taken by a knight.[3] On the other hand, the *greffier* de la Rochelle maintains that Suffolk said he would surrender only to "the bravest woman in the world." We may take our choice between these two versions.

[1]*Procès*, Vol. IV, pp. 171–2: *Journal du siège d'Orléans*.
[2]*Procès*, Vol. III, p. 97: Deposition of the Duke of Alençon.
[3]*Procès*, Vol. IV, p. 45: Le Herault Berri; and *Procès*, Vol. IV, p. 173: *Journal du siège*.

iii

Jargeau was thus the first of the Loire towns to fall into obedience to the Dauphin. Jeanne and d'Alençon rode back to Orleans, where she received a red cloak and a green tunic as a present from the captive Duke of Orleans in England; red and green being the colours of his house.[1] The honour was great, and Jeanne's weakness for finery no doubt gratified. But, even with a new red cloak, which must have looked very handsome floating over her armour, she was in no mood to dally at Orleans. She had, in fact, spent no more than one night and half a day of rest in the city before she was again urging d'Alençon to be on the march. At the hour of vespers she sent for him and told him that on the following afternoon she wanted to pay a visit to Meung; he was to arrange, she said, for the army to be ready to start at that time. When we consider that d'Alençon was a royal prince and the commander-in-chief, whereas Jeanne herself still held no official position, the issuing of such arbitrary orders strikes us as rather startling. D'Alençon, however, and the other captains, sincerely believed her to have been sent by God to restore the Dauphin to his kingdom; the common people believed in her completely, attaching themselves in great number of their own accord to the company which marched out of Orleans towards Meung on June 15th.[2] D'Alençon records briefly that he spent the night in a church near Meung, with only a handful of soldiers, running a great danger. Where Jeanne spent the night is not related.

They contented themselves with giving the English a mere fright at Meung, taking only the bridge from them, and letting the town itself go free.[3] They had a more important objective ahead of them: Beaugency, a major stronghold of the English, lying on the Loire between Meung and Blois. Talbot, who had

[1] *Procès*, Vol. V, pp. 112–13: Account-books of the Duke of Orleans.
[2] *Procès*, Vol. IV, p. 13: Perceval de Cagny.
[3] *Procès*, Vol. IV, p. 174: *Journal du siège d'Orléans*.

been there in command, had already removed himself to a safer place at Janville. The garrison he left behind him seemed little disposed to meet the then triumphant French in open battle. Retiring into the castle, they allowed the French to enter Beaugency unopposed, save by a few ambushes concealed within houses and behind masonry, harrying the French by surprise as they sought their billets, *combien qu'ilz ne se logèrent pas à leur ayse du tout*.[1]

All the following day (June 16th) the battle raged, ending by the capitulation of the English at midnight. They were allowed to retire to Meung on condition that they should not fight again for ten days. Here, again, it is difficult to understand why the French should voluntarily have allowed a large garrison to escape capture, when they might have held them all to ransom. Another event had occurred during the day which perhaps absorbed most of Jeanne's attention. This was the approach of Artus, Count of Richemont, Constable of France and brother of the Duke of Brittany, with a large following. Owing to previous difficulties with the Dauphin and La Trémoïlle, which had left Richemont with a justifiable grievance, there was some doubt in d'Alençon's mind as to whether the Constable should be received in a friendly spirit or no; it seems, in fact, that Jeanne was of the opinion that they must go out to fight him. This was going rather too far, and the French captains remarked that, if she insisted, she might well discover that many in the army would prefer the Constable to all the *pucelles* in France. It was not for Jeanne to be disconcerted by such an answer. D'Alençon, the Bastard, young Gui de Laval and his brother, were all constrained to accompany her to meet the Constable in the open, though no one knew what was to come of such a meeting. When the two companies came within sight of one another, both Jeanne and the Constable dismounted and advanced. Jeanne, according to her custom, knelt and embraced his knees. One may suppose, although it is not recorded, that the Constable made

[1] *Procès*, Vol. IV, p. 174: *Journal du siège d'Orléans*.

the sign of the cross, for he spoke to her, saying, "Jehanne, I have been told that you want to fight me. I do not know whether you come from God or not. If you come from God, I do not fear you in any way, for God knows my good intentions; if you come from the Devil, I fear you even less." They then appear to have composed their differences, for they all rode peaceably back to Beaugency together, and the sentinels that night were drawn from among the Constable's men, according to the usual custom of drawing the sentinels from the ranks of the latest arrivals.[1]

iv

At dawn (June 17th) the English took their humiliating departure from Beaugency, but, even as they were evacuating the town, one of La Hire's men arrived with the news that Talbot and Fastolf were rapidly approaching with a large army (i.e. about 5,000 men) to the succour of their friends at Beaugency. This piece of news appears to have dismayed the French captains, some of whom said that they had better send for their horses. Jeanne, however, took her usual point of view, so curiously compounded of common sense and religious inspiration. Her common sense suggested that, since Richemont was there and had been accepted, she had better make use of him. "*Ah, beau Connétable,*" she said to him, "I was not responsible for your coming, but since you have come, you shall be welcome." To the captains she said that even if the English dangled from the skies they should be caught, since God had sent them for their chastisement. She went further. The Dauphin, she said, should gain the greatest victory he had

[1]*Procès*, Vol. IV, p. 317: Account of Guillaume Gruel. Gruel was a devoted servant of the Constable, and M. Quicherat suggests that the details of Richemont's meeting with Jeanne should be accepted with reserve. The various accounts of the Constable's arrival differ in several particulars, Gruel himself making so capital and ludicrous a blunder as to say that his master was marching to assist in the relief of *Orleans*, which had taken place a week earlier.

gained for a long time, *"et m'a dit mon conseil qu'ils sont tous nostres."*[1]

She was right. The result was the battle of Patay (June 18th), the most serious blow the English had sustained since Orleans.

v

Descriptions of mediæval battles are wearisome and unreal in the extreme, but it so happens that a Burgundian follower of Fastolf has left us an account of the battle of Patay which, supplemented by the accounts of d'Alençon and the Bastard, lifts the dead old story into the vivid light of actuality. This Burgundian follower was a certain Jean de Wavrin du Forestel, the illegitimate son of a father who had been killed at his side at the battle of Agincourt. A soldier of repute and skill, he had assembled a company of mercenaries whose services were engaged now by the Duke of Burgundy, now by the English. In later life he took up his pen for the benefit of a nephew, and to this desire to inform the younger generation of the dramatic events which had taken place in the earlier half of the century we owe one of the most astute, though not always accurate, commentaries that we possess.[2] The interest is increased by the fact that we are for once reading a version given from the English point of view, exhibiting their difficulties and perplexities, as a change from the note of triumph habitually sounded by the French contemporary witnesses and chroniclers.

Following Jean de Wavrin, we learn that the English commanders at Janville were much distressed on receiving the news of the capture of Jargeau, of the semi-submission of Meung, and of the siege laid to Beaugency (*lesquelles nouvelles leur furent en moult grant desplaisance*). We learn, also, that they were greatly cheered by the arrival of Talbot, and that, after they had all dined together, the tables were cleared so that they might hold a council to discuss the situation. This

[1]*Procès*, Vol. III, pp. 98–9: Deposition of the Duke of Alençon.
[2]*Procès*, Vol. IV, pp. 406–24.

discussion proved both argumentative and acrimonious, largely owing to the insistence of Fastolf, who got up in his place to address the most bitter remonstrances to Talbot, saying that they were all well aware of the losses the English had sustained at Orleans, Jargeau, and other places, which rather suggests that the English authorities had attempted to falsify and diminish the news of these defeats. Fastolf, to whose discourse Talbot listened with a most disapproving and anxious ear, went on to say that in his opinion they had better leave the garrison of Beaugency to its fate and conclude the most favourable treaty they possibly could with the French, until the Duke of Bedford could supply them with his promised reinforcements.

Talbot, a fiery man, taking a leaf out of Jeanne's book, declared that, with the aid of God and Saint George, he would go and fight with anyone who was willing to follow him. Fastolf, seeing his remonstrances disregarded, rose and left the council table in a huff. The meeting, in short, broke up, all its members retiring into their own lodgings. A sulky and uncomfortable afternoon must have ensued. Nevertheless Talbot held firm: Fastolf, after all, was nothing but his second in command; he might protest, but, in the last resort, he was obliged to obey: Talbot had every right to hold to his own opinion. Orders were issued that the army should be ready to march on the following morning, to go wherever their commanders should ordain. As bidden, they turned out in full array, with standards and pennons, only to be kept waiting while their leaders withdrew into further council and Fastolf renewed his argument. His argument was even more urgently advanced than before. They were only a handful, he said, to oppose the French; if fortune went against them, all the conquests of Henry V would be undone; they would be far better advised to restrain themselves and to wait until they might be reinforced. Neither Talbot nor the others would listen. Fastolf had to give way; willynilly he had to order his men to march with the rest upon the road towards Meung. Patay lay between Janville and Meung, but even Fastolf for all his wisdom, even Talbot for all his daring, could not know what Patay was to mean to them as a name in history.

The English had no idea that Beaugency had already fallen. The French, better informed, knew both that the English garrison of Beaugency was in retreat, and that Talbot's army was advancing towards them. They were already perched at an advantage on a small rise of the ground—in Wavrin's words a *petite montagnette*—when Talbot's army came into sight across the plains of la Beauce—*celle Beauce qui est ample et large*. The ensuing conduct of both parties is typical of the mediæval methods which make warfare look like a game of chess rather than like ferocious business. The English, perceiving the French upon their monticule, drew rein, and disposed their archers into their accustomed formation (i.e. with their pikes stuck into the ground, the points sloped towards the enemy, in a sort of sharp stockade), and in this arrangement the two forces contemplated one another. Neither side seemed disposed to move. The English, at length, seeing the French quietly ensconced above them, sent two heralds with an offer to say that they had three knights willing to fight them if they had the courage to come down. It was an arrogant challenge, which was probably not intended to be taken seriously—a mere gambit, to which the French returned an equally conventional reply. "Go and find lodging for yourselves to-night," they said, "for it is already late; but to-morrow, God and Our Lady willing, we shall see you at closer quarters" (*de plus prez*).

The English thereupon retired to Meung, and spent the night bombarding the bridge which had previously been taken by the French.

They still had no information of the fall of Beaugency, and next morning were busily assembling shields and doors, as protection for their attacking party, when a courier arrived to tell them that the town and castle of Beaugency were already occupied by the French, and that even as he, the courier, was leaving, the French were on their way to offer battle.

On the reception of this news, orders were hastily given to

Q

abandon any renewal of the attack on the bridge at Meung, and to proceed instantly into the country, where every man according to his own position was to range himself *en ordonnance de belle bataille*. *Laquelle chose*, Wavrin adds complacently, *fut faite moulte agréablement*, and the English were able to take up their position in a narrow passage between two hedges in the vicinity of Patay.

The French, meanwhile, had lost the English host. La Beauce, that large and ample plain, thickly wooded, was a place in which anybody might be excused for losing sight of an army. Encouraged as usual by Jeanne, they had been quite ready to receive the enemy; they had, in fact, offered the enemy that bellicose appointment on the preceding evening. Nor had they gone back on their decision. D'Alençon himself, on the morning of Patay, had asked Jeanne, in the presence of the Bastard and the Constable, what he should do. Jeanne gave an unwontedly oracular reply: "Have, all of you, good spurs"— a reply which surprised her hearers into asking what she meant. Did she mean that they were to turn their backs, i.e. run away? "No," she answered, with a return of her habitual plain confidence, "it will be the English who will turn their backs. They will not defend themselves and will be defeated, and you will need spurs to pursue them."[1]

This was all very well, but spurs were of very little use if you could not find the enemy whom you were to pursue. The French scouts ranged about, sixty to eighty of them, mounted on the pick of the horses (*fleurs de coursiers*), and, as ill luck would have it for the English, put up a stag, who bounded off immediately into the English lines, a sight which the English evidently could not resist, especially in this game of hide-and-seek over the wide area of la Beauce, where neither army knew where to look for the other. It was scarcely to be expected that Englishmen, seeing a stag, should not set up a shout of delight. They set it up, with the result that for once the English love of sport turned against the hunter instead of against the hunted.

[1] *Procès*, Vol. III, p. 11: Deposition of Dunois.

The French, thus advised of their presence, were able to engage them before they could organise themselves into sufficient order of resistance, and the battle of Patay was won almost before it had begun. The whole thing was over by two o'clock in the afternoon.[1]

Fastolf was in flight, *demanant le plus grant deuil que jamais veisse faire à homme.* He succeeded in reaching the Duke of Bedford, who incontinently, and quite unjustly, deprived him of his Order of the Garter.[2] The English lost a number of killed and prisoners, which varies between two and four thousand. Lord Scales, Sir Thomas Ramston, Lord Hungerford, were taken prisoners; and so, more importantly, was Talbot himself, who surrendered to the men of Poton de Saintrailles.[3] This was the supreme triumph, and even the generous d'Alençon could not resist a slight gibe when "brave Talbot, the terror of the French," was brought before him. Jeanne and the Constable were present. "You did not think this morning," he said, "that such a thing would befall you?" D'Alençon himself, it must be remembered, had but recently tasted the displeasures of captivity among the English. Talbot gave a soldier's answer: "It is the fortune of war."[4]

Jeanne, according to Louis de Contes, her devoted but rather muddled little page, was characteristically and femininely

[1]*Procès*, Vol. IV, p. 374: Enguerran de Monstrelet.

[2]*Procès*, Vol. IV, p. 375: Enguerran de Monstrelet. The Garter was later restored to him, in consideration of the protests he had made to Talbot before the battle of Patay.

[3]*Procès*, Vol. IV, p. 319: Gruel: The Bastard of Orleans says 4,000; *Procès*, Vol. IV, p. 479: Walter Bower, 3,000; Perceval de Cagny, 2,000 dead and 400 to 500 prisoners; Jean Chartier, 2,000 to 3,000 dead and many prisoners; the *Chronique de la Pucelle*, over 2,200 dead; the *Journal du siège d'Orleans*, 2,200 dead; Guillaume Gruel, 2,200 dead; official letter to the city of Tours, 2,500 dead or prisoners; Wavrin, 2,000 dead and 200 prisoners; Monstrelet, 1,800 dead and 100 to 120 prisoners. We may decide on a wise mean between these varying estimates, but, however we may decide, it is clear that the English defeat was thorough and the losses considerable.

[4]*Procès*, Vol. III, p. 99: Deposition of the Duke of Alençon.

moved by the inevitable results of the battle she had advised. She was always ready to encourage the more prudent captains to battle; she was always ready to say that God was on their side; she was always ready to throw herself into danger with the best of them, but, once the heat and excitement were over, she was by no means ready to face the incidental consequences in a spirit of detachment. Either she wept for the unshriven souls of her vanquished enemies, or else she wept for their broken heads. On this occasion she wept for a broken English head to the extent of taking it on her knees and of obliging its owner to confess his sins before he died.[1]

vi

Jeanne slept at Ligneroles that night, and on the following day returned to her own Orleans. She ought, of course, to have insisted on marching straight against Paris.[2] With Talbot a prisoner, Fastolf in flight, the English army routed and their morale gone, as even the Anglo-Burgundian Wavrin observes (*considérant que par la renommée de Jehanne la Pucelle les courages anglois estoient fort altérés et faillis*), the opportunity was in her hands, if only she had chosen to take it. Even Bedford saw that the Dauphin ought to march on Paris. Even Bedford saw the necessity of getting the wretched and useless little Henry VI to come over to France to be crowned. But the career of Jeanne d'Arc, triumphant in so many ways, was also a career of missed opportunities. The common sense which ought to have guided her, had her intellect been of the more masculine instead of the more feminine type, frequently failed her at critical moments. Perhaps we should state it differently. Perhaps, instead of using the terms masculine and feminine, we should use mundane as opposed to spiritual; balanced as opposed to fanatical. She could be common-sensible enough in immediate

[1]*Procès*, Vol. III, pp. 71-2: Deposition of Louis de Contes.

[2]On this point I find myself in complete agreement with Mr. Andrew Lang.

crises; over the larger issues she appears all too frequently to have been the victim of her own *idées fixes*. She strikes me all too often as a person of inspiration but of unequal judgment; as a person with an objective but with no reasoned policy; as a person galloping headlong down a narrow road never lifting her eyes over the landscape beyond; as a person whose very weakness was her strength, her very strength her weakness. Thus, on this occasion, when she ought to have ridden straight to Paris, carrying d'Alençon, the Bastard, and her devoted army with her, she lost time because of her conviction that her first duty was to get her Dauphin crowned King of France. She would have been better advised to present her Dauphin with a united France of which to get himself crowned King. Any real military genius and strategist would have perceived it.

Of course, there is a great deal to be said in her defence. She was quite right to think that the Dauphin would never be the King until he was crowned as the King. Such ceremonies as the anointing with holy oil were of immense importance in the eyes of the fifteenth century. No King of France could be given his true title until he was consecrated and crowned, and had received the peculiar grace he was supposed to receive from the Holy Spirit through the holy oil. This holy oil, traditionally used for the anointing of the Kings of France, and contained, as it was, in the sacred vessel known as the Sainte Ampoule, was the very especial pride and property of the city of Reims, and constituted, in fact, the whole claim of that city to consecrate the sovereign within the walls of its cathedral. In such veneration was it held, that it was never allowed to leave Reims save on one sole occasion during thirteen centuries—to comfort the dying Louis XI, who, autocrat though he was, had been obliged to send to Rome for permission from the Pope.[1] The vessel itself was a little phial measuring only an inch and a

[1]Charles Cerf, *Histoire de Notre Dame de Reims*, Vol. II, pp. 484–5. The Sainte Ampoule was deliberately smashed by a deputy of the Convention, but some morsels of the glass, with the oil adhering to them, are said to have been preserved.

half long, the neck being closed by a stopper of red silk[1]; the holy contents had admittedly dried and shrivelled since a pigeon whiter than snow had arrived with the phial in its beak to the assistance of Saint Rémi at the baptism of Clovis.[2] But the size of the vessel and the state of the contents—*d'une consistance cérumineuse, d'une couleur rougeâtre*—bore no relation to the awe with which they were regarded. It was all very well for Saint Rémi himself, for Pope Anastatius the Second, for Saint Avitus, Bishop of Vienna, for Saint Nicet, Bishop of Treves, for Saint Gregory of Tours, for Fredegaire, his successor, for the authors of the life of Saint Arnoul, for Alcuin, author of the life of Saint Vaast, for the monk Horicon, for the authors of the *Gesta Dagoberti* and the *Gesta Francorum* to withhold their testimony on the subject of so miraculous an origin: the people of France knew better. They knew that the King was not the King until the necessary morsel of Saint Rémi's oil had been dug out of the Sainte Ampoule at the point of a golden needle. And Jeanne d'Arc was very much a daughter of France. She had always been very careful to address Charles VII as Dauphin and not as King before his coronation, and had in fact declared her intention of doing so. When we consider that she was only a peasant, and a peasant living in a credulous age, and an especially inspired peasant at that, we can begin to understand why her desire to lead the Dauphin to Reims exceeded, however unwisely, her desire to lead his army to Paris. Besides, there were other difficulties in her way, which did but increase her obstinacy. The fat La Trémoïlle crossed her whenever he could, jealously disapproving of any influence she might exercise over the weak puppet wavering between them; thus, thanks to his vindictive intervention, she completely failed to effect a reconciliation between Charles and the Constable de Richemont; and other leaders who, entirely on her account, had

---

[1]Charles Cerf, *Histoire de Notre Dame de Reims*, Vol. I, p. 285.
[2]Charles Cerf, *Histoire de Notre Dame de Reims*, Vol. II, p. 574.

come from all sides to offer their services to Charles at their own expense, met with black looks even if they were not actually turned away. The Constable, who *was* turned away, took his company of twelve hundred men with him. Such wanton sacrifice of much-needed help to La Trémoïlle's personal ambition drew general criticism, yet no one dared breathe a word outwardly against him.[1]

And not only did La Trémoïlle impede her, but Charles himself seemed to have but little idea of what she was doing for him, or of what she would expect him to do for her in return. When, after Patay, she met him (June 19th–22nd) at St. Benoit-sur-Loire, he reduced her to tears by the suggestion that she should now allow herself a rest.[2] It was not that he was ungrateful, for he expressed his pity for all the fatigues she had suffered on his behalf—indeed, he could do no less— it was that he was utterly unable to enter into sympathy with a flaming spirit such as Jeanne's. Besides, we cannot tell what La Trémoïlle was saying to him in private, nor can we justly estimate what indolence, lethargy, and even cowardice contributed to his disinclination.

Jeanne got her way in the end, but only after a week's delay. If Perceval de Cagny is to be believed, all sorts of difficulties were raised, some people saying, with truth, that many hostile towns lay on the road, others, with equal truth, that the Dauphin had no money to pay his men. The men, according to the loyal de Cagny, were ready to give their services for nothing, saying that they would go anywhere the Pucelle wished to lead them.

Jeanne, still according to de Cagny, ended by losing her patience; left the Dauphin at Gien, and, going off in despite, encamped for two days and nights, without him, in the fields.[3] This gesture seems to have stirred him into some activity, for on June 29th he finally took his departure from Gien, and on

[1]*Procès*, Vol. IV, pp. 70–1: Jean Chartier.
[2]*Procès*, Vol. III, p. 116: Deposition of Simon Charles.
[3]*Procès*, Vol. IV, pp. 17–18: Perceval de Cagny.

July 1st we find him and Jeanne together before the Burgundian city of Auxerre. Jeanne, it is said, was in favour of entering Auxerre by force, but, as the army stood in serious need of reprovisioning, an agreement was reached by which the city provided the necessary supplies on condition that it should be left in peace. It is also added that La Trémoïlle received two thousand crowns from the city as a bribe for his good offices in effecting this arrangement.[1]

It is not difficult to enter into Jeanne's feelings as she once more beheld Auxerre, that noble city with its two great churches towering so majestically on the slope above the river, the city in which she "on her way from Domremy, in her black and grey page's suit, had heard Mass with Jean de Metz and Bertrand de Poulengy," and to which "within four months she returned, the companion and counsellor of princes, at the head of an army which, in her presence, had never met with a single check."[2] No doubt the mediæval beauty of Auxerre did not appeal to Jeanne in the same way as it appeals to us, with our trained æsthetic appreciation and exaggerated sentiment for antiquity, but in a different way the dominance of the great Houses of God over the jumbled roofs of streets no less tortuous than the policy of her enemies, must have impressed her with a grandeur and single-mindedness as uncompromising as her own intentions.

More practically, she must have regretted the decision to leave an unsubjected city behind her, especially as she could foresee the possibility of Troyes, Châlons, and Reims itself holding out on learning that Auxerre had with impunity been allowed to do so.

vii

It is perhaps unnecessary to follow the march towards Reims in any detail; I cannot, however, resist the temptation of pausing before the Burgundian city of Troyes, where Jeanne

---

[1] *Procès*, Vol. IV, p. 181: *Journal du siège d'Orléans.*
[2] Andrew Lang, *The Maid of France*, p. 152.

came into contact with one of those curious characters abound-
ing among her contemporaries. Troyes was at the moment
under the influence of a Franciscan friar named Brother
Richard. This fiery and extraordinary personage had already
made a name for himself as a preacher in Paris, where he seems,
for three weeks, to have combined the rôles of a Solomon
Eagle and a Savonarola. Endowed with a magnificent voice,
he could speak in the open from five o'clock in the morning
till ten or eleven, without coming to an end of his eloquence
or showing any signs of fatigue. His audiences, who were
willing to spend the whole night under the stars rather than
miss his opening sentences, flocked in their thousands to hear
his denunciations, and to fling their vanities in armfuls on
brasiers lighted in the streets. Cards, dice, and personal orna-
ments such as the then extravagant head-dresses of women,
were willingly heaped upon the flames. Apart from his dema-
gogic powers of oratory, he was shrewd enough to claim definite
justifications for his pronouncements. He announced himself
as newly arrived from Jerusalem, where the brothers of his
order were in charge of the Holy Sepulchre, and where he had
met, or said he had met, bands of Jews setting out for Babylon
to visit the Antichrist who had been living for some years in
that city. The very name of Antichrist struck terror. What did
the Parisians care or know that Babylon had ceased to exist
some hundreds of years ago? A man who had met Jews actually
setting out from Jerusalem to Babylon was a man to be listened
to. Besides, he could foretell that the year 1430 would bring
forth the most marvellous things that had ever yet been seen.
It was very necessary, under such teaching, that they should
secure their salvation, and so they not only heaped their
finery and their games on the bonfires at street corners, but
also struck and wore leaden medals stamped with the mono-
gram of the name Jesus. Brother Richard's sway over Paris was
dramatic but short-lived. The religious terror he had evoked
was soon eclipsed by the more immediate dread that he might
have gone over to the side of the Dauphin—an excellent excuse

for resuming all the amusements he had forbidden, and for throwing his leaden medals into the Seine.[1]

Fortunately for the Dauphin and his army, Brother Richard had spent the previous Advent preaching at Troyes, where the population had interpreted one of his rhetorical flights so literally as to sow actual beans instead of only the metaphorical variety. "Sow, good people, sow beans in abundance," he had said to them, "for He who is to come will come before long." The odd result of this recommendation was that when the underfed army arrived before Troyes, in the following July, they found plenty to eat. They also found Brother Richard there in person, not at all sure what attitude he should adopt towards the notorious Pucelle. Not only were they rivals, in a sense, for popular favour, but the friar seems to have shared the suspicion which persisted in the minds of some people— that the Pucelle might be a witch. In any case, the citizens of Troyes were not at all disposed to admit either the Dauphin or his *coquarde*, as they termed Jeanne. The example of Auxerre was recent in their minds: if Auxerre could remain inviolate, so could Troyes, which was, moreover, a far more strongly fortified town. Jeanne, however, recommended a firm policy. She was summoned to the Dauphin's council and invited to give her advice. Let him wait for two days, she said, and he should receive the submission of the town, either through force or love. The Archbishop of Reims, who was travelling with them, said that they could willingly wait for six days if necessary, but was she quite sure? Jeanne was always sure. Nor were her certainties based on mere optimism, for, no sooner had she received their promise of patience, than she set about practical preparations which, as she rightly conjectured, would terrorise the people of Troyes into opening their gates to their lawful King.[2] These practical preparations were supported by one of her famous letters, addressed to the citizens (July 4th), saying that they need have no fear for their lives or property if only

[1]Siméon Luce, *Jeanne d'Arc à Domremy*, pp. ccxlvi–viii.
[2]*Procès*, Vol. IV, p. 75: Jean Chartier.

they would receive their King as they should; but if not, then on their lives she would promise them that with the aid of God all the cities of the kingdom would be entered and peace made, *qui que vienne contre.* "Answer quickly."[1] It was now that they sent Brother Richard to meet her, making the sign of the cross and sprinkling holy water, lest she might be a thing not sent by God. She reassured him. "Approach boldly," she said, "I shall not fly away."[2]

After this, Brother Richard attached himself to the moving train of the royal army, an allegiance which he found was not without material profit.

viii

Leaving a submissive Troyes behind him, the Dauphin went on to Châlons, which received him without any difficulty, thus proving how right Jeanne's judgment had been over the scare she had produced at Troyes. They were now in full Champagne, and prospects were bright for a warm welcome at Reims. For Jeanne's part, speaking personally, a homely little incident awaited her at Châlons: she met two friends from Domremy. They have both left an account, brief but vivid, of their meeting. One of them, Jean Morel, her godfather, states that she gave him her old red dress.[3] The other, Gérardin d'Epinal, states that she told him she feared nothing but treachery.[4] The remark is significant in the light of subsequent events, for at the moment she had, ostensibly, no immediate treachery to fear. All seemed to be going well in accordance with her plans when she met these two doubtless dazzled cronies at Châlons-sur-Marne. God still seemed to be wholly on her side. Swarms of white butterflies had recently been seen escorting

---

[1]*Procès*, Vol. IV, pp. 287–8: Jean Rogier.
[2]*Procès*, Vol. I, pp. 99–100.
[3]*Procès*, Vol. II, p. 391: Deposition of Jean Morel.
[4]*Procès*, Vol. II, p. 423: Deposition of Gérardin d'Epinal. According to Gérardin, he was with three other men from Domremy, but he does not say who they were. One of them, of course, must have been Jean Morel.

her banner. Little more than thirty miles separated her from the goal of Reims. The Archbishop of Reims had already written to his people, requesting them to welcome their King; the citizens of Châlons had written to their neighbours at Reims, giving the King a good character, and advising their neighbours to receive him in the same spirit as they had themselves displayed.[1]

Jeanne cannot have found much time to spend with her friends from Domremy, for she stayed only one night at Châlons-sur-Marne. On the following day she entered an excited and loyal Reims in the train of the Dauphin.

ix

The preparations for the coronation had to be undertaken in some haste—in such haste, in fact, that those concerned had but one night in which to make ready. Up till the very afternoon before the actual ceremony the citizens of Reims had not decided whether to deliver their keys to the Dauphin or not. That Saturday, July 16th, must have been enough to fluster the most soberly minded. For one thing, in the morning, they had their first sight of their archbishop, who had been their archbishop for twenty years without ever coming near them. A few hours later, in the afternoon, they had their first sight of their King and of his famous Pucelle, whom everybody stared at (*qui fut moult regardée de tous*),[2] not to mention the arrival of a whole army seeking billets in the city, or of personages such as the Duke of Bar—that same gay young René whose support Jeanne had in vain demanded at the court of Nancy, five months earlier in the year. On the top of all this excitement, with processions passing through the crowded streets, the order went forth for the ceremony to be performed on the following day. The moon was full, and all night long the city resounded to the blows of hammers and mallets.

[1]*Procès*, Vol. IV, pp. 297–8: Jean Rogier.
[2]*Procès*, Vol. IV, p. 185: *Journal du siège d'Orléans.*

CHARLES VII

From the portrait in the Louvre Museum, by Jean Foucquet

The cathedral itself was in its full glory. The building, its foundation-stone laid in 1212, interrupted since 1381, had been resumed in 1427, and was approaching completion. Little now remained to be done save the addition of a spire on each of the two towers flanking the great west door,[1] and these, for the occasion, were replaced by enormous fleurs-de-lis. The thirteenth-century organ was still in use. Much of the stained glass had already been in its place for over a century, so that the grave and archaic company of saints, apostles, evangelists, and kings looked down upon the aisles and transepts, while the mosaic of the *rosaces* blazed like living flowers in sunlight and fell in splashes of red, blue, and yellow against the columns and on the paving of the floor. Eighteen double lancets in the nave represented thirty-six bishops and thirty-six kings and queens, crowned and sceptred, dressed in richly ornamented cloaks and tunics, seated in high-backed chairs, according to the custom of portraying the dead in a position of repose. Bishops and kings they certainly were; but were any of them really queens? There appears to be some doubt on the subject. An historian of Reims with unconscious humour observes that *plusieurs de ces personnages, qui ont le même costume et les mêmes ornements que les rois, sont entièrement imberbes.*

For some seven hundred years these gorgeous fragilities, let into the solid stone, withstood the ravages of elements and time: *leur face extérieure, luttant sans discontinuité contre la pluie, la poussière, l'air, et le soleil, a cédé en mille endroits à ces influences malignes; mais rien n'a pu ébranler la solidité des panneaux, irrevocablement attachés à leur vêtement de fer, et bravant, dans leur imperturbable fermeté, toute la fureur des plus terribles orages.*[2]

Alas, the historian of Reims could not foresee the most terrible of storms, more terrible for being human, not elemental: the storm which in 1917 irrevocably destroyed, under the most cruel of bombardments, the beauty which awaited

[1]Charles Cerf, *Histoire de Notre Dame de Reims,* Vol. II, pp. 181–3 (2 vols. 1861). These projected spires were never added.
[2]Charles Cerf, *Histoire de Notre Dame de Reims,* Vol. II, pp. 181–3.

Charles VII and Jeanne d'Arc on the morning of Sunday, July 17th, 1429.

x

It is a noticeable but odd fact that mediæval chroniclers seldom if ever make any reference to the weather. They refer to the weather only in its more unpleasant and inconvenient aspects, such as excessive rains or the flooding of an otherwise fordable river. When they remain silent on the subject, we may suppose that the season was behaving according to its normal mood; thus, although it would add considerably to the vividness of our impressions were we to be told for certain whether the day of July 17th, 1429, was bright or clouded, we can only conjecture, in the absence of other evidence, that, the date being the height of summer and the situation being the favoured plain of Champagne, the day was warm and sunny, as might reasonably be expected *en cette heure et en ce lieu*. Had the heavens chosen to be overcast, or even to open themselves in tears, on such an occasion as the long-deferred translation of the Dauphin into the King, friendly chroniclers might possibly have suppressed the fact, but hostile chroniclers would certainly have seized with delight upon its symbolism. We may take it, therefore, that the day was gay when, at nine in the morning, Charles rode to the cathedral in full procession, accompanied by the Duke of Alençon, the Duke de la Trèmoïlle, the Count of Claremont, the Count of Vendôme, and the young de Lavals, representing the peers of France. The maréchal de Saint-Sévère, the maréchal de Rais, the seigneur de Graville, and Louis de Coulen, Admiral of France, had already gone to St. Rémy to escort the Abbot bearing the miraculously holy oil. They brought him, dressed in his pontifical vestments, richly ornamented with gold, to Notre Dame, where they were met by the Archbishop, surrounded by his clergy, who, receiving the vessel from the Abbot, placed it upon the altar. There were present also such other dignitaries of the Church as the Archbishop of Châlons and the Bishops of

Seez and Orleans, and an enormous concourse of knights and soldiers filling the vast cathedral.

The ceremony was conducted with all its accustomed pomp. The Duke of Alençon knighted the King; the seigneur d'Albret held the sword. The Archbishop of Reims performed his traditional duty. But a single figure drew all eyes, the cause, as they said, after God, of this coronation and of all that assembly[1]: Jeanne d'Arc, who kept her place standing beside the King, in armour, her standard in her hand. *"Il avait été à la peine,"* she said, when they asked why her standard had figured at the *sacre*, *" c'etait bien raison qu'il fut à l'honneur."*[2]

---

[1]*Procès*, Vol. IV, p. 186: *Journal du siège d'Orléans* and note.

[2]*Procès*, Vol. I, p. 187: *Interroguée pour quoy il fut plus porté en l'église de Rains, au sacre, que ceulx des autres cappitaines, respond: "Il avoit este à la paine, c'estoit bien raison que il fut à l'onneur."*

Chapter XII

REIMS TO PARIS

i

The coronation represented the peak of Jeanne's triumph. Not five months had elapsed since she had left Domremy, but during the course of that time she had forced herself into acceptance, had become a national heroine, and had accomplished two out of her four main promises. She had seen her father again, and had received his forgiveness, for that bewildered peasant had travelled from Domremy to Reims, where he had been lodged with much honour at the town's expense. She had stood beside her King in a position never accorded even to the greatest peer of France, and had fallen on her knees before him, weeping with emotion, while even those present had been moved to tears as the crown was placed upon his head to the sound of trumpets and the shouts of "*Noel!*" so that it seemed as though the vaulting of the roof would be rent.[1] That was her hour, and she had lived it to the full. It seemed also as though her victory would be pushed to its logical conclusion, for the plan was definitely to march towards Paris next day.[2] Jeanne herself had no doubt of reducing Paris to obedience. She had already laid the train by writing to the *haut et redoubté prince*, the Duke of Burgundy, three weeks earlier[3] and again on the very day of the coronation, begging him *à jointes mains* to make peace,[4] but, as events proved, she had here acted as her own worst enemy. Crossing her second letter, Burgundy sent envoys to Reims to negotiate, if not a permanent peace, then at least a truce; and Charles, gullible, optimistic, and only too thankful for any excuse for delay,

[1]*Procès,* Vol. V, p. 129: Letter from three gentlemen of Anjou to the wife and mother-in-law of Charles VII.
[2]*Procès,* Vol. V, p. 130, ibid.
[3]This letter no longer exists.
[4]*Procès,* Vol. V, pp. 126–7.

wasted four precious days in *pourparlers* with the Burgundians at Reims, while a large English army, under Cardinal Beaufort and the Duke of Bedford, was hastening towards Paris, strengthened by Burgundy's men from Picardy.

The Dukes of Burgundy and Bedford between them, in fact, fooled the King exactly as they pleased. Jeanne's fate was sealed. From Reims onwards her feet were set on the sharply sloping path which fetched up at the stake.

ii

Jeanne herself was in despair. She was fully conscious of the seriousness and urgency of the situation, but what could she do? I dare to suggest that after Reims the first great gale of her inspiration left her, and that she was no longer capable in quite her old way of making men listen to her voice. She seems to have been aware of something of the sort herself, for she told the Archbishop of Reims, as she rode between him and the Bastard, that she wished God her Creator would allow her to lay down her arms and return to serve her father and mother, keeping their sheep with her sister and her brothers, who would greatly rejoice on seeing her.[1] One may conjecture that the immediate reason for the expression of so uncharacteristically weak a wish lay in the recent meeting with her father at Reims. Although no record exists of their meeting, nor of the place in which it happened, nor of the words which passed between them, it is only reasonable to imagine that this strange reunion, humanly speaking, must have been fraught with great and difficult emotions on either side. Consider the experiences through which Jeanne had passed, and through which we have followed her almost day by day in those five

[1]*Procès*, Vol. III, pp. 14–15: Deposition of Dunois. Anatole France (*Vie de Jeanne d'Arc*, Vol. II, p. 17, note) suggests that some hagiographer of a clerk has here embellished the passage in the Bastard's recollections. As her sister is presumed to have been dead by then, and as two of her brothers were in her company at Reims, there seems to be some foundation for his scepticism.

R

packed months. But consider also the unrelieved and unrecorded days at Domremy, where there was nothing to do but to follow patiently on the same accustomed round of a peasant's year—sowing the crops, milking the cows, slicing the turnips, collecting the eggs; keeping on in the same old way although one's daughter had run away after the wildest of geese; no news coming through, save unbelievable rumours of her doings among men whose names were as awful as they were remote. Insufficient sympathy has, I think, been accorded to the parents of Jeanne d'Arc. Anxious, perplexed, and very human beings, they have been allowed to suffer an almost total eclipse in the shadow of their resplendent child. It is permissible to pause and to speculate for a moment on the feelings of Jacques d'Arc as on those of Jeanne herself, when, on the eve of the King's coronation, they met again in Reims, Jeanne no longer the disgraced and fugitive Jeannette, but the magnificent Pucelle who had earned her right to stand beside the King.

Was it difficult for her to readjust herself immediately to the position of a child, confronted by a father from whom she still had to obtain a verbal forgiveness? Where did they meet? Was it at Jacques' lodging at the *Ane Rayé*,[1] or did he have to be summoned because his Jeannette could not ride through the streets of Reims without provoking the wildest of demonstrations? The last time he had seen her she had been wearing her patched red dress. Now, she had a green tunic, armour, and a gold and crimson cloak. Then, she had

---

[1]*Procès*, Vol. V, p. 266: The *Ane Rayé* was in the rue du Parvis, and was later replaced by the *Maison Rouge*, ornamented by the following inaccurate inscription:

> L'an 1429,
> au sacre de Charles VII,
> dans cette hotellerie appelée alors l'Ane Rayé
> le père et la mère de Jeanne d'Arcq [sic]
> ont été logés et defrayés
> par le conseil de ville.

The inaccuracy consists in the mention of both her father and mother, the truth being that only Jeanne's father travelled to Reims.

ridden the farm-horses bareback; now, she had a charger of
her own, a household, pages, a majordomo, and her own
confessor. She was on terms of familiarity with princes; with
lords both spiritual and temporal; with the King himself,
who gave her sixty *livres tournois* as a present for her father.[1]
Did she show him her miraculous sword and her armour,
telling him how its weight had hurt her when first she had put
it on? Was it difficult for her, having been translated into so
different a world, to revert suddenly to the old idiom, or did
the familiar Lorraine accent carry her back into asking quite
naturally for news of her mother and of her friends Hauviette
and Mengette and all those whom she had left behind? We shall
never know. We know only that a fortnight later the King, at
her special request, accorded remission in perpetuity of all
taxes or other levies to the villages of Greux and Domremy,
and that their taxation-demands henceforth appeared cancelled
by the words: *Néant, la Pucelle*, written in the margin.[2]

Someone else witnessed the triumph of Jeanne at Reims:
Durand Lassois, that patient man who had been the first to
believe in her.

iii

All these things were pleasant, but they were not enough
to satisfy Jeanne. I have already suggested that after Reims
a new note seems to enter into the story, as though she were
striving now against odds she had very little hope of overcoming, her courageous spirit refusing to give in, but struggling on without that absolute conviction which had previously
raised her to so irresistible a state of exultation. Perhaps it
is not too much to suppose that her gift of prescience whispered
a subtle warning. Perhaps she was merely disheartened at
last by the heavy task of dragging the reluctant and untrustworthy Charles where she wanted him to go.

[1]*Procès*, Vol. V, p. 267: Account-books of Hémon Raquier.
[2]*Procès*, Vol. V, p. 138: Deed of Charles VII. This privilege was rescinded
only in the eighteenth century.

They left Reims together, four days too late, and reached Soissons two days later. From here it became apparent that, far from making straight for Paris, Charles intended to sneak back to the comfort and safety of the Loire. He would not even enter the important town of Compiègne, although it was prepared to surrender without resistance. By August 2nd he had arrived at Provins, where he stayed until the 5th. By then he had concluded a fifteen-days' truce with the Duke of Burgundy, who thereby undertook to surrender Paris peacefully to him on the fifteenth day.

Jeanne writes a letter to the citizens of Reims (August 5th) which reveals more poignantly than any comment her deep distress, anxiety, and scepticism. It is evident that she rightly has no confidence in the truce, the Duke of Burgundy, or his promises. It is really tragic to read between the lines of her letter, and to observe how she endeavours to preserve an uncritical loyalty towards the King, while still implying to her "dear and good friends" of Reims that she is fully alive to the situation, and assuring them that she will never abandon them as long as she lives. "Jehanne la Pucelle," she writes, "sends you news of herself, and begs and requests that you shall be in no doubt as to the good quarrel that she pursues for the blood royal, and I promise and guarantee [here the letter changes from the third person to the first person singular] that I will never abandon you while I live. It is true that the King has made a truce with the Duke of Burgundy for fifteen days, by which he is to deliver the city of Paris peacefully at the end of the fifteen days. Nevertheless do not be surprised that I should enter into it so briefly, for I am not in favour [*ne soy point contente*] of truces made in this way, and do not know whether I will keep it; but if I do keep it, it will only be to preserve the King's honour, that the blood royal should suffer no harm, for I will keep the King's army together in readiness, lest at the end of the fifteen days they should not make peace."[1]

[1]*Procès*, Vol. V, pp. 139–40.

Jeanne, of course, was perfectly right. The exact dates of the truce are unknown, but it is evident that Burgundy never had the slightest intention of delivering Paris into the hands of the King. All that he had done was to gain a fortnight of extra time for his allies the English. That Charles should have allowed himself to be taken in is both incredible and incomprehensible. It is suggested, not without good reason, that his evil genius, La Trémoïlle, had been bribed by Burgundy; and La Trémoïlle had many a hold besides his personal influence over the wretched Charles.

An unexpected move on the part of the English, however, checked Charles' retreat towards the Loire. His intention had been to cross the Seine by the bridge at Bray, near Provins, but, most fortunately for Jeanne and her supporters, the English elected to seize the bridge just before the King and his army could cross it.[1] This had the effect of cutting the road, and of throwing Charles back on Château Thierry, which at least was nearer to Paris. Jeanne and her friends the Dukes of Alençon and Bar, and the Counts of Clermont, Vendôme, and Lavals rejoiced, since the decision to cross the Seine had been taken entirely against her will.[2]

It now appeared as though the Duke of Bedford, having been given plenty of time to make his preparations, really intended to meet the French in the open field, for on August 7th he addressed a personal letter to Charles, challenging him in the most insulting terms to appoint a rendezvous either in the province of Brie, which was then in the joint occupation of both the English and the French armies, or in the neighbouring province of the Ile de France.[3] Not only did he suggest that Charles was no true King of France, not only did he call Charles in plain language a murderer (i.e. guilty of the assassination of the late Duke of Burgundy), not only did he accuse

[1]*Procès*, Vol. IV, p. 79: Jean Chartier.
[2]*Procès*, Vol. IV, p. 79: Jean Chartier; *Procès*, Vol. IV, p. 188: *Journal du siège d'Orleans.*
[3]*Procès*, Vol. IV, pp. 382–5: Enguerran de Monstrelet.

Charles of being the only cause of all the distress which had come upon the people of France, but he spared no epithets to qualify Jeanne, that "disorderly woman dressed as a man," who had been his principal helper in seducing his ignorant people. It might have been supposed that Charles' personal pride, sense of honour, chivalry, and gratitude would be stung into taking some action upon the receipt of such a letter. True, he did hang about for some days at Montépilloy, in the neighbourhood of Senlis (August 14th–16th), when a few skirmishes resulted between the outposts and patrols of the two armies, but neither Charles nor Bedford, in spite of his braggart letter, seemed in the least anxious to enter into a decisive engagement when it came to the point. After all the fanfare and advertisement, nothing much happened, except that La Trémoïlle fell off his horse, and was nearly, but not quite, taken prisoner.[1] Jeanne did her best. She went so far as to ride up to the English stockade and to strike it with the pole of her standard.[2] Seeing that this was of no avail, she sent to ask them to come out and fight: she could scarcely do more, even with d'Alençon gallantly backing her. In the end, the two armies withdrew in different directions—like two dogs who have stalked round and round one another growling with raised hackles, but who have finally decided on discretion rather than on valour.[3]

Bedford went back to Paris; Charles at last was persuaded to advance towards Compiègne. For the moment it looked as though Jeanne's fortunes were again in the ascendant. Important towns once more began dropping their keys at the feet of the King or his representatives. Senlis and Beauvais both made their subjection; Compiègne welcomed the King in person. Still Jeanne was uneasy: she mistrusted the length of the stay that Charles proposed to make at Compiègne, for by his manner she judged him so well satisfied with the favours

---

[1]*Procès*, Vol. IV, p. 195: *Journal du siège d'Orléans*.

[2]*Procès*, Vol. IV, p. 22: Perceval de Cagny.

[3]There were strategical reasons for this unheroic conduct on both sides, but I have thought it unnecessary to go into them here.

he had received from God that the wish to undertake anything further had failed him. She was not only uneasy, she was also preoccupied, and her preoccupation led her into a blunder— the serious blunder of dictating a letter to the Count of Armagnac even as she was about to mount her horse. This was not the moment to choose to reply to an enquiry from an important and friendly lord, and, moreover, the subject of the letter and the manner in which Jeanne in her impatience chose to answer it were alike unfortunate. For d'Armagnac had seen fit to ask her which of the three popes ought to be obeyed, and to request her to obtain guidance from Jesus Christ on the subject. Now Jeanne should never have admitted, even by implication, that she had any right to pronounce on a matter which was the sole business of the Church; still less should she have answered that she was too busy making war at the moment, but that as soon as she should be at rest in Paris, or elsewhere, she would make the necessary enquiries and would let him know.[1] Her judges, attacking her at her trial, were little impressed by the excuse that this ill-considered letter was hurriedly dictated because some bystanders were threatening to throw the Armagnac messenger into the river. It was a piece of presumption on which they could, and did, pronounce her guilty.

There is no doubt that Jeanne had little time or thought for anything but war. To d'Alençon she said that she wanted to go and see Paris closer[2]; hitherto, she had caught only a glimpse of Montmartre from the heights of Dammartin. D'Alençon, ever faithful, accompanied her to Saint Denis (August 23rd), and the King, hearing of their departure, sulkily removed himself to Senlis, seemingly under the influence of advice contrary to the wishes of Jeanne and d'Alençon.[3] It took d'Alençon ten days, and a repeated coming and going, to persuade him to join them at Saint Denis after

[1]*Procès*, Vol. I, pp. 82 and 243–4.
[2]*Procès*, Vol. IV, p. 24: Perceval de Cagny.
[3]*Procès*, Vol. IV, p. 25: Perceval de Cagny.

repeatedly broken promises to do so. Charles, as usual, was playing a double game; he could not break openly with d'Alençon and Jeanne, but he could, and did, continue his negotiations with the Duke of Burgundy, even to the point of concluding another truce with him (August 28th, 1429), embodying the peculiar arrangement that, although the French might be allowed to attack Paris, the duke should equally be allowed to send Burgundian troops to the assistance of the English in Paris. This really amounted to saying that although Jeanne, Charles' own servant, might endeavour to subject Paris on his behalf, he would yet authorise the Burgundians to help his enemies against his own servant in its defence. Perhaps he did not really believe that the Duke of Burgundy would avail himself of the permission, for at the same time we find him offering to "lend" him the town of Compiègne, an offer which cannot be considered in any light other than a bribe. Fortunately, Compiègne proved more loyal to France than did its King, and nothing which the Archbishop of Reims could say would induce its citizens to allow themselves to be lent. They replied very politely to the arguments of the archbishop, *d'une commune voix*, that they were the humble subjects of the King, anxious to obey and serve him both with their persons and their goods, but that they could not possibly submit themselves to the Duke of Burgundy, on account of his hatred, which they had incurred owing to their loyalty to His Majesty; therefore, in all submission, they would rather be destroyed with their women and their children than fall into the hands of the said duke.[1] Loyalty and fright could go no further. Loyalty and fright had pushed the citizens of Compiègne into refusing to obey the expressed wishes of the very sovereign they had just acknowledged. It had been hard enough for Charles' lieutenants to recover his towns for him; now that they had been recovered, he was doing his best to give them away again. One is tempted, over and over again, to ask, What did the man really want?

[1] *Procès*, Vol. V, p. 175: *Mémoire sur Guillaume de Flavy.*

Did he want his kingdom, or did he not? Was he a recreant, or merely a fool? It is very difficult—very difficult indeed—to follow the workings of Charles' mind; either his intentions were furtively cowardly and dishonourable, or, if honourable, then so impractical as to be insane. Nothing will persuade any reasonable historian, as nothing could persuade Jeanne, that any agreement with the Duke of Burgundy could be reached save at the point of the lance.

iv

Jeanne and d'Alençon were now at Saint Denis, and Saint Denis, as a place of sojourn, quite apart from its proximity to Paris, must have been entirely after Jeanne's own heart. Not only was its abbey the burial place of the French kings and the repository of the sacred standard of France, the *oriflamme,* but it contained, also, enough relics to satisfy the most credulous and superstitious soul. Among the secular relics was the heart of Bertrand du Guesclin; among the religious were a piece of the True Cross, the swaddling bands of the infant Christ, a shard of the pitcher in which the water had been changed into wine at Cana, a bar from the grid of Saint Laurence, a wooden cup belonging to Saint Louis, and the chin of Saint Mary Magdalen.[1]

Jeanne, profoundly believing as she was, cannot have failed to be impressed by this remarkable collection. It is not urging the imagination too far to suppose that she spent a fair proportion of her time in worship within the already venerable abbey. But, practical as well as mystical, she also found employment, during her ten days at Saint Denis, reconnoitring the defences of Paris in order to discover their weakest points. D'Alençon, when he was not away at Senlis trying to prevail upon Charles to join them, was constantly at her side. There had been skirmishes, but no serious attack was delivered until September 8th, and even then it is doubtful whether we are justified in regarding the attack as seriously

[1] Anatole France, *Vie de Jeanne d'Arc*, Vol. II, p. 53.

meant. The French captains appear to have acted in a most half-hearted way, neither beginning the battle early enough in the day nor employing the whole of the forces at their disposal, nor, even then, attacking in more than one place, i.e. between the gates of Saint Honoré and Saint Denis. According to the account of a contemporary witness,[1] "they could not have taken the place either by storm or siege," even had they been four times as numerous, and their intention was therefore to stir up a panic within the city itself, rather than to attempt to carry it by assault. We are not privileged to overhear the deliberations of the French captains, nor, consequently, to judge whether they intended a real attack or a mere demonstration; we can record only that the move against Paris on September 8th stands out as the first important reverse the royal arms had suffered since Jeanne first took the field at Orleans.

Jeanne's own part in the Paris business is not nearly so clear cut and well defined as usual. She had long been fretting to get to Paris, yet she admitted later, at her trial, that on the day of September 8th she had followed, not the counsel of her voices, but the request of certain lords (*gentilz hommes*) who wanted to make a *vaillance d'armes*.[2] Had she, then, gone to the attack without that real conviction which had always carried her to victory in the past? Is it superstitious to suggest that without the direct inspiration of her voices she lacked the necessary spark which lit her followers to seemingly impossible deeds? True, she adds that her own private intention was to go further and cross the *fosses* of Paris. But that private intention, on her own showing, was unsupported on this occasion by heavenly encouragement. Thus, although her personal courage and determination remained undiminished, one cannot help wondering whether, having regard to the peculiar resources of her strength, the whole difference did not lie between human tenacity and spiritual *afflatus*? In other

[1] *Procès*, Vol. IV, p. 458: Clement de Fauquemberque.
[2] *Procès*, Vol. I, p. 146.

words, could she work apparent miracles only when she genuinely felt the breath of God to be in her, and did she fail when she was acting, so to speak, on her own? And had that breath of God begun to fail her immediately after Reims? Had the poor vessel of her receptivity already overflowed? Had the effort already proved so great that she could no longer sustain it in its early vigour, although half her promises remained as yet unfulfilled? Were her sails already drooping in a flagging wind? Had she tired so soon, as she seemed to suggest by the wistful remark that she would gladly lay down her arms and go back to Domremy to look after her parents' sheep?[1]

There can be no question that her personal courage was as great as ever, even if her personal leadership had lost something of its miraculous quality. In the *fosses* of Paris she behaved with all the heroism she had displayed in the *fosses* of Orleans: at Paris, as at Orleans, she and her standard were in the thick of the battle, and her voice was raised, as before, in encouragement towards her men. Not only did she cross the dry *fosse*, but descended even into the second or wet *fosse*, probing it with a lance to discover the depth of water or of mud.[2] The external similarity between Paris and Orleans does not end with her exploits and example in the moat beneath the city walls. In the moat beneath the walls of Paris, as in the moat beneath the walls of the Tourelles at Orleans, she received a wound from an arrow—in the thigh this time instead of above the breast. *"Paillarde! ribaude!"* said the man who aimed the shot; and with another shot he pierced the foot

---

[1]Andrew Lang (*The Maid of France*, p. 180) raises an interesting point. He suggests that she "falsely denied having received any special command from her voices, and falsely reported that the French nobles intended to make no serious attack. Her object would be to save the character of her Saints . . . and to minimise the check to the arms of her King." But, as he rightly goes on to point out, we have the corroborative testimony of Clement de Fauquemberque, and we may add that when on a later occasion at Beaurevoir her voices refused to give her the counsel she wanted, she had no hesitation in admitting that she had disobeyed them.

[2]*Procès*, Vol. IV, p. 199: *Journal du siège d'Orléans.*

of her standard-bearer. This unlucky man was so incautious as to raise the visor of his helmet in order to remove the dart (*vireton*) which had hurt him, and in that uncovered moment a second arrow struck him between the eyes so that he fell dead.[1] But Jeanne, much against her will,[2] was carried out of danger by de Gaucourt and others. She went protesting, and saying that the place would have been taken but for her withdrawal. D'Alençon seems to have added his voice to those who forced her to retire,[3] but she evidently bore him no resentment, for early next morning we find her sending for him to beg him to give the order for a renewed assault, saying that, *par mon martin*, she would not leave Paris before she had captured it. Her *beau duc*, as usual, was ready to follow her, but even as they were still in discussion the Duke of Bar and the Count of Clermont arrived with a command from the King, to the effect that they were both to rejoin him immediately at Saint Denis. Most reluctantly they obeyed, but even now all hope had not left their hearts. They knew that by d'Alençon's orders a bridge had been thrown across the Seine near Saint Denis, and they still looked forward to the chance of invading the city that way. Unluckily for them, Charles also knew of the bridge, and, foreseeing their scheme, took the incredible step of having the bridge secretly destroyed by night.[4] How are we to explain Charles' conduct throughout? On the face of it he had played false by Jeanne at every turn. He put every obstacle in her way. How could his faithful servant possibly capture Paris for him under such conditions? His dealings with the Duke of Burgundy had been foolish and shady beyond belief. His destruction of d'Alençon's bridge was an act of overt treachery. One is almost forced to the conclusion that he never intended Jeanne to bring Paris to him, as it were a present in her hand. Still the question remains,

---

[1] *Procès*, Vol. IV, p. 465: *Le bourgeois de Paris*.
[2] *Procès*, Vol. IV, p. 27: Perceval de Cagny.
[3] *Procès*, Vol. IV, p. 199: *Journal du siège d'Orléans*.
[4] *Procès*, Vol. IV, p. 28: Perceval de Cagny.

Why? A teasing echo answers, Why? Mere indolence and cowardice can scarcely explain so apparently insane a course. Was bribery at the bottom of it? Was he genuinely hoaxed by the Duke of Burgundy? Was La Trémoïlle responsible? These questions are perhaps idle, since they cannot be answered, but they suggest themselves inevitably to our bewilderment.

At any rate, he succeeded in his object. By September 22nd he was back at Gien on his beloved Loire, and the army, for lack of funds, was being disbanded. Jeanne is sad to contemplate at this moment. Little more than an honoured captive, she remained in Charles' company, but it is no longer as the heroic, shining figure that she appears. On receiving the King's final command to abandon Paris and to accompany him in his retreat, she had discarded her armour, symbol of conquest, and had left it lying before the image of Our Lady in the cathedral of Saint Denis.[1] It was the supreme gesture of renunciation.

She parted from d'Alençon too. Their friendship, which had begun so gaily, and which had been preserved so loyally through all the dangers and difficulties they had weathered together, was broken by d'Alençon's departure from Gien to rejoin his wife in his *vicomté* of Beaumont. She had promised his wife that she would send him home safe and sound, and she had kept her word, but he and she, those young and hopeful comrades-in-arms, were never to meet again. The large and sinister shadow of their enemies falls across their gay, gallant, chivalrous, and platonic path. The Archbishop of Reims, the duc de la Trémoïlle, the seigneur de Gaucourt, *qui lors gouvernoient le corps du roy et le fait de sa guerre, ne vouldrent oncques consentir, ne faire, ne souffrir que la Pucelle et le duc d'Alençon fussent ensemble.*

Et la Pucelle demoura vers le roy, moult ennuyée du département et par especial du duc d'Alençon que elle amoit très fort et faisoit pour lui ce que elle n'eust fait pour ung autre.

Et ainsi fut le vouloir de la Pucelle et l'armée du roy rompue.[2]

[1]*Procès*, Vol. IV, p. 29: Perceval de Cagny.
[2]*Procès*, Vol. IV, pp. 29–30: Perceval de Cagny.

Chapter XIII

PARIS TO COMPIÈGNE

i

It would, in a sense, be better if we could here record that Jeanne had been allowed to satisfy the wish she had expressed to the Archbishop of Reims in the hearing of the Bastard of Orleans—the wish that she might now return to Domremy to look after her parents' sheep. It would be better for her in the sense of being more comfortable and less painful, but, dramatically speaking, the *catharsis* would not be complete. Jeanne d'Arc was meant to, dramatically, die. Not the least queerness of each individual human life is its insistence upon adjusting itself throughout to the key imposed upon it from the first. Jeanne's life had been led on the high planes of feeling, and it was fitting that death should meet her in the same high key; her career, if it was to be rounded off into the unity which it dramatically demanded, must end in an early and tragic death. There is something unsuitable, even offensive, in the idea of her returning to keep sheep when she had led armies, or of her giving herself docilely in marriage to a young man of Toul, or to another, when other, perhaps more worthy, men had been summarily drowned by the act of God for offering an insult to her virginity. Jeanne's life, as I see it, divides itself into four almost deliberately designed theatrical Acts: First Act, The Rise; Second Act, The Triumphs; Third Act, The Stagnant Interlude; Fourth Act, The Culmination of the Tragedy. The Third Act is the one that one would wish to cut out; one could wish to take a short-cut between the Second Act and the Fourth. Unfortunately the Third Act is the very one we have to consider now. Let us do so as briefly as possible.

It covers, in time, the period from July 1429 to May 1430, and is marked by no outstanding event save the abortive attempt on Paris in September with which we have already dealt. After this, it deteriorates into a dreary recital of poor Jeanne's attendance on the Court. She was no born lady-in-waiting. She was still full of militant ideas; she wanted to go into Normandy with d'Alençon, but the King's council would not hear of it; failing this, she had not yet given up the idea of capturing Paris. All these projects being officially blocked, for the very pertinent reason, amongst others, that the King could not allow her to make war against the Duke of Burgundy whilst the truce between them still held good, Jeanne could do nothing but resign herself to a life of un-welcome *fainéantise* at the heels of her *fainéant* King. Nine months went by; nine months nibbled away from her short predicted span. It is shocking and surprising to find that she endured it so meekly; surprising, because such endurance is not in character; shocking, because she is not being true to herself. The old Jeanne, surely, would have been in revolt; the old Jeanne would have forced even the most reluctant, *fainéant*, and involved of kings into some prosecution of action. The new Jeanne, the Jeanne who seems to have spent herself in her first original effort, tamely accepted conditions instead of vigorously rebelling against them. She submitted herself to a tame, cheap mode of life, trailing about after the King and Queen, being first taken to stay in the house of her darkest enemy, La Trémoïlle, at Selles-en-Berri, and then to Bourges, which must ironically have recalled the days when Charles, her hero, was known as the King of Bourges for want of a prouder title, a King so poor that even a cobbler of the town refused him credit for a pair of slippers, *et qu'il en avoit chaussez ung et pour tant qu'il ne le pebut payer contant, il lui redechaussit le dict houzel, et lui convint reprendre ses vielz houzels.*[1] If Jeanne had only realised it from the start, she would have put no more trust in Charles VII than in any man who could order a pair of new slippers knowing that he could not pay the cobbler for them. He came back now to Bourges in better case, certainly, but still with the lack of money pressing upon him,

[1] *Procès*, Vol. IV, p. 325: *Le doyen de Saint Thibaud de Metz.*

for, in justice, it should always be remembered, when we rail against his inactivity and disinclination for war, that his coffers were permanently depleted and that there were times when the crown jewels themselves were in pawn. We may imagine therefore that the Court of Charles VII was less splendid in fact than in name, even when he returned to his old haunt at Bourges with the holy oil upon his head and the victorious Pucelle of Orleans at his heels.

ii

Jeanne's hostess at Bourges, Marguerite La Touroulde, then a woman of nearly forty, had long been familiar with the penurious state of Charles' finances, for her husband, then Receiver-general, had once found himself with only four *écus* left, either of his own or the King's money. She herself was attached in some way to the service of the Queen. She and Jeanne seem to have got on very well together during the three weeks of Jeanne's stay in her house, and, as Marguerite was evidently a chatterbox only too willing to recount everything she knew of her illustrious guest, she has left us many details we do not learn from other sources. I cannot help suspecting that Marguerite was not averse to exaggerating the friendship which had sprung up between them, any more than she was averse to repeating popular gossip, such as that those who first brought Jeanne to Chinon had begun by thinking her mad, and had decided to throw her into a deep ditch—an account which does not tally at all well with the words of Jean de Metz and Bertrand de Poulengy. Perhaps the demoiselle La Touroulde lacked the power of selection, and perhaps, also, she was apt to represent Jeanne as more communicative than she really was; I fancy, in fact, that the hostess, an eager and inquisitive soul, besieged her guest with questions to which Jeanne good-manneredly replied, and which later could be advanced as proofs of intimacy and confidence. I estimate Marguerite La Touroulde, perhaps unjustly, as a kindly, rather bustling busybody, as self-important as she was worthy, to whom we must, however, be grateful for the little pen-picture she has left of one on whom no additional detail can be superfluous.

They slept together, according to custom. They went to church together, and to the public baths, where Marguerite decided cheerfully that Jeanne, so far as she could judge, was a virgin. (Evidently she hesitated to ask Jeanne the direct question, for she lays no claim to anything but her own powers of observation. How she, or any other, could possibly establish the fact of virginity from a mere look, however searching, at a girl of seventeen about to enter, or having just emerged from, her bath, is a point which I must leave to more physiologically experienced persons to settle.) When neither at church nor at the baths, they frequently talked together (*fabularentur ad invicem*), and, according to Marguerite, the topics of their conversation ranged over many outstanding points in Jeanne's short career. Thus it is to Marguerite that we owe the record of Jeanne's admonitions to the Duke of Lorraine (see Chapter VI, p. 108); to her that we owe one of Jeanne's own allusions to her examination at Poitiers, her answer to the doctors in theology: *Il y a ès livres de Notre Seigneur plus que ès votres*; to her that we owe the odd little bit of information that Jeanne hated dice, was extremely lavish in charity, and laughed at the women of Bourges who brought their rosaries to the house for her to touch, saying, "Touch them yourselves; they will benefit from your touch quite as much as from mine."[1] Marguerite, of course, gave this last piece of evidence as a proof that Jeanne had never arrogated holy powers to herself.

iii

The King was restless, and the three weeks spent in Bourges were succeeded by sojourns in various places—Montargis, Loches, Jargeau, Issoudun, and Meung-sur-Yèvre. Most of

[1] *Procès*, Vol. III, pp. 85–8: Deposition of Marguerite La Touroulde.

these names mean very little to us—at most, to the English
traveller on French roads, they may suggest a blue-and-white
sign with arrows pointing in opposite directions and a figure
expressed in kilometres—but to Jeanne they must by that
time have become extremely and personally familiar. Loches:
that was where she had knocked on the Dauphin's private
door, beseeching him to come with her to Reims. Jargeau:
that was where she had saved her dear d'Alençon's life, and
where Suffolk had been taken prisoner. How otiose and fretful
must have appeared the change from camp to Court! At
Meung-sur-Yèvre her prospects seemed to brighten a little
and her opportunity for activity to revive. It was to prove but a
flash in the pan, but Jeanne, with her hopes starting once more
into life, could not foresee this. For the moment, all she could
see was that she was to be allowed to take up her arms again, and,
ironically enough, in a more officially authorised position than
ever before: her name and that of the seigneur d'Albret were
linked as commanders of the army. For the army, although
still unpaid, was once more to be sent into the field. Charles'
Council in October decided that it was "very necessary to
recover the town of La Charité" from the enemy, but that it
was also necessary to take the town of Saint Pierre-le-Moutier
first.[1] Jeanne, thus released, rode off to Bourges with d'Albret
to assemble the army, and by October 25th was at her old
occupation of besieging a town. The unfortunate citizens of
Bourges, by royal command, were required to supply, promptly
and without delay, thirteen hundred gold écus to be sent
instantly to d'Albret and Jeanne—a command accompanied
by the ominous remark that it would be a great pity for the
said town and the whole province of Berry (grant dommaige pour
ladicte ville et tout le pays de Berry) if the siege of La Charité
had to be raised in default of this payment. Bourges, perhaps
wisely, decided to sell by auction the rights over a thirteenth
part of its retail wine-trade for a year.[2]

[1] Procès, Vol. III, pp. 217–18: Deposition of Jean d'Aulon.
[2] La Thaumassière, Histoire du Berry, p. 161.

Other towns sent contributions: Orleans, always generous to its deliverer, gave money and cloth; Clermont Ferrand, munitions of war; Jeanne wrote herself to Riom, asking for saltpetre, sulphur, and cross-bows.[1]

iv

Jean d'Aulon leaves an account of her at Saint Pierre-le-Moutier, an account in which his own part is not omitted, for there was something in that honest man which could never resist putting himself into the front of the stage. On this occasion he appears on crutches, having been wounded in the foot, but heroically struggles on to a horse and rides up to Jeanne, who, abandoned by all save four or five men, was watching the retreat of her discouraged troops. What, he asked, having ridden up to her, was she doing there alone? There is something in his question which suggests the old hen fussing after her chick. He is half cross with her for exposing herself to danger; half proud of her for doing it, as she had done so many times before. One sympathises with the irritability of Jean d'Aulon. It was no light task for him to look after a militant saint at the best of times, more especially when he was on crutches from a wound in his heel, and had hoisted himself on to a horse in order to rescue his troublesome, temerarious, and sublime charge. Jeanne, his chick and charge, took off her helmet before replying. She was not alone, she said then, for a company of fifty thousand was with her. Practical as ever, after this sudden flight among the heavenly hosts, she immediately added that he must call for faggots and fascines to enable them to cross the moat, and raised her voice to call her men back to the attack. It is a story which has to be told many times in speaking of Jeanne. The old magic worked once more: Saint Pierre-le-Moutier fell.[2]

[1]*Procès*, Vol. V, pp. 269–70, 146, and 147–8. Jeanne's letter to Riom is the one that was sealed with the imprint of a (?her) finger and a black hair. See Chapter I, pp. 4–5.
[2]*Procès*, Vol. III, pp. 217–18: Deposition of Jean d'Aulon.

V

She was less fortunate at La Charité, not perhaps entirely by her fault. According to her own account she had received no heavenly guidance about La Charité.[1] At her trial, she remained obstinately evasive on this point; she never definitely said that her voices had forbidden her to go there, although, in her honesty, she would not be persuaded to say that they had spoken. A loyal soul, she was always reluctant to state specifically that her counsel at a given moment had failed her. Without wishing to fall into the easy error of unduly stressing a theory, it does seem significant that her first serious failures under arms—at Paris and at La Charité—should have occurred after what I have represented as the peak of her career: the coronation at Reims. It does suggest rather that her inspiration was deserting her at last. At the same time it must be borne in mind that circumstances at Paris had been almost overwhelmingly against her—so overwhelmingly that nothing but the strongest supernatural power could have conquered; and at La Charité the same considerations must be given their fair chance. One must keep one's head and remain practical, otherwise romanticism will run the danger of being totally discounted when it tries most extravagantly to break out of the ledger. Jeanne herself evidently recognised this elementary truth, in her queer strong mixture of the visionary and the executive. Without vision, nothing can be; without the executive faculty, nothing, save on purely spiritual planes, can be accomplished either. It is useless to try and write about Jeanne d'Arc without keeping a sense of proportion equivalent to her own. Thus it is salutary to remember that, although in a moment of exaltation she might see fifty thousand angels surrounding her at Saint Pierre-le-Moutier, she was not so carried away as to forget to call for faggots next moment to bridge the *fosse*. And thus, again, not unduly romanticising her supernatural powers, one must soberly take into consideration

[1] *Procès*, Vol. I, pp. 109, 147 and 169.

that at La Charité the winter season was against her, money was short, and the repeated promises of money and supplies were made only to be broken.

vi

The attempt on La Charité ended in a sad failure—the siege had to be raised, and from the end of November 1429 until the spring of 1430 nothing but odd bits of information, picked mostly from account-books and letters, provides us with any guide as to Jeanne's pursuits and whereabouts. We know that the Court spent two months at Meung-sur-Yèvre, from November till January, and it is possible, and probable, that Jeanne remained there also, in the very ambiguous position of a dependant, honoured indeed, but unemployed. How did she occupy herself during that time? We do not know even where she was lodged—a piece of information usually supplied whenever she spent more than a few days in any place; no good woman such as Marguerite La Touroulde was brought forward later at the *procès de réhabilitation* to testify to the impeccable conduct and piety of her life during this distressing period when Satan might well have been expected to be doing his worst. At the same time it is worth noting how many women play a part just at this phase; we should scarcely notice their intrusion, were it not for our unconscious habit of regarding Jeanne's life as led entirely in the company of men. We have really grown so well accustomed to the rattle of armour that the rustle of a skirt comes as something of a surprise. The feminine life is a life we had forgotten; true, Jeanne, most wisely, had always been careful to safe-guard her reputation by sleeping with women under a roof when not sleeping under the stars with men; but, for the rest, she lived the life of a man so naturally that we cease to be conscious of her sex either one way or the other. It was even brouhgt against her at her trial that she had refused all offices of women in her room and private affairs, preferring men as her servants—a sly suggestion which she denied, with, as I believe, absolute truth.[1] At the same time she answered with equal frankness that men had always been of her government, meaning, obviously, that men had represented the strong, vital, public element in her life; women the soft, private, and subsidiary. In this respect she seems quite naturally to have looked upon men as another man would have looked upon them. Thus, when women do appear on the scene, it requires almost an effort to readjust ourselves to the idea that Jeanne was herself a woman, and to remember that this young fighting captain could consort with women in an even more natural freemasonry than she could consort with men. And in the months between September 1429 and April 1430 quite a number of women pass across Jeanne's stage. She had had those three weeks in the enforced intimacy of Marguerite La Touroulde. The Queen, meanwhile, had joined the King, which in itself must have imported a feminine softening into the Court. Then, Jeanne came into contact with that very uninteresting fraud, Catherine de la Rochelle. Jeanne met her twice, once at Jargeau and once at Montfauçon-en-Berri, and saw through her without any difficulty. Catherine de la Rochelle was not at all the kind of person designed to impose upon that sincere spirit and cutting mind. Her encounters with Jeanne must have been, from her point of view, destructive in the extreme. It is always distressing to have one's own falsities exposed, especially to oneself. She cannot have enjoyed being told to go back to her husband and look after her house and her children. She cannot have enjoyed hearing her offers of peace-making with the Duke of Burgundy snubbed as Jeanne snubbed them, saying, so rightly, that the only peace which could be made would be made at the point of the lance. Still less can she have enjoyed spending two successive nights with Jeanne, waiting for her own particular "white lady," dressed in cloth of gold, to appear to them both. Poor Catherine de la Rochelle: on the first night, Jeanne, having stayed awake

[1] *Procès*, Vol. I, pp. 293-4, Article LIV of the Act of Accusation.

till midnight, evidently got bored and went to sleep. In the morning, when she asked if the "white lady" had appeared, Catherine assured her that she had indeed appeared, but that she, Catherine, had been unable to awaken her, Jeanne, adding that the "white lady" would surely appear again next night. Here, I think, occurs one of the most typical instances of Jeanne's good peasant common sense, nor am I at all sure that it does not also mark her instinctive, humorous, and wise mistrust of a certain type of members of her sex: she spent most of the following day in sleep, in order to stay awake watching for the "white lady" during the whole of the following night. It is evident that she was determined not to let Catherine go to sleep either, for she kept asking her if the said lady was not soon going to put in an appearance. Poor Catherine kept on answering, "Yes, soon!" Her eyelids must have been drooping, but Jeanne, having slept all day, pitilessly kept her awake till dawn, and, of course, nothing came.[1]

Jeanne was not to be taken in by frauds. If she had been a more sophisticated person, one would be tempted to say that she had deliberately made a fool of Catherine de la Rochelle. As it is, she probably wanted to get at the truth of the matter, and took the best and quickest way she knew of doing so, putting her sincerity like a scythe through the humbug of the woman who had advised her not to go to La Charité "because it was too cold there."

Catherine, who had offered to discover hidden treasure for the King, was no good, and Jeanne told the King so, greatly to the displeasure of Brother Richard and of Catherine herself. Jeanne, an uncompromising person, had no patience with adventurers like Brother Richard and Catherine de la Rochelle. On the other hand, she would take trouble for people she was fond of, and threw the good notables of Tours into some consternation by writing to demand a marriage-dowry for her friend Héliote Poulnoir, the daughter of that Scottish

[1]*Procès*, Vol. I, pp. 106–9.

painter who had executed her standard and her pennon (see Appendix E, p. 397). It is amusing to read their embarrassment through the lines of their official report. A special meeting was summoned to deal with the situation—a very grave meeting, including the judge of Touraine, the councillor of the Queen of Sicily, four canons, representing the churches of Tours, and three leading citizens. It was decided that the painter himself should be consulted, and that the opinion of two other important burgesses should be sought—they being for the moment with the Court at Bourges, on the business of their city. The next meeting was held three weeks later, and was even more numerously attended. Héliote, perhaps wisely, had not waited on their deliberations, and the wedding had meanwhile taken place. A certain apologetic regret appears in their finding that the public funds of Tours must be expended on the needs of the city and on nothing else (*pour ce que les deniers de la ville convient emploier ès réparacions de la ville et non ailleurs*). This ruling evidently seemed to them a little too ungracious and too harsh, for they added that, for the love and honour of the Pucelle, the bride should be prayed for in the name of the city, and, moreover, should receive bread and wine, both white and red, on the day of her benediction. Colas de Montbazon was charged with the execution of this friendly office.[1]

Jeanne's effort on behalf of her friend, although partially unsuccessful, does her credit. She was evidently not so inhuman as we might sometimes be tempted to believe. She could bother about the wedding of a girl in Tours—a girl whose father had supplied what was, perhaps, her most precious

---

[1]*Procès*, Vol. V, pp. 154-6 and 271. *Extrait des comptes des deniers communs de la ville de Tours*. It is amusing to find the red wine described as "claret." This is nothing more than an adjective denoting the colour, *clairet*, and, I should think, indicates a local *vin rosé* or *vin gris* rather than *vin de Bordeaux*, to which the English give the generic and inaccurate name of claret, in the same way as they call all Rhine wines "hock," a term which becomes intelligible to the German only when he realises that we are employing our own abbreviation for Hochheimer.

and symbolic possession. It proves that she was neither ungrateful nor forgetful in small matters, which is more than can be said of many people, whether preoccupied with greater matters or not.

Nor, among strange women associated with Jeanne, must we forget La Pierronne, the unfortunate Breton visionary, who claimed that God appeared to her dressed in a long white robe with a scarlet tunic, and addressed her as one friend might speak to another. She knew Jeanne at just about this time, but was burnt for defending her, as well as for blasphemy, after Jeanne had been taken prisoner.[1]

vii

It would be suitable and pleasant to add the name of Sainte Colette de Corbie to the list of women who figured in Jeanne's life during this period, but unluckily we cannot do so with any certainty. It seems more than probable that Jeanne must have come across this very remarkable woman at Moulins in November 1429, and, although there is no evidence to prove their meeting, there is equally none to disprove it. It is almost incredible that these two women, two of the great saints of France, should have been in the same town on the same date—as we know they were— without contriving to meet. Of course, neither thought of herself as a "great saint"; it is we who set them together in that juxtaposition: Sainte Colette de Corbie, Sainte Jeanne d'Arc. There are sound reasons for assuming that Sainte Colette and Sainte Jeanne almost certainly met at Moulins in the Bourbonnais during the first fortnight of November 1429. There is the fact that Marie de Bourbon, who was Jeanne's friend, and who was also the foundress of Colette's convent at Moulins, happened to be at Moulins when Jeanne and Colette were both there, and so would naturally have been anxious to bring the two together. There is the further fact that Jeanne,

[1]*Procès*, Vol. IV, p. 467: *Journal d'un bourgeois de Paris.*

according to local tradition, prayed frequently and at great length in the chapel of the Poor Clares, the very Order to which Colette belonged, and the very chapel attached to Colette's convent. There is the further fact that Colette, quite apart from her miraculous gift of making clocks go slow and the sun rise too early, of rooting hostile men to the ground, and of teaching lambs to kneel down at the moment of the Elevation, had not led the life of a cloistered nun but of a very practical and active woman with an interest in public affairs—on occasion she had even interfered in the negotiations between the Dauphin and the Duke of Burgundy—so that the two saints would have had much in common besides their religious experiences. Even in religious experience they shared much: both had fallen under the usual suspicion of being witches; both had seen visions and had been directed by heavenly voices, though Colette's visitations had treated her less kindly than Jeanne's, striking her first with dumbness and then with blindness when she displayed a somewhat natural reluctance to obey their commands; there were even occasions when her chair was snatched from under her by invisible hands.[1] There were ample reasons for their wishing to meet, and there seems to be no reason why they should not have gratified the wish. I think we can take it, safely, that Colette de Corbie may be included among the women who crossed Jeanne's path during those unhappy months which filled the interim between the splendour of Reims and the downfall at Compiègne; and that Colette de Corbie, among all those women, was the most worthy of the friendship, however briefly, owing to circumstances, accorded.

viii

Jeanne's movements from December 1429 to April 1430 are sparsely recorded compared with the detail in which we have hitherto been able to follow them, and the events which

[1] Rev. Dominic Devas, O.F.M., *Sainte Colette.*

do give us some guide as to her occupations appear insignificant enough as the aftermath of her great doings. In December the King was so gracious as to confer a patent of nobility upon his *cara et delecta* Jeanne, her father, her mother, her brothers, and all their posterity.[1] I doubt very much whether this honour brought any particular gratification to Jeanne, who would certainly have preferred a document granting her full powers to proceed against the Duke of Burgundy and the English, nor is there any reason to believe that she herself ever availed herself of the privilege thus conferred. The only interest which this easy instance of the royal gratitude holds for us is the light it throws upon the pronunciation of Jeanne's name (see Chapter III, p. 28).

The act of ennoblement can scarcely be ranked as an occupation. It throws no light on what Jeanne was doing at the time; she appears in it as a passive rather than an active agent. As to her own movements, she may perhaps have spent Christmas Day at Jargeau[2]; she was certainly at Orleans on January 19th, when the city presented her with fifty-two pints of wine, six capons, nine partridges, thirteen rabbits, and a pheasant, plus a doublet for her brother.[3] The city of Orleans was always loyal and generous to its Pucelle. Jeanne herself, who went back to Orleans as often as she could, seems, in her frequent returns, to have expressed her especial affection for the city she had saved. It is suggested even that she "took the lease of a house in Orleans, perhaps as a home for her mother."[4] Having taken the whole city and made it historically hers, she could well afford to take a house in it as a *pied-à-terre*. A pheasant for her dinner; a doublet for her brother; a lodging

[1]*Procès*, Vol. V. pp. 150–3.

[2]*Procès*, Vol. IV, p. 474: *Le bourgeois de Paris*, an unreliable authority.

[3]*Procès*, Vol. V, p. 270.

[4]Andrew Lang, *The Maid of France*, p. 198, quoting Jules Doissel, *Note sur une maison de Jeanne d'Arc, Mem. de la Société Arch. et Hist. de l'Orléans*, Vol. XV, pp. 494–500. I have not personally had access to this work, but, having tested Mr. Lang and found him accurate and reliable in other particulars, I venture to give this reference without verifying it myself.

for her mother—Orleans was the last place in the whole of France to grudge such small benefits to its deliverer. Jeanne was always its welcome guest—so welcome, that it was perhaps fortunate for Pierre Cauchon, Bishop of Beauvais, that she should eventually have been bound to the stake at Rouen instead of at Orleans. Had she been bound to it at Orleans, I fancy that it would have been a case of "Water, water, quench fire!" while Pierre Cauchon found himself held down to the nostrils in the Loire at the same time as the waters of the same river were being poured from buckets over the pyre his orders had ignited. Orleans would have drowned the Bishop sooner than have burnt the Pucelle.

But the Bishop of Beauvais has not yet, properly speaking, walked on to the stage. His shadow is as yet only darkly and gigantically projected from the wings. He waits.

The Duke of Burgundy took advantage of the lull to celebrate his third marriage, with extravagant pomp, at Bruges (January 10th, 1430). Described as the richest prince in Christendom, he has three wives, twenty-four mistresses, and the rather moderate allowance of sixteen illegitimate children to his credit. On this occasion he was marrying Isabella of Portugal, who was brought to him from Portugal by a special embassy including his favourite painter, John Van Eyck. For eight days and nights the city of Bruges excelled itself in display: seventeen nations, who had their banking houses in the Flemish city, vied with one another in magnificence; the burghers vied with the nobles, so that fête succeeded fête, the streets were hung with the richest tapestries of Flanders, and wine ran night and day from fountains—Rhine wine from the mouth of a stone lion, Beaune from the mouth of a stag, while during meals a unicorn spouted rose-water and malmsey. As the crowning symbol of the fidelity he intended to bring to his marriage, the Duke instituted a new order of chivalry with the comforting motto *Autre n'auray*—the Order of the Golden Fleece, "conquered by Jason."[1]

[1] Michelet, *Jeanne d'Arc*, pp. 221-2.

Meanwhile, those three little bubbles of information about Jeanne rise to the surface and burst. She is ennobled; she spends Christmas at Jargeau; she is found at Orleans in January. Then there is a gap till March the 3rd, when she reappears at Sully as the originator of a letter to the Hussites of Bohemia.[1] Then on March 16th and again on March 28th she reappears as the incontestable dictator of two letters to her "very dear and good friends" at Reims. She is not at all happy or easy in her mind, and, as with most people who are not happy or easy in their minds, a certain irritability pierces through the tone of her letters. She is keeping something back from her dear and good friends: she would willingly send them good news, but is afraid the letters may be intercepted on the way. (*Je vous mandesse anquores augunes nouvelles de quoy vous seriés bien joyeux: mais je doubte que les letres ne fussent prises en chemin.*[2]) This is a short letter. In the next one she allows herself to be more outspoken, and quite openly mentions *ces traitrez Bourguignons adversaires*; but then, recollecting herself, refers again, darkly, to the *bonnes nouvelles* she will shortly send them *plus à plain*.[3] It is clear that neither Jeanne nor her friends at Reims trusted the Burgundians or their truces in the least; it is, in fact, quite clear that her friends at Reims were worried by the presence of a Burgundian party within their walls. The English were even entertaining the idea that they might take their own little King to be crowned at Reims. He was

[1]*Procès*, Vol. V, pp. 156–9. I say "originator" rather than "author" because for several reasons the letter as it exists in its present form could never have been dictated, although it might have been suggested, by Jeanne. There is only one phrase in it which I can believe to have proceeded straight from Jeanne; only one phrase which has her true accent, authoritative, Elizabethan: *Ich werde Ihnen sagen, was Ihr zu thun habt.* The rest of it is all a rather hysterically rendered diatribe, for which Jeanne may have provided the material but certainly not the style.

There is some disagreement as to the exact date of this letter. Quicherat gives it as March 3rd; Andrew Lang as March 23rd, quoting Th. de Sickel, *Bibliothèque de l'école des Chartres*, third series, Vol. II, p. 81.

[2]*Procès*, Vol. V, p. 160.

[3]*Procès*, Vol. V, pp. 161–2.

only eight, but he could serve as a figurehead. His head was as good as a grown-up head, when nothing was required of it but to support the crown of France and England during the brief though impressive ceremony of an hour. After that, he could go back to his lessons or his toys, leaving the Dukes of Burgundy and Bedford to do the rest. He need take, momentarily, no further part in the governance of his double kingdom.

On the other hand, the Dukes of Burgundy and Bedford had still to reckon with that inconvenient figure popularly called "la Pucelle." She had been kept waiting for more months than she could afford, and although her personal King, Charles VII, was easily persuaded and gullible, his evil genius, that limb of the Fiend, that *Pucelle de malheur*, was not gullible at all. Truces, however often renewed, failed entirely to convince her that people whom she regarded as enemies of France really desired the good of France and were not merely gaining time for their own advantage. Truces, however often renewed, were bound to come to an end some day. Danger could be staved off, but not indefinitely. It was becoming really necessary to clear this sorceress out of France. So long as she was in it, there could be no ease for either the Duke of Burgundy or the Duke of Bedford. Neither of them could get on with his affairs.

That was the Burgundian and the English point of view. Jeanne's point of view was quite different. Jeanne's point of view was that she wanted to get back into the field as soon as she possibly could. She quite agreed with her friends at Reims that the Burgundians were not to be trusted. At the same time, she was also forced, through loyalty, to agree with her King who was responsible for the truce. She could not, outwardly, disagree with him; she could only, inwardly, fret.

Nevertheless the time of her inactivity was drawing to an end, and at the end of March she left the King at Sully and joined a small force at Lagny-sur-Marne under the command of a French captain called Baretta, a Scotsman called Kennedy, and her old acquaintance, Ambroise de Loré. The rest of her band was scattered: she must have missed d'Alençon, the Bastard, and the others, but she was, at least, a soldier once more and not an impatient appendage to the Court. At first things seemed to be going well: Melun, which had been in the hands of the English for ten years, but which in the previous October had been given by the Duke of Bedford to Burgundy, suddenly rose of its own accord and threw out the Burgundians. This gesture was not unnaturally attributed to Jeanne's re-appearance in the field, and it must have added to her happiness to reflect that this first and signal success had occurred near the feast of Easter. She, to whom the feasts of the Church always meant so much, must indeed have felt that, with the great festival of Resurrection, the hopes of France had resurrected also. Her thoughts turned again towards Paris.

Meanwhile, she was at Melun, and it was while standing on the ramparts of that city that she received a visit from Saint Catherine and Saint Margaret, giving her perhaps the cruellest piece of news she had ever heard from their lips. They had accustomed her to encouragement and advice, but now they came with no advice, with nothing but the warning that before the feast of Saint John came round she would be taken. Coming at this moment, in the flush of victory and the ringing of the Easter bells not yet stilled upon the air, it must have been a bitter blow. She relates the circumstances herself in quiet, resigned phrases through which it is not difficult to discover the disheartenment which overcame her.[1]

It was one thing to fight on, even struggling against apathy, reluctance, and treachery; it was quite another thing to fight with the certainty of capture and failure ahead. For to Jeanne,

[1]*Procès*, Vol. I, p. 115: *Respond que en la sepmaine de Pasques derrenièrement passé, elle estant sur les fossés de Melun, luy fut dit par ses voix, c'est assavoir Saincte Katherine et Saincte Marguerite, qu'elle seroit prinse avant qu'il fust la saint Jéhan, et que ainsi falloit qui fust fait, et qu'elle ne s'esbahist, et print tout en gré, et que Dieu lui aideroit.*

of course, whatever her voices said was certainty, and their constant comfort and counsel had now been replaced by the gravest note of warning. They came to her nearly every day after that, she said, and repeated their solemn prophecy: that she must be taken; that she must not be surprised; that she must take everything as it came, and that God would help her. There was at least some comfort in that last assurance. It emboldened her to ask for further details. She wanted to know the hour of her capture, adding, rather piteously, that, had she known it, she would not have gone out. Oddly enough, she never seems to have made any enquiries about the place: it is only the hour which interests her. But they would not tell her, only repeated that it had to be, and that she must take it well (*print tout en gré*). She begged, also, that she might die when she was captured, and thus be spared the long vexation of prison, but to this they made no reply. Still, she added bravely, she would have gone out if the voices had commanded her to do so; she would not have gone willingly, but, all the same, she would have obeyed their orders to the end, whatever happened to her.[1]

She spent nearly a month waiting for the sword to fall, for it was not until May 23rd that she was taken into captivity.

ix

She had gone from Melun back to Lagny, where, with Kennedy, Baretta and Ambroise de Loré's lieutenant, she achieved a brilliant minor success against a small English marauding party. The engagement at Lagny laid up a store of future trouble for Jeanne, and drew the censure of the judges at her trial over an incident where, I think, censure seems to have been deserved. A Burgundian captain, named Franquet d'Arras, was taken prisoner, either by Jeanne herself or by one of her company, and exchanged by her for the landlord of the Bear Inn in Paris. Why she should have wanted the landlord

[1]*Procès,* Vol. I, pp. 115–16.

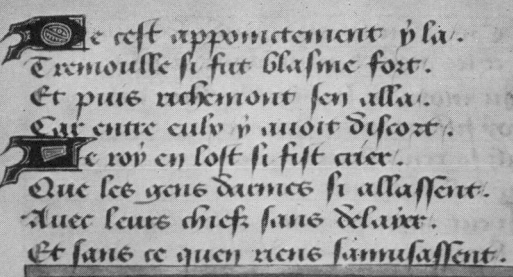

De cest appointement p la.
Tremoulle si fut blasme fort.
Et puis richemont sen alla.
Car entre eulx y auoit discort.

He roy en lost si fist crier.
Que les gens darmes si allassent.
Auec leurs chiefz sans delaier.
Et sans ce quen riens samusassent.

Comment la pucelle batit deux filles
de Joye et rompit son espee.

Ladicte pucelle en allant.
Si rencontra deuant sa veue.
Deux filleotes et vng galant.
Qui sa menoient vie dissolue.

Si frappa dessus ruddement.
Tant quelle peut de son espee.
Et sur gens darmes tellement.
Quelle fut en deux pars couppee.

De les batre nestoit que bon.
Et luy fut dit par lassemblee.
Que deuoit frapper dun baton.
Sans despecer sa bonne espee.

JEANNE BEATS THE COURTESANS

A page from " Les Vigiles de Charles VII" by Martial d'Auvergne

of the Bear Inn is not stated, but when she heard that he had died before he could be handed over, she said to the *bailli* of Senlis, "Since my man is dead, whom I wanted, do with this one [i.e. Franquet d'Arras] that which is required by justice." Franquet in consequence was given a trial lasting a fortnight, found guilty of murder, robbery, and treachery, and was executed.[1] No doubt he deserved his sentence, and, indeed, confessed his crimes himself, but I cannot see that the incident does any credit to Jeanne. If she was quite ready to spare Franquet when she thought she could exchange him for the other man, it was scarcely fair to make him suffer for a mishap which was certainly not his fault.

It is at Lagny that the miraculous sword of Fierbois makes its last appearance in Jeanne's history. She herself stated that she had had it there, but that after Lagny she had carried the sword of a Burgundian, which was a good sword, a proper sword with which to give good blows and buffets, *de bonnes buffes et de bons torchons.* When they asked her where she had lost the other one, she replied that that did not concern the trial and that she would not answer.[2] According to popular tradition, she had broken it across the back of a courtesan, but the chroniclers do not agree where this incident took place. They do agree, however, in saying that the King, on hearing of it, was displeased, and remarked that she ought to have used a stick; Jean Chartier picturesquely adds that the armourers found it impossible to mend it, which was an additional proof of its divine origin.[3]

It was at Lagny, too, that she was credited with the miracle of restoring a dead baby to life.[4]

From Lagny she went to Senlis. The King meanwhile was still trying to negotiate the peace which Jeanne had declared to be impossible save at the point of the lance, but even to his obstinacy it was becoming clear that neither the English nor the Burgundians had the slightest intention of agreeing

[1]*Procès*, Vol. I, pp. 158 and 264. [3]*Procès*, Vol. IV, p. 93: Jean Chartier.
[2]*Procès*, Vol. I, p. 77. [4]*Procès*, Vol. I, p. 105.

T

with him on terms favourable to the torn and wretched France. Nothing but a victory even more complete than Jeanne's first campaign had inaugurated at Orleans would drive the foreigner from the country and reduce the great duke to the status of a dutiful vassal. It looked as though this second campaign were about to begin, almost exactly a year after the first, but with what a difference to Jeanne! She had always known that a year was her allowance of time—she now knew more specifically that she was to be in the hands of her enemies before midsummer. It was now getting on for the end of April, and on the 23rd the little English king landed with his army at Calais.

It was obvious that the English and the Burgundian forces would wish to join; it was equally obvious that they would wish to capture the loyally recalcitrant town of Compiègne, which had refused to be handed over to Burgundy at the suggestion of Charles VII, and which, so long as it remained in the possession of the French, constituted a strong position from which to threaten Paris. (The map facing this page will make the geographical situation clearer than any amount of explanation in words.) It will be seen that Compiègne lies on the south, or Paris, side of the river Oise, near its confluence with the river Aisne, and that the question of bridges was vital to any army or armies wishing to operate in the Ile de France, or country lying on that side of the two rivers. Now both the English and the Burgundian armies were on the wrong sides of the rivers: the English, with some Burgundians, had arrived opposite Compiègne, the Oise dividing them from the town; the Duke of Burgundy, with his main force, had arrived at Noyon. Since he had marched from Montdidier to Noyon (via Gournay) it was reasonable to suppose that he would cross the Oise by the bridge at Pont l'Evêque, then held by the English, and would then swoop down on Choisy-le-Bac when, if he could carry out his intention of capturing it, Compiègne would lie open to his attack. To thwart this plan, Jeanne, with her old comrade Poton de Saintrailles, left

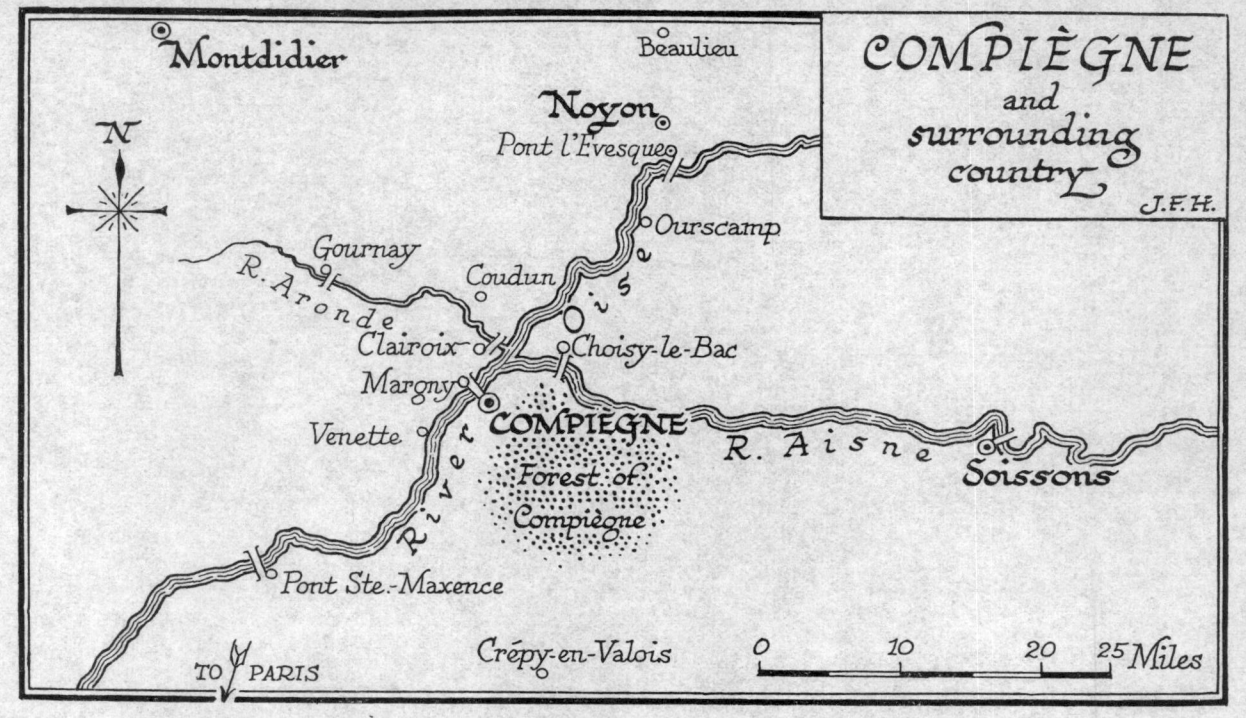

Montdidier

Beaulieu

Noyon

Pont l'Evesque

N

Ourscamp

Gournay

Coudun

R. Aronde

Oise

Clairoix

Choisy-le-Bac

Margny

COMPIÈGNE

Venette

R. Aisne

Soissons

Forest of
Compiègne

River

Pont Ste.-Maxence

Crépy-en-Valois

0   10   20   25 Miles

TO PARIS

COMPIÈGNE
and
surrounding
country

J.F.H.

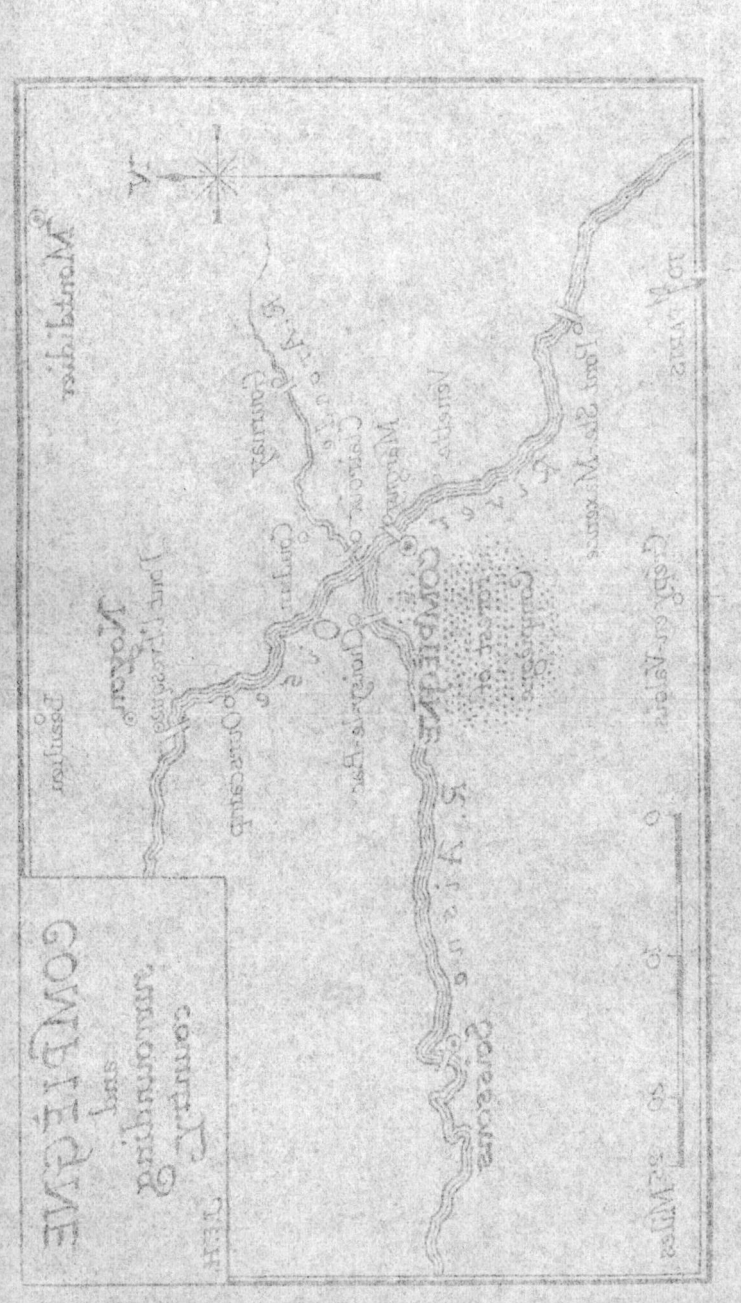

Compiègne for Pont l'Evêque, which they attacked at dawn (May 14th). In the old days, they might have carried the bridge, and, in fact, were on the point of doing so when the garrison of Noyon, arriving post-haste from two miles away, drove them back. Two days later Choisy capitulated to the Duke of Burgundy, who immediately destroyed the fortress and flung a bridge across the Oise.[1]

X

Choisy being now held by the Burgundians, it was very necessary for the French to recover it as soon as possible if they were not to be left without any bridge across the Aisne nearer than Soissons. Unless they could freely cross the Aisne, they could not take the Burgundians in the rear, but for the moment they were constrained to go round by Soissons, a little more than twenty miles away. Accompanied by the Count of Vendôme and by the Archbishop of Reims, in whose company she now rode for the last time, Jeanne accordingly rode to Soissons. The Count of Vendôme had been a good friend to her; it was he who had first introduced her into the presence of the Dauphin at Chinon; it was he who had rejoiced with her when Charles' scheme of retiring to the Loire was thwarted after the coronation.[2] The Archbishop had been a false friend; he had gone against her in secret whenever he could, and had flattered her wishes openly whenever he saw that no other choice would avail him. On the very day when he knew her to be a prisoner and safely out of the way, he hastened to write to the citizens of Reims, a most displeasing letter, since even then he dared not come out into the open and express his opinion of her in his own name, but must needs quote a young

---

[1]*Procès*, Vol. IV, pp. 397 and 399: Monstrelet. If I interpret Monstrelet rightly, this bridge was intended to give him a passage to Coudun, where we find him after his victory at Choisy. There was, of course, already a bridge at Choisy across the Aisne.

[2]*Procès*, Vol. IV, pp. 49–50: *La Chronique du hérault Berri.*

impostor known as *le Berger*, as having declared that God had allowed the Pucelle to be taken because she was so full of pride and had not acted according to God's will, but only according to her own.[1] A mean and poisonous man, one wonders what his private feelings had been when, as the representative of God on earth, he found himself constrained, by virtue of his holy office, to set the crown on Charles' head and saw the Pucelle standing in the place of honour?

He took his last leave of Jeanne at Soissons, but not before he had enjoyed the pleasure of seeing the fresh discomfiture which there awaited her. It was discomfiture rendered more bitter by treachery, for the captain of the town, a Picard named Guiscard Bournel, who was by way of holding Soissons for the King, refused to allow Jeanne and her followers to enter, and persuaded the citizens that they had arrived with the unavowed intention of remaining there as a garrison.[2] This meant that all hope of coming upon the Burgundians from the rear was destroyed, and that Jeanne had no choice but to return to Compiègne. Is it pushing a theory too far to suggest that in the days of her triumphs she would have found some means of getting her way with the people of Soissons, either by force or persuasion, as she had done with the people of Troyes? She made no attempt whatsoever to do so, and Bournel a few weeks later quietly sold the town in return for 4,000 *saluts d'or* advanced by the Duke of Burgundy.

The blow was more serious than might at first sight appear, for it involved more than the refusal of a safe passage across the Aisne. It meant that the army which Jeanne had got together was compelled to split up, since Compiègne could not maintain so large a company as well as its own considerable

---

[1] *Procès*, Vol. V, pp. 168–9. More fortunate than Jeanne, the *Berger* was spared the misery of long imprisonment and the farce of a protracted trial, but was tied up in a sack and thrown into a river by the English without more ado.

[2] *Procès*, Vol. IV, pp. 49–50: *La Chronique du hérault Berri*.

garrison, nor could the countryside support them. The various captains accordingly went off in different directions, Jeanne being apparently left alone with Baretta and a handful of men, probably not more than two or three hundred at the outside.[1] We do not know how long they had stayed at Compiègne, but at midnight on May 22nd–23rd we find them at Crépy-en-Valois about to ride in the secrecy of the dark through the thick forest towards Compiègne. The immediate reason for this nocturnal departure was the news that the Duke of Burgundy and the Earl of Arundel had arrived before Compiègne on the further side of the river, and that Jeanne had instantly decided to go and survey the situation for herself. Her own people tried to dissuade her, on account of their small number, from so daring an enterprise (*elle avoit pou gens pour passer parmi l'ost des Bourguignons et Englois*), but she answered with all her old headstrong spirit: "*Par mon martin, nous suymes assez; je iray voir mes bons amis de Compiègne.*"[2]

She reached Compiègne at dawn. They must have ridden fast, for, although the distance between Crépy and Compiègne is only some fifteen miles, they had no starlight to guide them beneath the trees, the moon was a slip only one day old, and, moreover, the hours between midnight and dawn are few towards the end of May. They entered the town without having encountered any resistance. Beyond this, we are not told how they passed the day until five o'clock in the evening, when the narrative resumes. It is suggested, with much probability, that they rested after their long ride, and that Jeanne heard Mass, and consulted with the governor of the town.[3] There is no actual authority for this supposition, but common sense dictates it. In the first place, they would naturally be tired after riding through the night, constantly on the alert, whether for rabbit-holes or Burgundians; in the second place, it was Jeanne's

[1]*Procès*, Vol. IV, p. 32: Perceval de Cagny.
[2]*Procès*, Vol. IV, pp. 32–3: Perceval de Cagny.
[3]Andrew Lang, *The Maid of France*, p. 211.

habit to hear Mass whenever she conveniently or inconveniently could, especially on feast-days—and this was the eve of Ascension; in the third place, her practical side would certainly have driven her, after her religious side had been satisfied, to summon the governor, de Flavy, and to demand from him an exposition of the tactical situation. Had she not done both these things, she would not have been acting according to the character we recognise in its entirety as Jeanne d'Arc. But, as she always acted true to her own character, whatever facet it chose at any given moment to display, save possibly over the unfortunate incident of Franquet d'Arras, we may suppose with Mr. Lang that first she made up for her sleepless night, then went to church, then went practically into the question of where the enemy was encamped. Unless, indeed, we ought to alter the order of the routine laid down for her by Mr. Lang, and suppose that she heard Mass before allowing herself any rest, which seems even more in keeping with her previous record.

Assuming that she did consult with the young, violent, and formidable de Flavy, and that he was in the mood to give her the information she needed, he must have told her that the bridge-head at Margny (here again the map facing p. 276 will make the situation clear) was held by the advance-guard of the Anglo-Burgundian army under the command of Baudot de Noyelle. This meant that the enemy had pushed very far forward against his objective—Compiègne. De Flavy must also have told her that the main force with the Duke of Burgundy lay at Coudun, in the valley of the Aronde. He must also have told her that Venette, five miles down the river, was held by the English, and Clairoix, five miles up it, by Jean de Luxembourg, comte de Ligny, though, of course, she cannot have been aware that Jean de Luxembourg, with the seigneur de Créqui and eight or ten other gentlemen, had already ridden down to Margny (*tous venus à cheval*) to decide by what means they could best besiege Compiègne, the rising ground behind Margny offering a specially good post of vantage for such observation.

(*Et regardoit par quelle manière on pourroit assieger ycelle ville.*[1])
Nor were the men at Margny aware that a French force, however
small, had issued from Compiègne and was advancing across
the bridge towards them. So little were they aware of this fact,
that most of them had put their arms aside, and were obliged
to scurry when the order came for the *escarmouche*. It is ironical
enough that Jeanne should have been taken in such a silly sally,
when a small outpost of the enemy was not even prepared for
her coming, and a dozen gentlemen-at-arms were riding about
in what sounds a very leisurely way, taking a look at Compiègne from the safe side of the river. It was the very presence
of these dozen gentlemen which brought about her undoing.
For the rest, her enterprise was such as she had often engaged in:
a surprise attack on a small and unsuspecting garrison, with an
open bridge and a friendly town behind her, was child's play
for the victor of Orleans and Patay. It seemed as though she
could charge the outpost, gallop into the village, and withdraw
across the bridge if she then wanted to, with practically no
danger either to herself or to her men. Lest she should be
pursued on her return journey, de Flavy had set archers and
men with cross-bows and culverins at the gate of Compiègne,
and more archers and cross-bow men in little boats bobbing on
the river.[2] The first part of the scheme went according to plan:
the defenders, taken by surprise, were driven back, with Jeanne
and her small company in pursuit. But unfortunately she had
been seen from the heights above by Luxembourg and de
Créqui, who sent back a message to their people at Clairoix
before coming down to join in the fray themselves. Créqui
was severely wounded in the face, and for a time it seemed as
though Jeanne would, as so often before, carry off the victory.
Three times she attacked, but meanwhile reinforcements were
arriving post-haste from Clairoix. It was now the turn of the
French to be surprised, and Jeanne's people, finding themselves
outnumbered, came to her in great distress, begging her to

[1]*Procès*, Vol. IV, p. 400: Monstrelet.
[2]Pierre Champion, *Guillaume de Flavy*, p. 46.

retire into Compiègne, or she and they would alike be lost.

It was the kind of appeal to which she had always responded with a salutary scorn. She received it with anger now. "*Taisez-vous*," she said to them; "their discomfiture depends only on you. Think only of falling upon them."[1] The answer was worthy of her, but either something of the old authority had gone out of her voice, or else the situation was really beyond redemption: she could not rally them, even if she managed to obtain a hearing at all. They were already in flight; they were taking to the boats, they were pouring back across the bridge into the town. Jeanne went after the fugitives, fighting desperately to defend their rear, as even a Burgundian chronicler testifies[2]: her last moments under arms were worthy of her gallantry. Her men were reaching the town; had reached it; had streamed into safety through the gates. At this point de Flavy, seeing that they were closely pursued by the enemy, and fearing that they might be followed and the battle carried within the walls, gave the fatal order to raise the drawbridge and close the gates.[3] Jeanne was cut off. She was almost alone. D'Aulon, his brother Poton, her own brother Pierre, and a few others were still with her. Englishmen and Burgundians surged round her. Still fighting, she gained the meadows. Hands were laid on her horse, and on her person; everyone was striving to take her; everyone was calling out "Yield to me!"[4] At last an archer belonging to the Bastard of Wendonne pulled her off her horse. The Pucelle of Orleans was a prisoner.[5]

[1]*Procès*, Vol. IV, pp. 33–4. Perceval de Cagny.

[2]*Procès*, Vol. IV, p. 401: Monstrelet.

[3]It has often been suggested that the closing of the gates was an act of treachery on the part of de Flavy. M. Quicherat discards this theory, for reasons which need not be gone into here, but which are sufficiently convincing (*Aperçus nouveaux sur Jeanne d'Arc*).

[4]*Procès*, Vol. IV, p. 34: Perceval de Cagny.

[5]The Bastard of Wendonne, Vendonne, Vendomme, or Wendomme, in Artois, has frequently and erroneously been represented as a scion of the royal house of Vendôme. He was, in fact, an ordinary soldier in the service of Jean de Luxembourg.

Chapter XIV

COMPIÈGNE TO ROUEN

i

Her capture aroused tremendous and immediate excitement, than which no greater tribute could have been paid to the fear and hatred she had inspired among her enemies for the past full year. They had called her by insulting names; they had pretended that she came from the Devil; they had threatened to burn her as a witch if they could catch her; they had jeered at her as a woman in men's clothes; they had affected to despise her, but now that she was actually in their power there could be no doubt that they regarded her as a major prize. They were frankly jubilant. *Ceux de la partie de Bourgogne et les Angloix en furent moult joyeux . . . car iloz ne redoubtoient nul capitainne ne aultre chief de guerre, tant comme ilz avoient tousjours fait jusques à che présent jour, ycelle Pucelle.*[1] Their manner towards her was marked by no contempt and no condescension. They did not in any way affect to underrate their capture. Among her first visitors was the great Duke of Burgundy himself, who had missed the fighting, but who had arrived from Coudun just after it was over, when the troops, English and Burgundian, were still in the fields opposite Compiègne shouting with joy *(faisans grans cris et rebaudissemens, pour la prinse de ladicte Pucelle)*.[2] He went at once to see Jeanne, and for the first time those so different antagonists met face to face. There is no record of what passed between them at their interview on that May evening in the quarters of Jean de Luxembourg. Enguerran de Monstrelet was present, but conveniently forgets what they said to one another. As it seems improbable that so biased a chronicler would forget what was said on so momentous an occasion, it is fair to assume either that the Duke confined his

[1]*Procès*, Vol. IV, p. 402: Monstrelet. It must be remembered that Monstrelet was a Burgundian, which makes his admission all the more remarkable.
[2]*Procès*, Vol. IV, p. 402: Monstrelet.

remarks to some banal enquiry after her comfort not worth recording, or that he made some perilous reference and got rapped over the knuckles for his pains.[1] We do know, however, that the Duke then went back to Coudun and dictated a letter to the citizens of Saint Quentin that same evening—a boastful letter, proclaiming that although his own side had lost no men either dead, wounded, or prisoners, the enemy had suffered severe losses both by death, drowning, and captivity. Through the pleasure of our blessed Creator, he says, the Pucelle is a prisoner, which, he is sure, will come as great news everywhere and will expose the error and wild credulity (*folle créance*) of those who inclined themselves favourably to that woman.[2]

He wrote to the Duke of Britanny too.[3] There was no pretence: the Duke of Burgundy was pleased; the Duke of Burgundy was very much relieved.

ii

After the shouts, the jubilations, and the letters, a far more vital point remained to be discussed: to whom did the notorious prisoner really belong? Safely locked up in the castle of Beaulieu en Vermandois as she was, with her faithful d'Aulon to attend her, claims and controversy raged round her person: *celle femme que l'on nomme communément Jehanne la Pucelle, prisonnière*. The claim was, so to speak, five deep:

(1) Her actual captor was an archer in the service of the Bastard of Wendomme.
(2) The Bastard of Wendomme was himself in the service of Jean de Luxembourg.
(3) Jean de Luxembourg, although a vassal of the Duke of Burgundy, was himself in the service of the King of England.[4]

[1]*Procès*, Vol. IV, p. 402: Monstrelet.
[2]*Procès*, Vol. V, pp. 166–7: Letter of the Duke of Burgundy, Count of Flanders, Artois, and Namur.
[3]*Procès*, Vol. V, p. 358.
[4]Andrew Lang, *The Maid of France*, note on p. 133, quoting *Bibl. Cotton*

(4) The King of England himself had a lien on French prisoners, including Charles VII in person.[1] Therefore he had a lien on Jeanne.

(5) As though this were not enough, the Bishop of Beauvais could claim that as Jeanne had been taken within his diocese, he had the right to demand her and conduct her trial. This meant that she could legally be handed over to the mercies of the Church.

In this extremely complicated situation, the archer who had actually dragged her off her horse and his immediate employer, the Bastard of Wendomme, quickly disappear. There remain only Jean de Luxembourg, the Duke of Burgundy, the King of England, and the Church to be considered. Jean de Luxembourg was easily bought off: it was he, in fact, who eventually pocketed the six thousand francs paid for Jeanne.[2] Sentimentalists who are shocked by these mercenary transactions should realise that, according to the current usage, Jean de Luxembourg could not really be blamed for not listening to his aunt, who threw herself at his feet, begging him not to dishonour himself.[3] He came of a noble house, but he was poor; the younger son of a younger son, he could not even count with any certainty on succeeding to his aunt's fortune, which he fully expected his elder brother to dispute. The prospect of a ransom was tempting; and, indeed, he could scarcely have refused to yield his prisoner to his feudal superior on demand. He had no choice, any more than the Duke of Burgundy had any choice (even had he desired it), when the King of England, whom he recognised as the King of

Cleopatra, F. iv, p. 52v, and Jeanne d'Arc et les archives anglaises, pp. 20–1, by the Abbé Henri Debout. I myself have no idea what Bibl. Cotton Cleopatra means, and can only hope that my readers are as erudite as Mr. Lang. So definitely in the service of the King of England was he that he appears in the English archives as John Jussingburgh, the recipient of five hundred livres d'or.

[1]Procès, Vol. I, p. 14.

[2]Procès, Vol. I, p. 13. The Bastard of Wendomme got two or three hundred pounds as well. The poor archer is never mentioned again; presumably he got nothing.

[3]Procès, Vol. I, p. 231.

France, demanded the person of Jeanne or another. The only person who can really be blamed in the whole affair is the miserable Charles VII. However dispassionate a point of view we may strive to preserve, there comes a moment when our indignation gets the upper hand. Charles owed everything to Jeanne. Admittedly, he had his difficulties to contend with. He had his own weak character, and his own strong false friends— two conflicting influences which tore him into pieces between them. He had his own poverty to consider. But all the same, when both these things have duly been taken into consideration, there still remains a residue of contemptible treachery which must for ever be associated with his name. He ought to have made some attempt to rescue Jeanne. He ought either to have ransomed her, which would, technically, have been easy and usual, even if expensive; or, if he could not afford that expense out of his exchequer, he could have exchanged her. He could, at any rate, have made some attempt to do so. He had, for instance, still got Talbot in his keeping ever since the battle of Patay. I am not suggesting that the English would have been prepared to exchange Jeanne for Talbot. Talbot as a prisoner was obviously of far less value than Jeanne: Talbot was just one among other captains, whereas Jeanne, although not a captain strictly speaking, was something incalculable and exceptional, a real danger, and, as such, a real prize. The English had enough sense to see that Talbot against Jeanne would not have weighed as a good exchange. Still, Charles should have tried it; he should have offered Talbot and other prisoners, and possibly a large sum of money, in order to recover Jeanne. He had pawned the crown jewels for meaner purposes. A bigger man would have pawned the richest towns of France for such a rescue.

Again, had he been a bigger man, he could have compelled the Archbishop of Reims, as Primate of France, to disqualify the Bishop of Beauvais as a traitor and a renegade. The Bishop of Beauvais had already been turned out of his see. He could have been suspended in the performance of his duties. Charles took no such step. His apologists have done their best to absolve him from the charge of criminal ingratitude, but theirs is an ungrateful task. They have not even the excuse to plead that Charles was temperamentally incapable of understanding the elements of loyalty, for when he wanted to be loyal he could be passionately and unwisely so. No one had ever dared to say a word against La Trémoïlle (*si n'y avoit personne qui en eust osé parler contre icely de la Trémoïlle,* says Cousinot), and, as for Agnès Sorel, when she was Charles' mistress, his loyalty to her was such that if any man wanted to damage an enemy, he had only to say that that enemy had spoken ill of the lady.[1]

But Charles, although he could run all risks for objects where his heart was really engaged, and could bribe the Duke of Burgundy with Compiègne as part of an unnecessary and foolish truce, lay low, small, mean, and evasive as he always was, when it came to the point of ransoming the most valuable prisoner in his kingdom. He left his best friend to her fate.

iii

That fate seems, to us, rapid and preordained. To its victim, it must have seemed protracted and slow. She who had been accustomed to carry her standard to victory was now incarcerated within walls. At first she was not unkindly treated. She was allowed to keep d'Aulon to serve her, and when she was removed from Beaulieu to Jean de Luxembourg's castle of Beaurevoir at the source of the Escaut, not far from Saint Quentin, a place of greater security,[2] she was put under the care of three women for whom she evidently conceived a great devotion. These were Jeanne de Luxembourg, the aged aunt of Jean; Jeanne de Béthune, his wife; and Jeanne de Bar,

---

[1] Thomas Basin, *Histoire des règnes de Charles VII et de Louis IX*, Vol. I, p. 312: *Car si l'un de ces chiens de cour en voulait à quelque honnête homme, il y avait un moyen sûr d'attirer sur lui la colère du roi: c'etait de dire qu'il avait mal parlé de la belle Agnès, chose tenue pour crime capital.*

[2] *Procès*, Vol. I, p. 163. She had tried to escape from Beaulieu, which was no doubt the reason they decided to remove her.

his step-daughter. The ladies of Luxembourg did all they could for their young namesake. They were greatly distressed by her obstinate refusal to abandon her masculine clothes, and tried by every means to persuade her into a more feminine frame of mind, giving her the choice between a woman's dress or a length of material from which to make it. Jeanne was not tempted by either of these inducements. She was reluctant to reject an offer so kindly meant, and stated at her trial that she would sooner have done it at their request than at the request of any other ladies in France, except the Queen's, but that God would not permit it.[1] From Jeanne, also, we hear of the old demoiselle de Luxembourg's remonstrance with her nephew when she begged him not to sell her to the English.[2] There can be no doubt that the ladies of Luxembourg treated their guest and prisoner with gentleness and affection. One wonders what they thought of Aimond de Macy, a young knight who later admitted naïvely that he had tried to treat her with familiarity when he saw her at Beaurevoir (*tentavit, cum ea ludendo, tangere mammas suas, nitendo ponere manus in sinu suo*), but whom she had pushed away with all her strength.[3]

Kind though the ladies were, it was not to be expected that Jeanne would accept captivity tamely. Apart from her personal feelings, she was terribly and constantly distressed by the thought of Compiègne abandoned by its King and threatened by the enemy. It was all very well for her to assure d'Aulon that the King of Heaven would never allow it to be retaken: ever practical, however much she might trust the King of Heaven, she wanted to go and see to things for herself. She had been told that everyone in the town over the age of seven would be put to fire and blood, and stated that she would sooner die than continue to live after such a destruction of good people. This was bad enough, but another dread came urging her to take the desperate step she was contemplating. She had known all along that negotiations were in progress for

[1]*Procès*, Vol. I, pp. 95–6 and 230.   [2]*Procès*, Vol. I, p. 231.
[3]*Procès*, Vol. IV, p. 35: Perceval de Cagny.

her sale to the English. She could not fail to know this, aware as she was that her friendly old hostess was doing her best to prevent it. At last she knew for certain that the transaction had been completed, and that she was indeed about to be handed over to the foreigner and the enemy by one who, Burgundian though he was, was yet her own countryman. At this, a kind of frenzy seems to have taken possession of her. On her own showing, she had no desire to commit suicide—she had only the desire to get away. To fall into English hands was the thing she most dreaded. It was in vain that her voices sought to restrain her. In vain that Saint Catherine assured her that she would not be delivered until she had seen the King of England. She had no desire to see him, and said so. Still, the voices would not authorise her to do as she wished. The argument continued daily for some time, Jeanne beseeching, the voices refusing their permission. Finally she took the law into her own hands, commended herself to God, and threw herself off the top of the castle tower.[1]

This leap from Beaurevoir constitutes one of the most inexplicable and curious episodes in her career. It is assumed that the height cannot have been less than sixty or seventy feet.[2] The act of accusation expressly states that she jumped from the top

[1] *Procès*, Vol. I, pp. 109–10, pp. 160–1, pp. 169 and 266.
[2] J. Quicherat, *Aperçus nouveaux sur Jeanne d'Arc*, p. 57. It will of course instantly occur to the reader that the height of the tower grew rapidly in popular legend, but in correction of that apparently plausible argument I must point out (1) that the actual height is never mentioned in contemporary documents, but is based by modern calculation on the analogy of towers of similar mediæval castles; (2) that the only contemporary reference to the height is found in the words *turris altæ*, which is phrasing it soberly and without the suggestion of any popular or legendary exaggeration; (3) that if, as I suppose, Jeanne was allowed to walk freely and alone on the roof of the tower, the height must have been such as to preclude all fear of her jumping down. I argue that the tower was high, and that she was allowed there alone, for, had the tower been low enough to admit the danger of her attempting a jump, she would have been accompanied and closely watched. The almost certain presence of a parapet, or at any rate battlements, would have given a vigilant guard plenty of time to prevent her from carrying out her intention.

(*a summitate unius turris altæ*), i.e. not from a window on the
way up, as we can readily understand when we reflect that any
window would have been heavily barred, even assuming, which
is unlikely, that it was anything more than a mere arrow-slit;
and also that her kind jailers probably allowed her freely to
take the air on the flat roof, never imagining that any prisoner,
however wild, would be so insane as to seek escape that way.
They had underrated Jeanne's courage and desperation. It is left
to our imagination to picture their consternation when they
discovered that she had disappeared, still more when they
found her lying insensible on the ground, for, apart from
Jeanne's own replies to questions, we have been left no first-
hand account of the happening. At first they thought her dead,
and, indeed, she later confessed that she had been unable to
eat anything for two or three days. She seems to have been
knocked thoroughly unconscious, perhaps even suffered slight
concussion, for she records that when the Burgundians saw that
she was alive they told her that she had leaped.[1] The simple
statement gives a good idea of the bewilderment she must have
experienced when first she reopened her eyes. Still, it seems a
small price to pay for so crazy an adventure. Far from falling
on her head and breaking her neck, she did not even sprain an
ankle, and as soon as Saint Catherine started telling her that
she must ask forgiveness of God, and that the people of
Compiègne would be relieved before Martinmas, November
11th, she began to eat again and was soon recovered.[2]

Now, how on earth are we to account for this extraordinary
story? There can be no doubt of its truth, for Jeanne never
sought to deny it and patiently answered all the questions put
to her during the trial, where it was greatly insisted on, the
accusation of attempted suicide providing a point of considerable value in the eyes of the Church, which will not allow any
human being, however wretched, the right to dispose of his own
life. Not that Jeanne, when she jumped from the tower of
Beaurevoir, intended to take her own life. She was far too good

[1]*Procès*, Vol. I, p. 110.   [2]*Procès*, Vol. I, p. 152.

a Catholic for that. Escape was all she thought of, and, determined upon escape, in defiance of her intermediary voices, she preferred for once to short-circuit them and to go to the fountain-head of God for protection and support. From whichever angle we look at the story, it is a very queer one. It is significant in so far as it proves that Jeanne, on occasion, could deliberately disobey the counsel of her chosen saints—a proof which surely disposes of the argument, so often advanced, that "her voices said what she wanted them to say." It disposes, almost *ipso facto*, of the argument, again so often advanced, that her voices were merely the subjective expression of her own inward desires. It proves that, on occasion, her saints could go against her, and that she could go against her saints. What are we to make of this? We can regard it either as a complication of the general problem or as a simplification of it; we can take it, in short, according to our individual temperament and mentality. The entirely credulous mentality will accept it as a final proof of the objective nature of Jeanne's inspiration. The more sceptical mentality will ponder over the psychological questions aroused, and will fail to come to any decision. For myself, being neither credulous nor sceptical, but trying to keep a balance, an *aurea mediocritas*, the whole story appears as one of the strongest arguments that can be advanced in favour of an objective rather than a subjective influence working on Jeanne. It seems to me, for instance, highly significant that her voices, although at the moment entirely opposed to her personal wishes, could still inspire her with the gift of prophecy, so far as to inform her that Compiègne would be relieved before Saint Martin's Day—as, indeed, it was. This was a thing that no one could exactly have foretold from a study of the situation, least of all Jeanne in her captivity, yet she appears to have known it. True, in this case she related it *after* the event, a circumstance which might well arouse our suspicion over anyone less impeccable: where Jeanne is concerned, we may, I think, take her word for any such serious statement. If she said Saint Catherine told her Compiègne would be relieved before a

U

certain date, we may accept without question that she did honestly believe that Saint Catherine had told her so. Her saints, therefore, although they forbade her to leap and risk her life, still kept her informed of what was going to happen. It is all very inexplicable and contradictory.

And even could we explain the psychological mystery, the physical aspect remains equally baffling. Several theories have been advanced to cover the facts, amongst them the suggestion that she attempted to let herself down—perhaps by bedclothes knotted together—but that the thing, whatever it was, broke (*mais ce par quoi elle se glissait rompit*).[1] As, however, the chronicler adds that she nearly broke her back, and suffered a long illness from her injuries, his evidence on this point may probably be safely discarded, especially taking into consideration that neither Jeanne nor her judges made any reference to ropes or bedclothes in the very exhaustive examination at the trial. It is suggested, also, by a modern author, who has the advantage of being a doctor, that at the age of nineteen her bones had not yet hardened, or, as he prefers to put it, "her epiphyseal cartilages had not ossified"—and that "if she fell on soft ground it is perfectly credible that she might not receive worse than a severe shock."[2] I confess that I find this contention less perfectly credible than does its originator. Let anyone stand on a tower the height of Beaurevoir, and ask himself if he would care to throw himself over with any reasonable hope of not being smashed at the bottom. Moreover, a leading orthopædic surgeon whom I questioned, emphatically replied that the suggestion that the bones were not yet hardened at nineteen is untenable, since, although ossification at the growth-lines is not complete at that age, the main portion of each bone is as hard and as breakable as in adult life.

Then there is M. Quicherat, who, as the greatest and most scholarly authority on Jeanne, cannot possibly be disregarded. M. Quicherat throws out a mysterious remark, to the effect that *une certaine maladie qui fait l'étonnement de la médecine* offers

[1]*Chronique dite des Cordeliers.*   [2]*Post-mortem*, by C. MacLaurin, p. 45.

parallel cases of tremendous falls without organic injury.[1] To what disease M. Quicherat refers here I have been unable to discover, nor can any of my medical acquaintances throw any light on the puzzle. The specialist whom I have already quoted has been kind enough to write me a long letter, from which the following are extracts:

"There is, as you say, a well-known condition in which bones are præternaturally brittle, but there is none in which they are abnormally resilient; they can, it is true, become extremely flexible in one condition of disease (osteomalacia), but that is the result of many pregnancies, or of severe deprivation of diet, and it causes gross deformities of the skeleton (flattened pelvis, stunted bent limbs, and so on). I do not think that it has ever been suggested that the Maid was a stunted cripple, has it?

"I have myself occasionally seen persons who have fallen from a considerable height without serious consequences. When I was a house surgeon at Guy's, I saw a porter from one of the hop-warehouses near by who fell to the pavement, from the fourth floor, and sustained only bruises, and a severe fright. I also saw a baby which fell from a third-floor window of Peabody Buildings, and was absolutely uninjured. Both patients were very thoroughly X-rayed.

"I have also seen, in my time, quite a number of persons who have suffered a crush-fracture of the body of a vertebra (usually the last dorsal or first lumbar), who have never, as far as they can remember, had any serious fall, or had any symptoms in consequence of their injury. Yet there the fracture is, in the radiogram, for all men to see—quite unmistakable. That can only mean that a vertebra can be broken in consequence of relatively slight force, in some cases, and the fracture may cause little disturbance, so much so that the causal injury is forgotten.

"Assuming, then, that the story about Joan of Arc is true, it is possible that she did suffer some bony injury, but that it caused no very disabling symptoms. And if, at that time, she was already strongly moved by religious ardour amounting almost to fanaticism —she might well have disregarded pain and disability of such a degree."

[1] *Aperçus nouveaux sur l'histoire de Jeanne d'Arc*, p. 58. J. Quicherat.

We are left, therefore, to take our choice of the explanations. Either it was some extraordinary chance which preserved Jeanne from injury, or else she did actually suffer some injury but remained unaware of it, or else she was upheld by some inexplicable agency. In any case, the incident is, to say the least of it, remarkable.

iv

Meanwhile, outside the confines of Beaurevoir, events had been moving towards an end which was finally to deliver Jeanne into the power of the Church. Even though delays were to arise later, no time had at first been wasted. Three days after her capture (May 26th) the Vicar-General of the Inquisition had addressed a letter to the Duke of Burgundy, demanding that she should be handed over,[1] and the University of Paris had likewise written, asking that La Pucelle should be submitted to the justice of the Church, to be duly tried for idolatry and other matters.[2] Jean de Luxembourg and the Bastard of Wendomme were also called upon to do their duty, i.e. to give their captive up. Delays ensuing, the tone of the letters becomes more and more peremptory, but by July we find a new protagonist taking charge of the situation, a protagonist who had no intention whatsoever of letting Jeanne slip through his fingers. Pierre Cauchon, Bishop of Beauvais, had every reason for wishing to square his account with the French King and his Pucelle. From the first, Pierre Cauchon had been marked for success. He had been associated with the University of Paris from the moment he went there at undergraduate age. In various stages, he proceeded from responsibility to responsibility. He was sent to Rome; he was given office after office. He progressed with certainty all along his particular line. As a churchman, he was doing well, but, even as a churchman, it sooner or later became necessary for him to decide on which secular side he would politically throw his weight. He chose the English side. Ever since his election to the see of Beauvais,

[1] *Procès*, Vol. I, pp. 12 and 13.   [2] *Procès*, Vol. I, p. 9.

in 1420, he had served the English cause in France, enjoying both the confidence of Bedford and presently the income of a thousand pounds as a member of the Council of Henry VI. Highly esteemed by the University of Paris, and in great favour with Pope Martin V, life was pleasant and successful enough until, in the summer of 1429, disaster fell upon him when his English friends were driven from Beauvais and he himself lost possession of his see. A fugitive at Rouen, he had time to reflect upon the wrongs he had suffered even as an indirect result of the triumphant campaigns of the idolatrous Pucelle. And Pierre Cauchon was not a man who readily forgave.

To this coldly revengeful prelate, therefore, the task now laid upon him by Bedford must have been congenial in the extreme. It must have afforded him great satisfaction to associate his own name with that of Henry VI, in demanding that "this woman who had been taken within his diocese and under his spiritual jurisdiction" should be delivered to him in order that he might conduct her trial as it behoved.[1] It must have been most agreeable to arrive in person at the camp of Jean de Luxembourg opposite Compiègne, as the accredited agent of Bedford, to put an end to all the shilly-shally and bargaining over the person of Jeanne. With the authority of Bedford and Henry VI behind him, he was in a position to dictate to Jean de Luxembourg and even to the great Burgundy himself. He came backed by the full authority of the English crown, and with promises of English money in his hand. The Burgundians, as we have seen, had no choice but to agree. Cauchon was unremitting and energetic in his efforts. He travelled, as he tells us, now to Compiègne, now to Beaurevoir, now to Rouen, and now to Flanders, and at the end of his mission he received seven hundred and sixty-five *livres tournois* for his expenses.[2]

[1]*Procès*, Vol. I, p. 14.
[2]*Procès*, Vol. V, pp. 194–5. These expenses were not incurred wholly in the pursuit of Jeanne. They represent Cauchon's bill from the beginning of May 1430 to the end of September 1430.

The delay in the actual delivery of Jeanne seems to have been largely due to the difficulty of raising the necessary money. It was raised, eventually, by a tax imposed on the Duchy of Normandy, to the tune of eighty thousand pounds, ten thousand *livres tournois* being used and converted into the payment for Jeanne la Pucelle, *sorcière, personne de guerre*.[1] It was not until November 1430 that she was finally handed over. There is no record of the exact date of her removal from Beaurevoir to another place of her captivity. We know only that some time during November 1430 she was taken from Beaurevoir to Arras, where she was shown the portrait of herself in armour, kneeling before her King (see Chapter I, p. 1). As she was depicted in full armour, we may imagine that this reminder of her glorious days hurt her considerably. *Nessun maggior dolore* . . . Where was that armour now? She had left it at Saint Denis in a mood of despair. Incidentally, it is worthy of remark that, although the early descriptions of her clothes are detailed and numerous, they cease altogether from the beginning of her decline. She must, for instance, have procured some kind of armour after she had abandoned her own at Saint Denis, for she was often in battle after that; but what happened to her after she had been taken at Compiègne? What did she wear in prison? What did she look like, deprived of her armour and her scarlet cloak? Did they leave her in possession of the tunic in the colours of Orleans? Or was the association with Orleans too dangerous a reminder? We know nothing for certain except that she wore boy's dress, and we may supplement this knowledge by reflecting that since she had now spent nearly six months in prison, wearing the same suit every day, she must have presented an exceedingly shabby appearance by the time she reached Arras. It is logical, I think, to assume that she had had no change of suit. Her jailers, however kind, would never have consented to supply her with new clothes of masculine fashion, and we know that she had

[1] *Procès*, Vol. V, p. 179. Details of the conversion are given in *Procès*, Vol. V, pp. 191–2.

steadily rejected the offer of any others. We know, also, that at Arras a certain Jean de Pressy and others, who remain anonymous, renewed the plea that she should adopt feminine clothes.[1] Her small human problems suggest themselves inevitably to our curiosity. How did she manage to cut her hair? It is unlikely that she would have been allowed anything in the nature of a knife, and equally unlikely that even the kind ladies of Beaurevoir, who for her own sake deplored her insistence on her masculine appearance, would have abetted her obstinacy by any loan of scissors from their work-baskets. These questions must remain for ever unanswered. All we can imagine for certain is that she must have arrived at Arras looking very shabby, very forlorn, and very young.

v

From Arras she was taken by stages to Rouen. First to the castle of Drugy near Saint Riquier,[2] then to the castle of Crotoy, on the sea at the mouth of the Somme. She had, of course, never seen the sea before, and it would be interesting to know what her feelings were on beholding for the first time this expanse of grey tossing water—the month was November, and the sea the English Channel. If ignorant children who have never seen the sea can still be astounded and impressed when confronted by its immensity, even to-day when photographs and cinemas might be expected to have bred a second-hand degree of familiarity in their minds, how much more must a girl like Jeanne, who belonged to an age of a very different type of wonder, who had never seen a photograph, and who could have formed no idea of the sea save by the very inadequate descriptions of illiterate travellers, have gazed in astonishment at its actuality. Add to this, that she was at that time a prisoner, and that to the yearning prisoner the sea and its ships must always romantically represent a symbol of

[1] *Procès*, Vol. I, pp. 95–6.
[2] *Procès*, Vol. V, pp. 358–9: Chronicle of Jean de la Chapelle.

freedom and escape. Add to this, again, that across the sea lay, somewhere, England, that dim strong island which had sent out such enemies of France as Henry V, Salisbury, Talbot, and Bedford, and which even now held her especial favourite, the Duke of Orleans, captive in one of its fortresses called the Tower of London. One thing taken with another, Jeanne's first sight of the English Channel must have been enough to move the firmest soul.

There was another point about the castle of Crotoy which cannot have failed emotionally to affect her: it was the very place where her friend d'Alençon had been incarcerated for five years as the prisoner of the English after the battle of Verneuil. Knowing this, she can scarcely have failed to think of him when she herself arrived there under similar, though more terrible, conditions. More terrible, for d'Alençon knew he could be ransomed; Jeanne, by that time, must have known that no ransom was forthcoming for her; she must have known, also, that no offered ransom would outbid the determination of the Church and the English. She must have thought with envy of d'Alençon's gay young figure, impatient, but daily expecting the release she could never hope to gain.

Still, the records prove that nowhere was she regarded as a mere mean prisoner, hustled unimportantly from place to place. At Drugy the monks of the local abbey attended upon her (*la visitèrent par honneur*), headed by their provost and their almoner, and followed by the principal citizens of Saint Riquier, all being much moved on seeing so innocent a person thus persecuted.[1] At Crotoy she received the ladies of Abbeville, who had come to see her as a marvel of their sex and who arrived by boat down the Somme, Jeanne expressed her appreciation, commended herself to their prayers, kissed them, and allowed them to take their departure in tears by boat again. So much impressed was she by their frankness, their candour, and their naïveté (*leur franchise, leur candeur, et leur naïveté*)

[1]*Procès*, Vol. V, pp. 360-1-2: *Histoire généalogique des comtes de Maieur d'Abbeville, par Jacques Samson (père Ignace de Jesus Maria.)*

that she came near to denying her own people in Lorraine. "Ha!" she exclaimed, "*que voicy un bon peuple! pleust à Dieu que je fusse si heureuse, lorsque je finiray mes jours, que je pusse estre enterrée en ce pays.*"[1] It is difficult not to allow oneself to be touched by the generous response of the shabby, boyish, important little captive towards these voluminous and prosperous matrons of Abbeville, who had come, in the first instance, one suspects, largely in order to satisfy their curiosity, although they may have gone away truly impressed and moved by their brief contact with a personality so entirely different from their own. Anyhow, they floated away on their barge, tears in their eyes, and Jeanne stayed behind, knowing that sooner or later she must be called upon to confront the dry damning assessors at Rouen.[2]

In one respect, Jeanne was fortunate during her brief stay at le Crotoy: she found a fellow-prisoner there, a remarkable man, Nicolas de Queuville, chancellor of the Cathedral of Amiens, whose celebrations of Mass in the prison Jeanne was allowed to attend, and to whom she was allowed to make her confession.[3] But it was not long before she followed the example of the ladies of Abbeville, embarking, like them, on the waters of the Somme, unlike them under guard, merely to be taken across the wide mouth of the river from le Crotoy to Saint Valery on the opposite bank. She does not appear to have paused at Saint Valery, but went straight on to Eu, where tradition says that she was lodged in the prison of the castle. Very little evidence is available about her journey. We know only that from Eu she was taken to Dieppe and from Dieppe —the last stage—to Rouen,[4] where she arrived some time during December 1430.

[1]*Procès*, Vol. V, p. 362.
[2]*Procès*, Vol. V, p. 361.
[3]*Procès*, Vol. III, p. 121: Deposition of Aimond de Macy.
[4]*Procès*, Vol. V, p. 363.

vi

The days of respectful and even kindly treatment were over.
She had now known captivity for some seven months, but
never captivity such as this. Spiritually and physically she
suffered as she had never suffered before. Spiritually, she was
now denied all the comforts of the Church. Physically, she
was denied the privilege which should have been accorded her
as one about to be tried by the Church, of being kept in the
ecclesiastical prison, where the Bishop of Rouen had at his
disposal a room for women, and where she might have been
placed under the care of women[1]; but was thrown, instead,
in irons into a common cell. The best that can be said for
the cell is that it was not a dungeon, since eight steps up
gave access to it (Massieu). Accounts of witnesses vary slightly
as to the exact nature of her fetters; some denied all knowledge of the matter; others, who had some means of judging
it, either by hearsay or by personal experience, agree that her
feet were chained; and some of these add that her feet were
padlocked to a long chain attached to a beam[2]; others go so
far as to say that at night an extra chain was passed round her
body. Did they allow her a bed or not? Here, again, accounts
differ. Jean Tiphaine, who visited her as a doctor during an
illness, says she had a bed, and so do others (Boisguillaume,
Massieu); Manchon, on the other hand, explicitly states that
she had none. Perhaps the discrepancy may be explained by
suggesting that they gave her a bed when she fell ill, and
allowed her to retain it once her illness had put it into their
heads that she might elude their vengeance by natural means.
For the rest, there can be no doubt whatsoever that she was

[1]Pierre Champion, *Procès de condamnation*, Vol. III, p. xxvi.

[2]*Procès*, Vol. II, p. 306: Depositions of Pierre Cusquel; *Procès*, Vol. III,
p. 48, Jean Tiphaine; *Procès*, Vol. II, p. 318, Nicolas Taquel; *Procès*, Vol. III,
p. 161, Boisguillaume; *Procès*, Vol. II, p. 302, Isambard de la Pierre; *Procès*,
Vol. III, p. 154, Massieu; and many others. It seems doubtful whether the
beam was really a beam, i.e. part of the structure of the prison, or merely a
heavy piece of wood.

most uncomfortably housed and harshly guarded. Marie Antoinette in the Conciergerie was not under more constant or less pitiful supervision. Day and night she was watched by five English soldiers of the lowest type, *houcepaillers*, who missed no opportunity of tormenting and mocking her.[1] Manchon heard her complaining both to the Bishop of Beauvais and to the Earl of Warwick that they had several times attempted to rape her, and heard her reminding Warwick that, but for his timely arrival in response to her cries for help, they would have achieved their object.[2] No one could approach her or speak to her without permission; the English dreaded lest she should escape, and, of the three keys to her cell, one was in the keeping of the Cardinal Bishop of Winchester.[3] There are further reports of an iron cage having been made for her, and, even if she was never put into it, we can scarcely doubt that her jubilant enemies took pleasure in describing it to her in all its horrid detail. The evidence for its existence is considerable. Thomas Marie and Jean Massieu had both heard of it; Massieu, indeed, claims to have derived his information from Etienne Castille, the very locksmith who made it, and credulously repeats the locksmith's statement that Jeanne was kept in it from the day of her arrival at Rouen until the beginning of the trial, standing upright, tied by the throat, hands, and feet. Thomas Marie had also heard of the cage from the locksmith who made it, and confirms the statement that the prisoner would be obliged to stand upright, but, less definite than Massieu, said no more than that "he believed" she had been kept in it. The most interesting witness on the subject of the cage, however, is Pierre Cusquel, a simple workman of

---

[1]*Procès*, Vol. III, p. 154: Deposition of Jean Massieu.

[2]Vallet de Viriville, *Procès de condamnation de Jeanne d'Arc*, p. 279: Deposition of Guillaume Manchon. To do Warwick justice, he appears to have reprimanded them severely, and to have replaced the two chief offenders by two others. The names of the soldiers have been recorded, doubtless incorrectly in some cases, as John Baroust or Berwoit, Nicholas Bertin, Julian Flosquet or Floquet, William Mouton and William Talbot. John Gray was their leader.

[3]*Procès*, Vol. II, p. 322: Deposition of Pierre Boucher.

Rouen, who twice had speech with her in her cell, owing to the fact that he was employed by Jean Son, the master mason of the prison. He seems to have been allowed to talk to her quite freely, and indeed privately, for he was able to warn her to answer very prudently as it concerned her life and death, and was also able to put questions to her and to receive her replies, during which time he could observe the cell at leisure, and is one of the witnesses who mentions the chain attaching her to a beam. He never saw her in the cage, but—and this is the value of his evidence—he does say that he saw the cage weighed in his house.[1] He is the only witness who claims to have seen the cage with his own eyes, the others are basing their stories on hearsay. Why the cage should have found its way to Cusquel's house for the purpose of being weighed, he does not explain. Possibly his connexion with the master mason had something to do with it.

Whatever else Jeanne might have to complain of in her prison, she could not complain of loneliness. Loneliness, which would have meant uninterrupted communion with her saints, she could have borne better. As it was, she had to endure the coarse and often ingenious banter and even the ill-treatment of the English guards,[2] constant visits from men who came on any pretext to satisfy their curiosity, threatening visits from men she knew to be her sworn enemies, nocturnal visits from mysterious figures she hesitated to trust. Trapped, friendless, she had nothing left to rely on but her courage and her wits. Neither failed her, but she knew very well that fate had closed round her as surely as the walls of her cell. It was partly her own superb honesty which made her captivity so hard, for she refused absolutely to give her word not to attempt an escape. Should she succeed in escaping, she said, no one

---

[1] *Procès*, Vol. II, p. 306; and *Procès*, Vol. III, pp. 179–82: Depositions of Pierre Cusquel.

[2] *Procès*, Vol. III, p. 161: Deposition of Boisguillaume: *Habebat custodes Anglicos de quibus conquerebatur multotiens, dicens quod eam multum opprimebant et male tractabant.*

could reproach her with having broken her word if she had given it to no one. Then, rather illogically, she complained of her chains and gyves. But when they told her that her previous attempts at escape had rendered necessary the order for a close guard and iron shackles, she replied, in her old uncompromising manner, that it was quite true she had wished to escape, and still wished it—that being within the right of any prisoner.[1] In no way would she condescend to placate or conciliate her jailers.

Many came to see her in prison. Pierre Daron and Pierre Manuel went together, and remarked to her, by way of jocularity (*dicendo eidem Johanna jocose*), that she would not have come to that place had she not been brought. Such wit was not perhaps in the best of taste when offered to a helpless prisoner chained to a heavy piece of wood, as Daron had occasion to observe, but they went on to question her about her foreknowledge of the day when she should be taken—questions which she answered patiently, seriously, and with good humour.[2] Far worse than these privileged and casual visitors, whose curiosity provided their only reason for wishing to get a sight of the witch, was the incessant attack maintained by those who had only too clear a reason for doing so. Sometimes they came openly and by daylight; sometimes, as we shall see, in disguise and by night. One of the open raids is described in some detail by that same Aimond de Macy who had already tried to take liberties with Jeanne at Beaurevoir, and who was to end by saying that he believed her to be in Paradise. Having seen her at Beaurevoir under the care of her kindly ladies, he was now to see her at Rouen surrounded by armed men. Indeed, the tramp of the company with whom he went must have resounded with ominous masculinity on the stone steps of Jeanne's tower. It was a distinguished company, for it included Jean de Luxembourg, his brother the Bishop of Thérouenne, and the Earls of Warwick and Stafford. It is difficult to

---

[1]*Procès*, Vol. I, p. 47.
[2]*Procès*, Vol. III, p. 200: Deposition of Pierre Daron.

imagine what Jean de Luxembourg's motive for the visit really was. Did he go merely to have another look at the young prisoner who had for so long enjoyed his hospitality? Ostensibly he went to tell her that he would ransom her, on condition that she would promise never to take arms again. Jeanne of course immediately saw through this empty offer, and very rightly pointed out that since he had neither the wish nor the power to do so, *en nom Dé*, he must be laughing at her. De Luxembourg insisting, Jeanne several times repeated what she had already said, then added that she well knew the English would bring her death about, in the belief that they would regain the kingdom of France after she was dead. "But," she said, "even if they were a hundred thousand Godons more than they are now, they should not have the kingdom."

This arrogant manner of speech, proceeding from a captive wholly in their power, provoked Stafford into drawing his dagger with the intent to stab her, but Warwick intervened.[1] It was not soft sentiment which made him save her life: the truest kindness would have been to let Stafford deal the blow. In Warwick's mind, she was reserved for other things.

vii

She had other visitors. The vexed question of her virginity was revived, and the Duchess of Bedford either came in person or sent other women to investigate the matter. Boisguillaume suggests that Bedford himself witnessed the inspection, hidden in a secret place. Whether this be true or not—and I very much doubt it—there was no privacy for poor Jeanne. Rouen was boiling with gossip, as was inevitable in a small town suddenly crowded with notables, where English archers brushed against French doctors in theology, and great churchmen, followed by their clerks, had grown as common a sight as the citizens going about their daily business. The witch incarcerated in the tower of Philip Augustus was naturally the

[1]*Procès*, Vol. III, p. 122: Deposition of Aimond de Macy.

current topic of conversation. They discussed the animosity of the English against her.[1] the partiality or the impartiality of her judges; they discussed her clothes[2]; they discussed her virtue. Not even her most private life was sacred from the public curiosity. In connexion with her virtue it was said that, though in fact a virgin, she had suffered some injury from riding on horseback.[3] They thrashed the questions of her morals up and down. Jeannotin Simon, for instance, a tailor who had been sent by the Duchess of Bedford with the ever-renewed offer of a woman's dress, related in the hearing of others that, when he went to try it on, she, indignant, had boxed his ears because he attempted gently to touch her breast.[4] The Jeannotins of Rouen were not likely to hold their tongues in discretion when they had the chance of boasting that they had actually seen the celebrated Pucelle in her cell. Even the normally humiliating fact of having been fetched a box on the ear acquired a certain news-value when it was the Pucelle who had fetched it.

One must not exaggerate the suffering caused to Jeanne by such indelicate publicity. In the first place, she probably knew nothing of the outside gossip running up and down the streets and across the squares of Rouen. In the second place, had it reached her ears, she, as a peasant, might have been flattered by it—even as peasants find some consolation in a worthy funeral in the midst of their sorrow. In the third place, it would be most rash to judge her sensibility on those particular points by the standard of our own. In the fourth place, and perhaps most pertinently, we may presume that the detachment of her intense spiritual life left her essentially indifferent to the vulgarity and intrusion of the world.

[1]*Procès*, Vol. III, p. 178 and others: Deposition of Jean Lemaire: *Fama erat in Rothomago*, etc.

[2]*Procès*, Vol. II, p. 306: Deposition of Pierre Cusquel: *Populos dicebat*, etc.

[3]*Procès*, Vol. III, p. 63: Deposition of Jean Monnet: *Fuit læsa in inferioribus de equitando*.

[4]*Procès*, Vol. III, p. 89: Deposition of Jean Marcel: *Eam accepit dulciter per mammam. Quæ fuit pro hoc indignata, et tradidit dicto Johannotino unam alapam.*

Similarly, I suppose, we should discount much of the physical hardship she was obliged to endure. Jeanne, we must always remember, was born tough and coarse. The rooms in her home at Domremy appear to us little better than prison cells. Few of us to-day would accept with gratitude as a lodging the cellar-like room which is shown (rightly or wrongly) as hers. It is advisable never to sentimentalise unduly over these matters.

It would, however, be difficult to exaggerate the suffering caused to her by the complete severance from the consolations of her Church, and by the tricks which the representatives of that Church played upon her both in public and in private. Of their public behaviour we shall speak presently; for the moment we are concerned only with what took place within that locked and guarded tower of Philip Augustus. We know, for instance, that Jean Massieu, who was charged with the function of taking her backwards and forwards between her prison and her judges, was severely rebuked by the Bishop of Beauvais' creature, d'Estivet, for allowing her to pause in prayer before the tabernacle in a chapel on her way, and was forbidden in unmistakable terms to allow her to do so again. D'Estivet told him, in short, that he would get him locked up in such a tower that he would be unable to see the sun or the moon for a month. (*Je te ferai mettre en telle tour, que tu ne verras lune ne soleil d'icy à ung mois.*[1]) We know, also, by overwhelming evidence which puts the story beyond a doubt, that this same d'Estivet and another displeasing personage named Nicolas Loiselleur made a practice of introducing themselves into her cell at dead of night under false pretences to gain her confidence. Loiselleur was by far the worst offender. It is difficult to restrain one's terms in writing of Loiselleur. A rat on a heap of garbage is not more distasteful than he. A priest, he pretended to be a countryman of Jeanne, and, having insinuated himself into her favour by giving her news of her province (*en lui disant nouvelles du pays à lui plaisantes*), he got himself appointed as her confessor, when, not content with betraying the secrets of the

[1] *Procès*, Vol. II, p. 16: Deposition of Jean Massieu.

confessional to the lawyers of the trial, he introduced the two notaries Manchon and Boisguillaume, with other witnesses, secretly into a room next door, where a spy-hole enabled them to hear all that Jeanne was saying or confessing[1] (. . . *une chambre prouchaine, ou estoit ung trou par lequel on pouvoit escouter, affin qu'ilz peussent rapporter ce qu'elle disoit ou confessoit audit Loyseleur . . . pour trouver moien de la prendre captieusement*). Such baseness makes Stafford's drawn dagger shine with honesty; such baseness seems incredible, even though it is recorded by Manchon, one of the two notaries concerned. Was Manchon telling the truth? Let us hope we may doubt it. But we cannot doubt the entire story. A twist is given to the screw when we learn that Loiselleur adopted the disguise of a shoemaker from Lorraine, and, persuading her that he was a fellow-prisoner, advised her not to put her faith in the churchmen, "for," he said, "if you put your faith in them they will destroy you." This is the testimony of Boisguillaume, who adds that the Bishop of Beauvais was surely privy to the deception, otherwise Loiselleur would never have dared to practise it, and, indeed, the English guards must have had orders to admit him. D'Estivet, he says, obtained Jeanne's confidence in the same way, by passing himself off as a fellow-prisoner. Among the many ugly stories connected with Jeanne's trial, this is surely one of the ugliest. The plea sometimes advanced,[2] that the rôle of a false confessor was compatible with inquisitorial procedure, can scarcely excuse the shameful part which Loiselleur and d'Estivet consented to play.

[1] *Procès*, Vol. II, p. 11: Deposition of Guillaume Manchon.
[2] e.g. by P. Champion, *Procès de condamnation de Jeanne d'Arc*, Vol. II, p. 332, note 22.

Chapter XV

THE TRIAL (1)

i

An entirely new set of characters has by now taken possession of the stage. All those familiar figures, who accompanied Jeanne during so many months, have disappeared—the gallant d'Alençon, the courteous Bastard, the fiery La Hire, the faithful fussy d'Aulon, the slippery King himself, the corpulent La Trémoïlle, and the crafty Regnault, Archbishop of Reims. In retrospect, even the last three gain something in glamour, for they were at least officially on Jeanne's side, different from the mean snarling pack that now surrounded her, showing their teeth. The English, too, move into a different position: from being the half-perceived enemy, skirmishing on the outskirts, their voices unknown and their countenances hidden, we are now in the heart of their own fastness, seeing Warwick and Stafford move freely as men in the place where they command. Their King is there amongst them. It is Jeanne who is the stranger, no longer among the people of her own party, deserted and alone.

It is, on the whole, a not very estimable crowd. Warwick and Stafford are well enough, straightforward soldiers who had caught an enemy and wanted her put to death, but the ecclesiastical and clerkly promoters and assessors, secretaries and scriveners, monkish lawyers and subtle theologians, all the team driven with such skill and intransigence by the Bishop of Beauvais, provoke a shudder of fear and contempt as one by one their dark figures slip in and take their place on the benches of the tribunal. The list is a long one, but only certain names detach themselves and stand out from the rank and file. Cauchon himself, cold, supple, implacable, losing his temper every now and then, enough to give a glimpse of the relentless man hidden beneath the suavity of the prelate; his fellow-judge,[1] Jean Lemaistre, Dominican Vicar in Rouen of the Inquisitor of France, uneasy, unwilling, hating the case, but compelled to do as he was told; the three clerks or notaries, Boisguillaume, Taquel, and Manchon, all three of them timid and terrorised[2]; the three assessors who, according to Manchon, were the most fanatically determined to ruin Jeanne, Jacques de Touraine, Nicolas Midi, who was later to die of leprosy, and Jean Beaupère, who had lost his right hand in an affray with bandits; Jean Massieu, whose business it was to bring the prisoner to the court, and who later, although a kindly man, a priest and the doyen of the Cathedral of Rouen, was to get into trouble for his *mauvaises mœurs* and *inconduite*; Estivet, the promoter of the case, a passionate partisan of the English, who not only introduced himself falsely into Jeanne's prison, as we have seen, but also allowed himself the pleasure of insulting her there on other occasions, calling her *putain* and *paillarde* and similar names which must have reminded her strongly of the greeting returned to her by the English from the forts of Orleans; the Abbé de Fécamp, of whom it was said that he seemed to be inspired by hatred of Jeanne and love of the English rather than by any zeal in the cause of justice; Thomas de Courcelles, a brilliantly gifted young man of intellectual attainments but weak character, a young man who, as Pius II, who admired him, later recorded, was "always looking at the ground, like one who would wish to pass unnoticed"; Guillaume Erard, violent and energetic, who received a payment of thirty-one *livres tournais* at the rate of twenty *sols tournais* a day from the Receiver-General of Normandy on behalf of the King of England for every day he had attended the trial of

[1] There were only two *judges*: Cauchon and Lemaistre. The others, although sometimes referred to as judges, were in reality only there in the capacity of advisers or assessors. Lemaistre had tried to get out of taking part in the trial; it was unfortunate for him that his superior, Jean Graverent, the chief inquisitor, was engaged on another trial at Coutances.

[2] Boisguillaume was the clerk for the trial, Taquel the clerk for the Inquisition, and Manchon the clerk for Cauchon.

celle femme qui se faisoit nommer Jehanne la Pucelle,[1] and whose eloquence was to be employed in the conduct of one of the most dramatic scenes of Jeanne's whole career. It is a mixed lot. Among them were men of intelligence, probity, and compassion, men who disapproved of the way the proceedings were conducted, men who would gladly have given justice and humanity a better chance. But there were few among them who dared even to hint at such opinions. The wrath of the Bishop of Beauvais was not a thing lightly to be incurred, and there is no doubt that he held them subdued and afraid. Jean de la Fontaine, for instance, who fell under the suspicion of having given Jeanne some advice which might enable her to defeat the intentions of her judges, was obliged to leave Rouen in haste. André Marguerie, for asking a question, was harshly told to hold his tongue. Nicolas de Houppeville was actually thrown into prison for venturing on a criticism behind Cauchon's back. Jean de Chatillon was told to keep quiet and let the judges speak, or he would only be allowed to attend the sittings when he was sent for. Isambard de la Pierre, attempting to direct Jeanne, was told to be silent in the Devil's name. (*Taceatis in nomine diaboli.*) Jean Lefèvre, bishop though he was, received the same rebuke from Cauchon for remarking that a certain question was a very big question, and that Jeanne was not bound to reply to it. There was no room in the same court for Cauchon and for liberty of speech. The slightest dissentient murmur was instantly suppressed. It was quite clear who meant to be master in that court, and they all knew it.

And behind the menacing figure of the Bishop was the whole power of the English. Rouen, to all intents and purposes, was an English town, and everybody in Rouen knew very well

[1]*Procès*, Vol. V, pp. 205–7. It would not be fair to represent Erard as the only one to be reimbursed by the English Treasury for his services during the trial. Amongst others, Beaupère, Jacques de Touraine, Midi, and de Courcelles were paid twenty *sols tournais* a day each; Beaupère got a further benefice of thirty *livres tournais* for the special clothes he had bought and three horses (*Procès*, Vol. V, p. 199). Lemaistre, that reluctant man, received twenty *salus d'or* (*Procès*, Vol. V, p. 202).

that the English had no intention of letting their prisoner go. They might lend her conveniently to the ecclesiastical court appointed by the University of Paris; that was a matter of form, and so long as Jeanne died they cared very little who condemned her. But from the first it had been explicitly laid down that, if she was not found guilty of crimes against the Catholic faith, she was to be returned to the secular power vested in the King of England,[1] which really amounted to saying that if they could not catch her on one count they would catch her on another. The stake or the Seine; but they greatly preferred the stake, and that she should go to it branded as a heretic and an idolater; therefore, whenever they thought they detected any signs of weakness or hesitation on the part of the religious tribunal, protests were registered, not always without hot words. Stafford's sword was ever ready to leave the scabbard. It was scarcely a spirit calculated to produce an atmosphere of calm and impartial deliberation in the hall of justice: Cauchon knew that the desires of the English exactly coincided with his own. He could act in as high-handed a manner as he chose.

Jeanne stood not the slightest chance from the first. Those who ask whether she was given a fair trial may here find their answer. She was given a trial conducted with all the impressive apparatus of ceremony, learning, and scholasticism that the Holy Catholic Church, the Court of the Inquisition and the University of Paris between them could command, but in essence the whole trial was a preordained and tragic farce. The most remarkable thing about it, to my mind, is that they troubled to give her a trial at all, let alone a trial in which one cardinal, six bishops, thirty-two doctors of theology, sixteen bachelors of theology, seven doctors of medicine, and one hundred and three other associates were involved,[2] and that the Burgundians had not sewn her into a sack and thrown her into

[1]*Procès*, Vol. I, p. 19: Letter of Henry VI, dated 3rd January, 1430: *Toutesvoies c'est nostre entencion de ravoir et reprendre pardevers nous icelle Jehanne, se ainsi estoit qu'elle ne fust convaincue ou actainte des cas dessudiz.*

[2]The complete list is given in Appendix F, p. 398.

the Oise at Compiègne forthwith. It is an astonishing tribute to her achievement, to the awe she had inspired, and to the position she had attained in the public mind, that it never occurred to them to apply such off-hand methods as were in current use for proletarian upstarts coming forward with the claim of unusual powers. At least they paid her the compliment of treating her seriously; at least they recognised her as an enemy that must be seriously, ceremoniously, and officially dealt with, not as a mere though inconvenient adventuress who could privily be put out of the way and no questions asked. She had made too much noise in France for that. She had made so much noise that the princes and prelates of Europe addressed letters to one another about her fate. She had worked herself, in fact, into the extremely anomalous situation of being a prisoner of the highest importance and yet a prisoner without authoritative defence. She had no one whatsoever to defend her. Charles VII, her natural protector, had disappeared completely out of the picture. She was granted no advocate at the trial[1]: no single witness was called on her behalf: no single member of the party favourable to her was among her judges: no one dared to raise his voice to assist or direct her: everyone was overawed either by Cauchon or by the English, frequently by both; no formal indictment was read to her until the end; her judges did their utmost to confuse her by a bombardment of inconsecutive and apparently irrelevant questions, whose drift must have been exceedingly difficult for her to perceive; alone, unable to read or to check the documents they prepared for her signature, she had to confront the whole assembly of learned, trained, and unscrupulous or cowardly men. Yet, tired and worn as she must have been—for she had spent some two months waiting in prison at Rouen, not to mention the six months she had spent as a captive before she ever arrived at Rouen—her wits failed her so little that she was even able to escape the traps they

---

[1]*Procès*, Vol. I, pp. 200–1. She was offered a counsel after the trial had lasted for over a month, but was told she must choose him from amongst the assessors present, and not unnaturally refused the offer.

subtly laid for her. Questions which appeared impossible to answer without exposing herself to charges of almost sacrilegious presumption, she could evade with unexceptionable sagacity.

"Do you consider yourself to be in a state of grace?" they asked her.

"If I am not, may God put me there; if I am, may He keep me in it."[1]

ii

Having thus presented the prisoner's point of view, and having insisted on the fact that the verdict was a foregone conclusion, it is only fair to consider also the point of view of the judges. In the first instance it is necessary to realise and to remember that the case was being tried, not on political, but on religious grounds. Although the English pressed so close and so revengeful round the court, watching Cauchon like lynxes to detect any possible sign of clemency dawning in those clever episcopal eyes, they bore, technically and officially, no part in the charges brought against the prisoner. She was being tried, not on a charge of high treason against the English King who, in their sight, was also King of France, but on a charge of heresy, blasphemy, idolatry, and sorcery, and to the mind of a mediæval churchman there could be no more heinous or dangerous profession than that of a heretic and a witch. On neither count could she reasonably expect to escape the burning. Her answers would have had to be very satisfactory, her recantations very complete, to make it impossible for the tribunal decently to hand her over to the waiting executioner. No doubt they would have preferred her to recant, when they could have condemned her to a minor penalty such as imprisonment for life or for a term of years, for the Church, on principle, was reluctant to shed human blood (*ecclesia abhorret a sanguinez*), but failing a recantation they were quite prepared to go all lengths. It is true that they were

[1] *Procès*, Vol. I, p. 65.

determined to do so if necessary, but it is also true that a genuine fear and conviction were at the root of their determination. This being so, it would be perfectly possible to make out a case proving that Cauchon personally had treated Jeanne with remarkably long-suffering leniency. He did, in fact, make repeated attempts to reconcile her to what he believed to be the only Church whose authority she ought, as a Catholic, to recognise. He could have condemned her long before he did. He knew quite well that any delay was resented by the English, and that he himself would be the first to suffer from any suspicion of clemency or partiality. The English were thick in Rouen. He was in close and constant contact with such dominating figures as the magnificent Warwick, the impetuous Stafford, and the Cardinal-Bishop of Winchester —men who had ample and daily opportunity of telling him exactly what they thought of the progress of the trial. Such comments cannot have been, and indeed were not, always agreeable. Yet he gave Jeanne chance after chance. He allowed over a month (April 18th to May 24th) in which to give her chances at intervals. On several occasions he addressed her in kindly terms, and never seems to have lost his temper with her even when she gave him plenty of provocation to do so.[1] I find no difficulty in believing that Cauchon, with the better side of himself, genuinely desired to restore an apostate to the right way of thinking, and that he took every risk thus to persuade her, before committing her definitely to the stake. I find no difficulty in believing that Cauchon quite sincerely found himself faced with a problem in which his worldly and his religious convictions were at war. The same tolerance might apply to many members of the tribunal. I find no difficulty in believing that the majority of these sons of the Church, including Cauchon himself, were genuinely persuaded that

---

[1] It is, of course, possible that the incidents when he did lose his temper were omitted from the *procès-verbal*. According to some of the later evidence, it seems not only possible but probable, e.g. see deposition of Frère Isambard de la Pierre, *infra*, p. 317.

Jeanne, as all others of her sect, had most perilously menaced and insulted their Mother. Men of the world and scholars though they might be, learning in the fifteenth century was no proof against the terror of superstition, nor could any considerations such as humane pity for youth, sex, or ignorance be allowed to obtain for a moment. The humane virtues in that rough age were but a trifling weight anyhow; and, when dread of the Powers of Darkness came into the balance, there could be little doubt on which side the scales would fall. One must accept, *a priori*, the principle that Jeanne had to be regarded either as saint or devil. There was no middle course. They elected to regard her as a devil. Ruthless suppression therefore became a stern and sacred duty. Where the Bishop of Beauvais and his fellows erred was in the unfairness in their conduct of the trial, not in their conviction that heresy and sorcery must be stamped out, or that Jeanne, as a guilty wretch, if they could not turn her from her wickedness, must be destroyed.

It must never be forgotten, either—a vital point which I have left to the end—that the trial of Jeanne as a sorceress really involved an attack on the King who had employed her.

iii

The argument is frequently advanced, and with some foundation, that Jeanne was not tried by *the Church* at all, but only by a small and hostile section of it. Even the most impartially minded arbitrator must find himself unable to deny the force of this assertion. It has already been pointed out that the tribunal, purporting to be a religious and non-political body, or at any rate a body constituted to deal with offences against the Church, not against the State, was actually composed entirely of men directly or indirectly ruled by the interests of the English cause. Whatever the authority of the Bishop of Beauvais within his own diocese, there is no getting away from the fact that, in the name of justice, the tribunal ought to have included at least a proportion of unprejudiced divines, even allowing that we might be going too far in expecting to find a proportion drawn from the party specifically favourable to Jeanne. Then there is no getting away from the further fact that Jeanne herself did several times appeal to be taken before the Pope—an appeal which was inadequately and even ludicrously answered by the objection that Rome was too far away[1]—nor from the fact that she did express herself willing, and even anxious, to be taken before the Council of Basle. That she appealed to be taken before the Pope is indisputable, for it is written in the official record of the trial; the information that she appealed to be taken before the Council of Basle we owe principally, with the corroboration of Manchon, to the favourable witness Isambard de la Pierre, testifying on her behalf nineteen years after her death. The evidence of these posthumous witnesses must always be taken with a grain of salt; nevertheless this particular account is so circumstantial and so credible that it is worth transcribing here in its entirety. It will be noticed that a definite accusation is brought, both by de la Pierre and by Jeanne herself, against Cauchon, of ordering the clerk to suppress the relative passage in his written report—a significant fact, in view of the charges often levelled against the judges, of corrupting the text both by falsifications and omissions.

Frère Isambard, on his own showing, was, if he is wholly to be believed, one of the very few who dared hold out a helping hand to the perplexed captive:

"Frère Isambard de la Pierre depones that once, he and several others being present, the said Jeanne was exhorted and admonished to submit herself to the Church. To which she replied that she would gladly submit herself to the Holy Father, requesting to be taken to him, and that she would not submit herself to the judgment of her enemies. And when Frère Isambard advised her to submit herself to the General

---

[1] *Procès*, Vol. I, p. 445: *Non poterat fieri quod iretur quæsitum dominum nostrum Papam ita remote.*

Council of Basle, the said Jeanne asked him what a general council was. He replied that it was a congregation of the universal Church and of Christianity, and that there were as many of her party in that council as of the English party. When she had heard and understood this, she began to exclaim, 'Oh! since there are some of our party, I will willingly go and submit to the Council of Basle.' And immediately, in great indignation and displeasure, the Bishop of Beauvais cried out, 'Be silent, *de par le diable!*' and he forbade the clerk to set down that she had made her submission to the General Council of Basle. Because of this and other things, Frère Isambard was horribly menaced by the English, and by their officers, that if he did not hold his tongue they would throw him into the Seine."[1]

This is one account given by Frère Isambard; later on he added that Jeanne said to the Bishop, "Oh, you write the things which are against me, but not the things which are in my favour."[2]

iv

Apart from these appeals, where she was acting entirely within her rights, it must be admitted that Jeanne made everything easy for them at every turn by playing into their hands. She almost saved them the trouble of condemning her by doing so over and over again out of her own mouth. Never did prisoner so generously, and even eagerly, provide evidence against herself. It was not through stupidity that she did it, for, when she wished, her answers to their questions would defeat them in their very shrewdness and bluntness, as surely as the answers of a practised lawyer—in much the same way as in the old days she had bewildered the captains by her habit of cutting straight through the recognised laws of military tactics. But more often she suffered under the enormous

[1]*Procès*, Vol. II, pp. 4-5: Deposition of Isambard de la Pierre.
[2]*Procès*, Vol. II, p. 350: Deposition of Isambard de la Pierre.

disadvantage of approaching every question with a single, believing, feeling heart, which the tortuosity of their own minds could not understand, but which the experience of their training could only too skilfully exploit. She suffered also from the disadvantage of betraying no fear even if she felt it, so that, far from trembling before her mighty judges, she treated them with a lack of ceremony which on occasions amounted to impertinence. It must have outraged them to find that she could joke and go gay (*de quo gavisa est ipsa Johanna*) in the midst of such solemnity. But so she did, for having caught Boisguillaume out in an inaccuracy over one of her answers, given eight days earlier—her memory being better than his, although he had it all written down in his own hand, and she, being unable either to write or read, had nothing but her recollection to rely on—she told him, in full court, that if he made such a mistake again, she would pull his ears.[1] It was a peasant's joke, perhaps; a countrified joke; not the sort of joke that the University of Paris would have thought very funny; but it must have considerably surprised an assembly of priests and jurists trying a girl for her life. On more serious questions, apart from pulling the ears of the clerk of the court, she could prove herself equally lacking in respect. Not content with refusing to take oaths they wanted her to take, not content with refusing to answer questions she felt disinclined to answer, she could go so far as to warn Cauchon himself to be very careful. "You say you are my judge; I do not know if you are or not; but be very careful not to judge me wrongly, for you would be putting yourself in grave danger. I am warning you of it now, so that if our Lord punishes you for it, I shall have done my duty in telling you."[2]

[1]*Procès*, Vol. III, p. 201: Deposition of Pierre Daron (corroborated by deposition of Jean Marcel, *Procès*, Vol. III, p. 89).

[2]*Procès*, Vol. I, pp. 154–5: *Vous dictes que vous estes mon juge, je ne scay se vous l'estes; mais advisez bien que ne jugés mal, que vous vous mectriés en grant danger; et vous en advertis, afin que se nostre Seigneur vous en chastie, que je fais mon debvoir de le vous dire.*

This was scarcely the language that the Bishop of Beauvais was accustomed to hearing used towards him. He was not accustomed to being told by peasants and prisoners what the Lord would or would not punish him for. He had probably never had so intractable a prisoner before him, and on the whole his patience towards Jeanne seems to have been commendable. He might, and did, lose his temper with his subordinates, but there is only one instance on record in which he lost his temper with the prisoner. Not that she ever made any concessions calculated to propitiate him. Indeed, by the first words she uttered at her first appearance at the trial she set the tone for what was to follow, and only for one brief hour of piteous panic did she depart from the calmly arrogant attitude of firmness and certainty she had from the first adopted.

v

The preliminaries of the trial had already lasted for nearly six weeks (January 9th to February 20th, 1431), during which ten sittings had been held, before Jeanne was brought before the court for the first time at its first public sitting, by Jean Massieu, shortly after eight o'clock in the morning on Wednesday, February 21st. Massieu had been sent to warn her on the previous day that her presence would be required, and she had returned the answer that she would willingly appear, but begged that ecclesiastics of the French party should be represented in equal numbers as ecclesiastics of the English, also that she might be allowed to hear Mass before appearing at the trial. One wonders what compassionate or taunting voice had been informing her of the composition of the tribunal, since her first request makes it clear that she knew she would have none but enemies to confront. In any case, the request, although faithfully repeated by Massieu, was ignored. The second request, at d'Estivet's instigation, was categorically refused. Without a friend, without even an adviser, the nineteen-year-old prisoner was led before the assembled tribunal in the Chapel Royal of the castle of Rouen.[1]

She was allowed to sit before them.

They did not take long to discover that they had no terrified, humble girl to deal with, but that the young captive of Rouen was in fact the very same person as the young captain of Patay and Orleans. Her first words revealed it. Asked to swear on the Gospels that she would answer nothing but the truth, she replied that she did not know what they wanted to ask her. "Perhaps," she added, "you may ask me things that I will not tell you."[2]

It was not a good beginning. They did not, however, insist too much. They got her to say that she would willingly tell the truth about her father and mother, and about everything she had done since she set out for France, and, after frequent admonitions, about everything which concerned the Catholic faith. With this they had to be content, seeing that she would not promise to answer anything about the revelations made to her by God, which, she said, she had told only to her King, and which she would tell to no other person, even if her head were to be cut off. They were possibly somewhat appeased by her remark that, before a week had passed, she would know whether she would tell them or not—an evasion with which, in the days to follow, they were to become familiar. Kneeling, with her hands on the Book, she was allowed to take the oath in its modified form, nor, in spite of other struggles on the subject, renewed on subsequent sittings, were they ever able to induce her to depart from her original determination.

The trial which thus opened is reported in its entirety in one of the most remarkable and enthralling of historical documents. It was transcribed in Latin, but large portions of it exist also in the original French minutes. On the first reading, we are left with the impression of an inconsecutive and incoherent jumble, which makes us sympathise with Jeanne in her complaints that they were trying to confuse her, and

[1]*Procès*, Vol. I, pp. 43-4.   [2]*Procès*, Vol. I, p. 45.

also that they were asking her questions which had nothing to do with the matter in hand—"Give me the chance to speak"; "*Ce n'est pas de votre procès*"; "Am I obliged to tell you that?" "*Passez outre*"—she objects repeatedly.[1] It must indeed have been puzzling for her to discover the general trend of their examination. Little by little, however, it must have become clear to her that certain subjects were recurrent: her insistence on adopting men's clothes; her refusal to abandon them; and of course, and above all, over and over again, the Voices, always the Voices. In one way or another, directly or indirectly, nearly all the questions could be linked up with the Voices. The source of her inspiration, the extent of her claim to be in real communication with God and His saints, her obedience or disobedience to the Church, her exaltation of herself as a holy person endowed with miraculous powers, her relations with the King—there was no subject which could not be associated with that dangerous, damning claim. And it was a point upon which she was absolutely unshakable. She had heard the voices; she had received their instructions; what she had done she had done at their bidding; God Himself had sent them to her; God Himself had sent her to France; she had not only heard the voices, but had seen the saints, seen them, spoken with them, touched them, smelt them, embraced them. . . . The wonder is that the trial went on for so long as it did. Jeanne had said enough to convict all the virgins in Lorraine.

It is to be noted, however, that on one point she was curiously reticent. Willing though she was to answer *ad nauseam* that the voices had told her this, that, or the other, she was correspondingly unwilling to answer questions of a more personal nature about the saints. The first time that the interrogation seemed to threaten an advance towards the heart of the mystery, she evinced great uneasiness and discomfort, and asked for a delay:

---

[1] According to the Bishop of Demetriades, this system of interrogation was deliberate, the examiners dodging from one subject to another in order to see if she would contradict herself.

"I am not telling you everything I know. I am more afraid of failing them, by saying something which might displease the voices, than of answering you."[1] Perhaps with the same instinct as had made her keep her own counsel as a child, she now shrank from the open discussion of the sacred subject. Asked if she had seen anything of them except their faces, she replied that she would sooner have her throat cut than say all she knew.[2] Perhaps, also, when her acute examiners tried to pin her down to any precise descriptions, she discovered to her chagrin that the image in her mind was not quite so definite as she had supposed; an argument which will certainly appeal to those who dismiss the apparitions as purely hallucinatory. It was easier to imagine golden gracious visions glimmering through a cloud of light than to say whether they had hair or not, or how they were dressed, or what age they were. Yet she maintained that she had seen them with her bodily eyes, as clearly as she saw the judges before her.[3] Whatever the explanation, her reluctance to discuss their personal attributes is manifest and consistent. She had several methods of getting herself out of the disagreeable situation. One method was by flat refusal. Another was by saying she had not received permission. Another was by asking for delay, trying to stave them off by promising an answer at a later date, when she should have had time to seek advice of her visitants. Another was by saying that she had already answered at Poitiers, and by appealing to them to produce the "Book of Poitiers," a document by which she evidently set great store, but which was never to reappear. (Small wonder, for several of the men who had examined her at Poitiers, and on whose recommendation she had been despatched to the relief of Orleans, were now sitting in judgment upon her.)

[1] *Procès*, Vol. I, p. 63.

[2] *Procès*, Vol. I, p. 93.

[3] *Procès*, Vol. I, p. 73: *Ego vidi eos oculis meis corporalibus, æque bene sicut ego video vos.*

Some extracts from the trial may speak for themselves[1]:

Question. When did you last hear the voice speaking to you?
Answer. Yesterday and to-day.
Q. At what time did you hear it yesterday?
A. I heard it three times: once in the morning, once at the hour of vespers, and the third time in the evening, at the hour of the Ave Maria. Very often I hear it more frequently than I tell you.
Q. What were you doing when you heard it yesterday morning?
A. I was asleep, and the voice woke me.
Q. Did it wake you by touching your arm? [A curious question, for how could a voice touch an arm? Probably a trap to make her admit physical contact.]
A. It woke me without touching me.
Q. Was the voice in your room?
A. I do not know. It was in the castle.
Q. Did you not thank it and go down on your knees? [This rather suggests that her guards had been giving information, true or false about her. What probably happened was that they presently saw her at her prayers.]
A. I did thank it, but I was sitting up in my bed. I clasped my hands and prayed for advice. The voice told me to answer boldly. [She repeated this statement four times running about answering boldly.]
Q. Did the voice not say certain things to you, before you prayed to it?

[1] These extracts are not consecutive, i.e. they do not all relate to the same day of the interrogation. For convenience, I have cast them into the form of question and answer, without, however, altering anything of the sense and preserving as much as possible of the actual words used in the original. The following specimen will show how the original reads:

Item interrogata depost quam horam audiverat vocem quæ veniebat ad eam: respondit: Ego audivi heri et hodie.

Item interrogata qua hora, hesterno die, ipsam vocem audiverat: respondit quod ter in illo die ipsam audiverat, semel de mane, semel in vesperis, et tertia vice cum pulsaretur pro Ave Maria de sero; et multotiens audit eam pluries quam dicat.

Interrogata quid heri de mane faciebat, cum illa vox venit ad eam: respondit quod ipsa dormiebat, et vox excitavit eam.

Interrogata si vox excitavit eam tangendo ejus brachia: respondit quod per vocem fuit excitata sine tactu.

X

A. Yes, but I did not understand them all. But when I was aroused from sleep it told me to answer boldly.[1]

Q. Has the voice forbidden you to answer fully about everything you may be asked?

A. I will not answer that. And I have had great revelations concerning the King which I will not tell you.

Q. Has the voice forbidden you to tell these revelations?

A. I have had no instructions. Give me fifteen days and I will answer.

Q. Do you see anything accompanying the voice?

A. I will not tell you all; I am not allowed to, nor does my oath apply to that.

Q. Are the said saints [Saint Catherine and Saint Margaret] dressed alike?

A. I will not tell you anything more about them now; I am not allowed to. If you do not believe me, go to Poitiers.

Q. Are they of the same age?

A. I am not allowed to say.

Q. Which of them appeared to you first?

A. I did not recognise them at once; I used to know which had appeared first, but I have forgotten; if I were allowed to tell you I would do so willingly. It is recorded in the register at Poitiers.

Q. What was Saint Michael like?

A. There is no answer for you about that as yet; I am not yet allowed to say. . . . I wish you had the copy of that book at Poitiers.

Q. How do you know that it is Saint Catherine and Saint Margaret who talk to you?

A. I have told you often enough that they are Saint Catherine and Saint Margaret—believe me if you like.

Q. Do you always see them in the same clothes?

A. I always see them in the same shape, their heads very richly crowned. I am allowed by our Lord to say this. I know nothing of their robes.

[1] I invite the attention of psychologists to this statement. It implies that Jeanne heard the voice, although confusedly, *before* she was properly awake. It implies, also, that she made some attempt to answer, for why should her examiners have suggested that it had said "certain things to her, before she prayed to it," if her guards had not reported that she was talking in her sleep? (This, of course, is pure conjecture, but with a good basis of probability.) Was she dreaming? The whole incident is suggestive.

Q. In what shape [*figuram*] do you see them?

A. I see their faces.

Q. Have they any hair?

A. C'est bon à savoir! [*Bonum est ad sciendum.*]

Q. Is their hair long and hanging down?

A. I do not know. I do not know whether they have any arms or other members.

Q. If they had no members, how could they speak?

A. I refer that to God.

Q. Does Saint Margaret speak English?

A. Why should she speak English, as she is not on the English side?

Q. What did Saint Michael look like when he appeared to you?

A. I did not see any crown, and I know nothing about his garments.

Q. Was he naked?

A. Do you think our Lord has nothing to dress him in?

Q. Had he any hair?

A. Why should it have been cut off?

She said, however, of Saint Michael that "*Il estoit en la fourme d'un très vray preud'homme,*" though she refused again to describe his clothes or anything else.[1] They attacked her again about the age and apparel of Saint Catherine and Saint Margaret, only to be told, "*Vous estes respondus de ce que vous en aurez de moy, et n'en airés autre chose.*"[2] They tried another trap after that, asking her whether those two saints hated the English, but she was too clever for them: "*Elles ayment ce que nostre Seigneur ayme, et haient ce que Dieu hait.*"[3] She could answer shrewdly, as well as boldly according to the saints' command.

vi

By her insistence on the reality of her revelations she had already placed herself in the gravest danger: there were two other major points, among the host of minor ones, which the judges were never tired of pursuing. These were the questions of her masculine dress and of her submission to the Church. It is difficult to understand exactly why the doctors and jurists

[1]*Procès*, Vol. I, p. 173. [2]*Procès*, Vol. I, pp. 177–8. [3]*Procès*, Vol. I, p. 178.

laid such stress upon her choice of clothes, until, towards the end of her trial, we come upon the explanation. At first it seems as though neither heresy nor sorcery could enter into it. It seems, indeed, hard to perceive what sin, crime, or vice could possibly be concerned. No unnatural form of immorality was ever alleged against her, and the reason she gave for her virile garb was surely convincing enough to any rational mind: simply that she ran less danger of rape than if she went about dressed as a woman. Still, to the judges, it bulked as a question of the first importance. Jeanne herself, not having the key to the riddle, was puzzled by their insistence, for when asked if a man's dress had been prescribed for her, she replied contemptuously that dress was a small thing, among the smallest things.[1] Unfortunately for her, no one else took this point of view. To the fifteenth-century mind, there was evidently something profoundly shocking in her choice; even the kind ladies of Beaurevoir, even the soft young Duchess of Bedford, had been distressed by it, and had done everything in their power to induce her to change her ways. Jeanne, in this respect as in many others, had passed into a practical reasonableness far beyond the scope of the fifteenth-century outlook. She had gone beyond: but to the jurists of Rouen it was still a point on which she could be badgered and bullied and persecuted out of all proportion; it was still a point where they could base their findings on the local laws of a Hebrew tribe. They went back to the Old Testament. They quoted Deuteronomy, chapter xxii: "The woman shall not wear that which pertaineth unto a man, neither shall a man put on a woman's garment: for all that do so are abomination unto the Lord thy God," quite forgetting that the next verse of the holy book passes on to a restriction as locally and topically practical as our modern Wild Birds' Protection Act, which we find pinned up to-day in the porch of our village churches: "If a bird's nest chance to be before thee in the way in any tree, or on the ground, whether they be young ones, or eggs, and the dam

[1]*Procès*, Vol. I, p. 74.

sitting upon the young, or upon the eggs, thou shalt not take the dam with the young." They quoted the New Testament also, with especial regard to her cropped hair (*capillos tonsos in rotundum*), drawing Saint Paul into the argument: "Every woman that prayeth or prophesieth with her head uncovered dishonoureth her head: for that is even all one as if she were shaven. . . . Doth not even nature itself teach you, that, if a man have long hair, it is a shame unto him? But if a woman have long hair, it is a glory to her: for her hair is given her for a covering."[1] Still Jeanne stuck to the contention that God and His angels were alone responsible, being clearly determined not to put the blame on any living soul, least of all on the King. In her answers on this subject a note of patient exasperation is, I think, discernible. It is compatible also with her remark that clothes were of the least importance:

Q. The first time you saw your King, did he ask you if it was by revelation that you had altered your dress?

A. I have already answered that. In any case, I do not remember. It is written at Poitiers.

Q. Do you remember whether the examiners of the other party [i.e. Charles' party] asked you about it?

A. I do not remember. They asked me where I had taken the man's dress, and I told them, at Vaucouleurs.

Q. Did neither the King, nor the Queen, nor others of your party not sometimes require you to abandon it?

A. That has nothing to do with your case.[2]

She was not going to be tricked into compromising the King, the Queen, or any of her friends.

In spite of her irritation, however, she was prepared to be reasonable about the dress:

Q. Since you ask to hear Mass, would it not be more seemly [*honestius*] that you should hear it in woman's clothes? Would you rather take woman's clothes and hear Mass, or retain man's clothes and not hear it?

A. Guarantee that I shall hear it if I dress as a woman, and then I will answer.

[1] 1 Corinthians xi.   [2] *Procès*, Vol. I, pp. 94-5.

Cautious Jeanne! she had little faith in their insinuations. The examiner[1] gave the required promise. It is easy to detect a note of mockery in her reply, when one remembers the ever-renewed arguments she had had with them over the taking of her oath: "And what would you say, if I had sworn and promised our King not to abandon this dress? Nevertheless, I answer you: have a dress made for me reaching the ground, without a train, and give it to me to wear at Mass; then on my return, I will resume the one I have."[2]

The offers came to nothing, though the point was being constantly revived.

vii

The question of her submission to the Church, which to our own way of thinking seems far more vital to the judges of an ecclesiastical court than the question whether she wore a skirt or breeches, was of course implicit throughout the whole of the trial, even though it appears to play a subordinate part in the interrogation, and was in fact not specifically mentioned until the trial had been going on for nearly four weeks. It was then (March 15th) that Cauchon and six others visited her in her prison, and asked her for the first time whether she would abide by the decision of the Church, as was her duty, should it be found that she had acted against the faith. She replied that her answers should be read by the clerks, and that she should then be told whether they contained anything opposed to the Christian faith, when she would lay the matter before her *conseil*, meaning her voices, and then would declare to them what the *conseil* had said.[3] She did add that she would not persist in any opposition to the Christian faith as ordained by God, but it was evident that she was not giving the answers

[1] We do not know which one it was. Cauchon, Lemaistre, La Fontaine, Nicolas Midi, and Isambard de la Pierre and two others were present on this occasion. The small number is due to the fact that the interrogation was taking place in Jeanne's prison.

[2] *Procès*, Vol. I, pp. 164–5.   [3] *Procès*, Vol. I, p. 162.

she ought to have given if she wished to save her life. She was, in fact, proving herself guilty of the major offence of adhering "steadfastly to the principle of private judgment which was in conflict with the attitude of simple obedience exacted by the Church."[1]

Father Thurston's clear and authoritative words really summarise the whole matter. In setting the judgment of her voices, i.e. her own private source of revelation, above the judgment of those appointed as God's representatives on earth, she was of course violating a major law of the Church. The Church Militant on earth permits no such direct appeal to the Church Triumphant in Heaven. By claiming to act under the direct guidance of Heaven, Jeanne was committing the unpardonable sin of short-circuiting the Bishop of Beauvais and all his colleagues. It was even apparent that she would, if given the chance, short-circuit the Pope himself, for, although she repeatedly asked to be led before him, she made it quite clear that, for all her veneration for His Holiness and his apostolic office, God alone would remain her authority in the last resort.

The first article of the Act of Accusation plainly sets forth the powers of the alarmed and resolute divines.

It is preceded by a formidable indictment. The jurists of the Inquisition and of the University of Paris certainly did their powers of invective justice on this occasion:

"That the woman commonly named Jeanne la Pucelle . . . shall be denounced and declared as a sorceress, diviner, pseudo-prophetess, invoker of evil spirits, conspiratrix, superstitious, implicated in and given to the practice of magic, wrong-headed as to our Catholic faith, schismatic as to the article *Unam Sanctum*, etc.,[2] and in several other articles of our faith sceptical and astray, sacrilegious, idolatrous, apostate, accursed and mischievous, blasphemous towards God and His saints,

[1] The Rev. Herbert Thurston, S.J., in an article on Mr. Shaw's *St. Joan*, in *Studies*, September 1924.
[2] The non-observance of this article is regarded as constituting the first principle of schism.

scandalous, seditious, disturber of peace, inciter of war, cruelly avid of human blood, inciting to bloodshed, having completely and shamelessly abandoned the decencies proper to her sex, and having immodestly adopted the dress and status of a man-at-arms; for that, and for other things abominable to God and men, a traitor to laws divine and natural and to the discipline of the Church, seductress of princes and the populace, having in contempt and disdain of God permitted herself to be venerated and adored, by giving her hands and her garments to be kissed, heretical, or at any rate vehemently suspected of heresy, for that she shall be punished and corrected according to divine and canonical laws. . . ."

Then follows the first article of the seventy which constitute the Act of Accusation. It expounds the authority of the Bishop of Beauvais to deal with offenders taken within his diocese, also of Lemaistre as Inquisitor of the Faith. Jeanne had already had the difference between the Church Militant and the Church Triumphant carefully explained to her, so that she could be under no misapprehension on that subject. Nevertheless her reply to the first article was given with her usual dauntless obstinacy:

"She fully believes that our Holy Father the Pope of Rome, the bishops, and other churchmen are appointed to guard the Christian faith and to punish those who transgress it, but, so far as her own actions are concerned, she will submit herself only to the Church in Heaven—that is to say, to God, to the Virgin Mary, and to the saints who are in Paradise. And she believes firmly that she has not transgressed the faith, nor would she wish to do so.[1]

---

[1] *Procès*, Vol. I, pp. 204–5. It is rather suspicious that the French minute ends thus: *Et croist fermement qu'elle n'ait point défailly en nostre foy chrestienne, et n'y vouldroit défaillir, et requiert* . . . There is nothing about *et requiert* in the official Latin version, which fact suggests strongly that Jeanne went on to ask for something which the clerks were forbidden to record. What was it she asked for? It is worth noticing that on another occasion (*Procès*, Vol. I, p. 185) the French minute runs: *Elle requiert qu'elle soit menée devant lui* (the Pope), but on this occasion the request was allowed to appear also in the Latin.

viii

Cauchon and his associates were hardly to be blamed for interpreting Jeanne's attitude towards the Church and its supreme head as subversive and schismatic in the extreme. It was not their fault if they could not attain to the simplified plane of their tired young prisoner, who could still see the wood where they had never been able to see anything but the trees. The foreground of their vision was so bulkily occupied by the Church Militant and by the ordinances essential to its preservation, that the Church Triumphant, as a working factor, was almost entirely blocked from sight. They rendered due homage to it, in its sublime consummation, but in cases such as the present it could scarcely be allowed to play any part in practical politics. What Jeanne did not, and could not, not would not, realise, was that practical politics entered into such fundamental matters at all. To her, the whole thing was quite logical and simple: one obeyed the Church and observed its rulings in daily life and throughout the Christian year, but in deep matters of the soul the last word lay with God, who knew better than even His Holiness in Rome. Admittedly, she had had the advantage of exceptionally direct instruction, and, having enjoyed that advantage, any other instruction must necessarily reach her at second-hand.

The Bishop of Beauvais and his kindred could naturally not be expected to see it from that point of view. For one thing, they perhaps sincerely regarded Jeanne as an instrument of evil, and, even if they did not thus sincerely regard her, they must at least have regarded her as a bad and rebellious daughter of the Church to which she professed to belong. In which case she was striking at the very roots of their delegated authority. If she was allowed to get away with her contentions, she would be creating a most pernicious precedent. "If the prelates of the Church do not see to it, subversion of the whole authority of the Church may ensue; men and women may arise on every side, pretending to revelations from God or His angels, sowing lies, and errors, as we have experienced many times since this woman arose and began to scandalise Christian people and to promulgate her impostures."[1] Of course they were worried. Jeanne's responses, cutting clean through all the safeguards of their orthodoxy, were the responses of a mind they could not deal with, save by the destruction of the body:

Q. Will you submit yourself in all your words and deeds, either good or evil, to the determination of our holy mother, the Church?
A. I love the Church, and would uphold it with all my strength for the Christian faith. It is not I who ought to be prevented from going to church or from hearing Mass!

The question being repeated, she held firm: "I refer myself to God who sent me, to Our Lady, and to all the blessèd saints in Paradise. As I see it, God and the Church are one and the same thing, and you ought not to make difficulties over that. Why do you make difficulties about it?"[2]

Q. Would you not consider yourself bound to answer the Pope, Vicar of God, the whole truth on anything you might be asked on matters of faith or touching your conscience?
A. Take me to him, and I will answer anything I ought to answer.

The reservation cannot have pleased them: it meant that Pope or no Pope, she still intended to act according to her private judgment.

In the end, they took to threatening her. She would be burnt, they said, if she persisted in her heresy. She answered—and the clerk wrote the words *Superba responsio* in the margin of his manuscript—"I will say no more about that. Were I to see the fire, I would still say all that I have said, and would not do otherwise."[3]

It may remain an open question whether they ever seriously

---

[1]*Procès*, Vol. I, p. 317.   [2]*Procès*, Vol. I, p. 175.

[3]*Procès*, Vol. I, p. 393: *Je ne vous en diray autre chose: et se je veoye le feu, si diroye-je tout ce que je vous dy, et n'en feroye autre chose.*

considered taking her to Rome or not. Most probably not, even if the English would have allowed them to do so. They had accumulated ample evidence without going to that trouble and expense, and, on the last day of March, they made quite certain that she in no way intended to repudiate her previous undutiful assertions. Would she obey the dictates of the Church on earth, they asked her for the last time? Her answers, as before, were unequivocal and clear: she will obey the Church, provided it does not command the impossible. She will never, for anything on earth, revoke the declarations she has made during the course of her trial about her visions and revelations. She will never, for anything on earth, obey the Church in the event of its commanding her to do anything contrary to the commandments which she says God has given her. She will refer always to God, were the Church to describe her revelations as illusory, diabolic, superstitious, or evil. She will submit herself to the Church Militant—that is to say to the Pope, the cardinals, archbishops, bishops and other clergy, but God must come first.[1]

Having received these answers, they retired to consider what now remained to be done about the trial as touching matters of faith.

ix

One very curious and suggestive incident remains to be recorded before the trial can be quickly taken through its stages towards its logical conclusion. This incident concerns the sign given to the King. It is an incident not so very important in itself, but interesting if only for the light it throws on to a most unexpected and almost impish facet of Jeanne's character. It is a facet which has revealed itself already once or twice in her brief history, a facet which shines like a brightly coloured jewel of imagination in the plain setting of her humorous common sense. For Jeanne was not, as a rule, an imaginative

[1] *Procès*, Vol. I, pp. 324-5-6 (abridged).

person. Even if we admit the theory that her visions and voices were entirely the product of the imagination, it was not of an imagination deliberately so employed by its owner; it was, rather, imposed upon her from without, and was not the outcome of any conscious effort on her part towards a flight of fancy. Over the sign given to the King, she seems to have let herself go. It seems as though, suddenly turned reckless, she had allowed herself deliberately to tease, confuse, and perplex the conscientious doctors. Were the subject not so solemn and serious, one might say that she had allowed herself to have a little fun with them—a sort of respite from the deadly routine of question and answer in the trial. It is the kind of fun one might imagine her having in her gay early mood at Poitiers; it is the more surprising when it makes its appearance within the grisly surroundings of Rouen. She becomes like a child telling a story to an open-mouthed circle of listeners, embroidering and embellishing as she goes.

Stated very briefly, Jeanne's story was that an angel from Heaven had accompanied her on the occasion of her first audience of the King, and had brought with him a crown finer than gold.

Her judges themselves had first put the idea into her mind. On March 1st they asked her whether she had seen a crown on the head of her King, when she first gave him the sign. This is the first mention of any such manifestation, and on this occasion there is no suggestion that the crown was brought by an angel. On February 27th, however, they had asked her whether there was an angel above the King's head when first she saw him, and had received the scornful answer, "By our Lady, if there was one, I was unaware of it and did not see it." By March 10th her tone has completely changed: this time she says the sign *was* brought by an angel from God, and by no other; that she curtsied to him, went down on her knees, and took off her cap. The sign itself, she says, was beautiful, honourable, and credible; the best and richest that could be. It would last a thousand years, and more. She would give on more exact details; she would not say if it was of gold, of silver, or of precious stones; she would only say that no man could describe so rich a thing. But it was evident that she was already beginning to let her inventiveness go, on the suggestion so carelessly provided by her judges. By this time the parable of the angel, the crown, and the King was definitely forming in her mind. It is as though she said to herself, "They want to discover what I really said to the King, and what was the convincing sign I gave him; I cannot, in loyalty, tell these his enemies that I reassured him as to his legitimacy; but some story they are determined to have, and, *en nom Dé*, they shall have it." The story that she could tell them was assuming shape, and on March 13th she let them have it in all its elaborated splendour.

They had tackled her once more on the subject. At first she demurred, asking if they wanted her to perjure herself? Tackled again, as to whether she had promised Saint Catherine not to reveal the sign, she replied that not only had she sworn and promised not to reveal it, but had done so of her own accord, because she was being too strongly urged to reveal it. Then they heard her muttering to herself that she would never speak of it again to any man.

In spite of this, they persisted, and with their persistence her scruples seem to have left her. Her last effort at honesty beaten down, she threw herself with true Jeannesque reckless-ness into the whole-hearted elaboration. She had always been very partial to crowns; crowns were almost an obsession with her—a childish and peasant-like obsession with the symbol of royalty and godhead; it is worth noting that however reluctant she was to describe the personal appearance of her saints, she was always ready to insist on the fact that they wore beautiful crowns.

The angel, she said, confirmed the rights of her King, bringing him the crown and telling him that the whole kingdom of France should be his entirely by the help of God and through the labours of herself, Jeanne; that he should put her to the task and should give her soldiers, otherwise he would not be so readily crowned and anointed.

After this brave opening she appears to have become a little confused, for she muddles up the fictitious arrival of the angel with the crown, and the actual coronation at Reims. It is rather a pathetic muddle, in so far as it betrays her rustic inexperience of crowns, kings, and coronations. I think that at this point, in the midst of her brave excursion into the wide opportunities of fiction, she got frightened, and tried to come down to earth again, with most confusing results. Having invented, or, rather, having taken up the judges' own invention of an angel and a crown, she remembered suddenly that she had in real life seen her King crowned by somebody who was anything but an angel. Therefore, in answer to the question as to how, exactly, the angel had brought the crown, and whether he had set it upon the King's head, she replied that the crown had been handed to an archbishop, the Archbishop of Reims, as it seems to her, in the King's presence, and that the Archbishop received it and gave it to the King, she, Jeanne, being present, and that the crown had been put into the King's treasury.

Now here was an obvious confusion of fact with fiction, and the judges were quick to see it. Where, they asked, was the crown brought?

Jeanne went hurriedly back to her fiction, and it is remarkable how circumstantial her details become after this brief attempt to reconcile fiction with fact.

The crown, she said, was brought into the King's room at Chinon. She could not remember the exact day; and, as to the hour, she could only remember that it was late.[1] It was either in April or in March, she thinks; and next month or in the present month (she is speaking on March 13th, 1431), it will be two years ago; and it was after Easter.

The crown itself by now is of pure gold, so rich and opulent

[1]This accords well with her statement that the *salle* was lit by torches. See *supra*, Chapter VII, p. 131.

that she cannot number or estimate its riches; it signifies that its King will hold the kingdom of France. No jeweller in the world could have made it so beautiful. She is a little cautious in her reply to the question whether it included precious stones: "I have already told you what I know about that." She had, in fact, told them nothing about that, but had evaded the answer on a previous occasion.

They asked her then whether the angel, bringing the crown, had arrived from on high or by earth, and she immediately became circumstantial again: the angel had arrived from on high, on God's command, and had entered by the door. He had bowed to the King, and had advanced from the door, walking on the floor on his way towards the King. The distance between the door and the King might be the length of a lance. (This rings curiously true: Jeanne knew the length of a lance, and would very naturally have visualised it as an instrument of measurement, ready to hand.) She followed the angel into the room, and said to the King, "Sire, here is your sign; take it."

She had been well prepared for this manifestation, for the angel had already appeared to her in her lodging at Chinon, before she ever gained audience of the King at all. In fact, they went together to find the King, the angel being accompanied by other angels, who were not seen by other people. She believed, however, that several persons had seen the angel, including the Archbishop of Reims, Charles de Bourbon, and the Dukes of La Trémoïlle and Alençon.[1] Several people saw the crown who did not see the angel.

Some of the angels accompanying the angel resembled one another, others were different, as she saw them; some were winged, and some wore crowns, others not; Saint Catherine

[1]Jeanne, here, makes a curious and uncharacteristic mistake: she states that the Duke of Alençon was among those who saw the angel. Now, the Duke of Alençon had not yet arrived at Chinon when her first interview with Charles VII took place. Either her memory, usually surprisingly accurate, was here at fault; or else we can find in this apparent error of memory an additional proof that she had made up the whole story.

and Saint Margaret came right into the room with the angels.

She wept when the angel left her, and wished he could have taken her soul with him, but he left her neither afraid nor frightened, only sorry for his departure.

The angel, she added, in reply to a further question, had never written her any letters.

This curious story can be explained only if we accept that Jeanne, driven into a corner, was taking refuge in fantasy based on allegory. The allegory is clear enough: she herself was the angel, bringing Charles the crown of France—as indeed she did. That she should have become confused at a given moment is comprehensible, since her intellect was nil though her genius was great. The nullity of her intellect rendered the story unmanageable for a brief and given moment: the flesh-and-blood figure of the Archbishop of Reims intruded, and so did the actual crown, which she had seen at Reims and knew to have been replaced in the royal treasury. They got between the image of the angel—whom, incidentally, she declared to have been Saint Michael—and of the miraculous crown set by the angel at Chinon upon Charles' head. Chinon and Reims, Archangel and Archbishop, crown symbolical and crown factual, all merged into a story too complicated and ambitious for her loyally ingenious brain. It was claimed that she later made full confession of the red herring she had attempted to draw across the path of the judges' enquiry. She could not tell the right truth, so she had made up another story. So they claimed; but, as the authenticity of their claim is doubtful, the full account has been relegated to an appendix.[1]

[1]See Appendix G, p. 405. It may here be noted also that Jeanne had most probably heard stories of angels, crowns, and kings. E.g. at the entry of Richard II into London in 1377, they erected a sham castle in the market of Cheapside, from which an angel descended to offer the King a golden crown. See Lingard's *History of England*, Vol. II, p. 274.

i

In the foregoing chapter very little has been said about the conduct of the trial itself, and the impression may perhaps have been unintentionally created that the interrogation confined itself to such major issues as the revelations by the voices, the physical manifestations of the saints, the insistence on Jeanne's masculine clothes, and the heresy implied in her independence of judgment. Such is not the case. Many other questions were raised, pursued, dropped, and frequently raised again, some of them seemingly insignificant, and only to be understood in their true purport if we bear continually in mind that they reach us out of a world of intellectual darkness in which men, frightened of the powers of evil, were using every scrap of evidence to condemn a girl as a heretic and a witch. Thus the endless questions about the Arbre des Dames and the Bois Chenu at Domremy, about the early employments, about the mandrake she was supposed to have carried in her bosom, about her standard, her sword, her rings, the Jhesus Maria heading to her letters, her prophecies, the death of Franquet d'Arras, and her leap from the tower at Beaurevoir—all had their bearing on the central enquiry, though at times their drift may seem puzzling to us and must quite certainly have seemed twice as puzzling to the poor ignorant uninstructed Jeanne. The question of her virginity alone might have offered scope for an enquiry all to itself, but that the official investigations negatively forbade pursuit in that direction. The *Pucelle* was a real *pucelle*: there could be no doubt about it. The fact had been established several times, at intervals, by witnesses whose authority the court could not dispute. Not to mention the ladies of Chinon and Tours, the Duchess of Bedford herself had more recently been involved in the enquiry, and also a member of their own council, the doctor of medicine, de la Chambre, who had had the opportunity of examining Jeanne during one of her two illnesses in prison, and who expressed himself some years later with more frankness than delicacy.[1] It was a pity, from the point of view of the clerics, that her virtue could not be assailed, for it was a well-known fact that the Devil could exert no power against the protective purity of a maid. Did not the snow-white unicorn, swifter than the swallow, whom no hunter could arrest on its course through the forest, come fawning to the call of a pure virgin and of a pure virgin only? Such facts were commonplaces of belief, and virginity a correspondingly priceless possession. Even William Caxton (incidentally her exact contemporary), never attempted to impugn the chastity of "this mayde who rode lyke a man and was a vaulyant captayn," but could only suggest that she tried to deceive her captors, "and then she sayd that she was with chylde, wher by she was respited a whyle; but in conclusyon it was founde that she was not with chylde, and then she was brent in Roen."[2]

ii

It is obviously impossible here to go into all the details of the trial; it is possible only to indicate its chronology and general outline in its various stages, with the inevitable culmination of the tragedy on the market-place.

The first public sitting, then, with the prisoner present for the first time, took place on February 21st in the royal chapel of the castle of Rouen. The court removed itself next day to the *salle d'honneur* or *chambre de parement*, near to the King's apartments. Henry VI and Jeanne were thus in closer proximity than they had ever been before, although there is no record

---

[1] *Procès*, Vol. III, p. 50: Deposition of Guillaume de la Chambre: *Scit ipse loquens, prout percipere potuit secundum artem medicinæ, quod erat incorrupta et virgo, quia eam vidit quasi nudam, cum visitaret eam de quadem infirmitate; et eam palpavit in renibus, et erat multum stricta, quantum percipere potuit ex aspectu.*

[2] *The Chronicles of England with the Fruit of Times.*

that they ever set eyes upon one another. She was being tried almost next door to the room where the little English King, then aged nine, was playing his games or doing his lessons in innocent ignorance of the complications unfolding themselves so close at hand. Westminster and Domremy were very far apart. Day after day, the court assembled in the same place at eight o'clock in the morning, the Bishop of Beauvais always present, though the number and personnel of his colleagues might vary, the prisoner always present since she had no choice. Day after day the proceedings started with the same argument about the oath—arguments which diminished in intensity as the obstinacy of the prisoner became more apparent, until finally they shrank from a set battle to a mere matter of form. After three sittings, the case was interrupted by the illness of the prisoner, so that between February 24th and 27th the proceedings had to be suspended. Jeanne had, in fact, been violently sick (*multum vomitum*), and the tribunal found itself obliged to look up and down its ranks for a doctor of medicine who could attend to the needs of the body while the needs of the soul remained temporarily in abeyance. They found one in the person of Jean Tiphaine, who had at first been reluctant to attend the trial, but who had finally given way owing to his fear of the English and their resentment. He had a considerable admiration for Jeanne and her spirited replies, and specially recalls a certain day when Jacques de Touraine asked her if she had ever been present when Englishmen were killed. "*En nom Dieu, si ay. Comme vous parlez doucement!*[1] Why did they not leave France and go back to their own country?" Upon hearing which, an English lord, whose name Tiphaine had forgotten, exclaimed, "Really, that is a good woman! If only she were English!"

Tiphaine was taken by d'Estivet to visit her in her cell, when, ill though she was, she accused the Bishop of Beauvais of having sent her a carp which she suspected of being the cause of her trouble. D'Estivet flew into a rage, and accused

[1]In French in the original. The incident is not recorded in the *procès-verbal*.

her of having eaten herrings and other things which she knew would disagree with her. Jeanne answered back, and they then appear to have abused one another soundly.[1]

The scene in the cell is vivid enough, Jeanne with her ankles chained, as Tiphaine tells us, and he himself trying to feel her pulse during the altercation, but it seems extremely unlikely that Cauchon could really have wished to poison her or even temporarily put her out of action. The last thing the judges or the English wanted was that she should die by natural means. Another doctor, Guillaume de la Chambre, records explicitly that the Bishop of Winchester and Lord Warwick sent for him when she fell ill, and that Warwick addressed him, saying, "I hear that Jeanne is ill and have sent for you that you may cure her. The King would not have her die a natural death on any account: he holds her dear, having bought her dearly. She must die only at the hands of justice, and must be burnt. Do whatever is necessary, and endeavour to restore her to health." Even the doctor's proposal to bleed the patient alarmed Lord Warwick: "Be very cautious of blood-letting. She is sly, and might bring her own death about."[2]

In spite of carps, herrings, and bleedings, in spite of having a return of her fever as the result of losing her temper with d'Estivet,[3] she recovered, and the sittings were resumed. By March 3rd the first part of the cross-examination was over, and for the next six days the judges held daily discussions in Cauchon's magnificent house, going over the evidence in detail, and deciding on what points she should be questioned further. At this point Cauchon, alleging that his other occupations might not allow him always to attend the trial, appointed Jean de la Fontaine as his delegate to conduct the enquiry, all Jeanne's most determined enemies being present—Beaupère, de Touraine, Nicolas Midi, de Courcelles, and the infamous Loiselleur. From this time onwards the scene of the trial shifts:

[1] *Procès*, Vol. III, pp. 48-9: Deposition of Jean Tiphaine.
[2] *Procès*, Vol. III, p. 51: Deposition of Guillaume de la Chambre.
[3] *Procès*, Vol. III, p. 51: Deposition of Guillaume de la Chambre.

it is no longer conducted in the castle hall, open to all the
assessors who chose to put in an appearance, but in Jeanne's
own prison, where space allowed only a handful of men to
attend at a time. The poor timid monk Lemaistre was compelled to take up his rôle as representative of the Grand
Inquisitor, more definitely than before, when he had appeared
as the mere associate of his formidable colleague the Bishop,
for Cauchon was now not always present, and Lemaistre, with
La Fontaine, was obliged to take the lead. Another difference
was that they now sometimes met twice a day instead of once;
morning and afternoon she had to answer their searching and
tricky questions. She was in chains; she was now deprived even
of the short walk from her prison to the judgment-hall; she
had been ill, and, because the season was Lent, she was fasting. Her spirit never flagged, but it was small wonder that
they heard her whispering to herself, when they pursued her
with questions about the sign given to the King, "I swear
I will never speak of it again to any man."[1]

She had very little respite now. They filled her cell almost
daily—on March 10th, twice on the 12th, on the 13th, twice
on the 14th, on the 15th, and twice on the 17th—nine sessions
in eight days. Nor was it like a trial in which witnesses are
called: the only witness was the prisoner. She must be on the
alert all the time, through all the weariness and the dread.
She was worn out; by March 14th she pleaded that, in the
event of her being taken to Paris for a renewed interrogation,
she might be allowed to say that she had already been examined
at Rouen and that she should no longer be persecuted by so
many questions.[2]

iii

After Passion Sunday, March 18th, she had a few days' rest,
while the learned doctors assembled once more in Cauchon's
house and deliberated over the register of the examination.

[1]*Procès*, Vol. I, p. 139.   [2]*Procès*, Vol. I, p. 154.

Having taken a week to do so, they repaired again to the prison (March 24th), and read the document, in French, to Jeanne, who, with only minor interruptions, acknowledged it as a true and accurate record of all she had said. A rare hint of weakness escaped her: "Give me a woman's dress to go to my mother's house, and I will accept it." She added that this was in order to be out of prison, when she could take counsel of what she was to do.[1]

The next day was Palm Sunday, and she asked repeatedly to be allowed to hear Mass, both then and on Easter Day. Of course they took advantage of these requests to revive the old vexed question of her clothes. Her distress pierces even through the clerkly formality of the register: "We asked her if she would abandon her masculine habit, were we to accord this favour. She replied that she had had no counsel about it, and could not yet take the said dress. And we asked her if she wanted to take counsel of her saints in order to receive a woman's dress. She answered that she might surely be permitted to hear Mass as she was, which she ardently desired; but that she could not change her dress, for it was not in her to do so. The doctors exhorted her again to adopt the habit suitable to her sex, but she replied that it was not in her to do so, and, if it were in her, she would do so readily. Then she was told to confer with her voices to know if she might resume woman's dress in order to receive the Eucharist at Easter, but she replied that, so far as it lay with her, she would not receive the Eucharist by exchanging her clothes for the clothes of a woman, and she asked again that she might be allowed to hear Mass dressed as a man, for, she said, the wearing of that dress did not oppress her soul, neither was it contrary to the Church."[2]

Imperative as was her desire to hear Mass, especially during that week, which must have represented the Passion to her even more vividly than to the most ardent and imaginative Christian, she refused to give way over this apparently

[1]*Procès*, Vol. I, p. 191.   [2]*Procès*, Vol. I, pp. 192-3.

insignificant point. It seems strange that she should have clung to her determination with such assiduity, even to the extent of forgoing the favour she most desired. One can understand her adoption of men's clothes as a reasonable and indeed necessary precaution for the preservation of her virginity; it is harder to understand her obstinacy at such a cost. Either it must have turned into a matter of principle by then, mixed up with all the other dictates of her voices, or else a very bitter experience must have convinced her that therein lay her only safety in a world of men.

iv

By March 27th they were back in the large hall, and an important discussion took place to decide whether the seventy articles dealing with her offences should first be read over to her, or whether she should be declared excommunicate without further delay. A fair proportion of the assessors expressing the opinion that the articles should be read, Cauchon addressed the prisoner, assuring her that the wise and learned doctors desired neither vengeance nor corporal punishment, but only to bring her back into the way of truth and salvation. She must take the oath they had always demanded of her, but, since she was not sufficiently experienced in such difficult matters, they would allow her to choose one or more from among those present to act as her adviser.

Jeanne replied with a courtesy and dignity which are all the more remarkable when we consider that she was scanning the faces of men who, for the past month, had been persecuting her both in public and in private. D'Estivet, de Courcelles, Beaupère, de la Fontaine, Jacques de Touraine, Midi—they were all there (Loiselleur was missing). It was not likely that she would choose an adviser in that company. Nor did she. "In the first place, I thank you in so far as you admonish me for my good. As to the counsel you offer me, I thank you also, but I have no intention of forsaking the counsel of our

Lord. As to the oath you want me to take, I am ready to swear that I will tell the truth about everything which concerns your trial." This was her usual reservation, and, as usual, they had to let her take the oath on her own terms.[1]

The reading of the articles was not finished until the following day, March 28th. On the 31st, Cauchon, accompanied by Beaupère, de Touraine, Midi, Lemaistre, de Courcelles, and Pierre Maurice, presented themselves in her prison and made yet another attempt to persuade her to revoke her own words. The next few days, until April 5th, were occupied in reducing d'Estivet's seventy articles to twelve, which were to serve as the basis for the ultimate verdict, and which were then handed to the assessors with the request that they should deliver their opinion within the week. By April 12th the reports were in Cauchon's hands. There could, of course, never have been any doubt about the decision, and indeed the word "heretic" seems to be scrawled in letters of blood all across the pages. Because, however, it had been suggested that Jeanne ought to be adjured once more— and they certainly gave her every chance—on the 18th of April they again visited her in her cell.

She had not seen them for over a fortnight. What that fortnight must have meant to her we can only conjecture; what we know for certain is that she was now seriously ill—so seriously that she herself thought that she might be dying. Cauchon addressed her with a surprising gentleness, which, personally, I do not believe to have been hypocritical. He not only renewed his offer of an adviser drawn from the ranks of the tribunal, but promised to send for any other suitable person whom she might choose to nominate—a thing he had never done before. This seems fair, though of course we are not in a position to judge how he would have acted had she really availed herself of the proposal; it is, I fear, only too likely that the chosen person might not have been considered "suitable," and that some plausible excuse would have been

[1]*Procès*, Vol. I, p. 201.

made. Fortunately, she ignored the offer, although she thanked him for the kind words he had spoken concerning the salvation of her soul, and confined herself to requesting that if she were indeed in danger of death through her illness, as she believed herself to be, she might be allowed confession and Communion, and might be buried in consecrated ground. She added, however, with her habitual reliance on the ultimate appeal, that if they would not give her a Christian burial, she would put her trust in God.

They told her that if she would not obey the Church, they would abandon her as a Saracen. She replied only that she was a good Christian, that she had been properly baptised, and that as a good Christian she would die.[1]

v

She did not die. Another fortnight passed, which time she spent in recovering, so far as a prison cell, irons, mental suffering, and the constant company of the English soldiers may be presumed to have permitted recovery, for the next sitting (May 2nd) took place, not in the prison, but in the *chambre de parement* as before. There is no record of what they had all been doing during that fortnight, so in all probability they had been waiting for the prisoner to regain her strength sufficiently to permit of her being again brought before them. Sixty-five of them were present, not counting the clerks, for it was a solemn occasion and Cauchon had especially desired their attendance to hear the exhortation which the Archdeacon of Evreux, Jean de Chatillon, had been instructed to deliver. Cauchon addressed them briefly, beseeching them to do everything in their power to restore the errant lamb to the fold. They then sent for Jeanne, and the Archdeacon prepared to deliver his sermon.

Jeanne merely said, *"Lisez vostre livre"*—for the Archdeacon had some papers in his hand, and to her, who could not read,

[1] *Procès*, Vol. I, pp. 375–80.

any fid of papers constituted a book—"*lisez vostre livre, et puis je vous respondray. Je me actens à Dieu, mon créatur, de tout: je l'ayme de tout mon cuer.*"[1]

It was not a bad sermon, considering the attitude of the Church; it was not an unkind sermon. It failed only in so far as it took the point of view of the professional, which was the churchman's, instead of the point of view of the amateur, which was Jeanne's—the mistake which they had all made throughout. They were still, in fact, quarrelling and quibbling over that vital difference between the Church Militant and the Church Triumphant. They could not grasp the simple fact— simple, at any rate, to Jeanne—that the one was subservient to the other; that the part was inferior to the whole. De Chatillon, well-meaning man, no longer young, with nearly thirty years' experience of the University of Paris behind him (Champion, *Procès*, note 72), spread himself in expounding the doctrine that it was most dangerous curiously to examine those things which are beyond one's understanding, or to put one's faith in new things, or even to invent new and strange things, since devils are in the habit of mixing themselves up in such forms of curiosity, either by occult suggestions, or by visible manifestations whenever they appear as angels of light.[2] It is the eternal sermon preached by the old to the young. Jeanne remained unshaken. They threatened her with the punishment of fire. She had nothing to say but that even were she to see the fire she would still say all that she had said, and would not do otherwise—the remark which caused the clerk to write *Superba responsio* in the margin. Cauchon's presidential patience on this occasion was exemplary. It was not in vain that he had encouraged his colleagues to instruct her freely for the salvation of her soul: they did everything they could to win her round. They talked about her clothes again, and about the Pope; they revived the story of the sign given to the King, and

[1] *Procès*, Vol. I, p. 385. Jeanne's comment is given in French, in the Latin text.

[2] *Procès*, Vol. I, p. 390.

suggested that she should refer it to the Archbishop of Reims, to the maréchal de Sainte-Sévère, to Charles de Bourbon, to La Trémoïlle, and even to La Hire. If she wanted to refer to others of her party, they said, they had only to write their account under seal. If three or four clerks or knights of her party were to be brought to her under safe-conduct, would she refer to them concerning her apparitions and other things included in the trial? Would she refer to and submit herself to the church of Poitiers, where her first examination had taken place? On the face of it, it seems as though they could not have made fairer or more extensive offers. She must have had good reason, unknown to us, for the extreme scepticism of her replies: "Give me a messenger, and I will write to them all about this trial"; "Send them to me, and I will answer you then"; "Do you think you can catch me by these means, and thus win me to you?"[1]

Perhaps her scepticism, whatever its source, was justified, for, in spite of a renewed offer a week later to let her appeal to the Archbishop of Reims, these supporters were allowed to remain undisturbed wherever they were, which was certainly not in the city of Rouen.

vi

At the end of the last sitting, after the admonition, Jeanne had asked for time to consider her final answer, and it appears that they must have granted her a week, for it was not until May the 8th, the anniversary of the day when, two years earlier, she had ridden out from a relieved and rejoicing Orleans, that she was taken before Cauchon and a mere handful of her judges in the Grosse Tour of the castle.[2] The reason for this change of scene was soon apparent: it was so that she might be shown the torture-chamber with the executioners waiting and ready beside their instruments. There were several counts on which

[1] *Procès*, Vol. I, pp. 393-7.
[2] Now known as the Tour Jeanne d'Arc.

torture might be applied to Jeanne (for the salvation of her soul, as they kindly explained to her) under the laws and rulings of the Inquisition. It could be applied when discrepancies had been observed in the replies given by the culprit, or when those replies were at variance with the known evidence; either of these two offences might be punished by the ordeal by water and by the stretching of the limbs with cords. Even this grim prospect failed to draw any recantation from Jeanne. "Truly," she said, "even if you were to tear my limbs asunder and drive my soul out of my body, I could not speak otherwise; and, if I did say anything, I should always say afterwards that you had forced me to it."[1]

Again we must commend Cauchon's restraint. Instead of ordering the torture to be applied there and then, he came to the conclusion that in the hardened state of her soul she would derive but little profit from its application, and sent her back to her cell until he could confer on the subject with his colleagues. This conference took place three days later, in Cauchon's own house, Jeanne not being present, when by ten voices to three it was decided that the measure was neither necessary nor expedient. The three who were in favour of putting her to the ordeal were Aubert Morel, Thomas de Courcelles, and Nicolas Loiselleur.[2]

This was on the 12th. Proceedings had to be suspended for a week while Beaupère, de Touraine, and Nicolas Midi went to Paris to expound the whole case to the University of Paris, and to return bringing the result of their deliberations. One hardly likes to speculate on what these constant delays must have meant to the prisoner shut away in her cell. On the 19th, she again not being present, a large meeting was held in the chapel of the archiepiscopal palace. The three delegates were back from Paris, bearing long, flowery, and unequivocal documents, addressed both to the King and to the Bishop of Beauvais. The University had come, it appeared, to the decision that the woman commonly called *la Pucelle* had so disseminated

[1] *Procès*, Vol. I, p. 400.   [2] *Procès*, Vol. I, p. 403.

her poison that it had infected the very Christian flock of almost the whole Western world.[1] Then followed the conclusions of the Faculties of Theology and Decretal on each of the twelve articles separately. They were utterly damning. Without one single dissentient voice, the assembled tribunal subscribed to the finding of the University—that if the prisoner persisted in her refusal to retract she must be considered as a heretic, sorceress, schismatic, and apostate.[2]

vii

It seemed that very little remained to do except deliver the sentence and see that it was carried out. As, however, the majority had been of the opinion that yet one supreme and final admonition should be addressed to Jeanne, and a final effort made to restore her to the fold of the Church, Cauchon and Lemaistre with the Bishops of Thérouenne and Noyon, and seven others, repaired to a room in the castle, near to her prison, where she was sent for to attend upon their pleasure. It was May the 23rd, exactly a year since she had been taken at Compiègne. She had first to listen to the long indictment founded upon the twelve articles of her accusation, read to her in French and explained to her point by point by Pierre Maurice, the canon of Rouen, and then to a long but not unkindly worded harangue from the same lips.[3] We must do Maurice the justice of acknowledging that he employed all the powers of his oratory to point out the error of her ways in language which the simplest mind could understand. But Jeanne's mind suffered from a form of simplicity with which Maurice was not and could not be in sympathy. She merely repeated her remark about not changing her attitude even if she were to see the fire lighted—again causing the clerk to write *Responsio superba* in the margin—though this time she strengthened her refusal by adding that even if she were

[1]*Procès*, Vol. I, p. 409.   [2]*Procès*, Vol. I, pp. 422–9.
[3]*Procès*, Vol. I, p. 441.

actually in the fire she would sustain everything she had said, to the death.[1]

On the following day, May 24th, the citizens of Rouen were privileged to witness a most extraordinary and dramatic scene. In the walled cemetery adjoining the abbey of Saint Ouen, two stands had been erected, one of which was filled up by such dignitaries as the Cardinal-Bishop of Winchester, the Bishops of Beauvais, Thérouenne, Noyon, and Norwich, supported by abbots, priors, and doctors both of law and theology. On the other one, two figures only drew the gaze of all—the figure of maître Guillaume Erard and the figure of the prisoner, dressed as a boy. The crowd was enormous, and seething with excitement; it was evident that, if things did not go exactly as they wished, trouble might be expected from the English. Lord Warwick was there, not far from the Bishop of Beauvais, and there were other Englishmen, not merely soldiers among the crowd, but on the stand among the notables. Nevertheless it may be supposed that they hushed to listen to the exhortation which maître Erard was about to deliver. If we may believe his servant, Frère Jean de Lenozoles, he did not at all relish the task, and wished himself in Flanders, away from so unpleasant an affair.

He chose as his text the words of St. John: "The branch cannot bear fruit of itself, except it abide in the vine . . ." and went on to show that every Catholic must abide in the true vine of the Church, planted by Christ at his right hand. The actual report of the sermon is missing, but thanks to the accounts of Massieu and Aimond de Macy, who were both present, it is possible to reconstruct its general trend and even to supply a few details. Thus Massieu relates that when the preacher was about half-way through, he cried out in a loud voice, saying, "Ah, France, you have been much abused, and Charles, who calls himself your King and ruler, has endorsed the words and deeds of this useless, infamous, and dishonoured woman, like the heretic and schismatic that he is; and not he

[1] *Procès*, Vol. I, p. 441.

only, but all his clergy, by whom she has been examined and not rebuked." He repeated these words about the King two or three times over, then, threatening Jeanne with his finger, added, "I am speaking to you, Jeanne, and telling you that your King is a heretic and a schismatic." This was more than her loyalty could stand. She interrupted him: "*Par ma foi*, I dare to say and to swear, on my life, that he is the most noble of all Christians, who best loves the faith and the Church, and is not as you say." Erard turned to Massieu, "Tell her to be quiet."[1]

The sermon over, he formally showed her the judges, who, as he said, had so often required of her that she should submit her words and deeds to the Church.

She said, "I will answer you. As for my submission to the Church, I have already given them my answer. Let all my words and deeds be sent to Rome, to our Holy Father the Pope, to whom, after God, I will refer myself. As to what I have said and done, I have done it through God. I charge no one, neither my King nor any other; if there is any fault, it is mine alone."

They told her that this would not suffice; that the Pope was too far away, and that the Ordinaries were judges, each in his own diocese. But as she refused to give any further reply, the Bishop of Beauvais at length rose and began to read the sentence.

He had got the greater part of the way through it, when Jeanne interrupted him. "For these reasons we declare you excommunicate and heretical, and pronounce that you shall be abandoned to secular justice, as a limb of Satan severed from the Church. . . ." After all these months and weeks of superb and undaunted resolution, the fatal words as she heard them rolling out, the sight of the executioner waiting with his cart, the cruel avid crowd, the upturned faces, were too much for her. She gave way completely, until nothing was left of her proud denials. She would defer in all things

[1]*Procès*, Vol. II, p. 17: Deposition of Jean Massieu.

to the Church and her judges. She would no longer support or believe in the apparitions and revelations she had pretended to have. She said this several times over, as though she wished to make quite sure that she had been perfectly understood, and said again that in everything she would follow her judges and the Church.

It is a little difficult to know precisely what happened then, for the excitement of the crowd seems to have broken out into a sort of tumult. Witnesses say that she called upon Saint Michael (Bouchier). Aimond de Macy (whose memory, however, was capable of making him confuse Nicolas Midi with Erard as the preacher) says that an English secretary named Lawrence Calot took a little document out of his sleeve, and offered it to Jeanne with a pen to sign. He had already heard her saying that they were taking a great deal of trouble to make her perjure herself. "But," she said then, according to de Macy, "I know neither how to read nor write." Calot still insisting, she took the pen and derisively drew a round O. Then Calot took her hand and made her trace another sign. De Macy had forgotten what the second sign was.

This story may or may not be true. The part about the secretary taking the document from his sleeve has a circumstantial air, but it is much more likely that the secretary was a Frenchman, perhaps Massieu, for what would a secretary of the King of England be doing with a ready prepared Act of Abjuration? What we learn from Massieu is that Erard first read out the document, and then, on Jeanne saying that she did not understand it and wanted advice, passed it to Massieu, who read it out to her again. Still following Massieu's account, it seems that the crowd began to murmur as it was seen that she was being urged to sign; the murmur grew to a tumult, and stones were thrown, though Massieu did not know at whom. The Bishop of Beauvais appeared to be angry with someone, for Massieu heard him saying, "You shall pay for this. I have been insulted. I will not proceed until I have been satisfied." Massieu did not know what had happened, and it is only from the evidences of the witnesses (Dudesart, Bouchier, de Mailly, Migiet, Marcel, Marguerie) that we learn of an altercation between the Bishop and an English churchman attached to the Bishop of Winchester. "You are favouring Jeanne." "You lie," said Cauchon, and the Bishop of Winchester had to intervene (de Mailly). Yet another witness (Bouchier) says that Cauchon threw his papers in anger on the ground, saying he would go no further that day. Meanwhile Jeanne still hesitated, and contradictory rumours ran through the crowd: had she signed or had she not? (de Lenozoles). Massieu and Erard were both telling her that she would be burnt if she did not sign. The English, seeing their victim about to escape them, grew restive. The Bishop of Noyon heard people saying that it was all trickery (*pure trufferie*), and that Jeanne was laughing at them. Although none of the accounts tally exactly, they tally sufficiently to give us the impression of a general confusion, and, if such confusion could exist in the minds of those whose lives were not concerned, what must have been the perplexity of the poor prisoner? De Courcelles, that evasive young man, took advantage of the confusion, in retrospect, years later, conveniently to forget everything which had happened: he "forgot" the terms of Erard's sermon, he "forgot" whether the Act of Abjuration had ever been read aloud to Jeanne or not. The one thing which does stand out as absolutely certain is that a document was produced, and that after some hesitation Jeanne signed it, either with a circle or a cross.

The question of how Jeanne signed her recantation has never been satisfactorily cleared up. According to Massieu,[1] she signed it with a cross. According to de Macy, she first signed it with a round O, and then, on Lawrence Calot taking her hand which still held the pen, he made her sign it with a different sign—presumably a cross.[2] The question very naturally arises, Why did she not sign it with her name? We know that she was able to write her signature, if nothing else.

[1] *Procès*, Vol. II, p. 17.   [2] *Procès*, Vol. III, p. 123.

Z

In an attempt at the elucidation of this mystery, the Rev. Father F. Wyndham (in *L'héroïsme de la bienheureuse Jeanne d'Arc*) advances the theory that in the days of her military career, before she had learnt to write so much as her name, she was in the habit of signing her dictated letters with a cross when she intended them to be read in exactly the opposite sense. In this way, he says, she could give her troops a warning which would be entirely missed by the uninstructed enemy, should the letter chance to fall into his hands. The cross which she first drew at the foot of her recantation would thus, in her own eyes, render it invalid. But what about the round O? Ah, that, says Father Wyndham, with the enthusiasm and ingenuity of the biographer developing a theory, meant absolute zero.

With some psychological shrewdness, the fruit of experience, they must have anticipated that something of the sort was likely to happen at the last moment. They certainly had the document ready, wherever it was lying concealed during the whole of Erard's address and during the first part of the sentence of condemnation. It was there somewhere, ready to be whipped out at the first sight of human weakness. The only question is, What exactly was written on that document which Jeanne found so hard to understand? Massieu, who ought to know, having read it himself, is quite positive that the words signed by Jeanne were not the words which are reproduced in the *procès-verbal*. The words written in the *procès-verbal* occupy nearly fifty lines of small print, and constitute a truly appalling self-indictment.[1] But five independent witnesses, who saw the original document when it was produced at Saint Ouen, agree that it was not more than six to eight lines in length—about as long, said Migiet, as a paternoster. Taquel, who was standing near Jeanne, and who kept his eyes fixed on her while it was being read aloud, says that there were about six lines of big writing. He adds, which nobody else mentions, that Jeanne repeated the words as Massieu read them, and it

[1]*Procès,* Vol. I, pp. 447–8.

is, I think, quite possible that she may have done so under her breath in the effort to understand.[1] Jean Monnet, who was sitting on the platform at the feet of his master, Beaupère, was able to see the document, which appeared to him *una parva schedula* of six or seven lines. Finally, de la Chambre, the doctor, who says that he was near enough to see the writing, also deposes to six or seven lines on a folded sheet of paper. Such unanimity of evidence is impressive, especially as none of these men had any motive whatsoever for wishing to throw any doubt on the abjuration as written in the *procès-verbal*. To do so deliberately would, in fact, have entailed committing perjury, a thing which the witnesses, churchmen as they were, would have been exceedingly reluctant to do. The obvious explanation is that Jeanne gave her consent only to a brief though comprehensive précis, and never saw the amplified version which went into the records of the trial. The judges, after all, had every reason for wishing to abbreviate her actual confession as much as possible: there was more likelihood of her understanding what she was being asked to sign, and less likelihood of her changing her mind half-way through. They had equally every reason for wishing to elaborate it in the official version, in order to leave no possible room for dispute or ambiguity, nor were their consciences so tender as to compel them to declare publicly what they had done.

There it was: the prisoner had recanted, she had humbled herself before Holy Church, she had saved her skin. Cauchon turned to the Cardinal to ask what he should do next; the Cardinal replied that he must receive her as a penitent.[2] In place of the sentence of condemnation which he had begun to read, Cauchon then delivered sentence in another form, which had been prepared at the same time as the little document presented to Jeanne. Released from the threat of

[1] *Procès*, Vol. I, p. 451. It may be observed, also, that in the final sentence Cauchon says she pronounced her abjuration with her own mouth—*per tuum proprium organum cum omni hæresi, vivæ vocis oraculo abjurasti*.
[2] *Procès*, Vol. III, pp. 64–5: Deposition of Jean Monnet.

excommunication, admitted once more into the bosom of the Church, she might well have been forgiven for thinking that some change in her condition would now take place. It was true that the Bishop, at the end of his pronouncement, had condemned her to perpetual imprisonment,[1] to the bread of pain and the water of sorrow, that she might expiate her faults to the end of her days, but even if, in the emotion of the moment, she grasped the full significance of these harsh terms, she at least had every justification for thinking that the nightmare days of her surveillance by the English were over. Dazed though she must have been, it was the first thing she thought of. Loiselleur himself had the impudence to come up to her, saying, "Jeanne, you have spent a good day, please God; you have saved your soul," but she disregarded him entirely, and called out, "*Or ça, entre vous gens d'Eglise,* take me to your prison, that I may no longer be in the hands of these English." But Cauchon—"Take her back to the place you brought her from."[2]

viii

The general excitement had by no means died down—indeed it had risen to even greater heights since the news had spread for certain that the witch had wriggled herself out of the grasp of justice. Jeanne herself was insulted by English soldiers as she was being led back to prison, with no interference from their captains. All the English leaders, in fact, were in a high

[1]At least one commentator on Jeanne does not agree with this interpretation of the Latin—The Rev. Herbert Thurston, S.J., in *Studies,* September 1924: "Mr. Shaw renders *carcer perpetuas,* to which Jeanne was sentenced after her recantation, as 'lifelong prison.' This is, undoubtedly, the natural and obvious translation; but the phrase, I submit, is shown by sundry Inquisition records to mean simply a permanent prison as opposed to the makeshift buildings which were casually employed for the purpose. The sentence imposed confinement in a public jail of which there were a few belonging to the Inquisition, and determined nothing as to the length of the incarceration."

[2]*Procès,* Vol. II, p. 14: Deposition of Guillaume Manchon.

state of indignation against the French, and especially against the Bishop of Beauvais, because Jeanne had not been declared guilty, condemned, and given over to the executioner. On his way back, accompanied by his colleagues, the angry English surged round him, threatening him with their swords, and saying that he had ill earned the money their King had spent on him. Warwick, in person, had protested: "The King is ill served," he said to Cauchon, "since Jeanne has escaped us." Someone tried to pacify him: "My Lord, do not trouble; we will soon have her again."[1]

Rouen must have been a split, divided city during the whole of the ensuing afternoon.

Jeanne was out of it; Jeanne was back in her dark cell. She was in irons again, chained to her block of wood; and of the five English soldiers who still guarded her, three spent the nights in the cell, and two outside the door.[2] Cauchon and Warwick might growl over her like dogs over a bone, the swords of the English flash in the May sunshine as the Bishop drew his pontifical robes disdainfully aside, the crowds disperse in an excited babble of argument and of divergent opinions hotly and rowdily expressed, but for the prisoner there was nothing but a broken despair. Her flesh was safe from the flames, but at what a cost! She had betrayed everything she held most sacred. Most bitter of all, she must have wondered whether her guardian saints had really deserted her; whether, in truth, the doctors had not been right when they said that her voices were not the voices of saints at all, but of delusive devils. One shrinks from contemplating the appalling loneliness of soul which must have overcome her in such a moment. The strain of the morning over, she had nothing to do but to look back on what she had done. The Church Militant had praised her, but had she really, in the eyes of the Church Triumphant, abominably sinned? Had her conduct, in fact,

[1] *Procès*, Vol. II, p. 376: Deposition of Jean Fave, "*Domine, non curetis; bene rehabebimus eam.*"

[2] *Procès*, Vol. II, p. 18: Deposition of Jean Massieu.

been comparable with that of Simon Peter? Had she denied her Lord? It must have been almost a relief when the entry of Lemaistre, Loiselleur, de Courcelles, Nicolas Midi, and Isambard de la Pierre jerked her out of such speculations.

They had come to tell her what great mercy God had shown to her that day, as also they themselves for granting her the grace and forgiveness of their Mother the Church, making it quite clear at the same time that any lapse from grace would shut the doors of the Church on her for ever. Then they came down to their first practical test of her repentance: she must put on a woman's dress, as it had been commanded. She was wholly submissive. She laid her man's dress aside, exchanging it for the other.[1] She allowed them to shave her head, so that the shameful symbol of her boyish crop might be removed. The Jeanne d'Arc of popular legend seemed to have disappeared for ever from the pages of history.

ix

It was thus with some surprise that the Bishop of Beauvais learned that the prisoner was to be seen in her male dress again. This news was brought to him some time between Thursday, May 24th, the day of the scene at Saint Ouen, and Whit-Sunday, May 27th. He immediately despatched Beaupère and Midi to bring her back to her senses, but, while they were waiting in the courtyard of the prison for the necessary keys to be brought, some Englishmen came up and started saying that anyone who would throw them both into the river would be finding useful employment. The one-handed Beaupère makes no bones about the effect produced by these remarks upon him and his fellow-canon (*les dessus dictz furent espouvantez*), and came away without having had speech of Jeanne.[2] Perhaps they were

---

[1]*Procès*, Vol. I, pp. 452–3. It seems likely that this was the occasion on which she boxed Jeannotin Simon's ears. See *supra*, Chapter XIV, p. 305.
[2]*Procès*, Vol. II, p. 21: Deposition of Jean Beaupère.

wise, for the temper of the English was extremely sore. André Marguerie met with very much the same reception. When he and some others whom he does not name presented themselves at the prison, full of curiosity, the English raised a great tumult (*magnum tumultum*); an English soldier raised his sword against him, and, fearing for their persons, they had to withdraw in haste.[1] Rouen cannot at all have been a comfortable place of residence for the French clerics during those days. Massieu and Manchon both testify to scenes of violent hostility: Massieu and the delegates coming away from the castle, very much astonished and alarmed (*moult esbahis et espaourez*), saying that the English had driven them away with swords and axes, shouting "Traitors!" and other terms of abuse.[2] Manchon says that eighty to a hundred Englishmen set upon them, calling them Armagnac traitors and false counsellors, and scaring him personally so much that he refused to return to the prison next day, when sent for, without one of Warwick's men to escort him.[3] This heated atmosphere was evidently not congenial to the people of the pen.

It is to Massieu, however, that we owe the most detailed account of what had been taking place within the prison while the malcontent English sulked or ruffled in the courtyard below. Massieu had treated Jeanne as kindly as he dared from the first, even to the extent of imperilling his own safety in order to oblige her. It was he who had always brought her from her prison to the hall of justice, he who had reconducted her, he who had taken her to Saint Ouen; no man connected with the trial, except possibly Ladvenu, had a better right to claim, as he claimed, a close familiarity with her. The story he tells of the change of clothes which so disturbed the Bishop of Beauvais and brought his deputies into such danger of a thrashing is so circumstantial and so pathetically human that we can scarcely doubt its veracity.

[1]*Procès*, Vol. III, p. 184. Deposition of André Marguerie.
[2]*Procès*, Vol. II, p. 19: Deposition of Jean Massieu.
[3]*Procès*, Vol. II. p. 14: Deposition of Guillaume Manchon.

He says that he had it from Jeanne herself—when Warwick and d'Estivet went away leaving him alone with her and he immediately took advantage of their privacy to ask her what had induced her to make this change. And she told him that after the abjuration, when she put on the woman's dress which was provided, her own clothes, the man's dress, were bundled into a sack, which was left in her cell in the keeping of the English guards. She seems to have been allowed to retain the prescribed garments without interference until the morning of Sunday, three days later, when she awoke and asked her jailers to free her of her chains as she wished to leave her bed for a purpose of nature (*ut surgeret a lecto et purgaret ventrem*). She had been sleeping in her clothes, but one of the soldiers took them from her, emptied the sack containing the man's dress, threw it on to her bed, telling her meanwhile to get up, and stuffed the woman's dress into the sack in its place. Then, according to what she told Massieu, she was obliged to put on her old dress, but protested as she did so, saying, "Sirs, you know that this is forbidden me; I cannot take it without falling into fault." But nothing that she could say would persuade them to restore the other, although she argued with them until noon, when the necessities of the body would no longer be denied and she was compelled to leave the room. And when she returned, she told Massieu, neither her supplications nor her requests were of any avail.[1]

The sympathetic Massieu is not the only one who affords us a sketch of Jeanne in prison. Isambard de la Pierre also saw her there, and heard her say that she had had much to suffer from the English since she had appeared in the guise of a woman, "and in fact," he added, "I saw her in great distress, her face wet with tears, so disfigured and outraged that I was filled with pity and compassion."[2] Ladvenu goes further—one hopes too far, though it is undeniable that he had heard her in confession on her last morning—he goes so far as to say that she told him

---

[1] *Procès*, Vol. II, pp. 18 and 333: Depositions of Jean Massieu.
[2] *Procès*, Vol. II, p. 5: Deposition of Isambard de la Pierre.

she had been raped by an English nobleman.[1] Luckily, his incredible assertion that she "scarcely knew the paternoster and Ave Maria" robs his well-meaning evidence of half its value.

x

These were not at all the stories which she told to Cauchon when, braving the English who had already molested his delegates on these several occasions, he entered her prison on Whit-Monday, May 28th, to conduct a personal enquiry. Of course we can never be sure that de Courcelles (who was present) or Boisguillaume, who drew up the Latin version, did not falsify the report of the proceedings on Cauchon's orders. In view of the evidence of de la Pierre, who was also present, and in view of the additional unpopularity which Cauchon would have incurred with the English, had he allowed too unflatteringly truthful a report to be perpetuated, it seems highly probable. Perhaps he merely left out any complaints that Jeanne proffered against the English as concerning her virtue, for, apart from that not very vital point, most of her answers as given in the official report have the same disastrously haughty ring as in her most uncompromising days. They have Jeanne's own recognisable stamp upon them. They found her dressed as a man, and, using that as a basis for their examination, immediately asked her when and why she had resumed that habit, and why she had ever adopted it, and by whose advice. She must have been tired of these questions.

"I took it of my own free will. No one constrained me to take it. I prefer to dress as a man than as a woman. . . . I never understood that I had sworn not to resume it. . . . I did so because I thought it more proper, being amongst men, than to dress as a woman. . . . I resumed it because you did not keep your word to me, that I should go to Mass and receive my

[1]*Procès*, Vol. II, p. 8: Deposition of Martin Ladvenu. Jeanne, however, alluded to her body "which has never been corrupted," within a few hours of her death.

Saviour, and that I should be taken out of irons. I would rather die than be in irons, but if you will let me go to Mass and take off my irons, and put me in a pleasant prison (*en prison gracieuse*), and let me have a woman, I will be good and do whatever the Church wants."

This last concession promised well, but the next question took her on to dangerous ground: "Since last Thursday (the day of the abjuration), have you heard the voices of Saints Catherine and Margaret?

Jeanne: "Yes."

"What did they say to you?"

"They told me that, through them, God sent me His pity of the betrayal to which I consented in making the abjuration and revocation to save my life, and that in saving my life I was damning myself. Before Thursday, they had told me what I should do, and what I did that day. They told me when I was on the platform that I should answer that preacher boldly; he was a false preacher, and he said I had done several things which I had not done. If I were to say that God had not sent me, I should be damning myself, for it is true that God did send me. My voices have told me, since then, that I did very wrong in doing that which I did, and that I must confess that I did wrong. It was fear of the fire which made me say that which I said. . . ."[1]

Against the words, *They told me that, through them, God sent me His pity*, Boisguillaume wrote, *Responsio mortifera*—fatal answer —in the margin.

[1]*Procès*, Vol. I, pp. 455–7. For a translation of the page from the trial, opposite, see Appendix G, p. 405.

A PAGE FROM THE TRIAL

Chapter XVII

THE LAST ACT

i

A few formalities remained to be accomplished, and the next day, Tuesday, May 29th, was given up to them. Forty-one voices were heard at the convocation summoned by Cauchon to attend in the archiepiscopal chapel, and in all those forty-one opinions there was only one opinion: "Relapsed heretic." The first speaker, Nicolas de Venderès, Archdeacon of Eu and Canon of Rouen Cathedral, expressed himself in terms which might seem misleading to any reader unversed in ecclesiastical law: *That Jeanne shall be abandoned to secular justice, with the request that they shall act mercifully towards her.*

This phrase does not mean what its amiable wording suggests. It is a mere formula, devised by the ingenuity of the Church, a euphemistic way of saying that the culprit shall be burnt. These niceties were perfectly understood between the ecclesiastical and the secular authorities. Thus, while it was recognised that the Church could neither shed blood nor put to death, it was equally well recognised that excommunication was its peculiar weapon, and that, once excommunicated, the outlaw could no longer claim either its protection or its jurisdiction. The handing over of an excommunicate to secular justice, therefore, meant that the Church blandly washed its hands of all further responsibility, knowing full well, as a contemporary judge neatly expressed it, that "what the one had begun, the other would complete."

According, then, to the verdict expressed with such unanimity by all present, it was enjoined upon them one and all to demand Jeanne's presence in the old market-place at eight o'clock on the following morning, that she might personally hear herself declared excommunicate and relapsed.[1]

[1] *Procès*, Vol. I, p. 468.

ii

Massieu must have been up early on Wednesday, May 30th, for by seven o'clock in the morning he had already written a letter addressed to the Bishop and Lemaistre, informing them that their command had been carried out, and that Jeanne had been formally and personally summoned to appear before them at eight. According to the official register, it was not until nine that the scene in the market-place began. What had been happening at the prison to account for this unpunctuality? Of some of the happenings we can speak with certainty; others must remain a matter of controversy and conjecture.[1] For the moment let us stick to what is sure.

What is sure is that Ladvenu, accompanied by a young monk named Toutmouillé, arrived early at the prison to hear Jeanne's confession. This, says Toutmouillé, Ladvenu did charitably and with care. Massieu was there, and on Ladvenu's request went off to find the Bishop of Beauvais for permission to administer the Sacraments to Jeanne. This permission took some little time to obtain, for it entailed calling some of the doctors together for deliberation, but resulted in the request being granted. Massieu was much displeased by the lack of reverence with which the Sacraments were brought by a clerk; on a paten, he says, wrapped in the linen used to cover the chalice, without any candles or any escort, without any surplice or stole. Ladvenu, displeased also, sent the clerk back to fetch light and a stole. Massieu watched her while she received Communion, "with great devotion and many tears."

It was Ladvenu's painful task to inform her of the manner of her death. She had always had a horror of fire, and now broke down, crying piteously (*doloreusement et piteusement*), "Alas, that

[1] This concerns the question whether Jeanne was visited in prison in the early morning by Venderès, Pierre Maurice, de Courcelles, le Camus, Loiselleur, and Cauchon, and, if so, what passed there between them. See *supra*, Chapter XV, p. 338; and Appendix H, p. 406.

I should be treated so horribly and cruelly; that my whole body, never yet corrupted, should to-day be consumed and burnt to ashes! Ha! a! I would rather be beheaded seven times, than thus be burnt."

At that moment, Cauchon came in, when she instantly said to him, "Bishop, I die through you." He tried to remonstrate with her, pointing out that she had brought her death upon herself by her broken promises, but she could only reproach him, saying that if he had put her into a prison of the Church and into the hands of competent and suitable keepers, this would never have happened (*cecy ne fust pas advenu*).[1]

Pierre Maurice came also. He had treated her gently once before, and she turned to him now for reassurance: "Maître Pierre, where shall I be to-night?" And on his asking her if she did not trust in God, she replied that she did, and that, God willing, she would be in Paradise.[2]

They took her out. A mob of English soldiers awaited her, armed with swords and sticks and axes, so that no one dared speak to her, except Massieu and Ladvenu, who went with her and kept close,[3] but were unable to restrain their tears. Isambard de la Pierre followed them. The market-place was crowded when they arrived there; one witness says that ten thousand citizens were present, and there seem to have been close on a thousand English soldiers (Manchon; Massieu). Three standings had been erected, one for the judges, one for the priests, and one, silent and sinister, for a stake heaped round with wood.[4] In front of this one was a board painted with the words: "Jehanne who called herself la Pucelle, liar, pernicious, deceiver of the people, sorceress, superstitious,

[1] *Procès*, Vol. II, pp. 3–4: Deposition of Jean Toutmouillé; and *Procès*, Vol. II, p. 8: Deposition of Martin Ladvenu.

[2] *Procès*, Vol. III, p. 191: Deposition of Jean Riquier. Riquier, a priest, says Maurice told him this.

[3] *Procès*, Vol. II, p. 14: Deposition of Guillaume Manchon.

[4] *Procès*, Vol. III, p. 55, and *Procès*, Vol. II, p. 8: Depositions of Jean de Mailly and Martin Ladvenu.

blasphemer of God, presumptuous, disbeliever in the faith of Jesus Christ, boastful, idolatrous, cruel, dissolute, invoker of devils, apostate, schismatic, and heretic."[1]

She was led first to the priests, and made to mount the platform where all could see her clearly. She was then solemnly addressed by Nicolas Midi, who took as his text 1 Corinthians, chapter xii., verse 26: *And whether one member suffer, all the members suffer with it.* She listened, says Massieu, very quietly until he came to the words, "Jeanne, go in peace, the Church can no longer protect you, and delivers you into secular hands." Then she knelt and prayed aloud to God, and asked that all manner of people might show her mercy, whether of her own party, or of the other, and would pray for her, for she forgave them all the harm they had done to her. She went on in this way for about half an hour, till even the judges were in tears and some of the English.[2] Loiselleur had already taken his departure, weeping, and but for the protection of Warwick would have been set upon as a traitor by a party of the English whom he happened to encounter.[3] Manchon left the scene, for he could not bear what was to follow; indeed, he says, he could not get over it for a month, and spent some of the money he had received for his services during the trial in buying a little missal, which he kept for years in memory of Jeanne, and which he used in saying prayers for her.[4] Massieu remained, and handed her the crude little cross made for her out of two pieces of wood by an English soldier, which she first kissed and then put against her breast, between the flesh and her gown. The official report, of course, only says drily that the Bishop of Beauvais then rose and, after advising her to pay heed to the counsel of those who instructed her for her salvation, more especially the two venerable brothers (Ladvenu and de la Pierre)

---

[1] *Procès*, Vol. IV, pp. 459–60: Clement de Fauquemberque.
[2] *Procès*, Vol. II, p. 19: Deposition of Jean Massieu.
[3] *Procès*, Vol. III, p. 162: Deposition of Boisguillaume; and *Procès*, Vol. II, p. 320: Deposition of Nicolas Taquel.
[4] *Procès*, Vol. II, p. 15: Deposition of Guillaume Planchon.

who were near her at that moment, read the final sentence by
which she was cast out, cut off, and abandoned.[1]

iii

The English, however, were growing impatient, and began
calling out, "Well, priest, do you mean us to dine here?"

No lay sentence was pronounced; that seems certain. None
is officially recorded, and all the witnesses agree that none was
delivered. Manchon says that she was led up to the *bailli* of
Rouen, who simply made a gesture with his hand, saying,
"Away with her."[2] It is true that Manchon was speaking from
hearsay, as he had already left, being overcome with his
emotion, but the general agreement is such as to dispel any
doubt. English hands seized her, and roughly propelled her
towards the scaffold where the stake and faggots were waiting,
and hoisted her upon it; it was built of plaster, and was very
high, so high that the executioner had some trouble in reaching
her, and was unable to do his work quickly.[3] Instead of a crown
of thorns, a tall paper cap, like a mitre, was set upon her head,
bearing the words: "Heretic, relapsed, apostate, idolatress."[4]
Massieu, Ladvenu, and de la Pierre went with her; de la Pierre,
at her request, and sent by Massieu, fetched the crucifix from
the neighbouring church of Saint Sauveur, and, mounting the
scaffold, held it up before her. She told him to get down when
the fire should be lighted, but to continue holding the crucifix up
so that she might see it.[5] Meanwhile, they bound her to the stake,
and some of the English laughed, as she called with a loud
voice upon Saint Catherine, Saint Margaret, and Saint Michael,
then cried out, "*Ah, Rouen! j'ay grant paour que tu ayes à souffrir*

[1] *Procès*, Vol. I, p. 473.
[2] *Procès*, Vol. II, p. 344: Deposition of Guillaume Manchon.
[3] *Procès*, Vol. II, p. 9: Deposition of Martin Ladvenu.
[4] *Procès*, Vol. IV, p. 459: Clement de Fauquemberque.
[5] *Procès*, Vol. II, p. 303: Deposition of Isambard de la Pierre.

de ma mort!"[1] Then as the flames crackled and rose, she called loudly and repeatedly upon Jesus; her head sank forward, and it was the last word she was heard to pronounce.

Many wept; John Tressart, secretary to the King of England, exclaimed, "We are lost; we have burnt a saint."[2] Strange things were seen to happen. The name of Jesus leapt written across the flames,[3] and an English soldier who had sworn to throw a faggot on to the pyre declared that he saw a white dove fly out of the flames and wing away in the direction of France.[4] Jean Alespée wished openly and with tears that his soul might be where he believed hers to be.[5] That no possible doubt could exist that the witch was dead—for the English greatly feared that a rumour of her escape might arise—the executioner was ordered to part the flames and show her charred and naked body hanging on the stake.[6] Ladvenu and Isambard de la Pierre had a busy afternoon. They had to deal with the Englishman who had seen the dove fly away; he had been so much upset that his comrades had removed him to comfort him with drink in a neighbouring tavern, but, that consolation failing, he sought out an English monk and made his confession in Frère Isambard's presence. They also had to deal with the executioner in person. He arrived at the house of the Frères Prêcheurs, looking for Ladvenu and de la Pierre, very frightened and

[1] *Procès*, Vol. III, p. 53: Deposition of Guillaume de la Chambre. Jeanne's words are in French in the text.

[2] *Procès*, Vo. II, p. 347: Deposition of Pierre Cusquel.

[3] *Procès*, Vol. II, p. 372: Deposition of Thomas Marie.

[4] *Procès*, Vol. II, p. 352: Deposition of Isambard de la Pierre.

[5] *Procès*, Vol. II, p. 375: Deposition of Jean Riquier.

[6] *Procès*, Vol. III, p. 191: Deposition of Jean Riquier. Jean Riquier is the only witness who gives this detail, but he is corroborated by the *Journal d'un bourgeois de Paris* (*Procès*, Vol. IV, p. 471), in the following terrible words: *fut liée à une estache qui estoit sur l'eschaffault qui estoit fait de plastre, et le feu sus lui; et là fut bientost estainte et sa robe toutte arse, et puis fut le feu tiré arrière; et fut veue de tout le peuple toutte nue, et tous les secrez qui peuent estre ou doibvent en femme, pour oster les doubtes du peuple. Et quant ilz l'orent assez à leur gré veue toutte morte liée à l'estache, le bourrel remist le feu grant sus sa poure charongne, qui tantost fut toute comburée, et os et char mis en cendre.*

contrite, saying that he was damned, having burnt a saint, and that God would never forgive him. He told them that, in spite of all the oil, sulphur, and fuel he had used, he could not reduce her entrails or her heart to ashes.[1] He had thrown everything which remained of her into the Seine.

[1]*Procès*, Vol. II, p. 352; and ibid., p. 7: Depositions of Isambard de la Pierre.

Chapter XVIII

AFTERMATH

i

That, then, is the story, told as straightforwardly as possible, but still it leaves us with all its deeper implications unexplained and even unexamined. It arouses many questions, which, if we could answer them, would carry us far along the road towards the solution of many mysteries. That, to me, is the fascination of France's national saint—not just the subject of a biography, not merely a picturesque figure in armour and a scarlet cloak, but a figure who challenges some of the profoundest tenets of what we do or do not believe. More, perhaps, than any other military figure in history, she forces us to think.

She makes us think, and she makes us question; she uncovers the dark places into which we may fear to look. We read, and, having read, are left with the essential queries: Does God on occasion manifest Himself by direct methods? Is the visible world the only world we have to consider? Is it possible for mortal man to get into touch with beings of another world? Is it possible that unearthly guidance may be vouchsafed to assist our human fallibility? Is it possible that certain beings are born with a sixth sense, a receptivity so far beyond that of their duller fellows that in order to explain it we take refuge in such words as "miraculous" and "supernatural"?

It is best to admit straight away that we can give no satisfactory or comprehensive answer to the general question. So far as Jeanne herself is concerned, we can accept her sincerity without scepticism; and, for the rest, attempt by methods of comparison to arrive at some conclusion—a conclusion which eludes us, and which must in the last resort be left to the individual judgment. By individual judgment I mean really that there are two possible lines of approach: the so-called scientific, and the so-called religious—two lines which may well prove to be not parallel but convergent. I believe that their discrepancies at present puzzle us only in so far as we fail to see far enough down the perspective which will eventually bring them to the sharp and understandable point of meeting.

It is with reluctance that I intrude my own convictions, but at a given moment it surely becomes imperative for any biographer of Saint Joan to make his own position clear, even at the expense of some declaration of personal faith, if only in order to avoid any suspicion of personal prejudice. The words in which I must clothe that declaration are trite, I know, but the conviction behind them is serious and sincere. I will state, therefore, briefly, that I am not, myself, what is called a "religious" person in the orthodox sense of the phrase, nor yet a member of any organised Church. I do, however, confronted with the ultimate enigma, believe, and believe deeply, in some mysterious central originating force which the natural weakness and insufficiency of human nature finds it necessary to symbolise in a name, an amalgam of fear and comfort, which you may call God or Gott or Dieu or Jah or Allah or X, or even "a pure mathematician," without any reason *necessarily* to identify that force with our own human conceptions of good and evil. It follows logically that, holding this belief, I share with my fellow-mortals the ancient superstition which no scientific explanation can destroy, but which no scientific explanation has as yet been able to account for: the belief in what we conveniently call the supernatural. I believe in it so profoundly as to quarrel with the expressions super-natural or extra-natural. For me there is only one comprehensive, stupendous unity of which we apprehend but the smallest segment. My readings into Joan of Arc have done nothing but increase my belief in the existence of that unity, and also the belief that certain persons are in touch with, or, shall we say, receptive to the influences of, a unity for which we have no adequate name, the greater whole of which our own imagination embraces but a tiny part. Without pretending to explain how or why these persons should be thus favoured, I accept the fact, with the logical corollary that Jeanne must be regarded as prominent among them—a bald and brief conclusion which I fear may be regarded as both unsatisfactory and evasive.

I have, however, already admitted that we are in no position to give anything resembling a satisfactory answer. I have suggested that neither of the two possible lines of approach —the scientific and the religious—is alone sufficient to resolve the mystery. The religious, of course, offers the quicker way out of the difficulty: blind acceptance, to some minds, is more agreeable than the more critical and enquiring attitude. The whole problem is simplified for those who can just believe that God sent three of His Saints to instruct Jeanne; for those who can throw themselves, in short, into the frame of mind of the good, believing Christian. Unfortunately for some of us, this attitude is impossible blindly to adopt. I have been painfully torn myself. There are moments when I am not at all sure that the religious line of approach may not, in the end, prove right; when I am not at all sure that instinct may not, as usual, be proved to have taken the short-cut rejected by reason. They may both arrive at the same point in the end; only, instinct may be found to have got there first. I am in the unfortunate position of anybody torn between an instinctive reliance on instinct, and a reasonable reliance on reason.

In the meantime it seems to me that the only spirit in which to approach the problem of Jeanne's voices and visions, in the present state of our understanding, is a spirit of complete open-mindedness and acknowledgment of our ignorance. Our ignorance and limitations, indeed, are still such that we may well question the audacity of approaching such a problem at all. We are in the position of a schoolboy who, having attained to some acquaintance with simple or even compound fractions, would aspire to comment on the higher mathematics. The outcome of such an attempt in the eyes of an informed mathematician would be piteous and laughable in the extreme. Just as piteous, in the eyes of succeeding and more enlightened generations, may be the attempts of the childish twentieth century to fumble towards the explanation of a phenomenon which to the more adult information of the future may offer no difficulties whatsoever. It is possible, conceivable, and indeed probable that with the expansion of our knowledge in the physical, psychological, and psychical worlds such problems may cease to be problems and may become the commonplace of ordinary information. With this hope in view, it would seem, therefore, as though any present effort of a groping understanding were a wasted effort, and as though we of the early twentieth century should be better advised to wait in patience for the coming of a fuller wisdom, a fulfilment of wisdom perhaps too remote ever to benefit our now existent selves, rather than waste our time only to expose ourselves to the antiquarian interest of our posterity as yet another example of commendable inquisitiveness but obsolete ignorance.

ii

At the same time, while thus humbly admitting our insufficiencies, we should be well advised to explore the information available from scientific, or pseudo-scientific, sources. The terminology of such sources is unfortunately enough to put the reader against them. The very word "psychic" has a malodour in rational nostrils, and is mixed up with tales of credulous devotees and fraudulent mediums in the popular mind. We have all heard such tales; and probably in a large percentage of cases our mistrust was justifiable.

Certain serious and respect-worthy essays, written with especial reference to Jeanne d'Arc, cannot, however, be ignored. It is impossible for any serious student of Jeanne d'Arc to overlook them, or to omit to search through them in the hope of discovering even one single instructive phrase. It is necessary, indeed, for the student of Jeanne d'Arc, if he wants to get as near to the truth as he can, to examine and compare reports and comments on experiences analogous to her own. For such experiences, one turns obviously to the records in the *Proceedings of the Society for Psychical Research.*[1]

These proceedings contribute two valuable articles: valuable, that is to say, for their bearing on Jeanne. Neither of them relates to any actual "sittings," and may thus be absolved from any suspicion in the mind of the reader. They are merely speculative essays based on authenticated historical events. The first article to which I allude is by Frederic Myers,[2] on the famous "Dæmon of Socrates." Socrates, as is well known, was guided in all the affairs of life by a monitory voice—a voice which on certain occasions gave him certain warnings, and on other occasions, by omitting to manifest at all, gave, through silence, approval of his actions. Myers, and rightly, is extremely cautious about attributing any exaggerated importance to the powers of this guiding voice. "We cannot," he says, " be sure that the monitory sign ever warned him of anything which no possible sagacity of the ordinary kind could have led him to discover." Throughout his essay he implies, in fact, that Socrates was drawing on what we should now call his sub-conscious, rather than receiving guidance from any exterior and dissociated force. "I believe that it is now possible," he says, ". . . to show that the messages which Socrates received were only advanced examples of a process which, if super-normal, is not abnormal, and which characterises that form of intelligence which we describe as genius. For genius is best defined—not as an unlimited capacity for taking pains,[3] but

---

[1] I will here add, hastily, in case of misunderstanding, that I have never had any dealings whatsoever with psychic matters; have never attended a séance in my life; have no acquaintance with any mediums or their controls; and am, in fact, completely innocent of any acquaintance with any such experiments.

[2] *Proceedings of the Society for Psychical Research,* Vol. V, Part XIV, p. 522 (Trübner & Co., 1889): F. W. H. Myers, *The Dæmon of Socrates.*

[3] Surely no familiar phrase was ever so unintelligent or so generally mis-quoted as this one! What Carlyle really wrote was, "Genius, which means the transcendent capacity of taking trouble, first of all" (*Frederick the Great,* Book IV, chapter iii). To quote it correctly, however, in no way redeems

rather as a mental constitution which allows a man to draw readily into conscious life the products of unconscious thought" —a pregnant phrase which grows the richer in suggestion the more one ponders over it. But then, as Myers goes on to observe, the case of Socrates is a marked one, and may be thought too exceptional for his argument. Socrates, after all, was one of the noblest intellects ever produced by Greece. Socrates, as he says, was too strangely above ordinary men to allow us to draw wider inferences from this example. "It might be well," he continues, "if we could add a case not complicated by such towering genius—a case where someone with no great gifts of nature, with no incomprehensible workings of the soul, had, nevertheless, by monitory voices been taught wisdom and raised to honour—and who, if so it might be, had testified to the reality of the inward message by some witness which the world could not gainsay. And such a case there is; there is a figure in history unique and marvellous, but marvellous in this point alone. One there has been who was born with no conspicuous strength of intellect, and in no high or powerful place, but to whom voices came from childhood onwards and brought at length a strange command—one who by mere obedience to that monitory call rose to be the saviour of a great nation—one to whose lot it fell to push that obedience to its limit, and to pledge life for truth; to perish at the stake rather than disown those voices or disobey that inward law.

"I speak, of course, of Joan of Arc.

"I must be excused for dwelling on this signal example; for I believe that only now, with the comprehension which we are gradually gaining of *the possibility of an impulse from the mind's deeper strata which is so far from madness that it is wiser than our sanity itself*—only now, I repeat, can we understand aright that familiar story" (the italics are mine). "We need not," he says, in conclusion, "assume that the voices which she heard were

the imperceptive idiocy of Carlyle's definition. The only word in the whole sentence which throws any light on the matter is the word "transcendent." Myers own definition comes, succinctly, far closer to the truth.

the offspring of any mind but her own, any more than we need assume that the figures in which her brave and pious impulses sometimes took external form were veritable saints" —a conclusion with which Jeanne herself would certainly and most vehemently have disagreed. But it must be remembered that he is taking the purely scientific, not the religious, point of view.

The gist of Myers' remarks, it is interesting to note, is that neither in the case of Socrates nor of Jeanne was there any trace of madness or hysteria. (Incidentally, in speaking of Socrates, he excludes all possibility of epilepsy.) He insists, also, on the fact that both Socrates and Jeanne, however different in their intellectual attainments, were persons of robust physical constitution. Their genius he admits, but, in his view, genius represents the supreme and ideal sanity rather than the derangement of a hysterical or over-excitable mind. Genius, to him, is the ready uprising of the subconscious into the realm of the conscious, and may take many forms of expression; thus, he has no hesitation in including such phenomena as the "lightning calculator" or "arithmetical prodigy, generally of tender years,[1] capable of performing in his head, and almost instantaneously, problems for which ordinary workers would require pencil and paper and a much longer time—problems which, in some cases, indeed, the ordinary student has no means whatever of solving, but which the calculating boy unriddles with ease and exactness"[2]; or

---

[1] In this connexion, it is worth noting that both musical and mathematical prodigies have given early evidence of their inexplicable gifts. It is scarcely necessary to quote the obvious example of Mozart. It is perhaps less generally known that Capablanca at the age of twelve was already the chess-champion of Cuba. It is probably something more than a mere coincidence which suggests some association between music and mathematics, extending possibly also to the very young child's aptitude for the creation of pattern-pictures—an aptitude which is liable to diminish after the age of ten. Anyhow, it is a large subject, upon which our views must necessarily remain speculative and inexact for some time to come.

[2] F. W. H. Myers, *Human Personality and its Survival after Death*, p. 51.

examples such as that of Sir John Herschel, who was attended by visions taking the form of geometrical patterns, both by daylight and in darkness. It is implicit in all that Myers has to say on the subject that he regards all such manifestations as analogous to, and therefore comparable with, the experiences which, in their different ways, guided Socrates and Saint Joan in the conduct of their lives. There is no hint of any supernatural or religious guidance. There is no suggestion of a diseased or hallucinatory brain. There is nothing but the suggestion that all such controversial problems may eventually be explained by the cold reason of greater psychological knowledge; the suggestion only that no mysterious agency is ever at work, other than the still unexplored or half-explored question of the dividing line between our conscious and our subconscious selves. Myers' approach, in fact, restricts itself purely to the scientific. The religious or supernatural element does not affect it at all.

In this, he finds support from Sir Francis Galton.[1] Galton is not talking specifically about Jeanne d'Arc, but he has certain observations to make which may throw some light on the insoluble problem of Jeanne's voices, visions, and their nature. He, like Myers, lays stress on the belief that the visionary faculty is by no means necessarily associated with a disordered mind. "The visionary tendency," he says, "is much more common among sane people than is generally suspected"; and again, "the familiar hallucinations of the insane are to be met with far more frequently than is commonly supposed, among people . . . in good working health." He quotes several examples drawn from his personal knowledge: a near relative of his own, for instance, "saw phantasmagoria very frequently, yet was eminently sane, and of such good constitution that her faculties were hardly impaired until near her death at ninety," and "another lady, apparently in vigorous health and belonging to a vigorous family," told him that during some past months she had been plagued by voices. The words were at first simple

[1] *Inquiries into Human Faculty and its Development.*

nonsense; then the word "pray" was frequently repeated. He instances, also, the case of Goethe, who, as a force of intellect, may surely stand not ingloriously in comparison with Socrates, and who, as is well known, could at will evoke the image of a rose "which would not keep its shape steady for a moment, but unfolded from within, throwing out a succession of petals mostly red but sometimes green, and . . . continued to do so without change in its brightness . . . so long as he cared to watch it."

All these instances, picked almost at random, suggest something very unexplained and odd in the workings of the human mind. What connexion, we may ask, can possibly exist between the short-cut of the lightning calculator, the precocity of Mozart, the schemes of Capablanca, the geometrical patterns of Herschel, the rose of Goethe, the dæmon of Socrates, and the voices of Jeanne d'Arc? What connexion, we may ask again, exists between such mundane warlike admonitions as were received by Jeanne and such admonitions as were received by, say, Bernadette of Lourdes—Bernadette, another peasant child of thirteen, going out to gather sticks for the fire, and being confronted by an apparition whom she, during a fortnight, was able to identify as the Virgin Mary, and under whose directions she discovered a spring so miraculous as still to draw thousands of pilgrims from all parts of Europe yearly in hopes of a cure? What binding thread links all these mysteries together? We cannot answer the question. We are, at present, working only on the data provided by analysis: the synthesis, so far, escapes us.

Therefore perhaps it is better to leave speculation, and to return to the sober scientific line of approach. It is comforting to read, when we are thinking specifically of Jeanne d'Arc, such phrases as these from Galton: "The power of visualising is higher in the female sex than in the male"; or, "The French appear to possess the visualising faculty in a high degree." Yet, somehow, these phrases do not help us far towards the real heart of the matter. We are still left wondering where the truth really lies. They may prove useful as sign-posts, but still there is nothing to tell us that two major roads do not run side by side.

The possible existence of a third road towards the explanation is based on physiological reasoning; physiological, with its reactions on the psychological. Andrew Lang, putting it delicately, suggests that Jeanne, when she first heard her voices, was "at a critical age, when, as I understand, female children are occasionally subject to illusions."[1] Putting it more frankly, he means that the arrival of her voices coincided with the onset of puberty. Yet another writer, more outspoken, suggests that in Jeanne's case puberty, with its usual symptoms, never arrived at all, but that the voices arrived instead, at the corresponding age, as a kind of sublimation of the ordinary physical processes of nature—an argument based on the very insufficient and indirect testimony of certain witnesses who averred that, to their knowledge, Jeanne had never suffered from the usual infirmity of women. This theory he supplements by suggesting that her vow of virginity was the outcome of her first realisation of her disability—in other words, "we can put the idea of virginity into the jargon of psycho-analysis by saying that Jeanne had well-marked repression of the sex-complex."[2] Unfortunately for this ingenious theory, its foundation is of the slightest. It arises from a paragraph in the evidence of Jean d'Aulon, which, although not veiled in what Gibbon calls the obscurity of a learned language, we will at least leave untranslated from the original French: *Dit encores plus qu'il a oy dire à plusieurs femmes, qui ladicte Pucelle ont veue par plusieurs foiz nue, et sceu de ses secretz, que oncques n'avoit en la secrecte maladie des femmes et que jamais nul n'en peut riens cognoistre ou appercevoir par ses habillemens, ne aultrement.*[3]

This testimony, to my mind, means nothing at all, except that Jeanne with exceptional modesty kept her private life

---

[1]*Proceedings of the Society for Psychical Research*, Vol. XI, pp. 198–212: Andrew Lang, *The Voices of Joan of Arc.*

[2] C. Maclaurin, *Post-mortem*, pp. 34–65.

[3]*Procès*, Vol. III, p. 219: Deposition of Jean d'Aulon.

to herself both in her speech and in her habits. It means no more than the rather naïf comment of another contemporary, Simon Charles, that, when she was on horseback in armour, she never dismounted for the purposes of nature, and that all the men-at-arms greatly wondered at the length of time she was able to remain in the saddle.[1] Simon Charles obviously underestimated the remarkable continence of women, as opposed to the lavish incontinence of men to which his quotidian experience was better accustomed. We must also take into consideration the fact that Jeanne was always sparing of both her meat and drink. The comments of her companions in arms provide ample testimony as to her frugality.

Still, there are certain physio-psychological aspects which cannot be ignored. We cannot, for instance, afford to neglect a comparison between Jeanne and some other "saints." We cannot afford to omit the notice of certain essential differences between them. It should be observed, in the first place, that Jeanne was neither an ecstatic, nor a mystic, nor in any sense of the word a "hysterical" person. We can find no signs in her of any exaggeration of feelings or temperament. Neither ecstasy nor despondency affected her unduly. She was neither disproportionately lifted up nor disproportionately cast down. True, at Poitiers she was gay with hope; but even at Melun when her voices grew gloomy with prognostication of imminent failure, she suffered no extreme blackness of despair. Throughout all her strange experiences she preserved a remarkably constant level. The darker passages of the soul seem never to have affected her life at all. If she suffered them, she left no record. Her faith was never, at any moment, eclipsed. Quite on the contrary, she was an essentially practical person, and the only unusual element in her life appears in the voices which commanded her to go into France, turn out the English, and crown the Dauphin. Apart from that, she was a very

---

[1]*Procès*, Vol. III, p. 118: Deposition of Simon Charles: *Dum erat in armis et eques, nunquam descendebat de equo pro necessariis naturæ; et mirabantur omnes armati quomodo poterat tantum stare supra equum.*

ordinary girl, and remained a very ordinary girl throughout. Her first character never changed at all, from the moment she left Domremy to the moment she got herself burnt at Rouen. Her replies to her judges at Rouen prove her to have remained always just what she was—a shrewd, suspicious, straightforward, roughly humorous peasant, with the only difference between herself and her kind, that God had intervened between herself and her cart-horses with His dictates.

In this, she differs in a remark-worthy manner from her fellow-saints. She never, for instance, used such conventional expressions as "my heavenly Spouse," or "my Betrothed," as are common to most women of mystical inclination. I think that possibly she had no need thus to sublimate her earthly desires in this pseudo-sexual fashion, since she found her outlet in her ardent devotion to the Dauphin and to the cause of France. She is the least sentimental of saints, and the most practical—which perhaps explains why you will always find a fresh bunch of humble flowers laid before the image, of, say, Saint Thérèse of Lisieux in any village church in France, whereas you will seldom find a similar bunch laid at the feet of Jeanne d'Arc. The roses and mignonette are not for her; only the laurels and the bays. She is a hard, not a soft, saint. There is nothing of the poetic quality in her, as in Saint Francis. She is too heroic and bracing to appeal intimately to the average mind. She makes the mistake of being always something over life-size; something which, however much she may command admiration and respect, can never be loved in quite the same personal way as the more human saints. Heroism may command the tributes of the populace, but sentimentality wins its heart. Jeanne never makes any appeal to sentimentality at all.

Even in her sainthood she remains severe and strict. As a little girl, she confided in no one. As an adolescent, she was determined, impatient, and frequently rough-tongued. Her piety is unquestioned, but her manners not always of the best. As Father Martindale has observed: "Saints retain all the human nature that is in them, all their personal, temperamental, hereditary, educational, characteristics. . . . They retain their tendency to gentleness or to imperiosity, to sense of humour or to sense of sublimity (or to both), to timidity or to audacity, as much as anyone else does; if they are vividly intelligent men, they do not become dolts; if they are very simple men, they do not become philosophers."[1] One cannot read the life of Saint Joan without recognising the truth of these words as applied to her. From beginning to end, she is all of a piece.

iii

The physiological road of approach really holds very little interest, especially in view of the insufficiency of the evidence. We are still left undecided as to the central nature of the problem: Did heavenly voices really converse with her, or did she draw solely on what we should loosely call her imagination, but what psychologists like Myers might prefer more technically to call her subliminal self?

We can only attempt some kind of an answer to the question by reflecting for a moment on the nature of the voices and visions. In the first place we may note that she declared them always to have been accompanied by a light—which is, I understand, a manifestation commonly claimed by those who are privileged to see visions. In the second place we may also note that she insisted very strongly on the fact of having apprehended them with the bodily senses—she "saw them with her bodily eyes," i.e. not only in her imagination; touched their limbs, felt their warmth, heard their voices, and smelt their agreeable odour. But, although Jeanne herself stuck consistently to this point, the sceptic is at liberty to dismiss it, if he wishes, as part of her general delusion. There is nothing absolutely conclusive in personal assertions which cannot be corroborated by independent evidence. On the other hand there is the very curious fact that she sometimes disobeyed her heavenly orders. If this be true, and if we disregard Mr. Lang's

[1]The Rev. C. C. Martindale, S.J., *What are Saints?* pp. 152-3.

theory (see Chapter XII, p. 253, footnote) that she only loyally *said* she had disobeyed them, in order to forestall any suspicion that her voices could ever have been at fault, we shall find it very hard to agree with the view that her voices only said what she wanted them to say, i.e. that they were no more than the expression of her own desires, and consequently of purely subjective origin. The arguments thus fall now in favour of subjective suggestion, and now in favour of a truly objective experience. It is most confusing. On the subjective side, it must be admitted that her few reluctant descriptions of the saints and their appearance conformed precisely to what might have been expected of a peasant's idea of celestial beings. On the subjective side, again, comes a point which I have never elsewhere seen mentioned: Why did Saint Michael continually, and Saint Gabriel occasionally, appear to her? In pursuance of the theory that certain favoured persons may be visited by the spirits of the dead, it may be argued that Saint Catherine and Saint Margaret, her two other familiars, might in fact have returned to earth in order to speak with her; but such an argument can in no way apply to Gabriel and Michael. Great archangels as Jeanne believed them to be, they remain the symbolic inventions of the human imagination: it is never claimed for them that they ever enjoyed a mortal existence. How, then, could the embodied semblance of these two mighty fictions have revisited an earth they had never inhabited as men? There is only one possible conclusion here: that Jeanne did indeed clothe them with mortal shape in her imagination, put crowns on their heads and wings on their shoulders— clothe them, in fact, in the very semblance she had been taught to expect of angels.

On the other hand, however, we have to remember that the first revelations came to her quite unexpectedly, to her surprise, alarm, and, indeed, consternation. They came unsought, and began by baffling her completely. Judging by her own account, there is no reason to suppose even that they were the outcome of some romantic serial story such as imaginative children love to tell themselves when alone. Many a child might have pictured itself, probably under another name, as the saviour of France; but Jeanne's instant rejection of the first warlike orders ("I said I was a poor girl, who did not know how to ride or how to conduct war") seems almost designed on purpose to enable us to dismiss this hypothesis. Besides, the voices began with no dramatic command; they began by telling her to be a good girl—surely a rather sober recommendation to be invented, even subconsciously, by a child avid for tales of adventure and derring-do?

It would seem, then, as though these strange manifestations were indeed imposed upon her from the outside, without any preparation or intention of her own. They happened, as it were, accidentally, and again we are left to wonder why. Certainly, she appears to have been an intensely pious child, and we know that she had been given religious instruction by that upright woman her mother, but was she any more conspicuously pious than many other girls of the same age and circumstances in the same century? Thousands of ignorant unlettered peasant girls of her day must have been equally and blindly pious; possibly equally virtuous; equally well informed as to the miseries of a war-ravaged France, even better informed if they chanced to live in the war-areas instead of at Domremy, which was relatively out of the way. But why the choice should have fallen upon Jeanne, who possessed no especial qualifications for her tremendous mission, remains a mystery which it seems impossible rationally to resolve.

iv

In saying that she possessed no especial qualifications it is necessary to make one important exception: she did possess the power to accomplish what she had undertaken. Her courage and conviction were superhuman. They were of the quality which admits no doubt and recognises no obstacle. Her own absolute faith was the secret of her strength. This is not at all the same thing as claiming for her that she was a great military genius, as even that cautious and experienced commander Marshal Foch has claimed. Her good sense we may freely acknowledge, and her gift, which Foch has pointed out, "of dealing with the situation as each new day presented it"; but, if we are to claim genius for her at all, we must be more comprehensive and less specific: we must grant her the genius of personality. No easier to define than charm or beauty, in Jeanne's case we can come somewhere near a definition by saying that this all-pervading forcefulness sprang from the intensity of her inner persuasions. This it is, as I have insisted in the foregoing pages, which raised her psychological value as a leader so far above her tactical or strategical value. It was her single-mindedness which enabled her to inspire disheartened men and to bend reluctant princes to her will.

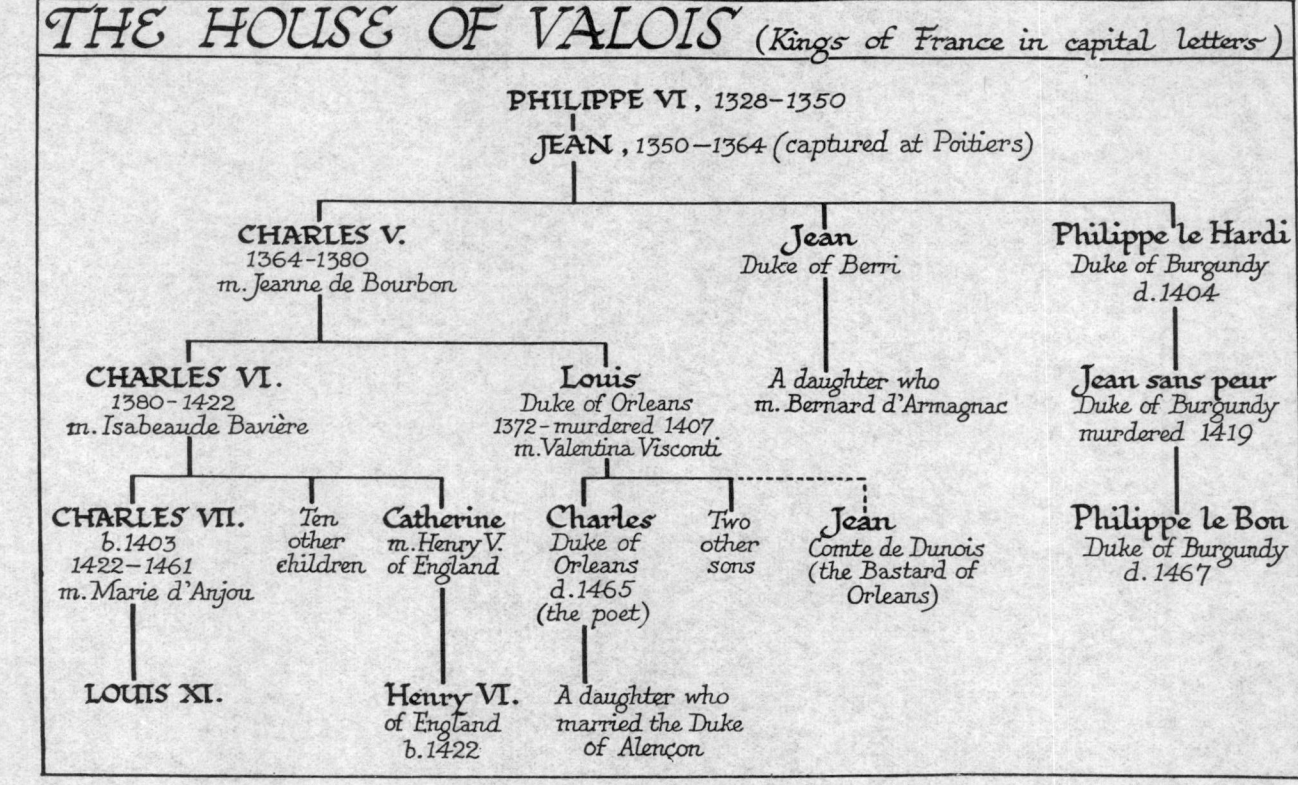

THE HOUSE OF VALOIS (Kings of France in capital letters)

PHILIPPE VI, 1328–1350

JEAN, 1350–1364 (captured at Poitiers)

- **CHARLES V.**
  1364–1380
  m. Jeanne de Bourbon
- **Jean**
  Duke of Berri
- **Philippe le Hardi**
  Duke of Burgundy
  d. 1404

- **CHARLES VI.**
  1380–1422
  m. Isabeaude Bavière
- **Louis**
  Duke of Orleans
  1372 – murdered 1407
  m. Valentina Visconti
- A daughter who
  m. Bernard d'Armagnac
- **Jean sans peur**
  Duke of Burgundy
  murdered 1419

- **CHARLES VII.**
  b. 1403
  1422–1461
  m. Marie d'Anjou
- Ten other children
- **Catherine**
  m. Henry V. of England
- **Charles**
  Duke of Orleans
  d. 1465
  (the poet)
- Two other sons
- **Jean**
  Comte de Dunois
  (the Bastard of Orleans)
- **Philippe le Bon**
  Duke of Burgundy
  d. 1467

- **LOUIS XI.**
- **Henry VI.**
  of England
  b. 1422
- A daughter who married the Duke of Alençon

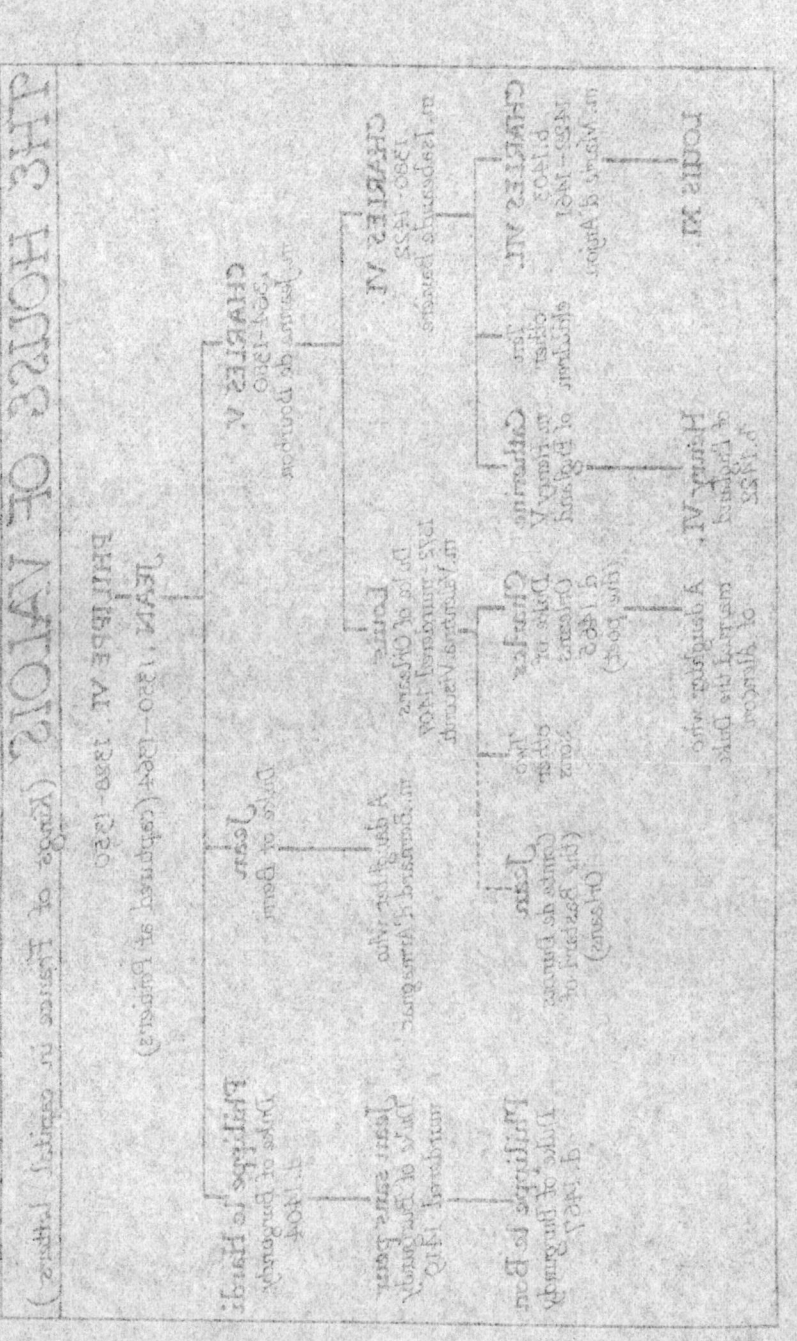

THE HOUSE OF VALOIS (Kings of France in italic capitals)

PHILIPPE VI, 1328-1350

JEAN, 1350-1364 (captured at Poitiers)

A MODERN JOAN OF ARC

(See Chap. V, p. 75)

I am indebted to the Rev. R. H. Steuart, S.J., for the following interesting letter about a peasant girl who did actually achieve something of the sort during the European War:

> DEAR MISS SACKVILLE-WEST,—The name of the girl in question is Claire Ferchaud—that at least is, I think, the right spelling. She claimed to have had a vision—or some sort of supernatural intimation—that the Allies would not win the War until the image of the Sacred Heart was added to the French flag—the tricolor! I understood that she succeeded in getting an interview with M. Poincaré, but I do not know what passed between them except that he was clearly unconvinced. Some people, clergy amongst them, believed at first in her "mission," but a *curé* to whom I spoke about the matter told me that she exhibited certain eccentricities and extravagances in her language and behaviour which before long lost her all her following. Of her subsequent history I know nothing. Such phenomena of quite sincere self-delusion are not uncommon in times of national crisis in France.

An account of Claire Ferchaud is given in the *Matin* of January 24th, 1932. She was a shepherd girl, born at Lamblade in 1895, who in 1915, at the age of twenty, heard voices in much the same way as Jeanne.

Appendix B

THE BREACH-OF-PROMISE ACTION

(See Chap. V, pp. 80–1)

I wish we knew more of the Toul affair. We cannot even be sure of the date when the case came into court. According to one computation at least, it was heard during the first days of February 1429, when Jeanne was on her way from Vaucouleurs to Nancy. One of Jeanne's most ardent admirers and ill-balanced biographers, Jean-Baptiste Joseph Ayroles, S.J., attempts an elaborate explanation which, in his eyes, partially covers the expedition to Nancy.[1] Père Ayroles suggests that Jacques d'Arc himself organised the breach-of-promise action, thus hoping by perjury to obtain (through the official interference of the diocese) that which he had been unable to attain by parental persuasion, i.e. the prevention of Jeanne's projected journey into France. With some ingenuity he almost induces us to believe that the distraught father pursued his daughter to Vaucouleurs, a suggestion which he supports in the first place by Jeanne's own statement that her father and mother nearly went out of their minds when she left for Vaucouleurs, and in the second place by the deposition of a then choirboy, later a priest, Jean le Fumeux, who stated that he remembered once seeing her father and mother at Vaucouleurs.[2] With the same ingenuity he argues (and this, I think, is the only point worth consideration in his case) that Jean de Metz, in escorting Jeanne as far as Toul on the first stage of her journey, leaving her to perform the four succeeding stages to Nancy without his escort, and returning post-haste to Vaucouleurs himself, must have had some very strong reason for his behaviour. This reason, Père Ayroles alleges, was his desire to observe how so controversial a person would comport herself before the tribunal, since there was an element of the greatest possible interest for all those desirous of estimating her true or

[1] *La vraie Jeanne d'Arc:* "La paysanne et l'inspirée," Vol. II, pp. 293–4.
[2] *Procès,* Vol. II, p. 460. Deposition of Jean le Fumeux.

false worth. Jean de Metz, in fact, would thus have been sent with her as a kind of spy, presumably by Robert de Baudricourt. To round off the explanation, a hint is thrown out that the motive of the Duke of Lorraine in sending a safe-conduct for Jeanne may not have been unconnected with his curiosity about the Toul affair.

The upshot of Père Ayroles' argument would be to fix the date of the breach-of-promise action as February 1429—not, in any case, a very important or interesting point, and it seems far more probable that it took place in July 1428.

Unfortunately for Père Ayroles, every clause in his argument, with one possible exception, is readily picked to pieces either by common sense or by a closer examination into the evidence. For one thing, it is scarcely likely that Jacques d'Arc would have devised the expedient of getting his own daughter dragged before the courts on so discreditable a charge: one is more ready to believe that he would have been, as he said, prepared to drown her in the defence of her virtue. For another, is it likely that, had he really been in Vaucouleurs with Jeanne at the time, and had he really engineered this summons to Toul, he would have allowed her to go off with Jean de Metz, and would not have gone also, in order to keep an eye on her? Thirdly, however, and most unfortunately for Père Ayroles, there is not a shred of reason for supposing that Jacques did pursue her to Vaucouleurs. True, he quotes the deposition of the choirboy Le Fumeux as to having once seen Jacques and Isabelle in Vaucouleurs; but conveniently forgets (*a*) that Jacques had probably journeyed to Vaucouleurs two years previous to Jeanne's arrival there, in order to transact business on behalf of his village with Robert de Baudricourt, so that Le Fumeux may equally well have seen him there on that occasion; and (*b*) that Jacques and Isabelle may well have gone to Vaucouleurs for no particular reason save a holiday jaunt. The only clause which seems to retain any sense at all is the one relative to Jean de Metz; for the rest, one hears nothing but the voice of the theorist determined to defend his case.

Père Ayroles even goes so far as to mention the names of two young men who might have been successively chosen by Jeanne's parents as their prospective son-in-law. These were the two young men whose testimony has already been quoted several times in the earlier chapters. Again, unfortunately for the reverend father, there is no word in either of their depositions to suggest any foundation that this was the fact. The first one, Michel Lebuin,[1] states that he knew her well; had sometimes accompanied her to Sainte Marie de Bermont; and knew that she frequently went to confession. The second young man suggested by Père Ayroles, Jean Waterin, also deposed[2] that he had known Jeanne well; had followed her father's plough with her; had played with her and the other children in the meadows, when, Jeanne withdrawing herself apart and, as it seemed to him, talking to God (*se trahebat ad partem et loquebatur Deo, ut sibi videbatur*), he joined with the others in making fun of her.

This is not at all the same thing as saying that they ever contemplated marriage with her.

---

[1] *Procès*, Vol. II, p. 439.　　　[2] *Procès*, Vol. II, p. 419.

Appendix C

LA PUCELLE

(See Chap. VII, p. 131)

"Gentil Dauphin, j'ai nom Jehanne la Pucelle." Thus she announced herself on first coming into the presence of Charles VII; a sobriquet which, once adopted at the outset of her public career, she never afterwards abandoned.

It is not surprising that she should have thus instantly and publicly declared herself as a virgin. If ever any woman justified a nickname based on so negative a profession, then surely she was the woman to do it. Not only had she taken a vow of virginity, but there were other reasons which dictated so wise and arrogant a declaration. The wisdom of it was obvious, for one whose career was going to take her into camp and Court, surrounded by soldiers and profligates; Jeanne was always sensible, and she knew about life. It was just as well to let the men know exactly how they stood. But there were other reasons which she would have been the last to disregard. Heavenly counsel had come to the support of worldly sagacity. Questioned later at her trial, she was able to reply that, even before the taking of Orleans, her voices had addressed her as Jeanne la Pucelle, daughter of God, and, as there is no reason to doubt her sincerity in this as in any other matter, it may be accepted that she believed the title to have received the sanction of Heaven in approval of her vow. Anyhow, having first adopted it officially at Chinon, she thereafter used it invariably in reference to herself. Even in her letter to the English, written before the taking of Orleans, it occurs no less than six times. And there can be no doubt but that she deserved it, whether personally or celestially bestowed, for, questioned again, she offered herself to examination, provided that such examination should be carried out by respectable women—as, indeed, it was, to their entire and doubtless critical satisfaction.

It is amusing that this single little word out of mediæval

French should have survived in current speech wholly in connexion with Jeanne. It is as though she had inadvertently conferred immortal life upon it. The dictionary (O. E. D.) gives it as *obs. exc. hist.*; yet to us, thanks to Jeanne, it is so familiar that we never stop to think about it. It is far more familiar to us in its French sense than in its English form, *puzzel*, which can mean something so surprisingly contradictory: a drab, slut, or courtesan—a contradiction which had evidently occurred to the author of the First Part of *King Henry VI*, and had given him the chance of a double pun on Jeanne and her king:

> Pucelle or puzzel, dolphin or dogfish,
> Your hearts I'll stamp out with my horse's heels,
> And make a quagmire of your mingled brains.
> Act I, scene iv.

JEANNE'S FIRST LETTER TO THE ENGLISH
March 22nd, 1429
(See Chap. VIII, pp. 151–4)

Au duc de Bethfort, soi disant régent le royaume de France ou à ses lieutenans estans devant la ville d'Orliens.

JHESUS, MARIA

Roy d'Angleterre, et vous, duc de Bethfort, qui vous dictes régent le royaume de France; vous, Guillaume de la Poule, conte de Suffort; Jehan, sire de Talebot; et vous, Thomas, sire d'Escales, qui vous dictes lieutenans dudit duc de Bethfort, faictes rason au Roy du ciel [de son sanc royal]; rendez à la Pucelle qui est cy envoiée de par Dieu, le roy du ciel, les clefs de toutes les bonnes villes que vous avez prises et violées en France. Elle est ci venue de par Dieu [le Roy du ciel] pour réclamer le sanc royal. Elle est toute preste de faire paix, se vous lui voulez faire raison, par ainsi que France vous mectrés jus et paierez de ce que l'avez tenue. Et entre vous, archiers, compaignons de guerre gentilz, et autres qui estes devant la [bonne] ville d'Orliens, alez-vous-en en vos païs, de par Dieu; et se ainsi ne le faictes, attendez nouvelles de la Pucelle qui vous ira voir briefment à vos bien grans dommaiges. Roy d'Angleterre, se ainsi ne le faictes, je suis chief de guerre, et en quelque lieu que je actaindray vos gens en France, je les en ferai aler, veuillent ou non veuillent, et si ne veullent obéir, je les ferai tous occire. Je suis cy envoiée de par Dieu, le roy du ciel, corps pour corps, pour vous bouter hors de toute France [encontre tous ceulx qui vouldroient porter traïson, malengin ne domaige au royaulme de France]. Et si veullent obéir, je les prandray à mercy. Et n'aïez point en vostre oppinion, que vous ne tendrez mie le royaume de France [de] Dieu, le Roy du ciel, filz [de] sainte Marie; ainz le tendra le roy Charles, vrai héritier; car Dieu, le Roy du ciel le veult, et lui est révélé par la Pucelle; lequel entrera à Paris à bonne compaignie. Se ne voulez croire les nouvelles de par Dieu et la Pucelle, en quelque lieu que vous trouverons, nous ferrons (*frapperons*) dedans [à horions[1]] et y ferons ung si grant hahay, que encore a-il mil ans que en France ne fu si grant,[2] se vous ne faictes raison.

Et croyez fermement que le Roy du ciel envoiera plus de force à la Pucelle, que vous ne lui sauriez mener de tous assaulx, à elle et à ses bonnes gens d'armes; et aux horions verra-on qui ara meilleur droit de Dieu du ciel [ou de vous]. Vous, duc de Bethfort, la Pucelle vous prie et vous requiert que vous ne vous faictes mie détruire. Si vous lui faictes raison, encore pourrez venir en sa compaignie, l'ou que les Franchois feront le plus bel fait que oncques fut fait pour la chrestienté. Et faictes response se vous voulez faire paix en la cité d'Orliens; et se ainsi ne le faictes, de vos bien grans domaiges vous souviengne briefment. Escript ce mardi [de la] sepmaine saincte.[3]

[De par la Pucelle.]

[1]Coup rudement déchargé (Littré).
[2]Fabre suggests that this phrase alludes to the invasion of France by Attila.
[3]At least five versions of this letter, with slight variants, are recorded. When it was read over to Jeanne during the trial (*Procès*, Vol. I, p. 55), she denied having dictated the words *rendez à la Pucelle; corps pour corps;* and *chef de guerre.*

Appendix E

THE STANDARD

(See Chap. VIII, p. 156)

It will be noticed that Jeanne's standard was painted, not embroidered. The work was entrusted to *Hauves Poulnoir, paintre, demourant à Tours*, for the sum of 25 *livres tournois*.[1] This Hauves Poulnoir or Poulvoir, was in reality a Scotsman named Hamish Power—a name with which French orthography was unable to cope, in spite of the presence of many Scotsmen in France at that time. His 25 *livres tournois* covered all his work on two banners, including the material, *ung grant estandart et ung petit pour la Pucelle*. The big standard, which was of white satin, was ornamented with a representation of Christ seated on the globe, supported by two angels, the groundwork being sprinkled with the golden lilies of France; the little banner, or *panon*, depicted the Annunciation, with an angel offering a lily to Our Lady.

[1] *Procès*, Vol. V, p. 258. The *livre tournois*, roughly speaking, was worth 6s. 8d., though, of course, its purchasing power was much greater.

Appendix F

LIST OF PERSONAGES CONCERNED IN THE TRIAL
(See Chap. XV, p. 311)

LES DEUX JUGES

Cauchon, Pierre, évêque de Beauvais; juge.

Lemaistre, Jean, bachelier en théologie, prieur des dominicains ou Frères Prêcheurs de Rouen, vice-inquisiteur; juge-adjoint.

OFFICIERS DE LA CAUSE

La Fontaine, Jean de, maître ès arts, licencié en droit canon, conseiller, commissaire et examinateur de la cause, délégué habituel de Cauchon.

Estivet, Jean d', chanoine de Beauvais et de Bayeux, promoteur de la cause, ou procureur général.

NOTAIRES

Manchon, Guillaume, prêtre, notaire impérial et apostolique près la cour ecclésiastique de Rouen, notaire pour Cauchon.

Colles, Guillaume, appelé aussi Bois-Guillaume; mêmes qualités.

Taquel, Nicolas; même profession, greffier ou notaire de la cause pour l'inquisition.

EXÉCUTEUR DES EXPLOITS

Massieu, Jean, prêtre, doyen de la cathédrale de Rouen.

ASSESSEURS OU CONSULTEURS
Docteurs en théologie

Adelie, Guillaume.

Beaupère, Jean.

Belorme, Martin, vicaire général du grand inquisiteur, à Paris.

Bonesgue, Jean de, aumônier de l'abbaye de Fécamp.

Boucher ou le Bouchier, Guillaume.

Carpentier ou Charpentier, Jean.

Castillon ou Chatillon, Jean Hulot de, archidiacre et chanoine d'Evreux.

Dierry, Pierre de, docteur en l'Université de Paris.

Du Fou, Jean.

Dupré, Richard.

Du Quesnay ou du Quesnoy, Maurice.

Duremort, Gilles de, abbé de la Ste-Trinité de Fécamp.

Emengard ou Ermengard, Erard.

Erard ou Evrard, Guillaume.

Feuillet, Gérard.

Fouchier, Jean.

Gilebert, Robert, anglais, doyen de la chapelle royale.

Graverand, Jean, dominicain, grand inquisiteur de France.

Gravestein, Jean.

Guesdon, Jacques, de l'ordre des FF. mineurs ou franciscains.

Houdenc, Pierre.

Lami, Nicolas.

Lefèvre ou Fabri, Jean.

Maurice, Pierre.

Midi, Nicolas, chanoine de Rouen.

Migiet, Pierre, prieur de Longueville-Giffard.

Nibat, Jean de.

Sabreuvois, Denis de.

Soquet, Jean.

Théroulde, Guillaume, abbé de Mortemer.

Touraine, Jacques de, nommé aussi J. Tessier ou Texier; en latin, Textoris.

Troyes, Jean de, doyen de la faculté de théologie de Paris.

Bacheliers en théologie

Baudrebois, Guillaume de.

Bourrilliet, Jean, dit François, prêtre, maître ès arts, licencié en décret.

Coppequesne ou Coupe-chêne, Nicolas.

Courcelles, Thomas de.

Duval, Jean.

Eude, Jean.

Grouchet, Richard de, chanoine de la Saussaye, au diocèse d'Evreux.

Haiton ou Heton, William, anglais.

Legagneur, Richard; en latin, Lucratoris.

Lemaistre, Guillaume.

Lemire ou le médecin: Medici, Nicolas.

Lermite, Guillaume.

Le Vautier, Jean.

Minier, Pierre.

Pigache, Jean.

Sauvage ou Saulvaige, Raoul. Radulfus Silvestris.

Docteurs en droits civil et canon (in utroque jure)

Bonnel, Guillaume, abbé de Cormeilles, au diocèse de Lisieux.

Conti, Guillaume de, abbé de la Trinité du Mont Ste-Catherine, près Rouen.

Guarin ou Guérin, Jean, chanoine de Rouen.

Roussel, Raoul, trésorier de l'eglise de Rouen.

Licenciés in utroque

Barbier, Robert, chanoine de Rouen.

Du Mesle, Guillaume, abbé de St-Ouen de Rouen.

Gastinel, Denis.

Labbé, Jean, dit Jean de Rouen, abbé de St-Georges de Boscherville.

La Crique, Pierre de.

Le Bourg, Guillaume, prieur de St-Lô de Rouen.

Moret, Jean, abbé de Préaux.

Docteurs en droit canon

Boisseau, Guérould, doyen de la faculté de décret à Paris.

Duchesne, Bertrand, religieux de l'Ordre de Cluny, doyen de Lihons en Santerre.

Fiefvet, Thomas.

Le Roux, Nicolas, abbé de Jumiéges.

Vaux, Pasquier des.

Licenciés en droit canon

Augny ou Auguy, Raoul, avocat en la cour ecclésiastique de Rouen.

Basset, Jean, official de Rouen.

Brullot, Jean, chantre de la cathédrale de Rouen.

Carré, Pierre, avocat en ladite cour.

Colombel, Jean, idem.

Dubut, Laurent, id.

Duchemin, Jean, id.

Ledoux, Jean, id.

Maréchal, Pierre.

Mauger ou Maugier, Jean, chanoine de Rouen.

Morel, Aubert, avocat en ladite cour.

Pinchon, Jean.

Postel ou Poustel, Guérould, avocat en ladite cour.

Saulx, Richard de, id.

Venderès, Nicolas de, archidiacre d'Eu en la cathédrale de Rouen.

Licenciés en droit civil

A l'Epee ou Alespée, Jean, chanoine de Rouen.

Carreau ou Carrel, Pierre.

Caval, Nicolas, chanoine de Rouen.

Cave, Pierre.

Cormeilles, Bureau de, avocat en la cour ecclésiastique de Rouen, chanoine de la cathédrale.

Crotay ou Crotoy, Geoffrey du, id.

Deschamps, Gilles, chancelier et chanoine de la cathédrale de Rouen.

Livet, Guillaume de, avocat à ladite cour.

Marguerie, André.

Maulin, Nicolas.

Tavernier, Jean, avocat à ladite cour.

Docteurs en médécine

Canivet ou Quenivet, Gilles.

De la Chambre, Guillaume.

De la Mare, Simon, maître ès arts et en médécine.

Desjardins, Guillaume.

L'écrivain, Roland. Rolandus Scriptoris.

Tiphaine ou Epiphanie, Jean.

Tybout, Henri, maître ès arts et en médécine à Paris.

Maîtres ès arts[1] (consultés ou mentionnés)

Abessore, Richard, à Paris.

Barrey, Jean, idem.

Bereth, Martin, maître ès arts à Paris, un anglais.

Gouda, Pierre de, id., recteur de l'Université.

Hébert, Michel, id., greffier de l'Université.

Lefourbeur, Raoul, notaire de l'inquisition à Paris.

Loutrée, Boémond de. Bohemundus de Lutrea, grand bedeau de la nation de France en l'Université de Paris.

Nourrisseur, Jacques, Université de Paris.

Oscohart, Guillaume, id.

Pelé, André, id.

Trophard, Jean, id.

Cardinal

Beaufort, Henri de, évêque de Winchester, cardinal du titre romain de St-Eusèbe, appelé aussi le cardinal d'Angleterre.

Évêques

Alnwick, William, évêque de Nordwich, en Angleterre.

Castiglione, Zanon de, évêque de Lisieux.

Luxembourg, Louis de, évêque de Thérouenne.

Mailly, Jean de, évêque de Noyon.

Montjeu, Philibert de, évêque de Coutances.

[1]Ce grade correspond à celui que nous nommons aujourd'hui licenciés ès lettres. Il n'y avait pas de docteurs ès arts, mais seulement des bacheliers et des maîtres.

Abbés et prieurs

Dacier, Jean, abbé de Ste-Corneille de Compiègne.

Frique, Thomas, abbé du Bec-Hélouin.

Jolivet ou Lejolivet, Robert, abbé du Mont St-Michel-au-péril-de-la-mer.

Prêtres ou clercs, consultés ou mentionnés

Amouret, Thomas, religieux dominicain.

Bats, Frère Jean de. Frater Johannes de Bastis.

Cateleu, Eustoche ou Eustache, prêtre.

Champrond, Enguerrand de, official de Coutances.

De la Pierre, Frère Isambard, dominicain.

Dudesart, Guillaume, chanoine de Rouen.

Foville, Nicolas de, id.

Guérould, Robert, notaire du chapitre de Rouen.

Hampton, John ou Jean de, prêtre anglais.

Ladvenu, Frère Martin, dominicain.

Le Cauchois, Guillaume, prêtre.

Le Duc, Laurent, id.

Legrand, Guillaume, id.

Lejeune, Regnauld, id.

Lermite, Frère Guillaume.

Le Roy, Jean, chanoine de Rouen.

Loiselleur, Nicolas, maître ès arts, chanoine de Rouen.

Mahommet, Jean, prêtre.

Manchon, Jean, chanoine de Mantes.

Morel ou Morelet, Robert, chanoine de Rouen.

Rosay, Jean, curé de Duclair.

Vacheret, Jean, grand bedeau de la faculté de théologie de Paris.

Valée, Frère Jean, dominicain.

Assistants ou témoins appelés

Bosquier, Pierre, religieux dominicain.

Brolbster ou Brewster, William, prêtre anglais.

Camus ou le Camus, Jacques, prêtre, chanoine de Reims.

Carbonnier, Jean.

Cochon, Pierre, prêtre, notaire de la cour de Rouen.

Fécard, Jean, avocat.

Hubant ou Hubent, Nicolas de, notaire apostolique.

Le Bateur, Matthew, prêtre du diocèse de Londres.

Lecras, Guillaume, prêtre, notaire en la cour de Rouen.

Le Danois ou Dani, Simon, prêtre, id.

Luxembourg, Jean de, comte de Ligny, seigneur de Beaurevoir, etc.

Mathieu, Jean, prêtre.

Milet, Adam, secrétaire du roi d'Angleterre.

Orient, Pierre.

Orsel, Louis, clerc du diocèse de Noyon.

Toutmouillé, Jean, dominicain.

TRANSLATION OF THE LATIN TEXT GIVEN IN
FACSIMILE OPPOSITE P. 364

. . . than to have the dress of a woman. Item, she said she had resumed it because the promises made to her had not been kept, viz. that she should hear Mass and receive the Body of Christ, and should be taken out of irons.

Asked if she had not previously abjured, and particularly sworn not to resume this male dress, she replied that she would sooner die than be in irons, but that if they would allow her to go to Mass, and would take her out of irons, she would be good and would do what the Church wanted.

Item, as we, the judges, had been informed by certain persons that she was not yet detached from the illusions of her supposed revelations, which she had previously renounced, we asked her whether she had not heard the voices of Saints Catherine and Margaret since Thursday: she replied that she had.

Fatal reply. Asked what they said to her, she replied that God sent to her, through Saints Catherine and Margaret, great pity for the great betrayal she had consented to in the abjuration and revocation to save her life, and that she was damning herself in order to save her life.

Item, she said that before Thursday her voices had told her what she would do, and what she did on that day. She said, also, that her voices told her, when she was on the scaffold or pulpit, before the populace, that she should boldly answer the preacher who was then preaching. This Johanna said that he was a false preacher, who said she had done several things she had not done. Item, she said that if she were to say that God did not send [her] . . .

THE SIGN GIVEN TO THE KING

(See Chap. XV, p. 338; and Chap. XVII, p. 366)

We have already seen what Jeanne said, or, rather, refused to say, about the mysterious revelation made by her at Chinon to Charles VII (pp. 132–6), and also the curious symbolical story she invented in order to escape from the pressing questions of her judges; but it is impossible not to round off the subject without referring to the controversial document appended to the report of the trial.

This document is dated Thursday, June 7th, 1431, and takes its place in the official record (*Quædam acta posterius*). It purports to be an account of Jeanne's last admissions, made on the morning of her death. According to this account, she was visited in the early hours by Loiseleur and Maurice, Ladvenu and Toutmouillé, Le Camus and de Courcelles finally accompanying Cauchon himself. Still according to this account, they extracted certain statements from her:

(1) that her voices and visions had deceived her (Ladvenu; Maurice; Toutmouillé; Le Camus; de Courcelles; Loiseleur);

(2) that the story of the angel and the crown was nothing but an invention (Ladvenu; Maurice; Toutmouillé; Loiseleur), and that she herself was the only angel.

Is this document a forgery or not? It was dismissed as such by de l'Averdy[1] owing to the fact that Manchon refused to sign it.[2] Quicherat, however, while admitting that it remains "an insoluble problem," is unwilling to class the document as a forgery from beginning to end. He prefers to regard it as a collection of fragments left over from a final interrogation which, for some reason, was not included in the report of Jeanne's last day on earth—May 30th—and observes, with

[1] *Notices des manuscrits*, Vol. III, pp. 447–60.

[2] *Procès*, Vol. II, p. 14: Deposition of Guillaume Manchon: *Il ne fut point à quelque certain examen de gens qui parlèrent à elle à part, comme personnes privées; néantmoins monseigneur de Beauvais le voulut contraindre à ce signer; laquelle chose ne voulut faire.*

much plausibility, that *un habile homme comme l'évêque de Beauvais exagère ou réduit la verité: il ne forge pas de toutes pièces le mensonge.*[1] In support of his view that the document represents a partial truth, he points out (1) that the testimony of de Courcelles, the *rédacteur* of the *procès-verbal*, is included; (2) that the document was accepted as genuine by the doctors at the Rehabilitation; (3) that Taquel, himself one of the notaries, mentions having been present in the cell during an interrogation on the morning of the martyrdom. (Why then, a point not raised by Quicherat, did they not get Taquel to attest the document, Manchon having refused to do so on the plea that he had not been present?) The suspicious fact, of course, remains that the document is not signed by any of the notaries; that Manchon flatly refused to sign it; and that, unlike the rest of the *procès-verbal*, it is not attested by any of the notaries on every page. We can scarcely blame Quicherat for calling the problem insoluble, yet at the same time it is impossible not to agree with him that the Bishop of Beauvais was not likely to forge such a document in its entirety, especially as he was quoting several witnesses, any one of whom might have betrayed him at any moment.

It is worth calling attention to one small point which Quicherat ignores in this place, though he alludes to it elsewhere, and which does not sound to me like an invention of Cauchon or another. This is Jeanne's remark, reported by Ladvenu, Maurice, and Toutmouillé, that her apparitions sometimes came to her in the guise of minute things (*quantitate minima: sub specie quarumdam rerum minimarum; minimus rebus*). Mr. Maclaurin[2] comments, with apologetic cynicism, that he "hates to suggest that these specks before the eyes may have been the result of toxæmia from the intestine induced by confinement and terror." M. Marcel Hébert[3] makes a more interesting contribution to the subject by drawing a comparison between Jeanne's statement and that of Saint Rose of Lima, who saw Jesus in the size of a finger.

[1] *Aperçus nouveaux*, pp. 138–144.
[2] *Post-mortem*, p. 60.   [3] *Jeanne d'Arc, a-t-elle abjuré?*

Appendix I

THE FAMILY OF JEANNE D'ARC

It may be asked, What happened to the family of Jeanne d'Arc after her death? We know that they were granted a patent of nobility in December 1429, under the name of du Lys. The patent, which conferred nobility on Jeanne herself, her father, mother, brothers, and all their kindred, with all their descendants both in the male and female line, makes no mention of armorial bearings, but we know from Jeanne that they were accorded the right to bear the lilies of France and a sword on a field azure.[1] She herself never exercised the privilege of bearing these arms, but her brothers did.

We know, further, that Jean and Pierre du Lys, her brothers, married and begot a numerous posterity. Jean, who succeeded Robert de Baudricourt as governor of Vaucouleurs from 1455 to 1468, was the grandfather of Claude du Lys, to whom, it is thought, we owe much of the preservation and restoration of Jeanne's birthplace. Pierre accompanied his mother to Orleans, where she died in 1458. He did not long outlive her, and his descendants peter out by the middle of the seventeenth century, or, at any rate, disappear from history.

Jacques d'Arc is said to have died, in 1431, of the sorrow caused him by his daughter's tragic death.

[1] *Procès,* Vol. I, p. 117.

WAS JEANNE D'ARC OF ROYAL BIRTH?

In 1805 and 1819 a certain M. P. Caze published two works on Jeanne d'Arc, the first work an opuscule, the second a work in two volumes. The gist of these labours goes to prove that in 1407 the Queen of France, Isabeau de Bavière, gave birth to a child named Jeanne, the adulterous offspring of her liaison with the Duke of Orleans; that this child was farmed out to some labourers in Lorraine named d'Arc; and that the *curé* of Domremy was deputed to inform her of her pre-ordained mission, while two well-born ladies from the neighbouring villages of Commercy and Gondrecourt played the part of Saint Catherine and Saint Margaret.

In 1932, M. Jean Jacoby, basing his conclusion on an apparently extensive study on the same subject, which had occupied some twenty years of his father's life, produced a volume entitled *Le secret de Jeanne d'Arc*. His thesis was in main the same as that of M. Caze, and, as a study in determination to prove a point, is well worth reading. His version of the story is as follows: In February 1403, Isabeau de Bavière, Queen of France, gave birth to a son, later known as Charles VII. Four years then elapsed, interrupting the stream of her fertility; but in November 1407 she again gave birth to a son, who received the name of Philippe, and who died on the same day as he was born. So far, at least, M. Jacoby is in accordance with accepted historical fact. But then the fascination of the thesis begins to work. This poor little prince has behaved in the most untactful way. To begin with, he never ought to have been born at all, since he is really the son of Louis d'Orléans and not of the mad King Charles VI. But, having been born, he commits the further mistake of living, not dying. He commits the equally grave mistake of being a girl, not a boy. So here is the Queen, landed with an illegitimate child, whom she has not the heart to destroy (*Isabelle est une épouse infidèle, mais non une mère dénaturée*);

a child, moreover, which insists on being of the wrong sex. What was to be done?

Prince Philippe de Valois officially died; the little living girl was taken away to Lorraine and handed over to the care of Jacques d'Arc and Isabelle Romée. She was christened Jeanne, a name which, as M. Jacoby gravely remarks, was in the Valois family. At some time during her childhood the secret of her birth was revealed to her—M. Jacoby is not very explicit as to the date or means—and henceforward everything becomes plain sailing. Her devotion to France is explained, since she is really a French princess; her devotion to the Dauphin likewise, since he is her brother; her devotion to the captive Duke of Orleans, since he is her brother also; and to the Bastard for the same reason. It becomes quite a family party. Most satisfactory of all, the famous "King's Secret" is explained.

Unfortunately for M. Jacoby, the foundations of his belief are of the slightest. Passing without comment over the fact that the accepted date of Jeanne's birth, January 1412, has to be altered to November 1407 to fit his theory, thus adding over four years to her age, what do we find as the basis of his allegations? We find:

(1) That Jeanne, in addressing the Duke of Alençon, remarked, "The more of the royal blood of France are together, the better." This M. Jacoby takes to mean that Jeanne was including herself with the Dauphin and d'Alençon.

(2) The opening of the comte d'Armagnac's letter to Jeanne, calling her *ma très chère dame*.

(3) Two lines in a poem by Martin le Franc:

> Et pour un fier prince conté -
> Non pas pour simple bergère.

(4) The title of princess by which an Italian, Lorenzo Buonincontro, refers to her.

(5) The support accorded her by the Archbishop of Embrun.

(6) The enormous ransom paid for her, and the words employed by Cauchon to the effect that "all prisoners, whether the King, the

Dauphin, or other princes," might be purchased or taken by the King of England.

(7) The fact that Jeanne wore the colours of Orleans and their heraldic nettles, and that the coat-of-arms granted to her family included the lilies of France.

(8) Her indifference to her d'Arc family after her departure from Domremy. The fact that her two brothers were continuously at her side, and that her father met her at Reims, does not seem to trouble M. Jacoby.

(9) Her adoption of the sobriquet *La Pucelle*, instead of the surname d'Arc or even Romée.

(10) Last, and above all, her popular name of Pucelle d'Orléans. This, according to M. Jacoby, means that Jeanne called herself la Pucelle d'Orléans just as the Bastard called himself le Bâtard d'Orléans, and for the same reason, i.e. that he was a child of that royal house.

One other observation of M. Jacoby must be recorded: "Public opinion already at that time knew perfectly well how to distinguish between the legend of the shepherdess and the princely reality." If this is so, it seems curious that no contemporary record should even allude to this surely interesting truth.

THE MIRACLES OF JEANNE D'ARC

How far is it possible to claim a genuine miracle for Jeanne? Let us recapitulate very briefly the occasions which have given rise to such a claim, apart from the major problem of the visions and voices.

(1) The recognition of Robert de Baudricourt. This, I think can easily be disposed of when we remember (*a*) that her father may have seen and subsequently described him; (*b*) that Jeanne may have heard many other people describe him, who was, after all, a prominent personage in the region; (*c*) that she may herself have seen him riding through the streets of Vaucouleurs before she was actually granted an interview. (See Chapter V, pp. 68–73.)

(2) The recognition of the Dauphin. This may be explained in the same way. Jeanne had been for eleven days in the company of Jean de Metz, Poulengy, and Colet de Vienne, himself a royal messenger, and it is improbable that she should not have questioned them about the physical appearance of the man she so desired to meet. It must be remembered, also, that she spent two days in Chinon before being admitted to his presence, when she would have had ample opportunity of questioning her hosts or the townsfolk about him. (See Chapter VII, pp. 130–1.)

(3) The sword of Fierbois. This is much more difficult to explain away. The sceptical may suggest that she had heard a local legend, and indeed such legends must have abounded in connexion with a church where grateful soldiers came to deposit their arms as votive offerings. Even so, the precision of her directions must continue to puzzle us much as they puzzled her contemporaries. (See Chapter VIII, pp. 154–6.)

(4) The change of wind at Orleans. It is impossible to take this "miracle" seriously. Jeanne was a country girl, well accustomed to observe impending changes in the weather.

Besides, the matter was probably greatly exaggerated by those, including the Bastard, who were determined to believe in her mission and to make others believe in it. (See Chapter IX, p. 175.)

(5) The child resuscitated at Lagny. Here, medical ignorance and subsequent exaggeration were probably responsible for the attribution of the "miracle." The child was said to have been dead for three days and to have been black in the face. Jeanne joined the girls of the town in their prayers before the image of Our Lady, when the child gasped, drew breath, lived long enough to be baptised, and then irrevocably died. Jeanne, therefore, was not solely responsible. "If," as Mr. Lang says, "it were a sin to pray, and were sorcery to receive a favourable answer, at least the prayer was collective, and all the maids of Lagny were greatly guilty." (See Chapter XIII, p. 275.)

(6) The leap from Beaurevoir. I have gone into this question at some length in the text (Chapter XIV, pp. 289–94), so need not recapitulate the facts here. On the whole, I find it the most difficult of Jeanne's "miracles" to explain away, but am still not convinced that it will never be found susceptible of rational explanation.

(7) The question of second-sight or prophecy. Here we have at least two examples, one of them fairly well established and the other established beyond any possible doubt. To take them in order:

(a) Jeanne's knowledge of the battle of Rouvray (see Chapter VII, p. 113) on the very day of its occurrence, and the information given by her to Baudricourt before the news could possibly have reached her by normal means. Our authorities for this are the *Journal du siège d'Orléans*[1] (*elle avoit sceu véritablement le jour et l'heure de la journée des Harens, ainsi qu'il fut trouvé par les lettres de Baudricourt*), and the *Chronique de la Pucelle*,[2] which is really very little more than a rehash of the *Journal du siège* and of Jean Chartier. There is thus no evidence given here *before* the event, or even on the day of the

[1] *Procès*, Vol. IV, pp. 125 and 128.   [2] *Procès*, Vol. IV, pp. 206 and 208.

event, to convince us that the chroniclers were not improving on the story in order to enhance the credit of their heroine. It is well known that chroniclers have not always been scrupulous about such embroideries, though, on the whole, the claims made for Jeanne have been far less extravagant than those frequently made for other saints. This particular point must remain inconclusive.

(b) Jeanne's prescience of her wound at Orleans. This is quite another matter. Here we have evidence, written in a letter a fortnight before the event, that she would be wounded in battle before Orleans though she would not lose her life[1] (ed quod ipsa ante Aureliam in conflictu telo vulnerabitur, sed inde non morietur). We have also the subsequent evidence of Paquerel, her confessor, to the effect that she told him overnight she would be wounded on the morrow, and that blood would flow from her body above the breast.[2] This is certainly not as convincing as, though far more precise than, the evidence of the letter, but in the circumstances it may be accepted as a corroboration of her foreknowledge. On the other hand, it may be argued that Jeanne thought it extremely likely that she would receive a wound at Orleans; it was the first time she ever went into battle, and she perhaps naturally felt some apprehension (in other words, was frightened), which her belief in her heavenly mission immediately qualified: "I shall be hurt, but I shall not die." How, indeed, could the appointed saviour of France lose her life at the very outset of her career? Such an idea was a contradiction in terms. It was natural that she should anticipate a wound; it was equally natural, Jeanne being what she was, that she would refuse to anticipate that wound as mortal. Without undue scepticism, we may suggest that this prophecy had its origin in likelihood rather than in supernatural instruction. Still, the fact remains that it was recorded a fortnight before the event. We cannot evade that

[1]Procès, Vol. IV, p. 426: Lettre du greffier de la Chambre des Comptes de Brabant, Lyon, April 22nd, 1429.
[2]Procès, Vol. III, p. 109: Deposition of Jean Paquerel.

fact, and it must remain as our most authentic example of her gift of prophecy. (See Chapter X, pp. 202 and 206.)

The other prophecies—that the siege of Orleans would be raised, the English driven from France, the Dauphin crowned at Reims, Paris restored to obedience, and the Duke of Orleans delivered from captivity—may be regarded as the confident expression of a wish rather than as in the nature of knowledge of the future. In point of fact, only two of these prophecies were fulfilled during Jeanne's lifetime—the raising of the siege, and the coronation at Reims—though, according to the Duke of Alençon, Jeanne always spoke as though they were all to be accomplished before her death.[1] Again according to d'Alençon, she was in the habit of saying that she would last a year only, or not much longer—a prophecy which came only too tragically true, although she went wrong in believing that all her tasks would be carried out during the one year of her activity.

The words addressed to the man who insulted her at the entrance to Chinon (see Chapter VII, p. 130) can scarcely be taken as anything but a coincidence. They cannot rank as prophecy. What, exactly, did Jeanne say? She said, "You deny God, and you so near to your death!" To Jeanne, bringing not peace, but a sword, any man-at-arms was a man near to his death. It was a remark she might have addressed to any irreverent soldier, and possibly did address to many whom she heard using oaths distasteful to her; only, in this case, the man happened to get drowned before he could get killed in battle, and the pious Paquerel recorded her words with gusto as an example of her divine inspiration.

With the warning of her impending captivity, given to her at Melun (see Chapter XIII, p. 273), we cannot deal here, since it comes under the general heading of revelations made by the

---

[1] *Procès*, Vol. III, p. 99: Deposition of the Duke of Alençon. This is borne out by a letter written by Pancrazio Justiniani, in Bruges, on May 10th, 1429, to his father Marco Justiniani who received it in Venice on June 18th (*Chronique d'Antonio Morosini*, Vol. III, pp. 54–5).

voices. We must not, however, forget the incident of the King's prayer (see Chapter VII, pp. 132–6), which, if we accept the report of the Abbréviateur du Procès, and others, as true, is explicable only by assuming telepathy or thought-reading. The "miracles," properly speaking, thus do not appear to amount to very much. The real miracle was the whole career, not a few isolated incidents.

CHRONOLOGICAL TABLE

The Hundred Years' War begins	1337
Kings of England:	
Edward III	1327–1377
Richard II	1377–1399
Henry IV	1399–1413
Henry V	1413–1422 Aug. 31st
Henry VI., b. 1421, succeeded aged nine months	1422–1461 (died 1471)
Kings of France:	
Charles V	1364–1380
Charles VI	1380–1422 Oct. 21st
Charles VII	1422–1461 July 22nd
BIRTH OF JEANNE D'ARC	1412 Jan. 6th probably
The Treaty of Troyes	1420
Jeanne first hears the voices	1424 Midsummer probably
First visit to Vaucouleurs	1428 May
Flight to Neufchâteau	1428 July
Second visit to Vaucouleurs	1429 Jan.–Feb.
Expedition to Nancy	1429 Feb.
(Battle of Rouvray, or Battle of the Herrings)	1429 Feb. 12th
Jeanne leaves Vaucouleurs for Chinon	1429 Feb. 23rd
At St. Urbain	1429 Feb. 24th
At Auxerre	1429 Feb. 27th (approx.)
At Gien	1429 March 1st (approx.)
At St. Catherine de Fierbois	1429 March 4th–5th
Arrival at Chinon	1429 March 6th
Received by the Dauphin	1429 March 9th (approx.)
At Chinon, Poitiers, Tours, and Blois	1429 March–April
Leaves Blois for Orleans	1429 April 25th
Arrival before Orleans	1429 April 28th
The night spent at Chécy	1429 April 28th–29th
Enters Orleans	1429 April 29th
At Orleans	1429 April 29th–May 10th
Journée des Tourelles	1429 May 7th
The siege raised	1429 May 8th
Departure from Orleans	1429 May 10th
At Tours	1429 May 10th–11th
At Loches	1429 ? May 12th–23rd

At or near Selles en Berri	1429	? May 24th–June 6th
At Romorantin	1429	June 6th
At Orleans	1429	? June 9th–10th
Capture of Jargeau	1429	June 11th–12th
At Orleans	1429	June 13th–14th
At Meung-sur-Loire	1429	June 15th
Capture of Beaugency	1429	June 16th–17th
Between Beaugency and Meung	1429	June 17th
Battle of Patay	1429	June 18th
At Orleans, Sully, St. Benoit, and Châteauneuf	1429	June 19th–24th
At Gien	1429	June 24th–27th
In camp in the fields	1429	? June 27th–29th
On the way to Reims	1429	June 30th
Before Auxerre	1429	July 1st, 2nd or 3rd
At St. Florentin	1429	July 4th
At St. Phal	1429	July 5th
Before Troyes	1429	July 5th–11th
Entry into Troyes	1429	? July 5th–12th
At Bussy-Lettré	1429	July 13th–14th
At Chalons-sur-Marne	1429	July 14th–15th
At Sept-Saulx	1429	July 16th
At Reims	1429	July 16th–21st
Charles VII crowned	1429	July 17th
Charles VII and Jeanne leave Reims	1429	July 21st
At Cerbeuy (St. Marcoul)	1429	July 21st
At Vailly	1429	July 22nd
At Soissons	1429	July 23rd–28th
At Château-Thierry	1429	July 29th
At Montmirail-en-Brie	1429	Aug. 1st
At Provins (Nangis, Bray)	1429	Aug. 2nd–5th
At Coulommiers and Château-Thierry	1429	Aug. 7th
At La Ferté Milon	1429	Aug. 10th
At Crépy-en-Valois	1429	Aug. 11th
At Lagny-le-Sec	1429	Aug. 12th
At Dammartin and Thieux	1429	Aug. 13th
At Baron and Montepilloy	1429	Aug. 14th
Battle of Montepilloy	1429	Aug. 14th–15th
At Crépy-en-Valois	1429	Aug. 16th–17th
At Compiègne	1429	Aug. 18th–23rd
At St. Denis and La Chapelle	1429	Aug 26th–Sept. 8th
Attack on Paris (Jeanne wounded)	1429	Sept. 8th
La Chapelle and St. Denis	1429	Sept. 9th

At St. Denis	1429	Sept. 10th and 13th
Departure from St. Denis for the Loire	1429	Sept. 13th
Lagny, Provins, Bray, Sens, Courtenay, Château-renard, Montargis, Gien	1429	Sept. 14th–21st
Meung-sur-Yèvre, Bourges	1429	October
St. Pierre-le-Moutier	1429	Oct. and Nov.
Moulins	1429	Nov. 9th
Attack on La Charité-sur-Loire	1429	Nov. 24th
Meung-sur-Yèvre	1429	Dec.
Orleans	1429	Dec. 19th
Jargeau?	1429	? Dec. 25th
Jeanne's family ennobled, with surname du Lys	1429	Dec. 29th
Sully	1430	March 3rd–28th
Leaves Sully	1430	March or April
Lagny—Battle of Lagny	1430	April
Melun	1430	April 17th–23rd
Senlis, Compiègne, Berenglise near Elincourt, Ste. Marguerite, Soissons, Crépy-en-Valois	1430	April
Compiègne and Pont l'Evêque	1430	May 14th–15th
Soissons	1430	? May 18th
Crépy-en-Valois	1430	? May 19th
Leaves Crépy-en-Valois	1430	May 22nd—midnight
Compiègne and assault on Margny; Jeanne taken prisoner	1430	May 23rd
Clairoix	1430	May 23rd–25th
At Beaulieu, a prisoner	1430	? May, June, July
Beaurevoir	1430	? Mid-July–mid-Nov.
Arras, St. Riquier, Drugy, Le Crotoy	1430	Nov.
St. Valéry, Eu, Dieppe, Rouen	1430	Dec.
Prisoner in a tower of castle of Phillipe Auguste, Rouen	1430	Dec. 25th ? to May 30th, 1431
Delivered to the Inquisition and the Church by the English	1431	Jan. 3rd
Trial begun	1431	Jan. 9th
The recantation	1431	May 24th
Burnt at the stake	1431	May 30th
Examination of witnesses for the rehabilitation begins, under the direction of Guillaume Bouillé	1450	

Resumed under Cardinal d'Estouteville, Bishop of Digne, and Jean Bréhal, Inquisitor of France	1452	
Continued by order of Pope Calixtus III	1455–6	
The sentence revoked by Pope Calixtus III	1456	July
Formal proposal entered for canonisation	1903	February
Pope Pius X gives her the title of Venerable	1904	January
Decree of beatification	1909	April 11th
Canonised by Pope Benedict XV	1920	May 16th

A SHORT BIBLIOGRAPHY

I. THE TRIAL: TEXTS AND TRANSLATIONS

Procès de condamnation et de réhabilitation de Jeanne d'Arc. JULES QUICHERAT. 5 volumes. (Jules Renouard et Cie, 1861.)
This is the standard work, and is referred to as *Procès* in my footnotes throughout. It is out of print and not easily obtainable.

Procès de condamnation de Jeanne d'Arc. PIERRE CHAMPION. 2 volumes. (Honoré et Edouard Champion, 1921.)
The first volume gives the Latin text; the second, an introduction, a French translation of the Latin text, and many notes.

Procès de condamnation de Jeanne d'Arc. M. VALLET DE VIRIVILLE. 1 volume. (Firmin Didot frères, 1867.)
A French translation, with notes.

Jeanne d'Arc, Maid of Orleans. DOUGLAS MURRAY. 1 volume. (Heinemann, 1902.) Out of print.
An English translation, with a short but interesting introduction.

Procès de réhabilitation de Jeanne d'Arc. JOSEPH FABRE. 2 volumes. (Delagrave, 1888.) Out of print.
A French translation of the evidence of the witnesses. Not as reliable or accurate as it might be, but is the only complete one I know of.

Les deux procès de condamnation, les enquêtes et la sentence de réhabilitation de Jeanne d'Arc. E. O'REILLY. 2 volumes. (Plon, 1868.)
A French translation with an introduction and notes. Confusing.

Chronique de la Pucelle, Geste des Nobles, and *Chronique normande.* M. VALLET DE VIRIVILLE. 1 volume. (Garnier frères.)

La vraie Jeanne d'Arc. J.-B. J. AYROLES, S.J. 5 volumes. (1890–1902.)
   (1) "La Pucelle devant l'église de son temps."
   (2) "La paysanne et l'inspirée."
   (3) "La libératrice."
   (4) "La vierge-guerrière."
   (5) "La martyre."
An immense, unreliable, and almost hysterically prejudiced work.

II. LIVES OF JEANNE D'ARC

The Maid of France. ANDREW LANG. 1 volume. (Longmans, Green & Co., 1908.)
Accurate and reliable as to facts and references; readable, Agreement with

Lang's opinions must remain a matter of personal taste. Inclines to be sentimental and picturesque. On the whole, the best English biography of Jeanne.

Vie de Jeanne d'Arc. ANATOLE FRANCE. 2 volumes. (Calmann-Levy, 1908.)
A controversial, brilliant work, which may infuriate, but can never bore, the reader. References as to sources of information unbelievably inaccurate: mistrust them all.

Joan of Arc. MILTON WALDMAN. 1 volume. (Longmans, Green & Co., 1935.)
The most recent biography in English. I am unable to comment on this book, which appeared while I was writing my own, so that I refrained from reading it.

Joan of Arc and England. JOHN LAMOND. 1 volume. (Rider & Co.)

Joan of Arc. GRACE JAMES. 1 volume. (Methuen.)

St. Joan of Arc. CHANOINE JUSTIN ROUSSEIL, translated by the REV. JOSEPH MURPHY, S.J. 1 volume. (Burns, Oates & Washbourne, 1925.)

Joan of Arc. A. BIGELOW PAINE. 2 volumes. (Macmillan, New York, 1925.)

Jeanne d'Arc. MRS. OLIPHANT. 1 volume. (Putnam, New York, 1896.)

Joan of Arc. HILAIRE BELLOC. 1 volume.

Jeanne d'Arc. GABRIEL HANOTAUX. 1 volume. (1911.)

Joan of Arc. FRANCIS C. LOWELL. 1 volume. (Boston, 1896.)

Jeanne d'Arc. H. WALLON. 2 volumes. (1860.)

The Maid of Orleans. REV. F. WYNDHAM. 1 volume. (1894.)

III. SPECIAL STUDIES

Jeanne d'Arc à Domremy. SIMÉON LUCE. 1 volume. (Champion, 1886.)
Indispensable; scholarly; interesting.

Aperçus nouveaux sur Jeanne d'Arc. JULES QUICHERAT. 1 volume. (Renouard, 1856.)
Various essays, all interesting, by Jeanne's most scholarly and incisive historian.

La première étape de Jeanne d'Arc. MARQUIS DE PIMODAN. 1 volume. (Champion, 1890 or thereabouts.)
A detailed study of the route followed by Jeanne and her companions on the first night of their journey to Chinon, from Vaucouleurs to St. Urbain.

Jeanne d'Arc écuyère. L. CHAMPION. 1 volume. (Berger-Levrault, 1901.)
A disappointing book on an interesting subject; contains some useful facts.

The France of Joan of Arc. LT.-COL. ANDREW HAGGARD. 1 volume. (Stanley Paul.)

For Joan of Arc. Essays by MARSHAL FOCH and others. 1 volume. (Sheed & Ward, 1930.)

"The Voices of Joan of Arc." ANDREW LANG. *Proceedings of the Society for Psychical Research,* Vol. XI, p. 198–212.

"The Dæmon of Socrates." FREDERIC MYERS. *Proceedings of the Society for Psychical Research,* Vol. V, Part XIV, p. 522. (1899.)

Human Personality and its Survival of Bodily Death. FREDERIC MYERS. (Longmans, Green & Co., 1920.)

Post-mortem. C. MACLAURIN. Essay on Jeanne. (Cape.)

L'héroïsme de la bienheureuse Jeanne d'Arc. REV. F. M. WYNDHAM. 1 volume. (1914.)

"Blessed Joan of Arc in English Opinion." REV. HERBERT THURSTON, S.J. Essay in *The Month,* May 1909.

"A Rationalised Joan of Arc." REV. HERBERT THURSTON. Review of Anatole France in *The Month,* July 1908.

Some Inexactitudes of Mr. G. G. Coulton. REV. HERBERT THURSTON, S.J. 1 volume. (Sheed & Ward, 1927.)

Le secret de Jeanne d'Arc. JACOBY. 1 volume. (Champion, 1932.)
An attempt to prove that Jeanne was the illegitimate daughter of the Duke of Orleans and Isabeau de Bavière.

Jeanne d'Arc médium. LÉON DENIS. 1 volume. (Jean Meyer, 1926.)

HISTORICAL

Histoire de Charles VII. G. DU FRESNE DE BEAUCOURT. 6 volumes. (Société bibliographique, 1881.)
A detailed work; in essence an attempt to whitewash Charles VII.

Histoire de Charles VII. M. VALLET DE VIRIVILLE. Vol. IV. (1861–5.)

Les Lorrains et la France au Moyen Age. COMTE MAURICE DE PANGE. 1 volume. (Champion.)

The Close of the Middle Ages. R. LODGE. 1 volume. (1901.)

Histoire du siège d'Orléans. J. B. M. JOLLOIS. 1 volume. (1833.)
Out of print; rare.

Louis d'Orléans. F. D. S. DARWIN. 1 volume. (John Murray, 1936.)

House of Orleans. M. CORYN. 1 volume. (Barker, 1936.)

Jeanne d'Arc. J. MICHELET. 1 volume.

La France pendant la guerre de cent ans. SIMÉON LUCE. (1890.)

Guillaume de Flavy. PIERRE CHAMPION. (1906.)

TOPOGRAPHICAL

Sainte Catherine de Fierbois. CHANOINE HENRI BAS and L'ABBÉ CHARLES PICHON. 1 volume. (Tours, 1920.)

Chinon. EUGENE PEPIN. 1 volume. (Laurens.)

Histoire et description de Notre Dame de Reims. CH. CERF. 2 volumes. (Reims, 1861.)

INDEX

accompanies Jeanne to Orleans, 169; at Orleans, 204; attends the coronation, 240; involved in the "sign given to the King" story, 337

CUSQUEL, PIERRE, quoted, 301–302

DARON, PIERRE, at Rouen, 303
DAUPHIN, THE, *see* Charles VII
DEMETRIADES, JEAN LEFÈVRE or FABRI, BISHOP OF, concerned in the trial, 310
Domremy, birthplace of Jeanne, its political situation, 25; disputes with Maxey-sur-Meuse, 26–27, 45; description of, 36–39; its troubles, 44–46; system of *pâturage* at, 46–48; Château de l'Ile, 47; burnt by Burgundians, 81; exempted from taxation, 245
DUMAY, ALISON, mistress of the Duke of Lorraine, 108; her tragic end, 109
DUPUY, JEAN, Jeanne's host at Tours, 151

EDWARD III, claims the French crown, 17
EPINAL, GERARDIN D', a Burgundian, 26, 83; meets Jeanne at Châlons, 237
ERARD, GUILLAUME, assessor at the trial, 309–310; preaches at St. Ouen, 352–353
ESTELLIN, BEATRICE, godmother to Jeanne, 34–35
ESTIVET, JEAN D', promoter of the trial, 306, 309; visits Jeanne in prison, 306–307; allusions to, 319, 341, 345, 362

FASTOLF, SIR JOHN, advances towards Orleans, 192; quarrels with Talbot, 226; a fugitive from Patay, 229

FÉCAMP, GILLES DE DUREMORT, ABBÉ DE, concerned in the trial, 309
FERCHAUD, CLAIRE, 75 and Appendix A
Fierbois, Jeanne at, 121–122; she sends for the sword of St. Catherine, 154–156; last appearance of sword, at Lagny, 275
FLAVY, GUILLAUME DE, governor of Compiègne, 280–282
FRANCE, ANATOLE, brilliant and untrustworthy, 14; inexactitudes quoted, 74 note, 121; explanation of Jeanne's conversation with Baudricourt, 104; on Charles VII, 125
FONTAINE, JEAN DE LA, examiner in the trial, 310, 343, 344
FOURNIER, JEAN, visits Jeanne in the Le Royers' house, 100–102

GALTON, SIR FRANCIS, quoted, 379–380
GAMACHES, SIEUR DE, resents Jeanne, 184; defends her, 206
GAUCOURT, MADAME DE, examines Jeanne, 141
GAUCOURT, RAOUL DE, counsellor of Charles VII and governor of Chinon, 127; lends Louis de Contes to Jeanne, 141; at Orleans, 197, 200, 204; dispute with Jeanne, 205; carries her out of danger at Paris, 254; instrumental in separating her from d'Alençon, 255
GIFFORD, 203
GIRESME, NICOLAS DE, Grand Prior of France, meets Jeanne at Orleans, 175; crosses to les Tourelles, 210
GIRON, ALAIN, at Orleans, 191
GLASDALE or GLANSDALE, SIR

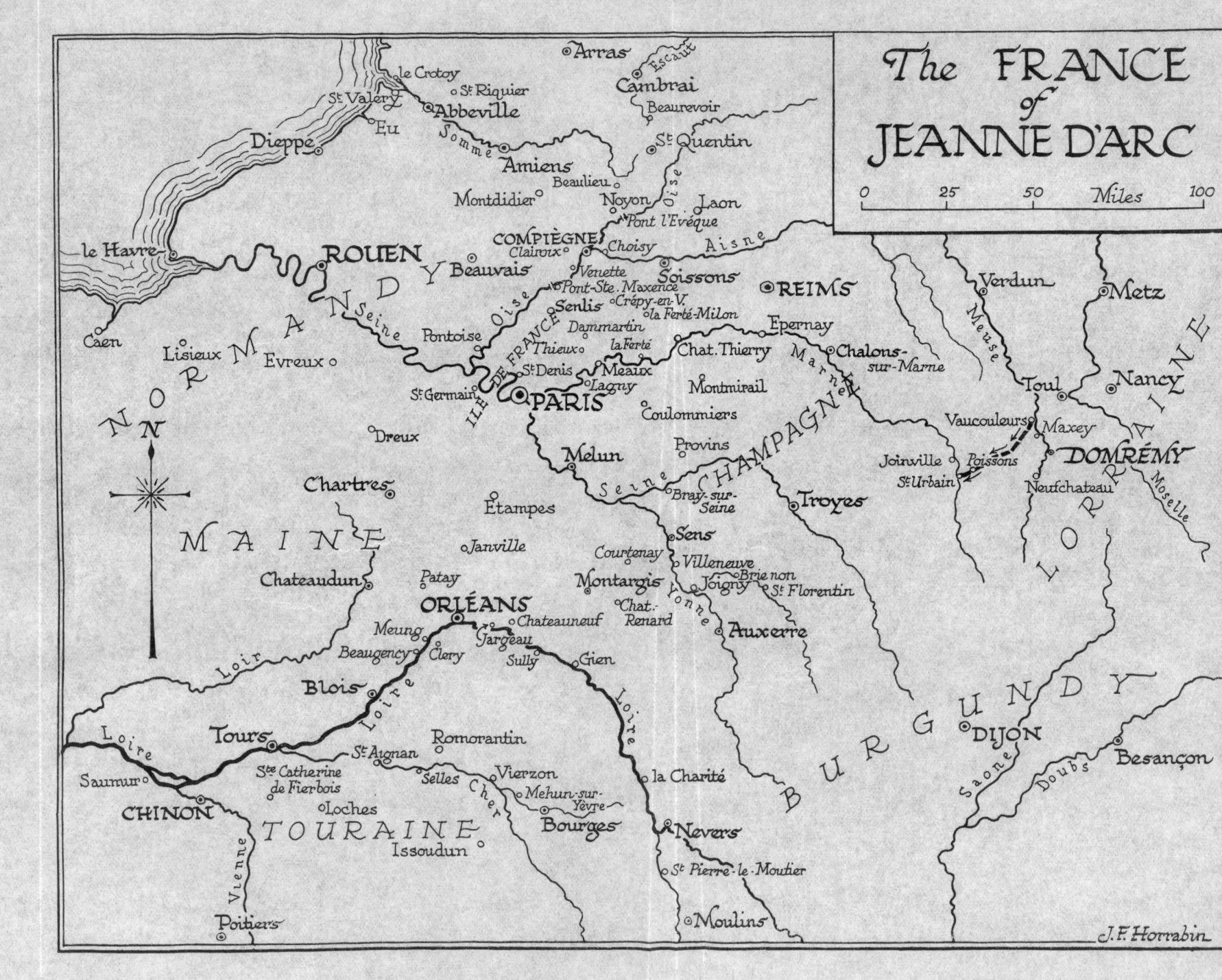

The FRANCE of JEANNE D'ARC

J.F. Horrabin

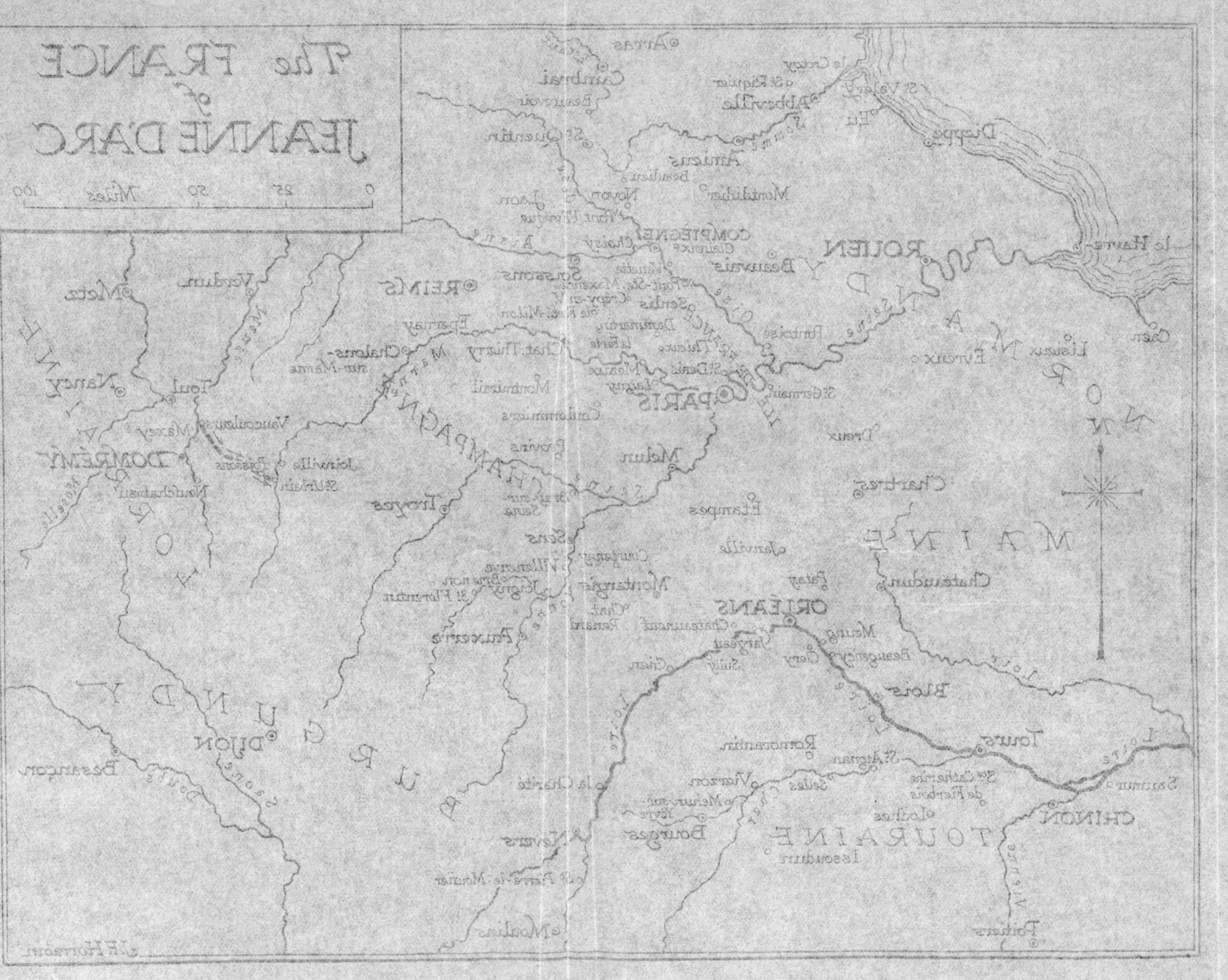